Transported to Another World
The Psychology of Anime Fans

Transported to Another World
The Psychology of Anime Fans

Stephen Reysen
Texas A&M University-Commerce

Courtney N. Plante
Bishop's University

Daniel Chadborn
New Mexico Highlands University

Sharon E. Roberts
Renison University College, University of Waterloo

Kathleen C. Gerbasi
Niagara County Community College

International Anime Research Project
Commerce, Texas, USA

ISBN-13: 978-0-9976288-1-4

Acknowledgments

Thank you to all of the anime fans who have participated in our studies in the past seven years. As a gesture of our gratitude, we're giving the PDF version of this book away for free (and will not be making any money on the print version of the book, as a way to make it as affordable as possible). We hope that seeing this book finally come to fruition will inspire you to continue participating in our future research and to encourage others you know to do the same!

Thank you to our research assistants who helped collect data at conventions and generally did all of the hard work on the ground: Amanda Gamboa, Jessica Gamboa, Tanner McCarter, Jessie Kierbow, Catherine Schroy, Thomas Brooks, Andrew Tague, and Justin Miller.

We're tremendously grateful to the conventions that opened their doors and allowed us to collect data in person: AnimeFest, A-Kon, and London (ON) ComicCon. We'd also like to extend a big thank you to FANS conference and *The Phoenix Papers* for welcoming psychology research into their conference and journal.

We are also appreciative of co-authors who have jumped on our various projects over the years: Dr. Iva Katzarska-Miller and Connor Leshner.

Portions of this research were supported by the Social Sciences and Humanities Research Council of Canada, the University of Waterloo, and by a Texas A&M University-Commerce Faculty Development Leave, and so we extend a great thank you to them for making this work possible!

Finally, thank you to all those who helped at one time or another to spread and promote our survey each year. Related to this, an enormous thank you to the various reddit moderators who allowed us to post on the various subreddits (sorry for bothering you every year).

Contents

Introduction

For the past seven years we at the International Anime Research Project have conducted a yearly survey of anime fans aimed at better understanding who they are and what makes them tick, so to speak. While this work has been tremendously successful, generating dozens of published scientific articles and yielding numerous fruitful datasets, it occurred to us that in all that time we haven't ever really stopped to step back to collect our thoughts on the project as a whole. It's easy to get caught up and hyper-focused on the nitty-gritty details of specific projects, but every so often it's necessary to gain some perspective and see the forest for the trees.

So, when the 2020 COVID pandemic struck and we found ourselves, like many researchers, unable to collect new data in-person, we finally had a chance to take our foot off the gas.[1] With less new incoming data, we had an opportunity to gather our thoughts and take stock of what exactly we'd learned from the past seven years of research. This book is a product of that reflection—an attempt to compile, organize, and reach some conclusions about the myriad threads of inquiry that have driven so many of our studies over these past years.

We should mention up front that our project is certainly not unique in being motivated by inquiries into our own interests. Indeed, we find ourselves in good company alongside researchers like Dr. Ru Igarashi. Dr. Igarashi is an experimental subatomic physicist from the University of Saskatchewan who conducted surveys about anime fans 1997 to 2007. In the beginning, Dr. Igarashi's surveys were simply meant to shed light on who fans were and what they were up to on the rec.arts.anime internet group. However, when the survey was eventually promoted by the Anime News Network, sample sizes grew considerably. Dr. Igarashi's surveys were extremely detailed (e.g., "How many video rental shops are accessible to you in your geographical area?") but primarily focused on how fans

---

[1] To be crystal clear, this is in no way meant to trivialize or make light of the horror that has been the COVID pandemic. Instead, we mean to show that, as researchers, it's often possible to find silver linings, however small, in almost every dark cloud.

consume and engage with anime.[2] As such, while many of these questions were not driven by theory (e.g., psychological models, media studies frameworks), Dr. Igarashi's work is significant as a sustained quantitative examination of the state of the (mainly Western) anime fandom.

This raises an important question: Why hasn't there been more theory-driven research about the psychology of fans—anime fans specifically and other media fans in general? In short, it's because researching fans has never really been a popular or respected topic within psychology.[3] If you peruse top-tier journals in social psychology you'll almost never find an article dedicated to fandom. We find this puzzling, given that almost everyone is a fan of *something* (e.g., sports, collectables, musicians, TV shows, cars). People spend countless hours, thousands of dollars, and often exert great effort in to engage with their fan interests. Indeed, the average person feels a stronger connection to their fan community than they do to their local neighborhood (Chadborn et al., 2018).

What's more, not only do fans spend much of their free time engaging with their fan interests, but these interests, in turn, have the power to influence their mind and shape their behavior. As an illustrative example, the manga *Silver Spoon*, a slice of life story about a city-dwelling student attending an agricultural school, spawned a boom in tourism for the city on which the story was based (Mason, 2016). Moreover, following the manga's release (and subsequent animation), student enrollment in agricultural schools increased (Donovan, 2014). If nothing else, examples like these should illustrate the need for psychologists to take seriously the importance of anime and its fandom to anime fans.

Placing this Book

Annett (2014) has suggested that there have been three waves, or generations, of fan scholarship. The first (researchers such as Bacon-Smith, Fiske, and Jenkins) sought to downplay negative conceptualizations of fans

---

[2] You'll need to use the internet archive's wayback machine to see the results, but it is a fascinating snapshot of the community at that time when the U.S. fandom was still relatively young—enough to make older fans nostalgic and younger fans perplexed.
[3] Speaking anecdotally to this point, several of this book's authors routinely get questioned by other psychologists at conventions or in our own departments about the validity of our research, usually with some variant of the question "Is this for real?"

as fanatical, mindless consumers of media[4] and instead reconceptualized fans as active and engaged consumers of media. The second wave (researchers such as Gray, Sandovss, and Harrington) pushed back against utopian conceptions of fans spawned by the first wave and noted the complexities of fan production (e.g., social hierarchies within fandoms). Finally, the third wave of scholars, rather than focusing on distinctions between passive vs. active and good vs. bad, have instead turned their attention to understanding how fandoms are integrated into peoples' everyday lives.

These three waves of scholarship, while influential in shifting the way academics think about fans, reflect the pop culture side of fan studies. They do not necessarily reflect the way other scholars, like psychologists, conceptualize fans.[5] For example, Schimmel et al. (2007) surveyed 65 fan scholars and discovered a split in the field revolving, at least in part, around disciplinary methodologies: Pop culture scholars mainly conduct qualitative research while psychologists mainly conduct quantitative research.[6] The study suggested that there is indeed a split in the way different fields study fans, often with little cross-communication between them.

From the psychological perspective, fan research has, until relatively recently, focused almost exclusively on sport fans. We suspect this is due to sport being among the most mainstream, accepted, and prevalent societal interests as well as the near-universal prevalence of sport across cultures. This makes collecting data about fans easy and makes it easy to make claims about fans worldwide when you're looking at a common interest.

---

[4] An example of this is reflected in the unflattering stereotype of an adult comic book fan who mindlessly buys anything bearing the image or logo of their favorite character and who goes to extremes in service of their interests—spending more than they can afford, behaving in ways that violate social norms (e.g., immaturely bickering with other fans at inappropriate times), and even blurring the line between fiction and reality.

[5] The authors of this book are all psychologists or in related social sciences fields, e.g., sociology, so we will tend to focus predominantly on the psychological perspective throughout this book.

[6] For readers unfamiliar with academia-speak, qualitative methods involve in-depth interviews with people or examining artifacts (e.g., show content) to get rich details and deep understanding about the experiences of individual people, while quantitative methods use surveys and experiments to gather numbers and statistics that condense, simplify, and allow claims to be made about what is typical or average in a group.

So, where does this book stand?

Put simply, our book is an attempt to inform the psychological literature on fans by examining a markedly non-sport fandom.[7] Furthermore, we offer a psychological perspective of the anime/manga fandom—a fandom which has been well-studied by pop cultural scholars but has been largely overlooked by psychologists. Lastly, to avoid falling into the trap of overcorrecting and treating the psychological perspective on anime as the only perspective, we have endeavored to include references to pop cultural studies about anime fan research where possible as a way of contextualizing our own work and to bridge the gap between them.[8]

Ultimately, qualitative and quantitative research go hand-in-hand in painting a complete picture. At present, much of the scholarship on anime/manga in academia is qualitative and tends to focus on content itself (e.g., analyzing the themes, characters, and symbols in anime/manga). For example, we picked up an article at random from the hundreds of papers on anime/manga and found an article by von Feigenblatt (2010), which posits that the interplay of sexuality and love portrayed in harem anime helped to move Japanese culture from arranged marriages to one of romantic love. The author describes three harem anime series and suggests that the themes were important as norms regarding marriage were changing.

Such an approach provides both an important context for anime and an understanding of the significance of the content itself within that context. However, the question itself is not a psychological one, in that it does not ask about the reaction of individual readers, changes in their attitudes, or their own beliefs about cultural norms. While our own work has not specifically addressed these questions from a psychological perspective, we have looked at topics such as hentai genre preference and questions about fans' beliefs about sex and gender roles, which could help shed light on a

---

[7] As it turns out, anime fans, like other predominantly "geek" or "nerd" fans, are not renowned for being big sport fans.

[8] Indeed, our position is that neither perspective holds a monopoly on truth when it comes to understanding fan culture. Different theoretical perspectives and methodologies allow for a richer, more complete picture than any one field can offer by itself. Our own emphasis on the psychological perspective should be seen as an attempt to add additional perspective to the conversation, not an attempt to devalue or downplay the pop cultural perspective.

topic such as this. Throughout this book, our emphasis is on the fans themselves: the psychological interplay between individuals, content, and fandoms. It is predominantly quantitative in nature[9] and focuses on general or average tendencies among fans rather than detail-rich descriptions about individual fan experiences.

A Short Note on Manga

We should also note up front that we do not make a distinction between anime fans and manga fans in this book. Over the years we've asked our participants whether they self-identify as anime fans and/or as manga fans, and we have asked them questions about anime and manga consumption separately. Comparing the results, time and time again, we find almost no differences in the outcomes of anime fans and manga fans. Our numbers show that while not all anime fans read manga, most manga fans have watched anime, which may explain why the groups differ so little. So, while we do find differences between some subgroups within the anime fandom (e.g., otaku vs. non-otaku, cosplayers vs. non-cosplayers), and note where these differences occur, we find no discernable difference between anime and manga fans. To be sure, pop cultural or media researchers may have documented significant differences that we do not. However, for the present, when we say anime fan, we are referring to anime and manga fans collectively.

What's in this Book?

In Chapter 1, we present a brief history of anime and a briefer history of cosplay. This is provided primarily for a bit of background on the subject, to bring readers who may be less familiar with anime as a cultural phenomenon up to speed on the subject. Importantly, as we are not historians, this chapter is primarily a broad-strokes summary of Jonathan Clements' excellent book *Anime: A History* (2018), which you should read if you would like a much better and more detailed history of anime than we provide here.

---

[9] Throughout this book we have strived to reduce the amount of numbers on the page and present the results in a manner that is straightforward and accessible to all. Rest assured that data and statistics were used in the process of reaching our conclusions, but we've spared you the statistical gobbledygook. If we've done our job well, you won't need any sort of formal training in statistics to understand what we're saying!

In Chapter 2 we lay out a brief primer on scientific studies and methodology. We explain some important concepts, such as measurement theory and study design, that will allow you to effectively scrutinize and think critically about the research presented in this book. Most importantly, we emphasize that our studies, and indeed the practice of science itself, is far from perfect. That said, we can be aware of the limitations of our research and ask what we can glean from the findings despite these imperfections.

Next, we move onto the research itself, beginning with Part II of the book, which is a look at the fandom's makeup and what fans, themselves, do. In Chapter 3, we explore demographic characteristics of the fans in our samples, such as the fact that anime fans tend to be young and, as a group, tend to remain fairly young, possibly due to a constant influx of new fans. This is followed by Chapter 4, where we examine anime fans' patterns of anime consumption. We cover topics such as where fans go to watch anime and how fans spend their money. We then take a deep dive into otaku-dom (Chapter 5) where we review definitions and descriptions of otaku and compare our own research to past research on the subject. One notable result, for example, finds that otaku and non-otaku fans show similar levels of overall well-being, despite stereotypes to the contrary! In Chapter 6 we take a look at fans' favorite characters and what this says about them. For example, we find that fans whose favorite characters were violent, nationalistic, and who embodied traditional gender norms were also more likely to endorse ethnocentric views themselves.

Similar to our deep dive into otaku-dom, in Chapter 7 we take a closer look at cosplayers. We find, for example, that about 30% of anime fans in our studies self-identified as coplayers, with a greater proportion of women than men reporting that they do so. In Chapter 8, we turn our attention to anime genre preferences, asking whether, like one's favorite character, one's favorite genre reveals aspects of themselves. Illustrating this idea, hentai genre fans were found to own more body pillows[10] and figurines! Finally, we round out this part of the book with a close look at hentai in Chapter 9, showing, for example, that hentai fans tend to be more politically liberal than non-hentai fans.

------

[10] A finding which, admittedly, many readers will find unsurprising!

In Part III of the book—fan psychology—we dive deep into a number of theoretically important psychological variables. We begin by considering the variables of fanship (one's connection to their fan interest) and fandom (one's connection to other fans) in Chapter 10, showing how they can predict important behaviors and attitudes in anime fans. Next, we examine the socialization of anime fans (Chapter 11). While sport fans tend to pick a team based on locality and one's parent's team, anime fans tend to become fans through other, very different means, such as through school clubs. In Chapter 12, we review the concept of global citizenship and explore the relation between various facets of the anime fandom and the tendency to see oneself as part of a global community. In Chapter 13, we turn to the darker side of the fandom in our analysis of elitism, entitlement, gatekeeping, and drama. In Chapter 14, we explore what motivates anime fans (e.g., belongingness) and what values they tend to hold (e.g., universalism). Ending Part III, we explore personality traits associated with anime fans in Chapter 15.

In Part IV of the book, we examine anime fans' well-being and factors that contribute to or hinder their ability to function. In Chapter 16, we explore the stereotypes that non-fans have of anime fans, revealing, for example, that anime fans are no longer stereotyped as sexual perverts as they once were, although they are *correctly* stereotyped as being somewhat introverted. In Chapter 17 we explore the stigma directed at anime fans and some of the ways that fans have developed to cope with this stigma. Rather dishearteningly for fans reading this book, these data show that people in general consider it somewhat undesirable to date an anime fan. In Chapter 18, we examine anime fans' experiences of bullying. We close this section in Chapter 19 with an overall look at the well-being of anime fans.

Finally, we end this book in Part V with a conclusion that pulls together the findings of this book and what we have learned from seven years of studying thousands of anime fans. We take stock of where we've come and where we will be going in the future, both as researchers and, in many cases, as anime fans ourselves.

Chapter 1
A Brief History of Anime and a Briefer History of Cosplay

As we stated in the introduction, we make no secret about the fact that we are, first and foremost, psychologists (or psychology-adjacent social scientists). This means that our bread-and-butter is conducting primarily quantitative studies that test hypotheses about relationships between psychological variables.

So, why the heck are we writing a chapter about the history of anime?

To be clear, we're not attempting to stray from our academic "lane." We fully intend to leave the history to the historians and make no claims about having any expertise with respect to historical methodology. While several of us are anime fans ourselves, the complete history of anime both extends back before any of us were even born and is, indeed, far too vast for our own limited experience with it to encapsulate.

Instead, what we offer is a very brief overview of the history of anime drawn primarily from the work of Jonathan Clements' *Anime: A History* (2018). Clements' expertise on the matter far exceeds our own, demonstrated by his more than 400 cited references and "thousands of pages of Japanese documentation" (p. 213). In fact, we draw so thoroughly from Clements' work that, as a blanket statement, any statements in this chapter without a citation should be taken as a reference to Clements (2018).[1]

Getting Started: What *is* Anime?

According to Clements, anime, as it is currently understood, includes not only cartoon films (e.g., the acetate cells of yesteryear and, more contemporarily, digital animation), but also includes frequently-overlooked media such as Claymation, stop-motion puppetry, and sand animation originating from Japan. What distinguishes it from other styles of animation (e.g., Western cartoons) is its complex stories and often dark content, which make it a more challenging and involved medium for viewers than what is

---

[1] We apologize in advance for any inaccuracies and sweeping generalizations in this chapter as a result of oversimplifying what is a long and very dense subject. For a fuller and more nuanced take on this subject, we would obviously encourage interested readers to get a copy of Clements' book for themselves!

traditionally associated with Western cartoons (e.g., Bugs Bunny, Mickey Mouse).

Speaking to the complexity of anime as a genre, Drazen (2014) recognizes a myriad of different anime themes and genres including, but not limited to, science-fiction, spaceships, robots, legends, romance (straight and gay), pornography, warrior and samurai, teenage girls, and religion.[2] Given this immensely broad range of content, we can state with reasonable confidence that there is an anime series out there for everyone.

While anime has its origins in Japan, today it represents a global phenomenon. For example, according to Clements, by 2009 Japanese animation companies had contracts with 138 different countries.[3,4] Condry (2013) similarly makes the case that anime is a global phenomenon, characterizing it not just as the global permeation of Japanese media, but as a cultural movement. Napier even goes so far to argue that, among the long, complex, and nuanced history of Japanese culture, "anime is one of the most important cultural expressions of contemporary Japanese society" (2005, pp. xvii-xviii).

The Early Years and World War II

It can be somewhat tricky to pinpoint the precise origin of anime. To be sure, the *term* anime arose in the mid-20th century in the wake of Tezuka Osamu's animated television cartoon *Astro Boy*, which first aired publicly on New Year's Day of 1963 (Schodt, 2007), a date which Clements states is viewed as an historically revolutionary event in Japanese culture.

Others disagree with the 1963 origin of anime. For example, Yasuo (2013) puts the origin of Japanese animation nearly half a century earlier, in 1917, with the first Japanese cartoons derived from drawing and cut out

---

[2] For convenience, Napier (2005) categorizes this vast array of genres into three broad modes of anime: apocalyptic (which may be material, spiritual, or pathological), elegiac (centered around loss and grief), and carnival (including elements of festivities and comedy).

[3] A few African and Central Asian countries comprise the majority of the exception to this trend.

[4] In fact, it's estimated that 60% of all cartoons worldwide are anime, illustrating the impact Japan has on the global animation market. The *Pokémon* series alone is watched in 68 countries and is the most-viewed cartoon series in the world (Napier, 2005).

techniques used in French and American films.[5] These early Japanese cartoons were silent and typically had moderators known as Benshi. The influence of these cartoons was so great that the Japanese Ministry of Education grew concerned about the content of the cartoons (e.g., *Playful Boy's Air Gun*), which they believed prompted undesirable behavior in children, such as playing at being thieves. As a result, regulations were enacted that laid out acceptable content for cartoons, including stories that involved parables, moral messages, and folk tales.

The Ministry also began to classify films as being either for children or for adults.[6] Consequently, by 1920, filmmakers began to focus their efforts primarily on films geared toward adult audiences, namely because they were more profitable. The Ministry of Communication, however, saw the value of harnessing cartoons—which children found entertaining—for public good, and supported the creation of educational cartoons on topics like how to mail things safely and how to save money.

In 1921, Kitayama developed Japan's first animation studio. It would not be long-lived, however, as in September 1923 the Great Kantō Earthquake destroyed much of the area around Tokyo and Yokohama, including the studio (National Film Archive of Japan, n.d.) and most of the cartoons it produced prior to the earthquake. In the wake of the earthquake, animation production moved away from Tokyo toward Osaka and Kyoto, which also conveniently allowed animators to escape much of the regulation and censorship. Nevertheless, the post-earthquake animators often received funding and requests from the Ministry of Education to make instructional films, which helped to support the developing animation industry.

At around the same time, Japan began to participate in the modern Olympics. This prompted an interest in sports like judo in both live films and in animation (e.g., Yasuji's 1928 *Animal Olympic Games*). The 1920s

---

[5] Others still may go further back, to the time when the first cartoons were shown in Japan, sometime between 1907 and 1912. Clements notes the difficulty in specifying exact dates due to limited record-keeping prior to 1977, lost records, foibles in peoples' retrospective memories, and language barriers.

[6] American readers will find this comparable to the controversial Hays code, which governed the content deemed appropriate and inappropriate for publicly-available motion pictures in America from 1934 to 1968 and, ultimately, was the precursor to the similarly controversial MPAA film rating system enacted 1968 and still used to this day.

also saw an increase in the use of personal cameras and amateur film clubs and magazines.[7] Technological advances in the 1930s added color to Japanese animation, and by 1937, Japanese technology had progressed to a color technology that would remain largely the same for about five decades.[8]

Politics would also play a considerable role in the development of animation in Japan. Events such as Japan's invasion of Manchuria in 1931 (Swift, n.d.), leaving the League of Nations in 1933, and imposing the Film Law in 1939 all affected the content of animation (e.g., rules prohibiting the showing of foreign films). Perhaps most importantly, however, Japan's entry into World War II influenced the content of films, with the government creating a film unit specifically tasked with making military-themed animated films on topics such as naval aviation, torpedo essentials, and ship identification. While these films were not intended for the public, they did represent considerable government financial support for the animation industry.[9]

World War II would have a significant impact not only on the funding of animation projects in Japan, but also on the content of anime itself. Following the national law that film had to contribute to national policy, Clements notes that the film *Sea Eagles* (which was supported by the Japanese Navy) was the "defining Japanese propaganda cartoon of the war era" (2018, p. 64). Other films, such as the 1942 film *Sankichi the Monkey: Air Combat*, featured monkeys fighting bears in air-to-air combat. Furthermore, while foreign films were banned in Japan during this time, the Japanese had acquired copies of *Fantasia* from a ship seized by the Japanese navy and the Chinese Wan brothers' *Princess Iron Fan*, both of

---

[7] Notably, however, these amateurs and their films were often stifled by the Japanese government, which restricted the content of what could be shown by levying penalties on people who violated content regulations.

[8] The addition of sound to animation was considerably more delayed in Japanese film, however. This is both because it was costly and because the Benshi opposed it, since it would make their jobs largely irrelevant.

[9] It is worth noting a similar occurrence in America, with the United States War Department commissioning Disney studios to make instructional cartoons (e.g., *Private Snafu*) for the War Department.

which were popular with Japanese audiences and would be both a contrast to, and influence, Japanese animation.[10]

Animation After World War II and Osamu Tezuka

In the wake of World War II, Japan was an occupied country. While the censorship imposed by this occupation undoubtedly stifled independent Japanese animation studios,[11] it did employ Japanese animators who were willing to make educational films for the occupation forces. Moreover, the American occupation force provided projectors and films about life in the United States and democracy. Clements states that 18 different foreign films, most of them American, played in Japanese theaters during the occupation, including *Snow White and the Seven Dwarfs, Bambi, Pinocchio,* and *Lady and the Tramp.* According to Yasuo (2013, para 6):

> It was during these years, as Japan began to recover from the disastrous war, that Ōkawa Hiroshi, president of the Tōei film company, saw Disney's *Snow White* (1937). He was overwhelmed by the gorgeous color of the film. In 1956, he built a modern studio—a white-walled palace with air conditioning, as people called it—and founded Tōei Dōga (now Tōei Animation). His ambition: to become "the Disney of the East."

Tōei Dōga chose *Hakujaden* (*The Legend of the White Snake*) as their first film. They sent a research team to the United States and invited several experts to travel to Japan as mentors. As a result, they were able to master the Disney system of "assembly-line production."

Despite limited development of Japanese animation during the occupation, there was a market for Japanese animation in the form of television advertising and commercials. This was especially the case toward the end of the 1950s, in no small part fueled by an increase in the number of Japanese television stations from one to four.

It was at this point that Japanese animation began to be recognized on the international stage. Mochinaga's *Little Black Sambo* won a prize at the Vancouver Film Festival, leading to a foreign contract from the Rankin Jr.

---

[10] Funnily enough, *Princess Iron Fan* was an anti-Japanese film. It was shown with the last line removed to make the film acceptable to the Japanese public (Stony Brook University, n.d.).

[11] During this time there were strikes amongst animators due to a shortage of jobs and insufficient supplies.

studio for Mochinaga to create 130, five-minute episodes of *Pinocchio* for American television. According to Clements, this started a trend that ran from 1960 onward for Japanese animators to contribute to dozens of American cartoons, including favorites such as *Frosty the Snowman, Rudolph the Red Nose Reindeer,* and *ThunderCats.*

Also in 1960, manga artist Osamu Tezuka turned his 500-page storyboard for *Saiyūki* into a feature-length animated film. The film was shown in 1961 in the United States under the name *Alakazam the Great.* The success of the film led Tezuka to leave the Toei studio and form his own studio, Mushi Pro.[12] Numerous other animators subsequently left Toei to work for Tezuka, since he offered better working conditions. With the success of other animated television series (e.g., *Otogi Manga Calendar,* a sort of "this day in history" program) demonstrating the viability of an animated television series in Japan, the stage was set for Tezuka's ground-breaking masterpiece, *Astro Boy* (*Mighty Atom*), which first aired on January 1, 1963.

Astro Boy began life as a manga in 1951. It is the tale of a robot boy built by a scientist to replace his dead son (Napier, 2005). Astro Boy was cute and cuddly and was patterned, in part, after the American cartoon *Mighty Mouse,* itself a parody of the popular American superhero *Superman* (Schodt, 2007). The resemblance is perhaps best seen whenever Astro Boy flies, as he extends his arm just as Mighty Mouse and Superman do.[13] *Astro Boy* ran four seasons and had 193 episodes (*Astro Boy,* n.d.). According to Tezuka Osamu Official (n.d.), "[*Astro Boy*] is one of Tezuka Osamu's monumental works that brought an epic-making change in the history of Japanese animation. This first animated TV series in Japan

---

[12] Tezuka is known in Japan as the "God of Manga" (Drazen, 2014; Schodt, 2007). Despite finishing medical school, he never practiced medicine, instead publishing more than 700 manga equaling over 150,000 pages.

[13] This is far from the only influence of American animation on Tezuka's work. His characters and their large eyes—now a hallmark of anime –were influenced by *Betty Boop* and Disney's *Bambi* (O'Luanaigh, 2010).

14

formed the basis for a long lasting and flourishing culture of Japanese animation."[14]

The impact of *Astro Boy* would soon spread to the United States. NBC Enterprises contracted 52 episodes, which were slated to run in various American markets. Illustrating some of the cross-cultural differences, however, half of the first 12 episodes were rejected for inappropriate content such as nudity and vivisection. In response, Tezuka was encouraged to make the *Astro Boy* cartoons "placeless" or "denationalized" so they would be easier to show to foreign audiences.

Back in Japan, Tezuka was forced to compete with American imports such as *The Flintstones* and *Popeye* for advertising. Since the U.S. imports were already produced and the cost of dubbing them was fairly inexpensive, it was difficult for Tezuka to remain competitive. Despite these difficulties, however, Tezuka was successful. With the proliferation of color television in the 1960's, Tezuka's first color episode released with very high ratings. Because of this, Tezuka was granted another contract from NBC Enterprises for a new series based on his 1950 manga, *Jungle Emperor* (*Kimba the White Lion*).[15] The contract imposed restrictions on Tezuka, including the fact that each episode had to be self-contained with no cliff-hangers; there were to be no scenes of animal cruelty, and all of the "bad guys" had to be White.

By the end of the decade Tezuka shifted gears, changing his focus to making adult anime (*1001 Nights* in 1969 and *Cleopatra: Queen of Sex* in 1970) in an unsuccessful attempt to increase revenues. His Mushi Pro studio employees ultimately unionized, the company declared bankruptcy, and in the late 1970's the new Mushi Production arose without Tezuka. Despite these setbacks, Tezuka formed Tezuka Productions and worked on various television and theatrical programs, including a 52 episodes colored version of *Mighty Atom*, until his death in 1989 (Schodt, 2007).

---

[14] The popularity of *Astro Boy* also gave rise to the Samurai-themed anime *Suzunosuke with the Red Breastplate*, which ran for 52 episodes in the early 1970s (Drazen, 2014; Ettinger, 2015).

[15] With a hint of irony, the studio which had inspired elements of Tezuka's style, Disney, would later be accused of appropriating his work, with *The Lion King* being alleged to be, at a minimum, *heavily* inspired by *Kimba the White Lion*.

While Tezuka paved the way for the popularity of Japanese television animation, his studio's work would not be the only one on the market. From the 1960's to the mid-1980s a growing variety of different anime series emerged across numerous genres ranging from adventures to comedies and from science fiction to ghost stories (Clements, 2018). For example, in 1968 *Star of the Giants* brought the theme of sports to anime in a story about a baseball team geared toward both children and adults (Clements, 2018). According to Drazen (2014), sports were banned in Japan after World War II for fear that they might promote militaristic attitudes. After Japan hosted the 1964 Olympics, however, there was an increased national interest in stories about athletics, especially those emphasizing the importance of training, effort, and determination as the keys to success, lessons congruent with the teachings of Confucius and which hold an important influence on Japanese culture.

The early 1970s saw the production of children's classics such as *Heidi* released in 1974. Often referred to as masterpiece anime, it was as popular as the science fiction anime series at the time, albeit sometimes overlooked or overshadowed in retrospect (Clements, 2018). During this period, toys were often marketed to accompany televised anime series, something which added an additional revenue stream that helped to support the burgeoning industry (Clements, 2018).[16] Speaking to the magnitude of this impact, an industrial section outside of Tokyo would be home to 44 different toy manufacturers alongside this trend. These toys often tied into the transformation and combination themes still popular in anime today (Clements, 2018).

The next wave of anime came in the late 1970s on the heels of George Lucas' hugely successful *Star Wars* (Drazen, 2014). Clements (2018) identifies 1977 as a boom time, when over 50 different anime titles appeared on television in a single year. By this point, anime had become popular enough that entire magazines had arisen, devoted solely to anime. As Clements says, "Arguably, 1977 was the first year in which 'anime' and anime fandom could assert a sense of itself as a culture, as a body of work with its own discourse, and its own developing sense of history" (p. 163).

---

[16] This tendency too would see a reprisal in American culture in the 1980s with the proliferation of shows like *G.I. Joe* and *My Little Pony*, which were often accused of being little more than prolonged commercials for toy manufacturers such as Hasbro, Inc.

"Modern" Anime: The 1980s and Beyond

The Japanese anime series *Star Blazers* (*Space Cruiser Yamato* in Japan) began on American television in 1979 (*Star Blazers*, n.d.). The series had a 26-week story arc and involved interpersonal relationships which interested American viewers in particular. Technological advances such as the home VCR and expanding cable channels created demand for additional anime in the U.S.[17] In the 1980s home VCR's and video stores made it possible for people to view anime from cassettes and contributed to the global spread of anime and its fan base (Drazen, 2014). The VCR also allowed people interested in learning the animation craft to watch anime in slow motion, and undoubtedly played an influential role for an entire generation of anime artists (Clements, 2018).

During the 80s many new anime motifs emerged including "bad boys on motorcycles," romances with female characters to give teenage boys characters to lust after, and, arguably the biggest seller of them all, pornography, the first of which was a 1984 *Lolita*-like anime "dominated by paedophile erotica" (Clements 2018, p. 170).[18] Revenue for anime erotica was robust and manufacturers could count on each of the 4800 video stores to take at least one copy of any given erotic film. In fact, while a typical erotic anime video would be less successful in terms of actual purchases than other, non-erotic anime films, erotic anime videos *rented* at a rate four times higher than other genres (Clements, 2018).[19]

In the mid-1990s, shows like *Sailor Moon* were becoming a hit not only in Japan, but also in the U.S., Canada, Poland, and Brazil, thanks in no small part to the internet. *Dragon Ball Z* was an even bigger hit than *Sailor Moon*, running from 1984-1995 with over 500 episodes. *Pokémon*, which developed alongside a video game, was a multimedia blockbuster that encompassed a series of video games, a television show, manga, films, and

---

[17] It is during this time that one of the classic anime series best known to American audiences rose to meet this demand: *Voltron* (*Five Lions* in Japan).

[18] Relevant to this, Clements points out that one advantage of anime is that the animator can create scenes and activities that would be too expensive (e.g., huge explosions) or illegal to stage with real people.

[19] For more about the reaction of modern anime fans to erotica and hentai in the anime fandom, see Chapter 9.

a collectable card game (Drazen, 2014).[20] The first film itself played on over 3,000 screens and had a revenue of over 85 million U.S. dollars (Clements 2018). The overwhelming success of *Pokémon* paved the way for related cartoons such as *Digimon* and *Cardcaptors* (Drazen, 2014), and, by the late 1990s, there were three economic strands of anime: child-oriented, adult-oriented, and anime made to appeal to both adults and children.

Continuing technological advances contributed to the distribution and availability of anime by making it easier to develop series such as *Cowboy Bebop* across multiple versions (mainstream and adult). New digital technology facilitated online shopping for anime, especially as it became more common for teens and young adults to have their own computers and access to the internet, allowing them to watch their shows without needing to put them on the family television. Fans could also create their own anime-inspired creations (e.g., anime music videos, webcomics), and it became possible for fans to add subtitles to existing anime in other languages (i.e., fansubbing), both of which could be quickly and easily shared online. Technology also increased the ease with which fans could digitally download anime and contributed to the makers' profit margins (Clements, 2018).

So, where does anime look to be going in the future? Clements (2018) predicts a steady stream of new anime, given that modern series typically only have a three-month run. He also imagines that in the future, there may be an increased demand for "silver anime," shows geared toward appealing to some of the aesthetics and tropes familiar to older viewers. Citing the Nomura Research Institute, Clements also indicates that three things will keep anime fans engaged: "Events, Holy Lands, and Legends" (p. 218). Events are conventions and other group activities like concerts and film festivals. Holy lands refer to specific anime sites and locations of particular importance to anime fans. Legends refer to signings, Q&As, photo

---

[20] In 1997 a television episode of *Pokémon* featured a "rapidly pulsating animation effect" (strobing), which played on nearly 30 million Japanese televisions and sent 150 viewers to the hospital with seizure symptoms. This event, referred to as "*Pokémon* shock," resulted in regulations about what kinds of visual effects were allowed in anime. Funnily enough, *Pokémon* was taken off the air for a while, although the strobing incident actually *increased* peoples' overall interest in *Pokémon* (Clements 2018, p. 177)!

opportunities, and physical interactions with anime celebrities such as artists and voice actors.

A Very Brief History of Cosplay

Another important aspect of fanship for many anime fans—one just as important as the series themselves to some fans—is the opportunity for individuals to cosplay. Cosplay (costume plus play or role-play) refers to fans dressing up as favorite characters from anime, manga, and other sources and can include activities such as costuming, performance art, masquerades, and posing for photographs (Ashcraft & Plunkett, 2014; Winge, 2006). Costumes are often hand-crafted, though they can also be purchased, in whole or in part (Han, 2020).

Winge (2006) describes the origins of cosplay as having both American and Japanese roots. In 1984, Nov Takahashi, founder and writer for an anime publishing company, attended the World Science Fiction Convention, Worldcon, in Los Angeles. There, he witnessed attendees dressed as various science-fiction and fantasy characters. When he returned to Japan and wrote about what he had seen, he encouraged Japanese fans to dress up and role-play as anime and manga characters. Ultimately, the term cosplay was used to describe the act, a term which was largely unknown outside of Japan until the 1990s (Aschcraft & Plunkett, 2014). However, there are other accounts of cosplay at Japanese science fiction events as early as 1974, and the term being used earlier than 1984, but these records were not reported in the literature due to a lack of translated works (see McCarthy & Ashmore, 2021).

Others place the origins of cosplay itself (the fan activity, not the word) considerably earlier, going as far back as 1910, when a woman wore an unusual costume on the streets of Tacoma, Washington (Ashcraft & Plunkett, 2014). While costuming and masquerading was not itself noteworthy, what made the woman's costume unique was the fact that it was patterned after a science fiction comic strip character, *Mr. Skygack*. She was not the first to do it—purportedly some others had done the same thing as early as 1908. Later, when the first Worldcon was held in 1939, two people, Myrtle Douglas and Forrest Ackerman, arrived wearing futuristic costumes, which Douglas had designed and made. While their goal was initially to get newspaper coverage for the convention itself, the idea of attending a convention in costume caught on. At the 1940

Worldcon, several more people attended in costumes, leading to a costume exhibition and forever solidifying the place of costuming in the science fiction fandom (Ashcraft & Plunkett, 2014).

Summarizing: Anime Today

It is difficult to definitively state precisely how globally popular anime and cosplay have become. We do have some clues, however. Anime Expo (formerly Anime Con) is the largest anime convention in the world (Jones, 2020) and in 2019 it had unique attendance of 115,000 and over 350,000 in turnstile attendance (Anime Expo, n.d.). The Facebook page *Anime Trending* (n.d.) has over one million followers and a search of Facebook yields countless anime groups ranging from small, local fan groups to international groups with more than a million followers (Facebook, n.d.).

While the World Cosplay Summit, an international cosplay competition, had only four countries (France, Germany, Italy, and Japan) in its first year in 2003; by 2019, 40 countries participated, representing every continent except Antarctica (World Cosplay Summit, n.d.). The World Cosplay Summit Facebook page has over 700,000 followers as of November, 2020 (Facebook, n.d.; World Cosplay Summit, n.d.). Entire cottage industries have taken root worldwide, with individual creators able to devote their career to creating accessories or entire outfits for interested cosplayers.

Conclusion

This chapter has shown that while we may not be able to precisely pinpoint the origins of anime as a medium, there is no doubting its global proliferation and influence. Long gone are the days when anime was relegated to a handful of commercials or short commissioned educational films for the Japanese government. Not only has anime exploded onto the international stage, but almost all accounts suggest that it shows no signs of slowing down or decreasing in popularity. As such, it is little wonder why scholars have taken such a keen interest in anime, both to understand how and why it rose to prominence and to understand its impact—both culturally and on the people who call themselves fans of it.

Chapter 2
One Does Not Simply Study a Fandom

At this point we can feel your eagerness to get to the delicious data-filled center of the book. However, before we can get to the data, we should take a brief detour to review (or, for some readers, introduce) the methodology through which the data were collected. While the detour may seem unnecessary at first, keep in mind that all the numbers in the world would be meaningless to you if they were collected in a haphazard way or if you didn't know how to interpret them!

This chapter aims to give someone without a research background both the vocabulary and the basic skills needed to think like a scientist. Consider it a crash course on research methods—just enough to let you think critically about the research presented in this book and to double-check our work.

We begin with an overview of what it means to take a scientific approach to the study of people before delving into some of the nuts and bolts of study design. We look at how to measure things that we can't see or touch, how to recruit people into our studies, how to use data from those people to make claims about people not in the study, and how to run different types of studies. We follow that up with a beginner's guide to understanding statistics.[1] Finally, after transforming you into a cold, calculating, scientific skeptic, we soften things up with a healthy dose of pragmatism through a talk about some of the realities of doing research in "The Real World." This includes learning the difference between healthy criticism and an unhealthy obsession with purity in scientific studies.

When all that's said and done, we close out the chapter by laying out our own studies for you to scrutinize. These very studies form the backbone of this book and are where we draw all of our findings from. Consider it our way of "showing our work" so you don't have to just take our word for it. We point out the strengths and drawbacks of our studies, what they can and

---

[1] We swear, they're not as scary as they're made out to be!

can't do as scientific tools, and hopefully spark some of ideas of your own for how researchers might conduct future studies that build upon them![2]

However, for now, let's go back to the very basics and discuss what it means to take a scientific approach to the study of the anime fandom.

Scientific Thinking

The word "science" gets thrown around a lot, often by the people least qualified to be making scientific claims.[3] Science is often treated like an impartial authority, invoked by someone as the ultimate way to shut down disagreement: "I win because *science* is on my side!"

So, what's the problem? Shouldn't we be using science to bolster our arguments—especially when it happens to be on our side?

In and of itself, there's nothing wrong with drawing upon empirical evidence to support your argument. The problem lies in the *way* science is used and understood by laypersons while doing this. Science is often treated like a club to be swung against an opponent. When used this way, science is treated like a list of facts about what is and is not true—and in this case, science says that I'm right and you're wrong.

However, that's *not* what science is! If this were this the case, science would just be an ever-growing mountain of unquestionable dogma and scientists would be little more than mindless drones endlessly memorizing those facts and adding to the pile.[4]

So, what *is* science, if it's *not* just a pile of facts?

At its core, science is a way of thinking. It's the deliberate attempt to understand the world in an organized, rational, systematic way. In this respect, scientists are not people who memorize a bunch of facts, they're people who spend years practicing how to think in a very specific way.

To help us, let's imagine how a scientist would approach a seemingly simple question: "Are anime fans psychologically well-adjusted?"

A scientist, starts, whenever possible, with existing theory and prior research. What studies have been done on anime fans? What do models about psychological well-being say about fans? If there's no prior research

---

[2] After all, what is science if not the continual process of standing upon those who came before us and improving upon their methods?

[3] Daytime television and social media, we're looking at you.

[4] Maybe it's because we're scientists ourselves, but we'd like to give scientists a little more credit than that!

on anime fans specifically, a scientist may start with the most relevant research they can find: What do we know about sport or music fans? Are there reasons to suspect that anime fans are categorically different from these other fans?

Right out of the gate, we can see that scientists try to build their answers on something solid. While theories are often far from perfect,[5] they do have the benefit of almost always being grounded upon some existing research. In a never-ending cycle known as the scientific method, researchers use these existing theories to generate hypotheses, which they then test by collecting data and, upon analyzing that data, they revise their theories accordingly, which generate new hypotheses.

Another important component of scientific thinking is a genuine willingness to embrace the possibility of being wrong. In fact, scientists don't just acknowledge the *possibility* that they might be wrong—they actively *try* to prove themselves wrong, a principle known as falsification. While people arguing online actively hunt for information that proves their point—a phenomenon known as confirmation bias—scientists go out of their way to design tests capable of proving definitively that they may be wrong. A good scientist only accepts a position if it can repeatedly withstand this sort of destructive testing and is willing to revise their position if the results show that they're incorrect. Scientists take this idea so seriously that the philosophy of science itself acknowledges that studies can *never* prove anything to be true, only false.[6] At most, studies can provide evidence to *support* one's particular theory, but they can never *prove* a theory to be true. This means that skepticism and doubt are baked into the

---

[5] It's worth pointing out that "theory" means something very different to scientists than it does for laypersons. Whereas laypersons treat theories like guesses, scientific theories are informed models about how the world works based on the best evidence available (e.g., atomic theory, theory of gravity).

[6] Philosopher Karl Popper famously asked folks to imagine testing the theory that "all swans are white." Intuitively, you might test this assertion by running out and collecting as many white swans as you can, with each additional white swan giving you confidence that the statement is true. A scientist, however, goes out in search of a black swan. Why? Because collecting millions of white swans doesn't eliminate the possibility that somewhere out there is a black swan. If, however, you are able to find a single black swan, the original statement is demonstrably false, and needs to be revised (e.g., most swans are white).

scientific method and that scientists entertain the possibility that, down the line, someone will come along and later disprove or force a revision to their theory.

If you've ever argued with someone online, you know that the same willingness to be wrong isn't so easy to find on social media!

Scientists also differ from those who rely on common sense in the approach that they take to gathering evidence to test their theories. If a layperson were asked to test whether anime fans are psychologically well-adjusted, they might immediately turn their attention to their own experience or to the anime fans they knew personally. Or, if they believed that anime fans were maladjusted, they might take to the internet to gather every example they could find of anime fans showing evidence of maladjustment.[7]

In both cases, it's worth asking whether the examples the layperson found accurately represents the anime fandom as a whole. Are most anime fans actually like you and your friends? Are anime fans like the people you find online when you search for "crazy anime fans"?

So, how do scientists collect their data? Ideally, they try to get the most complete, thorough, and accurate picture of the phenomenon. This means studying it in multiple ways, collecting as many examples as possible, and trying to collect their samples in a fair and systematic way to avoid basing their conclusions on a weird or biased example. For this reason, scientists recognize the problem inherent in judging all anime fans based of a handful of fans they're friends with or based on the fans they can find in an internet search for weird fans. Instead, they would try to get the largest sample of anime fans that they can, one that represents the population of all anime fans. They would then try to study that group from as many different angles as possible.

Related to this idea (and the fact that scientists are a skeptical bunch), scientists also differ from people who rely on "common sense" by seeking to replicate their prior findings. For most people going about their day-to-day lives, it's enough to test something once, figure out the answer, and then move forward with their answer. For our layperson judging anime fans,

---

[7] With the internet being as it is, they would surely find more than a few examples.

24

once they've made up their mind about anime fans, they're unlikely to spend more time thinking about the issue. After all, they have their answer.

Scientists, on the other hand, are the masters of double-checking their work. After all, it's always possible that a particular discovery was a fluke or caused by a weird idiosyncrasy of your procedure. To be as confident as possible in their conclusions, scientists try it again to see if the same thing happens. They try it again, but they might use different measures and different participants from different places. They encourage *other* researchers to try their procedures to see if they get the same results. In short, scientists rarely base their conclusions on a single study—ideally, they would want to run several versions of a study to test the consistency of the findings and rule out the possibility of a fluke.

At the risk of belaboring the point, we should mention one final difference between common sense thinking and scientists: probabilistic thinking. Probabilistic thinking involves understanding the concept of probability—the odds or chances of something happening. Scientists try to make predictions about complex systems (e.g., groups of people) that can include hundreds or even thousands of variables. Because of this complexity, it's almost impossible to make perfect predictions about a single outcome. Instead, scientists try to control some of the chaos and build models that allow them to predict a range of plausible outcomes, as well as an average outcome, in a particular system.

To see this in action, imagine medical scientists studying the lethality of a disease. A typical person is probably more interested in knowing "if I get this disease, will I, in particular, die from it?" Scientists, on the other hand, study groups of populations because doing so gives them the ability to use statistics to cut through the all of the different variables and draw conclusions about what tends to happen in *groups* of people: "males are 5x more likely to die from this disease than females" or "30% of people over the age of 60 who contract this disease die from it." In other words, scientists may struggle to accurately predict the outcomes of individual cases, but they tend to be pretty good at making predictions about collections or groups of outcomes. This is a result of probabilistic thinking.

To see a simple demonstration of this principle, imagine rolling two six-sided dice. It is practically impossible for a scientist to tell you what you will roll on the dice if you roll them once   there's just too many different variables involved (the angle the dice fall at, their starting orientation, how hard you throw them, etc.) However, scientists can confidently predict that if you *repeatedly* roll those dice, over time you will get far more "7s" than "2s," since there are many more ways to get a "7" than to get a "2." In a similar fashion, scientists may not be able to tell whether a specific patient will die from a disease, but they *can* predict that X% of people who get the disease will end up dying from it.

So, what does this probabilistic thinking have to do with our question about whether anime fans are psychologically maladjusted? Well, let's imagine our intrepid internet-searching layperson has found a handful of examples of maladjusted anime fans. They might conclude from this "well, clearly *all* anime fans are maladjusted!" An anime fan might argue back, saying "Hey, wait a minute! My friends and I are all anime fans and we're all well-adjusted! So, actually, you're wrong, anime fans are well-adjusted!" Arguing back and forth this way, bouncing between one extreme and the other, the two are unlikely to get anywhere, because the answer is not so black-and-white.

A scientist recognizes that absolute statements about *all* anime fans are almost certainly going to be wrong. All it takes is a single counterexample to prove that *not all* anime fans are maladjusted (or that not all anime fans are well-adjusted). Instead, a scientific approach would be to look at how well-adjusted the *average* anime fan is, to look at the *range* and *variability* of maladjustment across the anime fandom, and then see whether we can predict which anime fans are more or less likely to be well-adjusted.

It's extremely important to understand this probabilistic approach to scientific thinking because so many "common sense" people struggle with this concept when evaluating scientific claims. It's common, for example, for scientists to make claims like "smoking is a cause of lung cancer," only to have someone respond, "I've smoked my entire life and I haven't gotten lung cancer, so your conclusions are wrong!" The existence of a single counterexample (or even many counterexamples) does not *disprove* the claim that, on average, people who smoke are more likely to develop lung cancer than people who do not. While it's easy to recognize this principle in an example like the one above, people often forget this principle when it comes to scientific studies whose results go against their intuitions—for example, studies that make claims about groups that they've already made their minds up about.[8]

To wrap up this section: Thinking like a scientist isn't about memorizing a bunch of facts—it's about thinking in a particular way. It involves:

(1) Basing one's predictions on existing theory and research.

(2) An open-minded willingness to be wrong and to seek falsification.

(3) Systematic, unbiased observation and studying of a phenomenon.

(4) A willingness to repeatedly test the consistency of one's findings.

(5) Understanding probabilistic thinking, including making predictions about groups rather than focusing on individuals.

Now that we're armed with a scientific mindset, let's take a look at some of the nuts and bolts of research design and some of the decisions that go into running a scientific study. After all, even if you never plan to run your own study, knowing a bit about how studies are put together can help you be an informed critic of research!

Operationalization: Putting Numbers to Experience

At first glance, it seems pretty simple to run a study: Measure some things and see if the numbers you get are the ones you had been expecting. For example, if we wanted to test whether 12-year-olds are, on average, taller than 8-year-olds, it would take almost no effort at all to grab a ruler, line up a bunch of 8- and 12-year-olds, measure their height, and compare the two averages.

However, this is a question about height. A person's height is something physical and tangible. We can look at a person and see their height. Height is something we've been measuring for thousands of years, and we've developed standardized measurements and highly precise instruments to do just that. It's so trivial, in fact, that we take it for granted that a child measured to be 140 cm tall in Canada using a cotton tape measure will also be 140 cm tall if they're measured in India with a wooden ruler. Different

---

[8] The authors have spent more than decade studying numerous fan groups, including *My Little Pony* fans and furries—people who are fans of media featuring anthropomorphized animal characters. When their findings repeatedly show that *My Little Pony* fans and furries are, for the most part, happy, healthy, well-adjusted people, critics rush to find single examples of extremely maladjusted fans to somehow "disprove" the finding—demonstrating a lack of understanding this principle of probabilistic thinking.

people from different cultures using different instruments will agree on how tall this child is.

However, what if we wanted to test whether 12-year-olds are, on average, more *aggressive* than 8-year-olds? Suddenly, the task becomes a lot more difficult. After all, your aggression isn't a physical, tangible thing that we can touch, see, or feel. If we were to crack open a person's skull and plunk a ruler in there, we couldn't directly measure their aggression. Sure, we can see the *consequences* of a person's aggression (e.g., bullying, hitting, threatening others), but these are not aggression itself—they're acts caused by a person's aggressiveness, whatever *that* is!

So, what do we do? Should we limit ourselves only to studying the things we can touch, see, and feel? If that were the case, we'd have to throw out pretty much the entirety of the social sciences in one fell swoop. Concepts such as motivation, personality, love, prejudice, culture—all of these would suddenly be off the table for scientific study if we limited ourselves to only measuring physical things.

The solution to the problem, as you've probably guessed, is to measure things *indirectly*. In the case of aggression, this might involve measuring the aggressive behavior (e.g., hitting someone), or asking people to report aggressive thoughts and feelings (e.g., "I'm so mad I could throw something!"). True, none of these things are the pure essence of aggression itself, but they *are* related to aggression. If a child frequently punches other children, constantly thinks violent thoughts, and feels angry all the time, we will probably say this child has more aggression than the child who has never hit anyone, who thinks violence is wrong, and who never gets angry.

In other words, in the social sciences we often measure intangible concepts by measuring thoughts, feelings, and behaviors that are theoretically associated with those concepts. So, to make it more presently relevant, if we wanted to measure how much of an anime fan someone was—an intangible concept—we might choose to measure how much manga they own, or how many hours a day they spend watching anime, or how many anime conventions they've been to. The way we choose to measure our intangible concept is called "operationalization." In a nutshell, operationalization is the answer to the question "how are you going to put numbers to the thing you're trying to measure?"

There's no one correct way to operationalize a variable. Recall our example of measuring height: There are *lots* of ways to you can measure height! You can use a ruler, a tape measure, or simply compare an object relative to another object of known height. None of these is the agreed-upon "right" or "only" way to measure height. Likewise, when it comes to measuring intangible concepts, we can measure them in a variety of ways, including measuring behavior directly, asking people to self-report past behavior, giving them surveys to measure their thoughts, feelings, and beliefs, or we can even ask *others* to rate the person.

Of course, all of these measures have drawbacks. For example, what if we asked the question "Are you a very immoral person?" It's hard to imagine anyone saying "yes" to this question, even if they did happen to be an immoral person. Why? Because being immoral is generally considered undesirable, and participants typically don't want to paint themselves in an unfavorable light to others, including to researchers. That's why any time researchers rely on participants to self-report their thoughts, feelings, or prior behavior, they have to carefully design the questions to avoid pressuring participants to respond in a way that's desirable. Researchers are aware of these limitations, having taken courses and spent years learning to design questions to minimize these problems.

Other problems with question design are far more subtle. For example, imagine if a researcher wanted to test whether watching hours of anime is associated with a person's ability to speak Japanese. The researcher decides to ask the question in a fairly straightforward manner: "To what extent do you agree that watching anime has improved your understanding of Japanese?"

On the surface, the question might seem valid.[9] After all, if participants generally agree, why not conclude that, yes, watching anime is associated with a person's ability to speak Japanese? Well, let's look more closely at the original research question. We want to know whether watching anime is linked to a person's ability to speak Japanese—whether people who watch more anime speak more Japanese. To test this, we need at least two pieces of information. First, we need to know how much anime they watch. Then,

---

[9] In basic terms: Validity refers to whether you are measuring what you think you are measuring (accuracy), while reliability refers to whether the measure is consistent (e.g., the items fit together, you'll get a similar score today as you did yesterday).

we need to know how well they speak Japanese. If it were true that people who watched more anime also tend to speak better Japanese, we could conclude that the two are related to one another.

But, what did we *actually* ask participants? Whether they *thought* their anime-viewing improved their language ability. The answer to this question cannot tell us whether anime is actually related to a person's understanding of Japanese. After all, a person may *believe* that watching anime improves their ability to speak Japanese when, in fact, this may not the case at all! Believing something to be true is not the same thing as evidence supporting the idea that something is true. Were this the case, then a toddler's belief that broccoli is bad for them and candy is good for them would be proof that children should be eating an all-candy diet![10]

To this point, we've hopefully made it clear that operationalizing the variables in one's study is not something to be taken lightly. Researchers must be diligent in designing measures that capture the essence of what they're trying to measure without building biases or desirable responding into their scales. Which may lead readers to wonder, how do we know when a measure is perfect?

To which the answer, put simply, is "Never, because there are no perfect measures." Full stop.

It's a statement so stark that it takes a moment to fully absorb it. What do you mean there are no perfect measures? Of course there are! Maybe not in the soft social sciences, but surely, we can turn to the hard sciences for evidence of perfect measures. For example, we mentioned measuring height with a ruler. What could be simpler than a ruler?

When you think about it, however, the flaws in a basic measurement tool like a ruler become apparent. The ruler's composition, for example, can affect its measurement. Metal, for example, shrinks in the cold and expands in the heat. As such, the temperature of the room may affect the accuracy of the ruler. Likewise, cloth tape measures may expand if pulled tightly—not to mention researchers may disagree or be inconsistent in where they start and stop measuring (at the top of the skull? The tip of the hair? Should the participant be wearing shoes? Socks?).

---

[10] Or, for a more serious example, a person believing that they don't have a drinking problem doesn't necessarily mean that they don't have a drinking problem.

The problem becomes even worse by the fact that even "direct" measures of the concepts we're trying to measure are often not as direct as we'd like to think. For example, think of a thermometer, something we might consider to be a "direct" measure of temperature. However, what, exactly, does a classic mercury thermometer measure? If you remember back to high school science, you'll recall that temperature is thermal energy, the vibration of particles. A thermometer is not a measure of the speed of those vibrations—not directly, at least. Instead, a thermometer uses the volume of a known mass of mercury contained within a tube as an indirect way of measuring the average speed of the particles in the area around the thermometer.

The point of all of this isn't to say that we should abandon any hope of trying to measure things. Quite the contrary, in fact. It's to point out that scientists for millennia have been able to advance our understanding of the world *despite* using flawed and imperfect measurement devices. Ultimately, our goal shouldn't be to create a perfect measure. Instead, it should be to create or use measures that are best suited to the task at hand,[11] and to recognize that we can still gain valuable insights from studies that use imperfect measures.

Understanding this point is critical to being an informed critic of scientific research. For example, laypersons criticizing scientific studies often nitpick a study's measures[12] and claim "Well, the measures are flawed, therefore the entire study is flawed, and we don't have to listen to any of its conclusions!" Were we to adopt this criterion for all studies we would literally have no data left, since there *are* no perfect studies.

Instead of throwing the baby out with the bathwater, the best approach to critiquing the measures of a study is to scrutinize what they do well and what they do poorly. Even a bent or broken ruler has some functions, after all: If all the numbers have rubbed off my ruler, I may still be able to tell

---

[11] An analogy might be to use a desk scale to measure the weight of a feather and a truck scale to measure the weight of a vehicle. The truck scale is simply not designed to be sensitive enough to detect the mass of a feather, while the desk scale is not designed to handle the weight of a vehicle. These are flaws of both instruments, making them both imperfect. But, when used for their designed tasks, few would disagree that they do their job well enough for practical purposes!

[12] Especially when it's a study whose conclusions they disagree with!

that a 12-year-old is about 5 rulers tall while an 8-year-old is only 4 rulers tall. If a researcher decides to operationalize "anime fan" by asking "how many hours a day do you spend watching anime," this is far from a perfect measure. For example, it fails to take into account people who may not watch anime but, instead, read manga. However, if we believe that *most* anime fans watch at least *some* anime from time to time, then the measure can still function as a way of telling how much of an anime fan someone is. It may be far from perfect, and we'll want to craft measures that don't have this particular flaw in future studies. However, it is fairly rare for a measure to be so *completely* flawed that the study itself is absolutely worthless.

We'll talk more about the subject of imperfect measures and drawing conclusions from imperfect studies in the last section of this chapter. However, let us now turn our attention away from the measures we're using in our study and ask *who* we're studying in the first place.

Sampling: Who are We Talking About

As scientists, if we want to make claims about a group of people, we should at least try to study a sample of them. At first glance, this seems so straightforward as to almost not need to be said: If you want to study anime fans, go out and get a bunch of anime fans and ask them a whole lot of questions. What could be simpler?

As it turns out, the task is more complex than it would appear at first glance, owing primarily to the question of what scientists call "generalizability" or "external validity." Put simply, external validity is the question of whether or not the results of our study accurately tell us something about the state of the real world. When it comes to studying a specific group—like anime fans—it refers to whether or not the results of our specific study can be applied to anime fans as a group.

To see the problem at the core, it's helpful to make a distinction between what scientists call "the population" and "the sample." The population is every single member of the group that we're studying. It's the group we'd ultimately like to know more about and make claims about. If we want to study Americans, then our population is "all Americans." If we want to study "Bisexual Asian-Canadian women over the age of 50," then our target population would be all bisexual Asian-Canadian women over the age of 50. In an ideal world, we would take a census of our entire population—gathering up every member and surveying them to get a perfect picture of the state of the population.

In practice, however, this just isn't feasible. For example, even with all of the resources of the federal government and the legal system behind it, the national census is unable to reach every single member of a country's population. There are numerous reasons for this. For starters, sometimes people live in unexpected places, making it difficult to know where to find them. Other times they are motivated to evade or avoid being studied. Even if they can be reached, people may still resist being surveyed. In short, despite our best efforts, even the most thorough, well-funded, and legally-obligated attempt to fully study a population will fail to survey every member of that group.

What are the implications of this, and what hope do we—as mere social scientists—have of studying populations without the legal system and millions of dollars at our disposal?

This is where the concept of sampling and population representation comes in. Let's return to our original goal: We want to be able to make a claim about a population of people. Sure, the most accurate picture of that group could be achieved by sampling every single member of the group. However, what would our picture look like if we had managed to sample all but one member of the population? For example, let's say we were trying to figure out the age of the average college student. In our ambitious recruitment attempts, we were able to recruit the millions of college students throughout the country—all but one—and wound up with a calculated average age of 21 years old.

Based on this description, what would you estimate the average age of all college students—including our missing student—to be? Probably 21 years because we recognize that the addition of this one extra person is unlikely to significantly alter an average that's based on millions of people.[13] The same logic can be applied to the case where we were missing two, or even three people from our population. We thus recognize that a sample doesn't need to contain all members of a population to nevertheless be a fairly accurate representation of the population.

---

[13] Unless, of course, that person happened to be millions of years old!

But wait, we're talking about instances where our sample size is pretty close to the size of our entire population. What if, instead of nearly all of the population, we've only got a fraction of it? In the case of our college students, what if we only have a sample of 1,000 college students instead of several million?

At first blush, it would seem like we're in a pickle: Any conclusion we draw about the sample or any average we calculate could *easily* be overturned depending on the millions of other college students not in the study. So, how do we learn anything from such a small subsection of the population?

This is where a second concept comes in: representativeness. Representativeness is the extent to which our sample is an accurate microcosm of the general population. Imagine, for the sake of simplicity, that our entire college population consisted of one-third 20-year-olds, one-third 21-year-olds, and one-third 22-year-olds—thus yielding an average age of 21 years old. If, in our sample of 1,000 people, we ended up with a sample of one-third 20-year-olds, one-third 21-year-olds, and one-third 22-year-olds—we would end up with the same average—21 years old. This is because the sample accurately represents the population: it consists of the same proportions of people as the population does. As such, the same is an accurate reflection of the population.

At its core, this is one of the primary goals of every social scientist: To conduct studies using samples that accurately reflect the general population. Of course, in practice, this is easier said than done. After all, how can we know for sure if a sample is representative of a population if it's impossible to fully sample the population? If we knew exactly how many 20-, 21-, and 22-year-olds were in our population, we wouldn't have to sample it in the first place, would we?

Instead, scientists do their best to try and achieve the most representative samples possible through a myriad of different sampling techniques. It's beyond the scope of this chapter to outline all of these different techniques. It is worth mentioning a few that aim to get researchers "representative enough" samples to let them be reasonably confident in their conclusions about groups.

Random sampling is by far the "gold standard" of sampling. The idea is simple: If a person were to pick people out of a population completely at random, they should, in theory, form a sample that gets increasingly representative as the sample size goes up. How is this possible, you ask? How can random, blind chance lead to this? Because, in theory, if participants are sampled completely at random, then there is no reason for especially old or young people to wind up in the sample more often. There is no bias toward sampling men or women more. There is no bias toward race or religious belief or wealth. If it's truly random, then every person should be equally likely to wind up in the study, meaning that there is no reason for the sample to be biased in one direction or another (e.g., to have more or less of one type of person). This is why, above all else, researchers try their best to randomly sample from a population.

Of course, perfect random sampling is an idea that's almost impossible to live up to, practically speaking. This is because, in most cases, there isn't a list of all members of the population to randomly sample from. For example, if one wanted to randomly sample anime fans, how would they do so? There is no giant list of all anime fans from which to draw names at random.

Instead, in many instances, scientists try to do the next best thing: They try to recruit participants from a variety of different sources and to avoid, as best as possible, introducing biases into the way they recruit. This means recognizing, for example, that if a person were to only recruit anime fans from anime conventions, that they would only be recruiting those who have the *money* and *time* to make it to a convention. To compensate for this, researchers may try other avenues for recruitment, such as online sampling from anime fan websites, to try and include fans who otherwise might not be represented in convention samples. Wherever they sample from, they will tend to recruit their samples in as random a fashion as possible—trying to recruit people randomly at conventions or online to avoid preferentially sampling one group over another (e.g., only asking men at an anime convention or only emailing specific members of an online anime fan mailing list).

To be crystal clear, there are no perfect sampling methods—just as there are no perfect measurement techniques. Nothing short of sampling every member of a population will yield a perfect picture of the population itself. If we were to accept only those studies that had perfectly representative samples or which studied every member of a population, we would have to throw out the vast majority of everything we know from biology / medicine, psychology, sociology, economics, anthropology. Since we're not prepared to do that, a compromise has to be reached.

Ultimately, scientists end up engaging in a trade-off between what's reasonable to do in practice and confidence in one's findings. In fact, the imperfection of sampling is built directly into the statistical techniques used by researchers, who acknowledge the possibility that their conclusions might be wrong due to problems with sampling.

Like with studies involving imperfect measures, laypersons are often quick to dismiss studies they disagree with on the basis of the study's sample, often seeing studies in an all-or-nothing, black-or-white fashion: If a study has imperfect sampling, it should be ignored, goes the logic. "That sample is too small" they might argue, without considering the representativeness of the sample.[14] "You only recruited participants online" they might say, without pointing out a good reason to believe that online participants might differ from non-online participants. The point is, a study that makes a claim supported by data—even from an imperfect sample—is still more compelling evidence than no study at all. Ultimately, nitpicking a study's sample without a good rationale and, more importantly, compelling data to the contrary, does little to undermine the study's point. Anyone can say "that study wasn't perfect." It's much harder to provide compelling data that says otherwise—which is precisely the job of scientists.

We'll return to the question of what, exactly, researchers can learn from imperfect studies with flawed measures and sampling techniques in the last section of this chapter. For now, however, we turn to a brief overview of the use of studies as specific tools for testing specific claims and how, very often, people fail to grasp what specific studies can and cannot tell us.

Type of Study and Drawing Conclusions

Without tools, a tradesperson is nothing more than a person with a lot of ideas and experience. Scientists find themselves in a similar boat:

---

[14] In fact, it is almost *always* preferable to have a smaller, more representative sample than a larger, non-representative sample! As an example of this, which would be expected to give you a more accurate picture of what the average American is like: A sample of 1,000 90-year-old Harvard graduates or a sample of 100 Americans dialed at random? The first sample is technically larger, but is unlikely to represent the demographic composition of the American population as well as the sample of 100 Americans dialed at random.

knowledgeable and experienced, but ultimately nothing without the tools of data collection at their disposal. However, whereas the functions of a hammer or a screwdriver are pretty obvious to most people, the functions of different types of studies are not always so apparent.

It's worth pointing out, before diving into the function of studies, that, just like with measures, there are no perfect tools. A hammer, for example, is fantastic at what it does. It's purpose-built to drive in nails. The same hammer, however, is pretty awful being a screwdriver: It's specialization at one task also makes it ill-suited to perform another task. This illustrates an important point about tools in general and about studies specifically: A tool's inability to perform one specific task well and another task poorly does not make it a useless tool.

With this introduction in mind, let's discuss what studies, as tools, are designed to do.

Studies are the means by which scientists gather data about the world. Broadly speaking, studies can serve two broad, overlapping functions: exploration and hypothesis-testing. Exploration refers to collecting data to gain an accurate picture or initial understanding of a topic. Say, for example, you were interested in trying to understand the motivations of a bunch of anime fans, but you, yourself, were not an anime fan—or a fan of anything, really.[15] Ideally, you would like to form a theory about what motivates anime fans, but in this case, there is so little information available on the subject and you have no experience of your own to draw upon that you might as well be shooting in the dark.

This is where exploratory research comes in. It represents a first look at a subject. Exploratory research tends to be fairly broad in scope, casting a large net that often covers a wide range of topics. The questions being asked tend to be fairly open-ended in nature, encouraging participants to explain their thoughts, draw upon their own experience, and include any lay theories they have about a subject. In essence, exploratory research is an act of humility on the part of the researcher, in that it involves recognizing that they don't know enough about a subject to even know what questions are worth asking. Exploratory research helps researchers get a more accurate

---

[15] Full disclosure: At least one of the authors of this book is a self-admitted anime fan, and most of the authors are, themselves, media fans of one type or another. This is just a hypothetical scenario!

picture of the phenomena they're studying and the questions needing to be answered in a field.

Scientists rarely conduct exploratory research and call it a day, however. Once they have enough data, they develop models and theories to try and explain the phenomenon. More often than not, these theories involve relationships between important variables. For example, exploratory research might reveal that a lot of anime fans watch anime together. Having made this observation, a researcher might then theorize that fans are motivated by sharing fan experiences together and predict that bigger fans spend more time watching anime with their friends. It then remains for them to test the hypotheses generated by their theories.

Hypothesis-testing studies typically involve looking for relationships between two or more variables. To use our previous example, we might hypothesize that anime fans who identify more strongly as fans also spend more time watching anime with their friends. Testing this hypothesis involves measuring these two variables (how strongly one identifies as an anime fan and how frequently one watches anime with their friends) and then testing whether there is a significant relationship between them. There are a multitude of ways researchers can measure these two variables (remember operationalization) and there are, likewise, a multitude of ways they could structure the study to test for this relationship. Far from being trivial decisions, how the scientist structures the study will significantly impact the kinds of conclusions they can draw about their hypothesis.

One way the researchers could structure their study is a cross-sectional study. Cross-sectional studies are the most straightforward studies you can conduct. They involve measuring the variables in question at one point in time—the classic example being a survey. The strength of cross-sectional studies is that they're fairly easy to conduct: Give a group of people a survey, then analyze the data to test whether the variables you measured are related to one another.

There's a drawback to the ease of conducting a cross-sectional study, however: You cannot draw causal conclusions. Let's imagine that the researcher did a survey and found that, yes, people who identified more strongly as anime fans were also the same people who said they spend more time watching anime with their friends. The study allows us to conclude that these two variables are related, just as our hypothesis predicted.

However, can we conclude that watching anime with your friends *causes* people to become bigger anime fans? No. The cross-sectional study only allows researchers to know *that* the two variables are related to one another. The nature of this relationship remains a mystery because there are at least three possible—and equally plausible—explanations. One explanation is that, yes, watching anime with one's friends causes them to become bigger anime fans. An alternative explanation is that being a bigger anime fan causes someone to drag more of their friends over to watch anime with them. Another possibility is that some unmeasured variable is related to both of these things, causing them to appear directly related. For example, it might be the case that open-minded people are both more likely to become anime fans *and* are more likely to have more friends that they can watch anime with.

What should we do if they want to test the *causal* relationship that watching anime with friends *causes* people to become bigger anime fans?

Two types of studies lend themselves well to this particular purpose. The first is the longitudinal study, which is really just a repeated cross-sectional study. In a longitudinal study, researchers give the same survey to the same group of participants on two or more occasions. Researchers can then see how responses change over time, allowing them to test which variable came first: Does spending more time watching anime with friends come before being a big anime fan, or vice-versa? While longitudinal studies do allow researchers to get a better picture of temporal order, they are incredibly difficult to run: You need to track down the same participants months or years after the initial study, which can be very difficult. These studies also can't rule out the possibility that a third, unexplored variable was causing the relationship to happen. After all, it's still possible that as a person becomes more open-minded over time, they also become more open to watching anime and have more friends to watch anime with.

The other type of study—experiments—are ideally-suited to testing causal claims about variables. Without writing a textbook on the subject, experiments involve the following logic: If X causes Y to happen, then if the researcher manipulates the value of X, the value of Y should move in a proportional manner. If it doesn't, then X cannot be said to cause Y. In other words, in an experiment, the researcher manipulates the "causing" variable to look for changes in the outcome variable. Experiments are especially good at letting researchers establish the temporal order of variables (i.e., which came first), but also have the additional benefit of ruling out those pesky third variables in the process: By randomly assigning[16] participants to the different conditions of your manipulation, third variables are removed from the equation, since it's unlikely that all of the open-minded people will wind up in one condition and that none of the open-minded people will wind up in the other condition just by sheer dumb luck.

If experiments are so great, why bother with anything else?

Like with cross-sectional studies and longitudinal studies, experiments have their own basket of drawbacks. The most pressing of these is that it is often impractical, unethical, or outright impossible to manipulate some variables. For example, it may be possible for researchers to manipulate whether people watch anime with their friends or alone in the laboratory on one or two occasions, but it's impractical for researchers to insist, for the next three months, that anime fans *only* watch anime by themselves or *only* with their friends to test the long-term effects. Fans would be unwilling to let researchers to have that kind of control over their life, nor would there even be a way for researchers to know for sure that fans were following the researchers' instructions.

In addition to being impractical, it may simply be impossible to do the manipulation in question. For example, if we wanted to know whether anime fans today became anime fans because they watched anime with their friends in the past, it's impossible to run the clock back to before people were anime fans to run the experiment. The experiment could be run with non-fans to see if we can create new fans in the lab, sure, but there's no way of knowing whether the fans we created in the lab over the course of an hour or two would go on to become lifelong fans months or years later.

In sum, there are numerous tools at researchers' disposal. However, like a craftsperson, it takes skill to know when to use a hammer and when to use

---

[16] Random assignment is a key part of an experiment: Participants have to wind up in one condition or the other by a completely random means (e.g., flipping a coin, using a random number generator). If participants get to choose which condition they're in, or if they're assigned to condition by some other variable (e.g., what time of day they came into the study), then it's not a true experiment and it cannot rule out that third variable.

a screwdriver. For many of the sorts of claims you'll see throughout this book, we conducted a combination of exploratory research—aimed at giving us an accurate picture of what the anime fandom looked like—as well as cross-sectional research, aimed at testing theories about the relationship between important variables.

Our choice of cross-sectional methodologies does largely limit our ability to make causal claims about the relationship between our theoretical variables. Correlation, as they say, is not causation. At best, in most cases we can only claim that two variables *are* related, but not which one *caused* the other. This is something that we—as scientists—are mindful of when we design our studies.[17] The decision represents a compromise between several priorities, including the inability to practically manipulate some of the variables in question, the need to be able to conduct the study on a large scale (to get a large and representative sample of anime fans), and the fact that, theoretically speaking, many of the relationships we theorize between variables are thought to be bidirectional. To put it another way, it can be simultaneously true that watching anime causes people to identify more strongly as fans *and* that being a bigger fan causes people to watch more anime. In most cases throughout this book, we're not really concerned about the causal direction, in part, because the nature of our methods does not permit us to draw causal conclusions.

Since we're talking about two variables being related to one another, let's take a moment to talk about how we're able to use the numbers we've collected to determine whether or not two variables are "significantly related" to one another. Don't worry, you don't need to know anything about statistics, and we promise it will be pain-free!

Data Analysis: Making Sense of the Numbers

Whether you're a scientist or a layperson, it's valuable to have at least a rudimentary understanding of statistics. This is because you are confronted with statistical claims on a day-to-day basis. Whether we're talking about the relative effectiveness of one brand of toothpaste over another[18] or the results of a recent opinion poll, we often learn about the world and make decisions about it based on statistics. As such, it behooves us to learn at

---

[17] Though that doesn't stop laypersons from pointing out to us that correlation does not equal causation—as if this was somehow something we didn't already know!

[18] Really, what does it mean for a tooth to be "3x whiter?"

least a little bit about what they are and how to interpret them, especially when reading a book whose conclusions are founded entirely on statistics!

The first thing to understand about statistics is the difference between descriptive statistics and inferential statistics. When most people think about statistics, they're thinking about descriptive statistics. These are numbers which summarize something about a population. For example, if I were to sample the height of all the boys in a class, that average would be a descriptive statistic. It is a single number which summarizes all of the height data in a single number: "If you see a boy from this class, you can expect him to be about 150cm tall." While the most common descriptive statistics involve central tendency (i.e., what is a typical / popular / common value for most members of this group?), there are also statistics summarizing variability around that central tendency (i.e., are most people pretty close to average, or do people differ wildly from the average value?)

Descriptive statistics are, for the most part, fairly straightforward and intuitive. Most people can understand descriptive statistics like "56% of people say they support this new bill" or "the average car costs $28,000." However, recall that scientists are more than mere fact finders. Descriptive statistics, in and of themselves, are not terribly interesting to most scientists.

To understand why, let's consider a scientist studying anime fans. The scientist gives a bunch of anime fans a scale that measures their overall well-being on a scale from 0-10. After giving that measure to a bunch of anime fans, the scientist discovers that the average anime fan scores 7 out of 10. What does this number mean? Are anime fans doing well? Poorly? By itself, this number doesn't tell us a whole lot. Without any sort of comparison point or additional information, 7 out of 10 is just a number: Yes, it's higher than the midpoint of the scale, but it's lower than the maximum value.

Remember, scientists aim to test hypotheses. This is where inferential statistics come in. What if, instead of just trying to measure the well-being of anime fans, the researchers asked, "do anime fans experience higher well-being than non-fans?" This is a *much* more interesting question, one that hints at the possibility that watching anime may be associated with well-being (perhaps causing, or being caused by, higher well-being).

As such, our intrepid young scientist runs out and collects a second sample of non-anime fans for comparison. In this sample, they discover that the average non-anime fan scores 6 out of 10 on the same well-being measure—one point lower than the average anime fan does. "Great," our scientist thinks to themselves, "this settles it!" Anime fans experience better well-being than non-anime fans, right?

Not so fast! While it's true that the average well-being score for the sample of anime fans is higher than the average well-being score for the sample of non-anime fans, remember that these are just *samples*. It's impractical and implausible to measure every single anime fan and every single non-anime fan. As such, we're making guesses about what the average anime fan and the average non-anime fan based on these samples. We should expect there to be a bit of "noise" in our guesses, since our samples are not perfect representations of all anime and non-anime fans.[19]

Recall that the scientist found that the average anime fan scored 7 out of 10 on well-being. However, what if they ran the study again, with a different set of anime fans? Perhaps the next time they end up with an average score of 5 out of 10. Or 9 out of 10. The same could be true for the non-anime fan sample: In the first sample they averaged 6 out of 10, but in subsequent samples averages may be as low as 4 out of 10 and as high as 8 out of 10. Now we've got a predicament: Depending on the sample we use, we could conclude that anime fans score higher, about the same as, or lower than non-anime fans in terms of well-being. How can we conclude anything from this?

Inferential statistics helps to resolve this problem. In a nutshell, inferential statistics use information about *both* the central tendency and the *variability* of scores from the two groups to calculate how *likely* it is that the two groups are equal. To see, in a very basic sense how this works, let's go back to our first two samples, with anime fans scoring 7 out of 10 and non-anime fans scoring 6 out of 10.

---

[19] As a simple example: If we recruited all of our anime fans from a convention, we might only be getting a sample of anime fans who had enough money to go to a convention. Our sample would probably overestimate how much money the average anime fan had! This isn't a problem of sample size: This bias would be true whether we looked at 10 or 1,000 convention-going anime fans! In small samples, however, the problem is worse, because it increases the chance that one or two unusual fans can have a disproportionately strong influence on your estimate. Imagine, for example, getting a random millionaire in your sample. This millionaire will have a bigger effect on your estimate of the average anime fan's income if you only study 10 fans than if you study 1,000 fans.

Imagine a scenario where there was very little variability in both groups. In the anime fans, the average score is 7 out of 10, and virtually every anime fan scores close to 7 out of 10 (e.g., 6.8, 7.2, 7.1, 6.9, 7.0, etc.). Imagine the same is true for the non-anime fan scores, which are all very close to 6 out of 10. Because all the scores are very close to the average, we can be reasonably sure that if the scientist were to grab *another* sample of anime fans, they would probably also end up with an average score very close to 7, and that the non-anime fans would end up with an average score very close to 6. Because of this low variability in our samples, we can be reasonably confident that if the scientist were to run their study over and over again, they would again and again find that anime fans score higher than the non-anime fans. We could conclude that the two groups are statistically significantly different, meaning that they're different enough from one another that it was probably not due to a fluke or a lucky sample. With a bit of math, we can determine whether we could reasonably expect (e.g., more than 95% of the time) to get the same results if we ran the same study again.

In contrast, imagine a scenario with a *huge* amount of variability in both groups. In the anime fans, with an average score of 7 out of 10, imagine participants scored all over the place (9.9, 4.1, 5.3, 8.7, 7.8, 6.2). Because of how "noisy" and chaotic the scores are, there's a fairly good chance that if the scientist were to scoop up another random sample of anime fans, they might end up with a higher or lower average score just by random chance.[20] For this same reason, there's a much greater chance that, if the scientist were to run this study again, they may well end up with non-anime fans scoring higher than anime fans. Inferential statistics would allow us to conclude, based on this high variability information, that these two samples are not statistically significantly different from one another: Even though the anime fans scored higher in this one sample, we cannot be reasonably confident that the same would hold true if we ran the study again with new samples.

This is the strength of inferential statistics: They allow scientists to test hypotheses and determine whether the data they collect more strongly

---

[20] This becomes less of a problem if the researchers grab large samples rather than smaller samples, which is one of the reasons why larger samples are preferred in research!

support the predictions of their theories or the predictions of competing theories. Rather than simply eyeballing the results and having to rely on subjective opinion to decide whether the data support or refute a hypothesis, inferential statistics provide scientists with a mathematical way to determine which model is a better fit for the data.[21]

It's worth briefly mentioning a few more important concepts before we finish up this section. The first is the concept of correlation—a term that people often misuse to the point that it's physically painful to listen to.[22] A correlation is a number which represents how strongly two different variables are related to one another. In other words, you must always talk about a correlation *between* X and Y—it is not possible to look for a correlation in just a single variable.

Correlations are a sort of mathematical pattern-finding procedure that essentially asks, "how do the people who score higher / lower on X score on Y?" If people who score higher on X also tend to score higher on Y, we call this a positive correlation. If people who score higher on X tend to score lower on Y, we call this a negative correlation. Finally, if people who score higher on X score about the same as everyone else on Y, then we say there is no correlation. Correlations are measured with a score from -1 (the strongest possible negative correlation) to +1 (the strongest possible positive correlation), with a score of 0 indicating that there is absolutely no relationship between two variables. It is the absolute value of a correlation that tells you how strong it is. In other words, a correlation of +.60 is as strong as a correlation of -.60 (and a correlation of -.60 is stronger than a correlation of +.32).

To imagine some examples, let's call "the value of a car" our variable Y. Different cars will have different values, Y—some will be worth more and some will be worth less. We can ask whether different variables, X, are associated with different values, Y. Let's say that "X" is the amount of insurance that you pay for your car. Chances are that, in this case, X will be

---

[21] Of course, we're glossing over a *lot* of the nuances and complexities of statistics. But for the purpose of this book, our focus is on giving you enough information to understand what is meant by "statistical significance" and how scientists determine whether two things are statistically significantly different or not.

[22] Seriously! If this book does nothing else besides make a few people stop misusing the term correlation, it will have been worth the effort to write it!

strongly positively correlated with Y: Cars that you pay more for insurance on probably also cost more. It may not be a perfect correlation (there may be a few examples of expensive cars with cheap insurance or vice-versa), but for the most part, there is a positive trend in the data: as X goes up, so does Y.

In contrast, let's imagine that X is the age of the car. As the age of the car, X, goes up, the value of the car, Y, tends to go down. Again, there will be some exceptions to this: Really old, collectible cars may be worth a lot, while really new, economical cars may be particularly cheap. However, for the most part, there is a negative correlation between a car's age and its value: As X goes up, Y goes down.

Finally, let's imagine that X is a car's paint color, on a scale from "yellow" to "blue." Higher X scores mean more "blue," while lower X scores mean more "yellow." In this case, there's no reason to believe that, all else equal, a blue car costs more than a yellow car, or vice-versa. In this case, we would say that there is zero correlation between these two variables: As X goes up, Y scores do not differ.

Scientists can combine the concept of correlations with inferential statistics as a way to test hypotheses. For example, if a scientist wanted to test the hypothesis that consuming violent media was related to a person's aggression, they would set up a study which measured the correlation between violent media exposure and aggression in a bunch of participants. They would get an estimate of this correlation (e.g., +.20) and wound run inferential statistics to determine whether this correlation is statistically significantly different from a correlation of 0. If the correlation is determined to be statistically significantly bigger than a correlation of 0, scientists would conclude that, yes, a relationship exists. If the correlation does not differ statistically significantly from 0, they would conclude that no such relationship exists.[23]

A final point to consider when it comes to statistics and statistical thinking is the concept of probabilistic thinking—a concept we introduced earlier in this chapter. Probabilistic thinking involves thinking about thoughts / behaviors / outcomes as being caused by a multitude of factors interacting at once—so many, in fact, that we can often treat the outcomes

---

[23] We generally consider correlations around .30 small, .50 moderate, and .70 strong.

as being at least partially due to random chance. For example, imagine we are trying to predict the outcome of "getting a high-paying job." At first glance, it may seem impossible to predict who gets good jobs and who does not: People wind up at the jobs they're at for a variety of reasons.

However, despite all the chaos in the world, it is possible for scientists to use statistics and carefully designed studies to "cut through the noise" and make some predictions. For example, we can assume that educated people are more likely than people with no education to wind up at a high-paying job. Of course, there are plenty of examples of people without post-secondary education getting really good jobs for a variety of reasons (e.g., being related to the owner of the company, being charming and charismatic, being willing to work a very dangerous job). However, for the most part, all else equal, a highly-educated person can probably expect to earn more at their job than a person with no formal education. The existence of counterexamples (e.g., people without post-secondary education who get paid more) does not change the fact that, on average, educated people tend to get paid more.

Building upon this idea, scientists also recognize that numerous factors can interact in complex ways to predict outcomes. In the above example we considered a person's education. We could look at the interplay of a lot of different factors: education, the jobs of one's parents, where a person grew up, languages spoken, race, sex, religious affiliation, proficiency with technology, willingness to take risks, age, the economy, and the list goes on! In short, while scientists may try to cut through the "noise" and look at one or two variables at a time, scientists recognize that the world is a very complex place, and often aim to build models that take many relevant factors into account at once.

This is important, because a scientist looking at only one or two variables does not mean they believe that all other variables are irrelevant. Rather, it is often impractical to measure everything, or it is necessary to statistically control for the effects of other variables to be able to properly test whether a variable being studied is correlated with some outcome of interest. Keep this in mind as you read this book, otherwise you'll end up sending us letters telling us what we already know: Yes, we know that being an anime fan is not the *only* thing that relates to a person's well-being!

Limitations and the Fallacy of the Perfect Study

By now we've reviewed several important components of scientific thinking, including reviewing central tenants of scientific thinking, how we measure things in science, how we design our studies, and how we analyze them. We've also mentioned throughout these concepts that all of these processes involve trade-offs, limitations, and accepting imperfections. We haven't shied away from the fact that conducting scientific studies is a messy task riddled with imperfections. Let's be crystal clear: There are *no* perfect studies.

Before you spiral into a crisis about everything you've ever learned about science, however, let us reassure you with an example. Let's say we wanted to test a theory that becoming more involved in the anime fandom leads to better well-being on average. One simple way to do this might be to conduct a survey study: Go to a few popular anime forums and ask anime fans two questions: One asking them to rate, on a 10-point scale, how involved they are in the anime fandom and a second question asking them to rate, on a 10-point scale, their psychological well-being. Crunch the numbers and, sure enough, we find a significant positive correlation: People who scored higher on fandom involvement also scored higher on measures of psychological well-being. The data would seem to support our hypothesis, as they panned out in a direction consistent with hypotheses generated by our theory.

With a bit of critical thinking, however, we can easily challenge the study in several ways. For example, the study only looked at a subset of anime fans—specifically those who lurk in forums (and presumably interact with the fandom already). The study may miss out on all the anime fans who aren't actively involved in the forums and who may nevertheless be quite happy (something that might work against our correlation if we measured those people).

You could also argue that the measure of fandom involvement and well-being were woefully inadequate. How can a person measure involvement in the fandom on a 10-point scale, especially if we don't define what we mean by "fandom" or "involvement"? Do different people use these terms in different ways when they answer the question? Moreover, our measure of well-being is only asking about psychological well-being. What about physical well-being, or relationship well-being, or how well someone is doing financially? Surely these need to be taken into account in a measure of well-being, otherwise we're only getting part of the story!

Furthermore, the study itself was cross-sectional in design. As such, it's only able to, at best, show that two variables are related, it can never show that fandom involvement *causes* better well-being!

Your first response may be to throw away the study on these grounds, dismissing its findings as worthless in light of these flaws. Remember, though, that a screwdriver, while not designed to drive in nails, can still be used as a hammer in a pinch. It may not be ideal, but it's certainly better than nothing!

We acknowledge that we must always rely on imperfect studies in science, so we must also recognize that no one study can be expected to do everything. Studies involve trade-offs between desirable elements: The more you aim for the control and precision of a laboratory experiment, the more artificial and unnatural your study will be, and the less it will seem to apply to the "real world." The more you try to make the study longitudinal so you can track long-term changes, the more you're going to have to deal with losing or missing participants over time. The more you try to precisely measure your concepts with more and more measures, the more likely participants are to become tired, bored, or annoyed[24] with the survey and to just stop answering.

The imperfection of studies allows us a glimmer of hope, since it means that no one study bears the burden of single-handedly supporting or disproving a theory. Instead, scientists compare the relative weight of all the evidence for and against a theory. While our admittedly weak study linking fandom and well-being is a fairly modest piece of evidence in favor of our hypothesis, it is nevertheless a piece of evidence. If there is no study showing that fandom and well-being are *not* connected, the majority of the evidence is in favor of the hypothesis.

To be sure, at this point it might only take one or two simple studies showing no relationship to outweigh our fairly weak evidence supporting a

---

[24] One of the most common complaints we hear about psychological studies is that researchers seem to ask the same question over and over again, just in slightly different ways. This is the drawback to trying to be as precise and nuanced as possible in your measures. After asking about well-being in 10 different ways, participants really aren't interested in answering any more questions about their well-being!

relationship between fandom and well-being. However, until that evidence is collected, we must side in favor of where the bulk of the current evidence lies. Furthermore, if we conduct multiple imperfect studies that all point to the same result, there will be an even greater threshold for evidence to the contrary needed. Because, ultimately, scientists employ the famous philosophical tool of Occam's razor: If there are two bodies of evidence, a massive body of evidence showing that X causes Y and a single study showing that X does not cause Y, which is more likely: That X causes Y, and the single opposing study was a fluke, or that X actually doesn't cause Y, and *all* of the studies which say that it does represent hundreds of coincidences and flukes?

Keep in mind, however, that running the exact same study over and over again is not terribly compelling. After all, if you use the exact same sampling procedure and the exact same measures, one should expect to get the same results. It would be far *more* compelling would be if you got the same results using *different* measures, *different* samples, and *different* procedures.

So, imagine, as a follow-up study, we again tested the hypothesis that anime fandom involvement was associated with well-being. This time, however, instead of online fans we go to a fan convention, which gives us a smaller sample than our online sample. Instead of measuring fandom involvement with a single 10-point scale, we give fans a list of 30 different fandom activities and asked them to indicate, for each one, how frequently they engaged in it. Furthermore, instead of measuring well-being on a single 10-point scale of psychological well-being, we also measure self-esteem, mood, relationship quality, economic well-being, and how their day is going.

This study has its own unique problems, including the fact that participants may get sick of answering questions about their well-being, it's still a cross-sectional study, and now the study only looks at convention-going fans instead of online fans. But what if, despite these drawbacks, we still find that people who scored higher in fandom involvement also scored higher in well-being? Now we have to ask ourselves which is more likely: That anime fandom involvement is associated with well-being, or that two different studies, each using different measures and samples, happened to coincidentally find a statistically significant correlation due to chance alone when there isn't a real relationship between fandom and well-being in the real world?

If you're feeling particularly critical, you could argue that both studies had the same critical flaw: neither one can determine causation because they are both cross-sectional studies. This is completely correct! However, researchers in the field can draw upon *other* research to support this causal direction. For example, perhaps there have been laboratory experiments done on undergraduate students showing that putting them in study groups—as opposed to studying alone—improves their mood. Of course, this study isn't about anime fans, and it takes place in a lab and not in the real world. However, just like every other imperfect instrument we've used, it does provide evidence for the causal direction of our effect—that having other people around improves our well-being. As long as we have good reason to believe that study groups and anime fans may have something in common (e.g., they're social groups), we can use this as evidence to support the causal direction in our hypothesis. While it's not perfect, a growing body of imperfect evidence in favor of a hypothesis holds far more water in science than no evidence to the contrary.

If you take only one thing away from this chapter, let it be that science is more about comparing relative piles of evidence than it is about critiquing studies until you can ignore them. The studies upon which this book is based are far from perfect. As you'll read in the next section, they all involve cross-sectional designs, meaning that none of them, by themselves, is sufficient to make causal claims. They are limited by only being conducted in English. Some involve convention-going samples only, while others only involve online samples. Some measure the concepts involved in overly simplistic ways, or in overly complex ways that may have annoyed participants.

Despite these flaws, however, the findings in this book represent some of the best evidence to date about the make-up of the anime fandom, the psychological processes underlying involvement in the anime fandom, the activities engaged in by anime fans, and the beliefs and attitudes of anime fans. Future researchers may run similar studies or other studies, some of which will provide additional support for our findings and strengthen them, while others may provide convincing evidence against our current findings. We recognize and accept this: Science is a wonderfully dynamic process, as the theories of today are gradually replaced or improved with better supported theories tomorrow. We are not personally attached to the findings presented in this book and would be perfectly content with having researchers in the future conduct better studies that counteract the conclusions we reach here. The possibility of being wrong is what makes science so interesting!

Having laid our cards out on the table, and having armed you with the tools needed to critically scrutinize scientific studies, let's finish this chapter with a brief overview of the studies upon which the rest of this book is based.

The Present Studies

The findings in this book represent a culmination of eight studies conducted over the past seven years. Each of the studies consists of a survey of about 200-250 questions on a variety of subjects. We typically recruit participants for these studies from two different locations. The first is in-person at various regional anime conventions—a feat which typically involves months of planning in advance, including getting in touch with the convention organizers, getting permission to conduct research, and bringing a team of research assistants to assist in recruitment and survey collection amidst the chaos of a fan convention. The second main source of participants is online through anime forums and websites, which typically involves getting permission from the administrator or owner of the website before posting a recruitment letter asking for volunteers to participate in the study. All told, a typical survey study brings in between several hundred and several thousand participants—a very respectable, healthy sample size for a psychological study of this type!

One exception to the above studies was one of our first studies, conducted back in 2013, when we were just beginning this line of research. At the time, we had been wanting to test whether there was any truth to the stereotypes people commonly held about various fan groups, including anime fans. As such, we conducted an online survey of undergraduate students, asking them for their opinions about anime fans. This included their assumptions about the personality, behavior, and appearance of anime fans and whether they believed in common media-perpetuated stereotypes of anime fans.

It's important to note that before conducting any of these studies, we are diligent in ensuring that all of our protocols, questions, and recruitment procedures have been approved of by the institutional review boards of our respective universities. These oversight committees ensure that the research is being conducted in a way that minimizes the risk of harm to our participants. It also ensures that there is scientific merit to the research being conducted and is not simply wasting participants' time without any interest in furthering our understanding of psychology more broadly and the anime fandom more specifically.

Information about each specific study can be found in the following. For ease of presentation, we do not state for each finding in this book which specific study it came from. This information is available upon request from the authors, as are detailed summaries of every analysis conducted for this book. Additionally, we should note again that these studies were conducted in English. A good chunk of the participants in these studies are from Western, English speaking countries (e.g., U.S., UK, Canada). For example, the percentage of participants from the U.S. ranges from 54.9% to 86.4% in our data. Please keep this in mind as you read this book.

Year
2013

Con/Online
Online: Undergraduate Students

Sample Size
629

Survey Topics
Stereotypes of fans (traits, physical features, awkwardness, demographics, orientation, behaviors, well-being), prejudice, experience with fans. Included sample focused exclusively on anime fans.

Other Comments
179 questions; Only college students who had heard of the anime fandom, compared to Renaissance Faire Performers, eSport Enthusiasts.

Year
2014

Con/Online
Online / Convention (A-Kon)

Sample Size
4574:
3184 anime fans
1059 furries
511 fantasy sport fans

Survey Topics
Demographics, content consumption, personality, fantasy engagement, entitlement, social awkwardness, well-being, fandom / fanship, stereotype adherence, prejudice toward other fan groups, cosplay, character identification.

Other Comments
225 questions; Compared furries, anime fans, and fantasy sport fans in a large-scale, 3-fandom study; Anime fans recruited from large regional fan convention in Southern U.S. and various anime forums / discussion boards.

Table 2.1. Description of studies.

Year
2015
Con/Online
Online / Convention (A-Kon)
Sample Size
967:
328 con-going
639 online
Survey Topics
Demographics, content consumption, friendships in the fandom, functions of the anime fandom, display of fandom, stigma and disclosure of fan identity, waifu/husbandos, fandom/fanship, distinctiveness, typicality, well-being, character identification, bullying, loneliness.
Other Comments
210 questions; recruited from regional convention in southern U.S. and from anime websites.
Year
2016
Con/Online
Online / Convention (A-Kon)
Sample Size
737:
321 con-going
416 online
Survey Topics
Demographics, humanity, content consumption, genre preferences, fandom/fanship, sexism, experienced discrimination, obsession, attitudes toward fandom issues, spoilers, merchandise, paranormal beliefs, maturity, hostility, dark personality traits, health, well-being, socially desirable responding, fantasizing, prejudice toward other fandoms.
Other Comments
231 questions; recruited from regional convention in southern U.S. and from anime websites.

Table 2.1. Description of studies (continued).

Year
2017
Con/Online
Online / Convention (AnimeFest)
Sample Size
1115:
393 con-going
722 online
Survey Topics
Demographics, anime-related interests, content consumption, fandom/fanship, discrimination, favorite character, identification with / attitudes toward favorite character, technology use, problems in day-to-day life, sexism, spending habits, drama, political attitudes, well-being, prejudice toward other fan groups.
Other Comments
257 questions; recruited from a different regional convention in southern U.S. and from anime websites.
Year
2018
Con/Online
Online / Convention (AnimeFest)
Sample Size
2232:
369 con-going
1863 online
Survey Topics
Demographics, anime-related interests, spending, content consumption, motivation to be an anime fan, status, gatekeeping, elitism, attitudes toward LGBTQ+ people, helping, openness about sex, genre preferences, global citizenship, immersion, fandom norms, values, dreams, fandom/fanship, porn consumption, well-being, rituals, ratings of worst fanbases, favorite character.
Other Comments
236 questions; recruited from same regional convention in southern U.S. and from anime websites.

Table 2.1. Description of studies (continued).

Year
2019

Con/Online
Online / Convention (AnimeFest)

Sample Size
1019:
718 con-going
301 online

Survey Topics
Demographics, fandom/fanship, humanity, personality traits, LGBTQ+ prejudice, autism, well-being, disclosure of stigmatized identities, problems in day-to-day life, content consumption, fantasy engagement, identifying with characters, interdependence/independence, distress in life, fandom prejudice, private and public collective self-esteem, school performance.

Other Comments
202 questions; recruited from regional convention in southern U.S., convention in Canada, and from anime websites.

Year
2020

Con/Online
Online

Sample Size
2,852

Survey Topics
Demographics, subgroup identification, fan behavior, era preference, fandom/fanship, trajectory of fan interest, consumption habits, self-disparaging humor, word-of-mouth transmission, attitudes toward loli/shota, drama, well-being, autism, show preference, cosplaying and cosplay motivation, elitism, gatekeeping.

Other Comments
227 questions; Online data collection due to COVID-19 pandemic, collected through anime forums / websites.

Table 2.1. Description of studies (continued).

Chapter 3
Demographics

It's easy to fall into the trap of painting all members of a group with the same broad stroke. After all, this is precisely how the human mind works— it looks for patterns and construct prototypes that allow us to more quickly and easily recognize, predict, and interact with the world around us. When you think of a chair, for example, you likely think of a wooden piece of furniture with four legs under it. It's what we've come to expect when we imagine a chair, and it's the chair against which all other chairs are compared.

Our ability to create mental prototypes is useful for a myriad of reasons, the most of important of which is that it streamlines our thinking. When we encounter a new chair in the world, we quickly make certain assumptions about it, including the fact that it can support our weight and that it was built precisely to be sat upon. It's helpful to be able to do this, lest we be forced to re-learn what a chair is every time we encountered a new one.

This same tendency, however, can lead us astray. To continue with our chair example, there are some chairs with only three legs, or recliners, or chairs with wheels on them. If we assume that all chairs look and act the same, we're going to make some mistakes, including sitting on things that look like chairs but are not chairs, or not realizing that something is a chair because it doesn't look like a typical chair. In short, our use of prototypes can lead to misconceptions and prejudices about everything from pieces of furniture to people.

The problem is bad enough even when these prototypes and the assumptions we make based on them are grounded in reality; as the chair example demonstrates, we can still be led astray by a prototype founded on true information (e.g., most chairs do, in fact, have four legs).[1] The problem becomes amplified, however, when the prototypes themselves are less and less grounded in reality.

---

[1] For an easy demonstration of this principle, consider the average height of men and women. On average, men are taller than women. This is an empirically-supported, true statement. It is *not* true, however, to say that every man is therefore taller than every woman!

For example, most of us have beliefs about different groups of people (e.g., racial groups, gender, social classes, fan groups, religious groups, etc.). However, much of what people know about these groups is based on startlingly little data. More often than not, we form our opinions about an entire group of people based on a handful of personal experiences with a few members of that group. Worse, we sometimes base our opinions on *second-hand* accounts of other peoples' experience with group members, or from media portrayals of group members, which may have no basis in reality whatsoever.

As a result, social groups—especially disadvantaged groups—often struggle with misconceptions and stigma directed toward their group. This is as true for the anime fandom as it is for other groups, a point we investigate at great length in Chapters 16 and 17.

Let's not get ahead of ourselves by focusing on the misconceptions people have about anime fans, though. After all, it's far more useful to define a group based on what it *is* rather than on what it *is not*. With that goal in mind, in this chapter we aim to provide a sociodemographic "snapshot" of the, mainly, Western anime fandom.

We begin by looking at the fandom's makeup in terms of age and years of fandom involvement, considering whether the fandom is comprised primarily of young folks or a mix of older and younger members. This also includes assessing how long anime fans have been fans and when they first became anime fans. Next, we delve into a number of important identities, including race, gender, and sexual orientation. Given that being an anime fan itself puts one in a position of belonging to a somewhat stigmatized minority, it's worth asking how much of the fandom is comprised of other notable disadvantaged groups. We then investigate other important intrapersonal and interpersonal demographics, including the relationship status of anime fans, their relative wealth, social status, education level, and their political affiliation. Finally, recognizing that fandoms rarely exist in an isolated bubble, we look at the extent to which anime fans spill over into other fandoms and related interests.

Throughout this chapter we'll be challenging the picture of anime fans as a single homogenous group. After all, any two anime fans may share a love for anime but have entirely different tastes and preferences. Along those same lines, we also shouldn't expect them to look the same, think the same, identify the same, and have the same political affiliations.

Age and Years of Involvement

One of the simplest and most straightforward pieces of demographic information we collect about anime fans is their age. In fact, it's nearly always the first question we ask fans—in no small part because, for ethical reasons, participants in our studies must be 18 years of age or older.[2] Despite the ease of asking this question, however, there are some important caveats right out of the gate that need to be taken into account when interpreting its results.

As just one example, we often conduct a given study both online and in-person at a convention. At first glance, it might seem simple enough to just merge the two datasets and calculate the overall average age of all of our participants. In doing so, however, you would overlook an interesting finding: Convention-going anime fans tend to be older than online anime fans. In our 2019 study, for example, online anime fans were 24.9 years old on average, whereas the average convention-going anime fan was 27.6 years old—a statistically significant difference of more than two and a half years! While the size of this difference may vary somewhat from year to year, it has been consistent for every year of the study!

There are many plausible reasons for why this age gap between convention-going and online anime fans exists. One possibility is that younger people are less likely to have a stable, well-paying career and expendable income. Since it costs more to attend a convention than it does to participate in an online forum, conventions filter out those who lack the money to attend—something which selectively impacts younger fans.

Another possibility stems from differences in how long someone has been a fan or how big a fan someone is. For example, older fans are likely

---

[2] If you think that this requirement creates a "blind spot" in our understanding of anime fans by leaving out pre-teen and teenage anime fans, you're absolutely correct! Unfortunately, it's a largely unavoidable part of doing research. Ethics boards typically only allow research to be conducted on minors with parental consent. Since it's usually impossible to get parental consent online or at a convention (where a minor's parents may not be in attendance), there's not a lot we can do to overcome this limitation. For this reason, the results of our studies should always be taken with a grain of salt: They apply to "adult anime fans" only. That said, it's an interesting exercise to speculate on how and why 16-year-old anime fans should differ from an 18-year-old anime fans!

to have been fans for longer than younger fans and may, thus, be "bigger" fans.[3] It may also be the case that "bigger" anime fans are more attracted to the idea of attending a convention. Speaking to this idea, convention-going anime fans have, on average, been anime fans for longer than online anime fans (see Table 3.1).[4]

Year	Con-Going	Online	Difference
2015	13.3	12.1	1.2
2016	13.7	11.1	2.6
2017	12.7	10.1	2.6
2018	13.8	10.2	3.6
2019	13.8	11.0	2.8

Table 3.1. Average number of years a person has been an anime fan, broken down by convention-going and online anime fan samples across five years of research.

Another possibility is that older fans may have more friends who are anime fans, and people with more friends in the fandom may be more willing or able to attend an anime convention.[5] A myriad of plausible third variables such as these exist, and until we measure them all, we have no way to know for sure which ones fully explain this difference. It's unlikely any one of the reasons given above can entirely account for the difference between online and convention-going anime fans' age. Instead, it's more likely that each of these variables contributes, in their own small way, to the overall difference between convention-going and online anime fans that we commonly observe. Regardless of the specific reason, it's sufficient to say

---

[3] Assuming that less-serious fans are not as likely as more passionate fans to hang around in a fandom for, say, 20 years!

[4] Speaking to our earlier point about the prevalence of minors in the anime fandom: If the average age of a convention-going anime fan is 27.6 years old and if the average con-going fan has been a fan for 13.8 years, it suggests that the average con-going anime fan has been a fan since they were around 14 years old. While we might not be able to study minors directly, we *can* learn a bit about them through these sorts of analyses!

[5] From personal experience, it's more affordable to attend a convention if you're splitting the cost of a room with friends! Moreover, a person who is only semi-decided about whether to attend a convention may be "pushed over the edge" when they find out their friends are going.

that there are differences between online and convention-going anime fans, and we will be noting these differences throughout the book.

To switch gears just a bit, an age-related question we're commonly asked is whether or not the fandom is "getting older" as a group. One of the benefits of studying age data year after year is that it allows us to test this idea empirically. In theory, if we saw the average age of the fandom increase by about a year each year we did a study, it would lead us to conclude that the anime fandom is a fairly static population: It's the same group of people getting older over time.

On the other hand, if the average age of the fandom stays about the same over time, it would mean that the fandom is fairly dynamic: Older fans may be leaving the fandom, or there may be an influx of younger fans pouring into the group.

Figure 3.1 answers the question pretty clearly by comparing anime fans to two other related fandoms: the *My Little Pony* (brony) fandom and the furry fandom. Bronies are a fairly static group of fans who primarily got into the show when its newest generation began in 2010. By the time the show's third season was in swing, there were few new incoming fans—by that point, people were either on board the *My Little Pony* train or they weren't. As such, you can see that over a 7-year period, the average age of the brony fandom increased by nearly 4.5 years—suggesting that while there were likely some newer, younger bronies still trickling into the fandom,[6] the group was, for the most part, the same group of fans who aged alongside the show.

---

[6] Or turning 18 and being allowed to participate in our study for the first time!

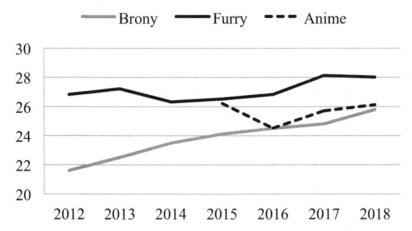

Figure 3.1. Average age of convention-going bronies, furries, and anime fans by year of study.

In stark contrast, look at the furry fandom—a fandom which does not orient around a single show but, instead, is based around a multitude of different shows, artists, and media. Over the same 7-year period, the average age of the fandom only increased by about 1 year. This suggests a fairly dynamic fandom, one with a steady influx of younger fans and possibly some loss of older fans.

So, where do anime fans fit in? Looking at the line for anime fans, we can see that it more closely resembles the furry line than the brony line. In fact, over 4 years, the age of the average anime fan was virtually unchanged. Given that there's arguably more new anime than ever before being produced and released to an ever-growing audience, this is fairly unsurprising in retrospect: The anime fandom is growing by continually capturing the interest of new young fans.

If this is the case, we should expect to find that the anime fandom is pretty heavily comprised of younger fans, with a steady tapering off of older fans. As Figure 3.2 reveals, this is exactly what we find! In fact, among adult anime fans, nearly 60% are between the ages of 18-21![7] In

---

[7] If we were able to include anime fans under the age of 18, we imagine the age of the average anime fan would be *far* lower. While we can't be sure exactly what the left side of

short, there is ample evidence that the anime fandom is comprised of teenage and young adult fans, with a fairly constant influx of new, young fans and a gradual trailing off of older fans.[8]

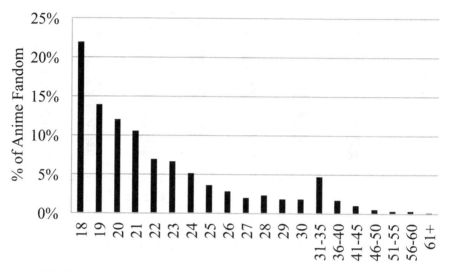

Figure 3.2. Age of anime fans.

Some additional evidence supports this interpretation of an influx of young fans and a falling off of older fans. In a recent study we asked anime fans to quantify their trajectory in the fandom. Specifically, we asked them to think about how big of an anime fan they were on a 7-point scale 10 years ago, 5 years ago, 1 year ago, and today. We also asked the fans to estimate how big of an anime fan they expect to be 1 year from now, 5 years from now, and 10 years from now. As Figure 3.3 shows, most anime

the figure would look like, we can be reasonably confident that there are *at least* as many teenage anime fans as there are anime fans in the 18-20 year range, since most fans report becoming an anime fan when they were young teens.

[8] Of course, we need to be careful about how we interpret this "falling off" of older fans. Recall that our sampling is drawn from online forums and anime fan conventions. It's entirely possible that many more older anime fans are still around, but simply do not visit forums or attend fan conventions. As such, we may simply be failing to study this part of the fandom!

fans show an upward trajectory of fan interest from the past to the present. In other words, they've become bigger anime fans over time.

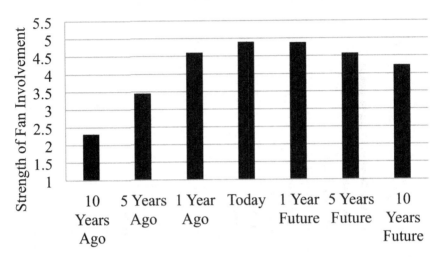

Figure 3.3. Trajectory of fan interest in a 2020 study of anime fans (1-7).

What about the future? While few anime fans expect themselves to entirely abandon their interest in anime altogether, the data do show that most anime fans *expect* their interest to decline at least a bit over time. Of course, these data are far from perfect evidence that people lose interest in anime and leave the fandom as they get older. After all, studies have shown that people are notoriously inaccurate when it comes to predicting their future thoughts, feelings, and behavior (e.g., Wilson & Gilbert, 2005). Nevertheless, it suggests that fans at least *expect* to become less interested in the fandom with time, and that there may be reasons to at least hypothesize that older fans may have reasons to become less active in the fandom with age.

In fact, when we analyzed the trajectory data for younger fans and older fans separately, we find that older fans may already be in the midst of this slide out of the fandom! While younger fans typically report being at the peak of their fan interest today, older fans tend to report that they were bigger fans in the past, stating that their fan interest has diminished today by comparison. Moreover, older fans also predict a steeper decline in their

66

future interest in the fandom than younger fans do. In other words, the way out of the fandom may be an increasingly-steep decline that younger fans can't fully appreciate until they're there themselves.

Taken together, while we can't know for sure whether older fans do, in fact, drop out of the fandom,[9] the available evidence suggests that this may be the case and may explain why the fandom's age distribution—comprised overwhelmingly by young fans—looks the way that it does.

Before we finish this section, let's consider how these findings about the anime fandom's age composition stacks up against other fan groups. For one thing, we find that anime fans are consistently the youngest of the fan groups we've studied. To be sure, adult *My Little Pony* fans, furries, and fantasy sport fans are all similarly comprised of teens and young adults. Even among these groups, anime fans consistently report being several years younger on average. This is likely due to the fact that anime fans also tend to report getting into anime at a younger age. To illustrate: While the average furry recalls that they became interested in the furry fandom at around the age of 16, the average anime fan recalls becoming interested in the anime fandom at around the age of 14, two years earlier. Likewise, anime fans actually recall joining the fandom itself (e.g., a forum, a local group) at a younger age (approximately 16 years) than furries (approximately 20 years).

There are at least two possible reasons for this tendency for anime fans to get into the fandom at younger ages. One is the relatively "mainstream" nature of anime compared to other fan cultures. It's common for furries to say that they were oblivious about the furry fandom's existence until they "stumbled" into it by accident. In contrast, anime content is readily available on TV, major streaming platforms like Netflix and Crunchyroll, and manga can be readily purchased at most bookstores. As such, anime is everywhere, making it easier for a potential fan to discover it at a younger age.

The other reason why anime fans may get into the fandom younger is because there is simply more anime content out there than there is for many of the other fandoms we study. It may take a while for a future furry to

---

[9] It's incredibly difficult to study this, given that people who have left the anime fandom typically aren't around on anime websites or anime conventions to answer surveys about their choice to leave the fandom!

discover furry content that they like because it is often niche or only available on specific forums for people with particular interests. In contrast, there is an overwhelming assortment of anime available, ranging from grounded slice-of-life stories to fantasy and science fiction and everything in-between. These different genres can usually be consumed in one's desired media format (manga, television series—often subtitled or dubbed into a variety of languages). As such, unlike the furry fandom, where it may be harder to find content that caters to a person's specific interest, it's increasingly likely that a potential anime fan will more quickly stumble upon something anime-themed that scratches their particular itch.

We'll discuss more differences between fandoms throughout this chapter, as well as discussing many of the overlaps between the anime fandom and related fandoms at the end of the chapter. For now, however, let's move on from age and consider other facets of the anime fandom's makeup.

Race and Ethnicity

Given that anime has its origins in Japan, one might expect the biggest consumers of anime to be Japanese people. While this is likely the case on a global scale, our research is focused predominantly on Western anime fans—in particular, fans from the United States and Canada. This is largely an artifact of us (the researchers) living in North America, primarily speaking English, and only having the financial means to make it out to American fan conventions. As such, keep in mind that the research discussed here (and throughout the book) refers to the (mainly) *Western* anime fandom, not necessarily to anime fans from Japan.

Based on the 2017 American Community Survey data from the United States Census Bureau's Population Estimates Program, the proportion of self-identified Asian people in America is 6.9% (with 6.5% of the Asian population, or about 0.45% of the total American population, being from Japan specifically). In our largest study of anime fans, we conducted in 2014, the proportion of online anime fans who self-identified as Asian was 19.5%, a number nearly triple that of the general American population.[10] The results also found that 72.9% of the fandom self-identified as White. African American/Black participants made up 3.5% of the fandom,

---

[10] This suggests that while the North American anime fandom may be predominantly White as a product of existing in countries that are predominantly White, the average self-identified Asian person is more likely to be an anime fan than the average White person is.

Indigenous/Native Americans made up 2.4%, Hispanic participants made up 8.5%, Middle Eastern participants made up 1.6%, and East Indian participants made up 1.1%.

Put simply, these data show that the Western anime fandom is predominantly White, but there is a sizable contingent of racially diverse folks, the largest group of which is, by far, Asian people. While data from convention-going anime fans suggest that the proportion of White fans is somewhat lower (approximately 68%), this may be an artifact of the convention's location in Texas, where a sizable Latinx[11] population exists (self-identified Hispanic participants made up 8.6% of that sample).

We should also note that our findings differ from much earlier research on the anime fandom conducted by other researchers. For example, in a 1994 article, Annalee Newitz reported on a survey of anime fans in which Asian and White fans were approximately equal in proportion. In contrast, ethnicity data from a more recent 2011 study by Annett reveals an ethnicity composition that is virtually the same as our own. This suggests that, demographically speaking, the anime fandom may have shifted to become "more White" over time.[12]

Despite the North American anime fandom becoming "more White" over time, compared to other fan groups we've studied, the anime fandom had the largest proportion of Asian members by far (see Table 3.2). A multitude of possible explanations for the demographic composition of the other fan groups include historical elements and cultural norms governing the acceptability of participating in each of the respective fandoms.

Together, these data suggest that the anime fandom, while predominantly White in the Western world, nevertheless includes a sizable proportion of Asian (and by extension, Japanese) participants relative to other fandoms. Moreover, the anime fandom also includes a sizable contingent of members of racially diverse backgrounds who, when combined with Asian fans, make up more than one-third of the fandom.

---

[11] There is currently deliberation about whether the preferred term for this demographic is Latinx. The wording on the original surveys did not use this term but instead used the term "Hispanic," which is why you see both terms used here.

[12] Given the history of anime's introduction to North America, which originally necessitated importing and translating anime from Japan before it was eventually popularized on larger networks, this demographic shift makes sense.

Ethnicity	Furry	Fantasy Sport	Anime
White	89.6%	68.4%	72.9%
Asian	3.8%	7.9%	19.5%
Black	3.2%	7.6%	3.5%
Native American	4.6%	4.4%	2.4%
Hispanic	3.4%	18.5%	8.5%
Middle East	0.8%	0.6%	1.6%
East Indian	0.1%	0.2%	1.1%

Table 3.2. Ethnic composition of furry, fantasy sport fan, and anime fandoms.

Sex and Gender

The past ten or so years represent considerable advancement in how society understands the concepts of sex and gender. To be sure, the notion of sex and gender as theoretically distinct is far from new, especially among scholars who specialize in this area. What is new, however, is the growing societal acceptance of this idea—both among laypersons and among scientists in other disciplines.[13]

The influence of these ideas can certainly be seen in our own research, which has advanced in leaps and bounds thanks to input from LGBTQ+ organizations and colleagues. In our early years, we, like many social scientists, focused our attention almost exclusively on participant sex, asking simply whether or not participants "identify biologically" as male, female, intersex, or other.

Since then, our questions about sex and gender have advanced considerably. Perhaps most importantly, we no longer ask just about participants' sex, but also ask about their gender.[14] We offer options beyond just "man" or "woman," including a variety of transgender, genderqueer, non-binary, and agender options that reflect the full gamut of gender identities. Finally, we no longer treat the question as a forced choice of only one of the options, but instead ask participants to check off any boxes that they feel represent them.

---

[13] We also recognize that language is ever-evolving, so the terms we used appropriately at the time of publication may not stand the test of time.

[14] In fact, we've moved away from being interested in a participant's sex to instead focus on fans' gender identity.

The result of these improvements has been a far more nuanced and complete picture of the anime fandom than we were able to achieve before. To illustrate, our earliest study indicated that 68.0% of anime fans identified as male, 30.4% identified as female, and the remaining 1.6% identified either as intersex or "other." These data allow us to say that the anime fandom is populated with more than twice as many males as females. Beyond that, however, it has very little to say on the subject of gender— including the relative proportion of masculine / feminine gender identities, the presence of transgender people in the fandom, or the concepts of gender fluidity, agender individuals, and gender queerness. Given that these topics are being more carefully studied in other fandoms, and given that many other fandoms (e.g., the science fiction fandom) have long been bastions for genderqueer people and have fostered critical discussions about gender, a nuanced take on gender is long overdue in the psychological literature on the anime fandom.

Identity	Online	American Con	Canadian Con
Male	72.4%	51.3%	47.4%
Female	20.9%	37.1%	42.2%
Transgender	3.6%	5.0%	4.8%
Non-Binary	3.7%	4.7%	4.8%
Genderqueer	1.0%	2.9%	3.0%
Genderfluid	2.0%	3.3%	4.1%
Agender	2.0%	0.9%	1.5%
Other	2.7%	2.9%	1.8%

Table 3.3. Identity in online and convention-going anime fans from Canada and the United States, 2019. Participants were permitted to select as many options as they identified with.

As Table 3.3 illustrates, while the online fandom tends to be predominantly male-dominated, convention spaces tend to be far more equally attended between males and females. The data also reveal that a significant proportion of the fandom, both convention-going and online, identify as transgender—upwards of 4-5%. This is a number 7-8 times higher than the 0.6% estimated proportion of transgender people in the general population (Flores et al., 2016). This number becomes even larger

71

when participants are asked, in a forced choice, to indicate whether they most closely identify with being cis-male, cis-female, transgender, or other; in this case, 5.3-9.0% of participants indicated that they identified as transgender across samples. This information about the prevalence of transgender people in the anime fandom would have been completely lost had participants solely been given the options "male, female, intersex, or other."

The prevalence rates of transgender, agender, genderfluid, and non-binary people observed in the anime fandom are comparable to rates we've observed in other fandoms (e.g., bronies, furries). As such, questions about the sizable transgender population in the anime fandom should be less focused on the anime fandom specifically and more focused on why transgender individuals are more prevalent in alternative media-based fan cultures more generally.

One possible explanation is that fandoms, themselves, foster norms of inclusivity and tolerance. This could be the result of a history of ostracism, bullying, and stigma associated with being part of a minority fandom (more on this in Chapters 17 & 18). Were this the case, it could be that those with a history of being bullied or ostracized may not wish to perpetuate the same judgment or cruelty onto others and may instead seek to create a fandom that is inclusive and welcoming for fans from all walks of life. This, in turn, would make these fandoms particularly inviting places for members of stigmatized groups.

A second possibility is that the alternative, non-mainstream nature of fandoms like the anime fandom makes them particularly appealing as spaces for people who, themselves, hold identities that run counter to what's societally common. This alternative interest, coupled with the largely fantasy-based (or, at very least, fictional) nature of the content around which the fandoms are based may make fandoms a place where members of historically discriminated / disadvantaged groups can be who they want without scrutiny or criticism.[15]

A final possibility is that fandoms are not magnets for members of gender-diverse groups, but rather members of gender-diverse communities

---

[15] Or, to put it another way: It's hard for people who don't fit in to make fun of someone who also doesn't fit in. The shared experience of being on the outside looking in may foster bonding and camaraderie.

may be more prevalent than we otherwise think, and people simply feel free to express it in fandom spaces. According to this position, far more people might identify as transgender, gender non-conforming, non-binary, or agender in the general population if they knew that these identities existed and if they had the opportunity to express this part of themselves without fear of judgment or ostracism. Fandoms such as the anime fandom may provide safe spaces within which people can explore their gender identity relatively consequence-free, allowing people who otherwise might not realize they belonged to these gender-diverse communities to discover this about themselves.

At the moment, these hypotheses are untested attempts to explain what is now well-documented: transgender and genderqueer people are prevalent in the anime fandom and related, predominantly online, media-based fan groups. Future research, including a considerable amount of qualitative research focusing on better understanding the lived experiences of transgender people in fandoms, can shed light on these hypotheses to see which ones hold water empirically.

Sexual Orientation

Before delving into the statistics about sexual orientation in the anime fandom, we'd like to make two observations to help set up expectations. First, entire categories of manga/anime have been dedicated both to yaoi and yuri—that is, content prominently featuring gay and lesbian characters. The very fact that these stories are numerous enough to exist as distinct genres illustrates that there are plenty of anime fans who are interested in stories about gay and lesbian couples. This, in and of itself, is enough to warrant questioning whether there might be a sizable contingent of lesbian, gay, and bisexual anime fans.[16]

The second observation is that many of the fan groups we've been comparing anime fans to (and which, as we'll see later, overlap with the anime fandom) have a fairly sizeable LGBTQ+ presence themselves. For instance, about 15% of the brony fandom self-identifies either as gay, lesbian, or bisexual (Edwards et al., 2019). Among furries, the number is even higher, with more than 65% of furries identifying as LGBTQ+ (Plante

---

[16] It's possible, of course, that at least some of this attraction is the result of heterosexual fantasies (e.g., men attracted to lesbian relationships or women attracted to gay relationships).

et al., 2015). For context, only about 4% of the general population of the United States identifies as gay, lesbian, or bisexual (Gates, 2017; Storrs, 2016). Put simply, fandoms which are demographically comparable to the anime fandom and overlap conceptually and demographically with the anime fandom report a robust (and in some cases majority) LGBTQ+ presence. That alone is reason enough to test whether the prevalence of LGBTQ+ folks in the anime fandom is higher than observed in the general population.

As the data show in Table 3.4, there is ample support for the prediction that there are considerably more LGBTQ+ anime fans than what is found in the general population. While majority of anime fans are straight, it is far from being overwhelming.[17] About 5% of anime fans identify as gay or lesbian, with considerably more identifying as either bisexual or pansexual.[18] Anime fans are also about 4-8 times more likely to identify as asexual than the approximately 1% of Americans who do (Gates, 2017).

Orientation	Con-Going	Online
Straight	58.1%	65.8%
Gay/Lesbian	5.0%	5.0%
Bisexual	17.1%	13.6%
Asexual	4.6%	8.0%
Pansexual	10.2%	5.3%
Other / I don't know	5.0%	2.3%

Table 3.4. Sexual orientation of convention-going and anime fans from a 2019 study.

Table 3.4 also suggests that there may be greater LGBTQ+ representation among convention-going anime fans than among online anime fans. There are a myriad of potential reasons for this, but one

---

[17] Not that it's a competition, of course!

[18] Pansexual refers to sexual attraction to a person regardless of their sex or gender. The term is sometimes seen as distinct from the term bisexual, which some see as referring to a sexual attraction to men or women but not to non-binary identities. For the purposes of our research, we do not provide definitions for the terms, but rather provide the labels themselves and allow participants to identify with the one that they feel most accurately describes them.

plausible explanation is that LGBTQ+ anime fans may benefit especially from face-to-face interaction and social support from the fandom. As we'll discuss in Chapter 19, the anime fandom provides fans with the resources needed to be resilient in the face of setbacks in day-to-day life. Since LGBTQ+ people often find themselves facing considerable stress because of their stigmatized identity (Meyer, 2003), they, like members of other fan groups, may find it especially beneficial to engage in fan-related activities with like-minded others (Mock et al., 2013). In contrast, straight fans may be less interested—or simply have less need—for face-to-face interaction and support network building, and may be content to interact with the fandom predominantly online.[19]

A final result on the subject of sexual orientation pertains to gender differences. Specifically, while 88.2% of men in the anime fandom identify as straight, only 56.5% of women in the fandom identify as straight. To put it another way, women in the fandom are nearly 4 times more likely than men in the fandom to identify as LGBTQ+. These findings largely align both with what we observe in other fandoms (e.g., furries, Plante et al., 2015) and with a general tendency for women to be less likely than men to be exclusively heterosexual (Chandra et al., 2011; Copen et al., 2016).

Relationship Status

It's one thing to know *who* anime fans are attracted to, but it's another thing entirely to know whether they find themselves in a relationship. As Table 3.5 makes clear, the answer to the question largely depends on whether we're talking about online or convention-going fans. While the majority of online anime fans are single, the majority of con-going anime fans are in a relationship of sorts. These numbers are comparable to other fan groups of comparable age (Edwards et al., 2019), although anime fans tended to be somewhat more likely to be single than those in other fan groups.

---

[19] Note that we're speaking only about average tendencies here! We're not suggesting that straight fans do not benefit from the social support provided by the fandom or that they have little interest in face-to-face interaction—far from it! They may simply have less need for it than LGBTQ+ fans.

Relationship Status	Con-Going	Online
Single	45%	73%
Dating	27%	15%
Polyamorous	6%	1%
Married	19%	9%

Table 3.5. Relationship status of con-going and online anime fans in a 2019 study.

An uncharitable interpretation of these data lends credibility to the stereotype of anime fans as desperately single[20] because they lack social skills—a topic we return to later in Chapter 16. A far more charitable interpretation, one grounded in empirical data, offers several other explanations for the prevalence among anime fans—particularly among online anime fans.

First, recall that anime fans are a fairly young group—the youngest, on average, of the fandoms we've studied. This is important because studies have shown that in recent years, people have been waiting longer and longer to commit themselves to relationships and to get married (Cohn et al., 2011; Levenson, 2010). This is often for financial reasons, but also because of changing cultural norms about when people are expected to get married. Regardless of the specific reason why younger folks are less likely to be in a relationship, the very fact that anime fans are younger than other fan groups can explain, at least in part, why anime fans are also less likely to be married or in long-term committed relationships.

Another possible explanation for the sizable contingent of single people in the anime fandom has to do with gender and sexual orientation in the fandom. Remember that the largest single demographic of the anime fandom—in particular the online anime fandom—is straight men. As such, straight men in the anime fandom, especially those who predominantly interact with other anime fans online, may find themselves in a "target-sparse" environment, given that there are fewer women in the online anime fandom and given that women in the fandom are far more likely than men

---

[20] The authors recognize that many people—including one of the authors themselves—are not in a relationship by choice and have little interest in being in a relationship. We do not wish to stigmatize single people, but rather are pointing out a popular negative societal belief that there is something wrong with people who are single or not in a relationship.

in the fandom to be bisexual or lesbian. As a result, the demographic make-up of the online fandom may simply be one that lends itself to a great number of men looking to find one of a few[21] straight women who might be compatible with them.

What does that mean for the single, straight men in the online anime fandom who are looking for a partner? Our advice to them is to perhaps consider looking elsewhere for a partner with other shared interests and then introduce to anime or, if possible, make it out to more in-person events (e.g., conventions, meet-ups) where you're more likely to meet more women in the fandom!

Socioeconomic Status

Among the most important pieces of demographic information about a person—from a social science standpoint, at least—is their socioeconomic status. Socioeconomic status refers to a person's class, wealth, education, and overall social standing. While interesting in and of itself, socioeconomic status is of particular importance because of its ability to predict everything from their political beliefs (Ballew et al., 2020) to their well-being (Pinquart & Sörensen, 2000). As such, no demographic look at the anime fandom would be complete without considering the living situation, economic status, and education of its members.

When it comes to living situation, it's helpful to compare anime fans to a similar fan group, furries, something we do in Figure 3.4. Nearly half of anime fans indicated that they currently lived with their parents, a number comparable to furries and to other groups we've studied (e.g., bronies: Edwards et al., 2019). The reason for this should be fairly apparent by now, given our consideration of other demographic variables. Since anime fans are, as a group, fairly young, it's unlikely that many of them can afford to move out and live on their own. This is amplified by a significant downturn in the economy in the past decade and young peoples' difficulty finding sustainable employment in recent years (Levenson, 2010). Speaking to this point, 36% of 18-to-34-year-olds in the U.S. report either currently living at home or being forced to move back home (Fry, 2016). With this context in mind, the half of anime fans who currently live with their parents can hardly be considered unusual for people their age.

---

[21] Relatively speaking.

■ Furries ■ Anime Fans

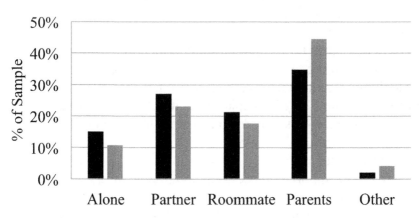

Figure 3.4. Living arrangements of furries and anime fans in a 2014 study of anime fans.

These findings are reinforced by data about anime fans' income. Anime fans, both online and convention-going, earn an average of about $28,000 USD annually.[22] This is comparable, albeit slightly less, than the average income of furries, about $32,000 USD annually (Plante et al., 2012).

While it's useful to know how much a person makes annually, especially when considering whether they can afford to move out on their own or buy a house, it's often just as useful to know how wealthy a person *feels*. After all, feeling frustrated or privileged is driven by whether you feel like you're getting more or less than you deserve and by what those around you are making.[23]

---

[22] Interestingly, this seems to fly in the face of our earlier hypothesis that older anime fans are better able to afford an anime convention than younger anime fans. One possible explanation is that while older convention-going anime fans earn about as much as younger non-convention-going anime fans, the older fans may have other resources that make it feasible to attend (e.g., living with a partner who can help pay rent, having connections to people who can share the cost of a hotel).

[23] As a little thought experiment to test this, imagine you received a $1,000 bonus at work. Most people would be pretty happy to get that extra bit of money. However, if everyone else at your company received $5,000, you would suddenly be dissatisfied with the same

How do anime fans *feel* like they're doing—or, to put it technically, what is their *subjective* socioeconomic status? One of the main ways we assess this is by giving fans an image of a ladder with 10 rungs on it and asking them to imagine that this ladder represents the society they live in. At the bottom of the ladder are the people who are the worst off in society—the poor, the homeless, and the unemployed. On the top of the ladder are the rich and powerful. With that in mind, they are asked to select which rung of the ladder they feel best represents where they currently stand.

The average anime fan rated themselves about mid-way up the ladder, somewhere between run 5 and 6. More surprising, online anime fans scored significantly higher ($M = 5.74$) than con-going anime fans ($M = 4.93$), despite the fact that online and con-going fans were indistinguishable with respect to their annual income or with respect to the size of their houses (a measure based on the number of bathrooms they had in their last house). Thus, while anime fans, in general, tend to rate themselves as being fairly middle class, online anime fans tend to be "middle middle" class while online anime fans rate themselves "lower middle class."[24]

One final component of socioeconomic status involves a person's level of education, as more educated people tend to earn more on average (Statistics Canada, 2017). As Table 3.6 reveals, anime fans, like other fan groups studied, are fairly well-educated, with more than three-quarters of anime fans currently in (or having completed) some amount of college. While con-going anime fans were more likely to have some college education than online anime fans—likely owing to their older age—online anime fans reported having parents who were more likely to have gone to college, something that typically predicts better college attendance and overall socioeconomic status.

---

amount of money that brought you so much happiness just a moment earlier. This is a phenomenon known as *relative deprivation*.

[24] Again, these findings might seem a bit surprising, but one can possibly make sense of them by considering who they're comparing themselves to. Those who attend anime conventions tend to be older and may be comparing themselves to others who already own their own home. In contrast, younger online fans may be comparing themselves to others their age and see themselves as doing okay for someone their age. As an analogy, a disappointingly low income for a 30-year-old might be an exceptionally good income for an 18-year-old.

Education Level	Anime Fans	Furries	Fantasy Sport
Some High School	2.0%	2.0%	0.5%
Ongoing High School	6.0%	2.1%	0.5%
High School Grad	14.7%	16.8%	10.0%
Some College	20.8%	24.8%	24.2%
Associate's Degree	5.0%	11.4%	5.9%
Ongoing College	28.5%	13.2%	7.1%
Bachelor's Degree	15.2%	20.4%	33.5%
Some Grad School	1.4%	2.3%	2.4%
Ongoing Grad School	2.6%	2.2%	3.6%
Advanced Degree	4.0%	4.7%	12.4%

Table 3.6. Education status of anime fans, furries, and fantasy sport fans.

Taken together, the socioeconomic status of anime fans paints a fairly clear picture of the average anime fan as a fairly well-educated middle-class person with some expendable income to support their hobby but not necessarily enough to move out with, at least in their early 20s. This profile—especially the data about educational attainment—is in line with stereotypes about anime fans being nerds (see Chapter 16 for more on this). This would also explain the significant overlap between anime fans and other facets of "nerd" culture, something we discuss later in this chapter.

While at first glance anime fans might seem in a poor financial situation due to living at home and making fairly unremarkable salaries, this is not unique to anime fans and is rather a characteristic of millennials in the current economy. It is also not likely to be a permanent situation: Given that many anime fans are currently in college or have recently graduated from college, many can expect to see a fairly significant increase in their salary as they leave their 20s and enter their 30s—something which largely destroys many of the unflattering stereotypes about anime fans as NEETs.[25]

---

[25] An acronym referring to people who are "not in education, employment, or training."

Political and Religious Beliefs

Other important variables for demographic research are the political and religious beliefs of a group. More than simply cataloguing the various opinions in the fandom, knowing the political and religious landscape of a group can yield important predictions about the group's norms, values, and behaviors, such as whether the group values charity and helping others in need (see Chapter 12 for more on this). Studying the group's beliefs can also reveal whether the group is a fairly homogeneous block of like-minded people or a loosely-held together club of people with a single shared interest who otherwise see eye-to-eye on very little else.

We could certainly delve into the subtleties and nuances of political opinions on an issue-by-issue basis but doing so would be both beyond the scope of this book and would shift the focus of this book from a psychological perspective to a political science perspective. For this reason, our own research has largely simplified the complex issue of political beliefs to a general tendency toward more conservative or liberal ideology along a single dimension.[26]

Despite being an overly simplistic representation of political beliefs, the data nevertheless paint a compelling picture. On the one hand, anime fans are about 3-4 times more likely to self-identify on the "liberal" side of the continuum than they are to identify on the conservative side—something that's true for both online and anime fans. They also tend to score more liberal on social issues, whereas on economic grounds they tend to be far more divided.[27]

On the other hand, despite being somewhat left-leaning politically, when asked whether they identify with a particular political party, 61.5% of congoing anime fans and 72.4% of online anime fans reported that they didn't. Unsurprisingly, those who scored fairly politically liberal were more likely

---

[26] We recognize that this system doesn't allow for important distinctions like "classical liberal" or "neoliberal." As psychologists, we're less interested in peoples' actual issue-by-issue beliefs and are, instead, more interested in the labels of "conservative" or "liberal" that people apply to themselves. This is also why we don't provide participants with definitions of these terms, and instead allow them to use them how they would in day-to-day life.

[27] On both scales, convention-going anime fans tend to score more liberal than online anime fans.

to identify with the American Democratic Party while those who scored fairly conservative were more likely to identify with the American Republican Party. Those who ascribed to neither party were far more likely to reside in the middle-ground, even if slightly leaning toward the liberal side of "middle-ground."

So, what's going on? Anime fans are both fairly liberal, but also don't identify with a political party? These findings are in line with the fact that, as a group, anime fans are fairly young, and younger people—especially in recent decades—tend to be far more liberal (Fisher, 2020) or, at very least, are less likely to become conservative over time than they are to become more liberal over time (Peterson et al., 2020). These findings are also consistent with another recent trend in young adults, one owing to skepticism about party efficacy—a tendency to eschew political party identification (CIRCLE, 2018). In this regard, anime fans are like any typical group of young adults in America.[28]

As we mentioned earlier, political orientation is important because it predicts numerous thoughts, attitudes, and behaviors. When comparing politically liberal anime fans to politically conservative anime fans, we find a number of interesting differences. Liberals, for example, are more likely than conservatives to welcome new members of the fandom, to be open-minded to changes in the fandom, and to be more opposed to elitism and gatekeeping behavior. Liberal fans are also more open to the idea of discussing sexual content and sexual behavior in the fandom with others. Liberal fans are also more likely to spend money on merchandise and content—something which may stem from more conservative fans possibly having a greater need to conceal their interest from others (e.g., their families) or simply being less interested in some merchandise (e.g., body pillows).

In closing out this section, let's take a look at an orientation related to one's political beliefs: religious orientation. The story of anime fans' religious beliefs is telling in the relative lack of a story. On a 7-point scale of religiosity, anime fans scored particularly low—an average score of only about 2.48. Measured another way, only 20.7% of online anime fans

---

[28] Speaking further to the idea that left-leaning political ideology is hardly unique to the anime fandom, similar results have been found for the brony fandom (Edwards et al., 2019) and the furry fandom (Plante et al., 2015).

identified as Christian and 3.8% identified with another major religion. In contrast, 64.1% reported having no religious affiliation and 7.1% indicated being agnostic or atheist.

While it's true that younger Americans are becoming decreasingly religious with each generation, recent studies put the number of 18-29-year-old Americans with no religious affiliation at 39% (Cooper et al., 2016). The rates of non-affiliated anime fans are thus significantly higher than the general population. While certainly not a defining feature of anime fans, this lack of religious belief is nevertheless a prevalent feature of the fandom, one warranting future research.

Other Demographics

Before we discuss the overlap of anime fans with other fan interests in the final section of this chapter, let's go over a few more scattered demographic details about the anime fandom. These are findings that either don't fit elsewhere in the book, which introduce concepts that will be discussed later in the book, or that add a bit of color to the picture of the anime fandom that we're painting.

First off, a bit about anime fans' physical appearance. This was prompted by research we'll discuss in greater detail in Chapter 16, when we directly challenge several prominent stereotypes about anime fans. The data revealed that a 56.2% of anime fans wear glasses (about 66% of U.S. population wear corrective lenses). It also revealed that the body-mass index (BMI) of anime fans was comparable to that of other fan groups (e.g., furries), an average of 27.8, a value categorized by those who use the scale as being "overweight."[29] Given that the study was based on a sample largely taken from the United States, and contrasted against the fact that 71.7% of American adults are either overweight or obese (Fryar et al., 2018), these results seem to say less about anime fans specifically and more about the American population from which is was predominantly drawn.

In a 2017 study, we asked anime fans, among other things, whether they currently worked in the anime industry. This was a part of a larger project

---

[29] We are aware that there are numerous problems with the use of the BMI, including a tendency for laypersons and researchers alike to over-rely on the measure as an indicator overall health despite the fact that this is a gross misuse of the scale, given its intended purpose. The question was used here primarily as a means of allowing for a simple comparison to other, existing datasets.

assessing fan entitlement (see Chapter 13 for more on this project). The study revealed that about 5% of anime fans claim to work in the anime industry in one form or another. While this seems exceptionally high at first, the deliberately vague wording of the question allowed anyone from manga artists to comic bookstore employees to potentially claim that they worked in the industry. It does suggest, however, that at least a small contingent of the anime fandom may well be involved in the creation and/or distribution of anime to the fandom. Coupled with the fact that 38% of convention-going anime fans and 27% of online anime fans describe themselves as artists, it seems plausible that at least a small minority of anime fans are, themselves, content creators, some of whom may do so at a professional level.

About 1 in 3 anime fans self-identifies as "manga otaku" and around 30% identify as "anime otaku," with online and convention-going anime fans being about the same in prevalence. We discuss otaku culture in Chapter 5, including the origins of the term, its significance in contemporary anime culture, and distinctions between otaku and non-otaku anime fans.

Among anime fans studied at a 2017 fan convention, approximately 40% described themselves as cosplayers. Distinctions between cosplaying and non-cosplaying anime fans, the psychology of cosplay, common cosplay behaviors, and attitudes toward cosplay are discussed in Chapter 7.

Finally, we can look at few specific characteristics of anime fans and how they differ between online fans and convention-going fans. First, convention-going fans are more likely (31%) to be fans of hentai content than online fans are (24%).[30] Convention-going fans are also about twice as likely to be fans of maid cafés than online fans are (14% vs. 7%). Both convention-going and online anime fans score very high on scales assessing their day-to-day technology use (e.g., social media, computers, cell phones), although, perhaps surprisingly, convention-going fans report significantly higher technology use in day-to-day life.

Perhaps least interesting of all to readers, but most interesting to us from a methodological point of view, a small minority of anime fans failed to properly complete a "validity check." Put simply, a validity check question

---

[30] We discuss hentai and its role in the anime fandom in Chapter 9.

is designed to test whether the survey-taker is both reading the questions and answering them sincerely. Sometimes they involve asking two completely opposing questions to see whether people are simply agreeing with every question on the survey (e.g., "I believe that cilantro tastes delicious" and "I think cilantro tastes horrible"). Other times, they involve a test of following instructions (e.g., "For this question, circle the number 3").

Con-going fans were more likely than online anime fans (17.3% vs. 10.0%) to fail the validity check question in our survey. This has at least two interesting implications. First, doing research at an anime convention may leave fans more distracted and less able to focus on the survey itself while they're doing it, causing them to miss the validity checks. Second, and more positively, the data suggest that while a minority of anime fans miss these validity check questions, most of the participants in our studies take the time to read and properly respond to the questions in the survey!

Other Fandoms / Interests

We'll finish this chapter by discussing some of the considerable overlap between anime fans and other conceptually related fandoms and interests. After all, throughout this chapter (and, indeed, throughout the rest of this book), we make the comparison between anime fans and other fans. The reason we make these comparisons is two-fold.

First and foremost: From a psychological perspective, a fan group is a fan group. While the content of each fan group will differ (sometimes considerably) from one another, fans are often driven by many of the same underlying psychological principles (Reysen, Plante, & Chadborn, 2017; Wann, 1995). To be sure, this doesn't mean that every fan group engages in the same behaviors, nor are they all motivated for exactly the same reasons (e.g., Plante, Chadborn, & Reysen, 2018). However, most fans do participate in their fandom to receive the same set of social benefits (e.g., social support; Mock et al., 2013). As such, it makes sense that a person who's motivated to participate in, and receives benefits from, one fan group may similarly be driven to pursue other fan groups.

The second reason we compare anime fans to other fan groups is because, in terms of the content itself, there is often considerable blurring of the boundaries between various types of media. For example, the furry fandom has its origins in the science fiction conventions of the 1970s and 1980s, creating considerable overlap between furry culture and science fiction culture.[31] However, furries also overlap with elements of high fantasy, with furry characters frequently finding themselves embedded in worlds that feature magic, knights, and dragons. Furry characters find themselves in the domain of anime, with the concept of "neko" characters (catgirls) being both a popular trope in both anime and furry. Likewise, anime prominently features elements of cyberpunk, science fiction, vampires, dragons, and other mythical creatures from fantasy.

For this reason, it should come as no surprise that 6.1% of anime fans self-identify as furries, 8.9% as *My Little Pony* fans, and approximately 50% as science fiction fans.[32] In fact, when studying other fan groups, we also see the reverse also tends to hold true. Among furries, for example, the #1 stated non-furry fan interest is in anime and manga (FurScience, 2017). Furthermore, among *My Little Pony* fans, nearly half identified as fans of anime (Edwards et al., 2019).

Despite this overlap with other fan groups, however, not all anime fans feel positively toward other fan groups. This may be because these other fan groups are often highly stigmatized (e.g., Mock et al., 2013), and anime fans—themselves stigmatized (see Chapter 17 for more on this)—may simply be trying to distance themselves from any group that could make them look bad by association. To this end, despite the fact that 6.1% of anime fans are furries, too, furries were looked at somewhat negatively by anime fans (an average score of 46 / 100 on a scale measuring positivity toward other groups). In contrast, furries tend to hold anime fans in high regard (73 / 100).

We can also look at a breakdown of how anime fans identify with specific subgroups, interests, and hobbies. For example, nearly 75% of online and con-going anime fans called themselves as gamers, although

---

[31] Indeed, Fred Patten was an early promoter of anime/manga in the U.S. as well as a prominent figure in the furry fandom (and science fiction fan) (Horbinski, 2019).

[32] This tendency to identify with other fan groups somewhat depended on whether one was an online or a convention-going fan, but also depended on the fandom itself. For example, while there was no difference between online and convention-going anime fans with respect to identifying as science-fiction fans, convention-going anime fans were about twice as likely to identify as bronies, twice as likely to be steampunk fans, and almost three times more likely to be furries. This may be the result of conventions being popular draws for people from related fan groups (e.g., as a place where furries can wear a fursuit and not stand out alongside cosplayers).

con-going anime fans were significantly more likely than online anime fans (62% vs. 44%) to describe themselves as "casual gamers," console gamers (59% vs. 45%), and mobile gamers (34% vs. 25%). Online anime fans were more likely to identify as PC gamers though (53% vs. 69%). About 7-8% of anime fans also identify as having an interest in e-sports. As these data make clear, gaming is an inextricable part of anime culture, even if there are small demographic differences in how fans play and what types of games they choose to play.

Finally, anime fans are also creators of content. In addition to the previously-mentioned fact that as many as one-quarter to one-third of anime fans consider themselves to be artists, 40% of anime fans also consider themselves to be writers and an additional 20-25% call themselves musicians.

Conclusion

The data in this chapter illustrate why we shouldn't treat anime fans as single, homogeneous group. While we can say that they tend to have more in common than different with respect to variables like age, politics, and religious beliefs, there is also considerable variability when it comes to gender and sexual orientation, ethnicity, income, and interests.

Keep this variability in mind as you continue through this book. While we tend to look at averages and aggregate data about the "average" anime fan in psychological research, there are almost certainly no fans who are "entirely average" across all of the variables. That said, the existence of variability and extreme examples of anime fans should not be taken as representative of the average anime fan, nor can it be said that anime fans don't have at least *some* fairly common features—even if they aren't universal.

Chapter 4
Anime Consumption

Fans are people who have a passionate interest in something—an interest that's so strong that they use their interest as a label for themselves.

Most people intuitively understand this idea, to the point where if we were to ask them what exactly fans *do*, the answer would seem pretty obvious: Fans consume whatever thing they're fans of, right? Football fans watch football, *My Little Pony* fans watch *My Little Pony*, and anime fans should watch anime and read manga. Seems simple enough!

However, people who spend a lot of time immersed in fan culture know that fans often do far more than just consume relevant content. For example, while furries—fans of media featuring anthropomorphized animal characters—frequently watch shows and read stories involving walking, talking animal characters, nearly all furries create their own character, known as a fursona (Plante et al., 2015). Furthermore, while bronies—adult fans of the television show *My Little Pony*—report watching the show fairly regularly, they also write fanfiction, attend conventions, and engage in charity events (Edwards et al., 2019). Music fans likewise remix songs from their favorite artists, and fantasy sport fans take on the role of a hypothetical team manager in fantasy football leagues.

In short, being a fan involves behavior that goes beyond just media consumption. We'll delve into many of these behaviors in other chapters. For now, however, we'll start by focusing on consumption behaviors, recognizing that even the simple act of consuming interest-relevant content is far more complex than it seems at first glance.

We begin by looking at how anime fans consume anime itself—the type of anime viewed, frequency of viewing, and attitudes and beliefs about consumption habits. Next, we'll broaden our focus to include consumption of non-canon material (e.g., fan-made content). As we continue to expand our analysis outward, we'll bring fandom interaction into the consumption process, looking at the mediums and methods through which fans collectively consume and engage with anime content. Finally, we consider the spending habits of anime fans and their tendency to collect trinkets, figurines, clothing, and pretty much anything else adorned with the likeness of their favorite characters.

Anime Consumption

It should come as no surprise to readers that anime fans enjoy watching anime-themed media. In fact, according to our 2020 study, the fan-related activities most frequently engaged in by anime fans were, respectively, watching officially-released anime series (89.1% of fans doing so with some regularity), listening to the soundtracks of those series (81.0%), and reading officially-released manga (76.0%). Consuming official content was more popular than all other fan activities.[1] Since anime fans are, by definition, people who enjoy consuming anime-themed media, it only makes sense that this activity itself is the activity around which all other activities are based.

While it may be obvious that anime fans spend the bulk of their fan-related time consuming the content around which their fandom is based, this shouldn't be treated as a given in every fandom. For example, when asked to what extent they spent all of their free time consuming fan-related content, anime fans did score statistically significantly higher (3.47 / 7.00) than furries (3.33 / 7.00) and fantasy sport fans (2.41 / 7.00), but their average score was less than the midpoint of the scale itself. This suggests that while anime fans *do* enjoy consuming anime, and while it is the most frequent single fan activity engaged in among anime fans, it is far and away not the *only* fan activity anime fans engage in.[2]

With respect to *what* anime fans prefer to watch, we discuss in later chapters some of the genre differences in the anime fandom and what a person's preference for one genre over another can tell us about them (Chapter 8). For now, we'll speak broadly about preferences for one generation of anime over another.

In our 2020 study we divided anime up by decade, starting back in the 1960s and advancing to the 2010s. Participants were asked to what extent

---

[1] Other activities include going to meet-ups and conventions (21.4%), producing (18.4%) or consuming (61.4%) fan-made content, chatting with others fans in forums (34.0%) or chatrooms (40.6%), playing anime-related games (57.9%), and collecting merchandise (38.4%).

[2] Although it is worth noting that, among the fan groups studied, anime fans were the *most* enthusiastic and excitable about their particular fan interest, with anime fans being the most easily overexcited (4.22 / 7.00) and obsessive (4.52 / 7.00) about the content than either furries (3.88 / 7.00 and 3.74 / 7.00 respectively) or fantasy sport fans (3.35 / 7.00 and 3.70 / 7.00 respectively).

they watched anime from each decade. This allowed us to not only compare which decades of anime were the most popular among fans, but, when combined with demographic data, which fans were watching anime from which decade.

The results painted a very clear trend: Recent anime tends to overwhelmingly be more popular than older, "classic" anime among current anime fans (see Figure 4.1). In fact, going back from the 1990s to the 1980s, we see a drop in viewership of more than half when it comes to watching series from that era with at least some frequency.

One possible explanation for this finding is the relatively recent growth in the popularity of anime in North American culture in recent decades. While it was possible for a person in North America to get their hands on a particular anime series or manga in earlier decades, it was often much harder to find translated versions of most anime. Moreover, prior to the advent of the internet, even if a person *wanted* to get into anime, it was not always clear how one could do so: Without knowing someone who was already interested and who had established ways of accessing translated anime and getting news about anime from Japan itself, figuring out where to get started was a particularly daunting task.

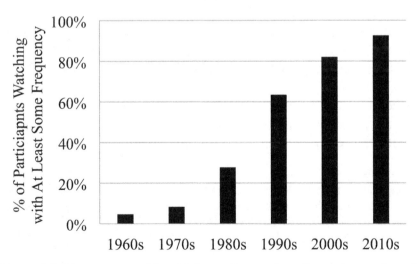

Figure 4.1. Frequency with which modern anime fans view anime from different decades.

In the 1990s, however, anime became increasingly popular and gained some mainstream appeal in North America, helped in no small part with the proliferation of blockbuster series like *Pokémon*, *Sailor Moon*, and *Dragon Ball Z*, especially on networks which catered predominantly to children. As the first generation of North Americans to grow up seeing an abundance of anime on mainstream TV, millennials and those in subsequent generations created a lucrative market for anime in North America.

Speaking to this idea, the same 2020 study similarly found that participant age was negatively correlated with frequency of viewing anime by ascending decade. Or, to put it in a simpler way: Older anime fans are less likely to watch newer content while younger anime fans are more likely to watch newer content and less likely to watch older content. It seems anime fans prefer to watch the series that were popular when they were growing up, a trend mirrored in other fandoms.[3]

We know that anime fans tend to watch anime series that were popular as they were growing up. However, *how* do anime fans get their hands on all of this anime?

According to our 2020 study, the most common way is through unofficial streaming services (63.29%), followed by paid (56.28%) or ad-based (43.76%) streaming services. Less common were unofficial downloads (40.25%), buying the series on DVD or Blu-ray (21.46%), or waiting for it to come on TV (16.13%). In fact, it is a bit of an open secret in the anime fandom (at least in North America) how common it is for anime fans to watch anime through less-than-legal means, usually through the internet.[4]

At this point we can ask whether the fans we recruit through conventions differ from the fans we recruit online through forums and anime-related websites with respect to their anime consumption habits. The short answer

---

[3] Some suggest that the furry fandom can be divided into generations based on the furry-themed piece of media that led to each generation's interest in anthropomorphized animal characters, including the era of Disney's *Robin Hood*, *Redwall*, and *Watership Down*, the era of *The Lion King*, *Sonic the Hedgehog*, and *Pokémon / Digimon*, and, most recently, the *Zootopia* era).

[4] This also facilitates binge-viewing, something the vast majority of anime fans admit to when watching anime. Streaming services allow for this sort of binge-watching in a way that simply wasn't possible on traditional TV networks.

is no. Across numerous studies, we repeatedly find that con-going fans watch just as much anime and read just as much manga as online anime fans do. So, differences between these groups have little to do with the *frequency* of consumption.

What *does* differ between the two groups is *how* they consume anime. Con-going fans report more engagement when watching anime than online fans. Con-going fans also report becoming more immersed in the fictional worlds of anime.[5]

One possible explanation for this difference is the fact that con-going fans are also more likely than online fans to co-view anime with other people (e.g., with a close friend or at local meet-ups). This "shared fantasy" may make the fictional worlds of anime more compelling for fans, while the opportunity to discuss and compare notes on characters and story points may add depth to the experience.

This co-viewing explanation may not fully account for the difference between con-going fans and online fans, however: A separate study found that while con-going fans do co-view anime with other fans more frequently and talk about anime with their friends more often, online anime fans spend more time than con-going fans reading up on anime-related news and reading reviews of anime online. To be sure, there's likely a difference between chatting about anime with one's best friend and reading reviews and forum posts about it online. Whether this difference can fully explain the results between online and con-going anime fans with respect to how they become immersed in anime will likely be a subject for future research.

---

[5] It's important to note that while anime fans tended to get fairly immersed into the shows they watch and the manga they read, this immersion is a far cry from blurring the lines between fantasy and reality. It's fairly normal for people to immerse themselves in the media they consume (Green & Brock, 2000; Plante et al., 2017). In fact, it's arguably the reason *why* people consume media in the first place—to feel sadness, excitement, or fear. Evidence from our study shows that anime fans scored just above the mid-point of the immersion scale, suggesting that anime fans do become immersed in the stories but they rarely do so to the point of losing their grasp on reality. While anime fans do tend to engage more frequently in fantasy than other fan groups we've studied, it is far more likely to be healthy, moderate levels of fantasy than pathological, reality-blurring forms of fantasy.

Moving on, we've been asked by anime fans to answer a particularly contentious question about consumption habits in the anime fandom: Should anime, most of which is produced in Japanese, be watched by English-speakers in the original Japanese with English subtitles (subbed) or with English actors dubbing over the Japanese actors (dubbed)?

It's hard to know exactly where the great rift between subbing and dubbing first arose, though it may be a product of perceived purity of the style: Those who support subbing claim that some of the important nuances and cultural differences in tone are lost with the use of English voice actors. Those who support dubbing, on the other hand, argue that attention is drawn away from important action or subtleties in animation when the viewer is forced to spend most of their time reading from the bottom of the screen.

Regardless of the reasons for the rift, there does appear to be a "winner" in the debate: In a 2016 study, fans showed a fairly strong preference for subtitles (49.5%) over dubbing (10.0%), though many fans (40.4%) also indicated that they were ambivalent on the issue. In other words, a good portion of fans are happy with either subbing or dubbing, but among those who had a preference for one over the other, they are five times more likely to prefer subtitled anime over dubbed anime.[6]

Despite having fairly strong views about subtitles and dubbing, however, anime fans did show a modicum of restraint when it came to judging those who didn't share their view. When asked whether fans who like dubbing over subbing were not "real" fans of anime, anime fans overwhelmingly disagreed with the idea. There is, however, evidence to suggest that one's preference for dubbed or subbed anime *can* tell us a bit about the fan themselves. For example, in that same 2016 study, one's preferred genre predicted the extent to which they preferred subbing or dubbing. For example, fans of hentai were far more likely to endorse subtitles over dubbing[7] while fans of action-themed anime were the least likely to endorse

---

[6] The preference for subbing was even more pronounced among online fans than for convention-going fans. We have no strong hypotheses for why this might be the case, though it remains a subject for future study.

[7] Dub-preferers, on the other hand, were more likely to own a body pillow!

subtitles over dubbing.[8] Other questions revealed that those who watch dubbed anime tend to consume more anime as a whole than those who preferred subbed anime.

To finish this section on a fairly non-contentious point, anime fans in our 2016 study strongly agreed that they disliked people who intentionally spoil shows, although they wouldn't go out of their way to avoid websites that might contain spoilers. This stance is hardly unique to anime fans (e.g., Richler, 2013), and while some psychologists have suggested that spoilers may not adversely affect a person's enjoyment of a story the way people expect them to (Leavitt & Christenfeld, 2011), anime fans, like many people, nevertheless hate being spoiled.

So, while anime fans they may disagree about which genre reigns supreme, about where to go to watch their favorite show, or about whether the show should be subbed or dubbed, they can at least agree that you shut up and not spoil the ending of the show they're watching!

Fan Content

In the years we've spent studying different fan groups we've observed numerous differences in the extent to which different fandoms foster fan-made content. In fandoms which revolve around a single show or a sole piece of source material, it makes sense that fans would adhere fairly closely to the show's canon and prefer fan-made content that remains fairly close to the source material. For instance, while *My Little Pony* fans sometimes created their own characters and stories, fans often balked at and panned characters who violated the rules, relationships, or boundaries of the show's canon. What's more, there often seemed to be a preference for content that was similar in appearance to the show's art style and for stories that tended to be in the same ballpark as the show itself.[9]

In contrast, we've also studied fandoms which, rather than focusing on one specific show or story, were based around a broader theme or aesthetic.

---

[8] We could argue that this seems obvious in retrospect, as action fans likely wouldn't want to let reading get in the way of the action scenes. However, one could extend the same argument when it comes to hentai, where fans are the most likely to prefer subbing!

[9] Which isn't to say that there aren't plenty of examples of very popular original characters or stories that deviated considerably from the show's style or canon. However, all else equal, fans of the show seemed to prefer fan-made content which offered more of the show and characters they already loved.

Such fandoms include science fiction, steampunk, or the group we've studied the most—furries. Given the broadness of the fandom's collective interest, there seems to be far more openness toward fan-made content. This includes crossovers between different series and more acceptance of fan-made characters and storylines that don't follow any particular show or story. As an example of this, furries have been fairly amicable to the introduction of entirely new species into the fandom's collective repertoire, species which have not appeared in any mainstream show, story, or comic (e.g., Dutch angel dragons, protogens).[10]

Where do anime fans fall within these two extremes? The anime fandom isn't quite like the brony fandom in that it's broader and not based on any one specific show or canon, and it contains a great deal of smaller, more independent studios and content creators. However, the anime fandom does tend to be centered around a lot of big-studio, "official" series that form a foundation for the fandom. As such, we might expect anime fans to be fairly open to the idea of fan-made content while still preferring official content.

Speaking to this idea, our 2020 study revealed that 61.4% of anime fans consume fan-made anime content with at least some frequency, with 33.2% saying they did so often. Another 21.8% of anime fans said that they collected unofficial merchandise and 18.4% said that they sometimes created fan-made content themselves. While these numbers are smaller than the number of anime fans who watch "official" anime and read "official" manga, it's telling that more anime fans consume fan-made content than play anime-themed games, participate in anime chatrooms or forums, or collect official merchandise.

In fact, the tendency may be even stronger for convention-going fans than it is for online fans. Among participants in our 2015 study, those recruited from conventions read more fanfiction than online fans did—though the two groups didn't differ with respect to how much fan art they looked at. Con-going fans were also more likely to be artists and content creators themselves than those recruited online.

---

[10] In another striking example, more than 95% of furries create fursonas, original furry-themed characters or avatars (Plante et al., 2015).

One possible explanation for this difference is that those who create fanfiction and fan-made products may be more likely to attend conventions to network with other creators or to sell their products—although research from our 2016 study suggests that this difference is likely to be fairly small (5% of con-going fans identify as dealers, whereas 3% of online fans identify as dealers). Regardless, these data provide additional evidence that fans whose primary way of interacting with the fandom is through websites and online forums may differ from convention-going fans in how they engage with anime-related content.

Online Interactions and Conventions

To this point, we've noted some of the differences between online and convention-going fans with respect to consuming anime content. Perhaps, then, it's time to look directly at differences between these groups with respect to their use of anime-themed websites and attendance at anime conventions.

Speaking to the former point, approximately 76% of anime fans say they read an anime forum with at least some frequency, while 34% say that they sometimes post in anime forums. In essence, these findings show that more than half of the people who frequent anime forums are "lurkers" so to speak—watching, but never commenting themselves. Another 41% or so of anime fans say they chat with other anime fans online with at least some frequency. Moreover, to no one's great surprise, anime fans recruited through anime websites were far more likely than those recruited from anime conventions to read blogs, reviews, and news sites about anime. They're also more likely to actively post in forums and participate in online discussions about anime.

Speaking to the latter point, a far smaller proportion of anime fans attend conventions. In a 2020 online sample of anime fans, only about 21% said they made it out to anime conventions with some frequency; 15% said they made it out to cartoon-themed cons more broadly and 13% made it out to other conventions.[11] Local meet-ups didn't fare much better, with only about 12% of anime fans sometimes making it out to a local meet-up or gathering of anime fans.

---

[11] For obvious reasons, we didn't bother to ask convention-going fans whether they have ever attended a fan convention.

The data suggest that those who go to anime conventions tend to do so fairly regularly. Across two studies, the average convention-going anime fan had attended between 8 and 9 anime conventions in their lifetime, numbers that nearly doubled the 3-5 conventions that online anime fans say they had attended.[12]

As we mentioned in Chapter 3 there are numerous reasons why a person may choose not to attend an anime convention. One reason is prohibitive cost: travel, hotel, and registration expenses can make conventions cost hundreds or even thousands of dollars. Speaking to this point, the average participant recruited from an anime convention had spent $403 USD in the past 12 months on anime conventions and would be willing to spend approximately $950 per year to attend conventions if they had the money to do so. For people who lack this sort of expendable income, cost can be an insurmountable hurdle, or at very least one that isn't worth the money in their eyes.

Is money the only factor influencing whether or not a fan chooses to attend a fan convention? To assess a myriad of factors, we used available data from our 2015 study to construct a statistical model predicting whether or not a participant was recruited at an anime convention or online. The model revealed five factors which predicted a higher likelihood of being a person who attends an anime convention:

(1) Having a higher proportion of friends that you see face-to-face (not online) who are, themselves, anime fans.

(2) Identifying more with the anime fan community (but not necessarily being a bigger fan of anime itself).

(3) Having your anime fan identity be a more salient part of your day-to-day life.

(4) Having an alternate persona that you identify with in the anime fandom.

(5) Having a history of being bullied.

Among these predictors, the first two—having anime friends and identifying with the anime community—were by far the strongest predictors of convention attendance. These results suggest that those most

---

[12] Of course, con-going samples tend to be older than online samples, and so you could argue that they've simply had more time to attend more conventions!

compelled to spend the money to attend an anime convention are those for whom their interest in anime overlaps considerably with their own identity and with their social groups. In contrast, those for whom anime-viewing was more of a solitary activity or for whom there was little opportunity to interact with other fans were perhaps less compelled—or saw less reason—to attend anime conventions.

Merchandise

In finishing this chapter on consumption, we would be remiss if we didn't take a look at fan spending on anime-related merchandise. After all, merchandise is a considerable part of many fan cultures: Sport fans purchase the jerseys of their favorite players. Fans of book series routinely pay for the signatures of their favorite authors. *Doctor Who* fans adorn their shelves, walls, and clothing with the iconic TARDIS.[13] Video game fans purchase figurines, posters, and even get tattoos of the fictional characters from their favorite games.

Anime fans are thus unremarkable in similarly surrounding themselves with hundreds of dollars worth of merchandise related to their favorite characters and series. However, before we delve into exactly what they spend this money on, let's take a quick detour and ask why anime fans—and fans in general—do this. Why spend money just to get a figurine that will end up collecting dust on one's shelf? Why buy a t-shirt when only a handful of strangers will ever understand what it's a reference to? Why get a tattoo or cover your walls in artwork or affix $10 stickers to the back of your $20,000 car?

Based on prior theories of fan culture and consumerism (e.g., Jindra, 1994; Pimentel & Reynolds, 2004), Edwards et al. (2019) suggest five functions that fan consumption serves.

The first is purely for display purposes. This is when fans surround themselves with the trappings of their fandom to communicate their membership to others. Think of sport fans wearing their favorite team's jersey around town to signal to other fans that they, too, are a fan. In cases where the fan group itself is stigmatized, symbols and in-jokes make it

---

[13] For those who don't know, the TARDIS is the blue police box that doubles as a time and space-travelling vessel for the titular Doctor Who and his companions.

possible for fans to signal one another without tipping off others, something that creates a bond between fans.[14]

The second function of fan consumption is knowledge-sharing. In this regard, merchandise becomes a conversation-starter, a way of capturing the interest of other people in the hopes of potentially recruiting new fans into the fold.[15] For example, an anime fan may have a cool-looking figure on their shelf. When their friend comes over and sees it, the friend may ask where that cool figure comes from. This creates an opening for the fan to educate their friend about the thing they're passionate about, and even potentially get their friend involved in it, helping grow the fandom itself.

The third function of fan consumption is that of a ritual activity, something that creates a sense of routine, order, structure, and predictability for fans. This ranges from fans agreeing to attend the same convention every year to fans swarming to get their hands on a new collectible. For example, among *Pokémon* fans it's common for fans to eagerly await and buy the newest game(s) en masse when they come out.[16]

The fourth function of fan consumption is that of collection—the sense of enjoyment that comes from just finding and securing valued or significant fan-related objects. This often includes the desire for completionism—to own a complete set of figures, a box set of DVDs, the entirety of a manga series, or simply wanting to create a shrine or special, significant place which serves as an icon of one's fan interest.

The final function of fan consumption is to show devotion through sacrifice. Given the costs associated with obtaining particular pieces of merchandise, a fan can show their devotion to an interest (e.g., being a "real fan") by sufficiently sacrificing enough of their time and money to show that they're not simply a "bandwagon" fan. Related to this idea, donning merchandise—especially that which is likely to lead to ostracism and bullying—might be seen as a way to "suffer" for one's fan identity—to

---

[14] Funnily enough, these same display rituals can also spur on friendly competition among fans looking to one-up each other through quantity or quality of their merchandise.

[15] When put this way, fan cultures can sometimes trend dangerously toward sounding like cults!

[16] One of the authors had a roommate who camped out in front of a game store for hours to do exactly that! He later had another roommate who waited months for a figure from their favourite anime-themed video game to be available for purchase.

show that one is willing to endure hardship (e.g., wearing an embarrassing shirt) to prove one's devotion to the fan interest.[17]

In sum, this model proposes that merchandise and consumption behavior serve a number of important social psychological functions for fans. Or, to put it another way, fans often consume for reasons beyond consumption's sake. Fans attach great importance to both their fan interest and to symbols of that interest, something evident from the amount of money that they're willing to spend on fan-related merchandise.

Some of the most common, popular merchandise owned by anime fans is artwork. This is, in no small part, due to the fact that anime itself is a visual medium with distinct styles that lends itself nicely to printed artwork. Art can easily be displayed on the walls of a person's home or in stickers on their vehicles, and ranges from very affordable prints to very exclusive, one-of-a-kind commissions from the fandom's top artists. In terms of the cost of production, art is relatively cheap[18] and easy to transport (e.g., compared to figurines, costumes), making it easy to bring to conventions for sale or to mail out in bulk.

It's not hard to empirically illustrate the popularity of art consumption in the anime fandom. For example, despite having access to millions of free pieces of artwork online through art repositories and image-sharing sites, anime fans still spend a considerable amount on artwork. Convention-going fans spend an average of $150 per year on physical art and $58 per year on digital art, while online anime fans spent $41 and $15 annually on physical and digital art, respectively.

While this may seem like a lot to spend just on artwork, anime fans often have limited budgets or limited access to the art they would like to buy: con-going anime fans indicated a willingness to spend an average of $592

---

[17] A look at some of the t-shirts worn by anime fans leaves little other explanation, such as the trend of wearing shirts that are intentionally cringe-inducing (e.g., ahegao).

[18] To be clear, this is referring only to the material cost of art (e.g., printing, paper, ink). This is not to say that art itself has little value: We recognize fully the thousands of hours of practice and craftsmanship needed to produce high-quality art and believe that, if anything, artists in most fandoms are undervalued, underappreciated, and underpaid! Tip your artists, folks!

per year on physical art and $897 per year on digital art if they had the ability to do so (online fans reported $98 and $68 respectively).[19]

Anime fans also support artists in the fandom, with convention-going and online fans paying an average of $17 and $8 per year on websites like Patreon to support their favorite artists and being willing to spend as much as $75 and $33 per year if they had the ability to do so.

So, why do con-going anime fans routinely spend more on art than online fans do? There are at least three possible explanations, some of which should be familiar to you by now. The first is that con-going anime fans may have more expendable income that they are willing to spend on their interests. A second is that con-going fans represent bigger, more committed fans than online fans, who may be a bit more casual in their interest and feel less need to spend money on it. A third possibility is that the social, face-to-face interaction afforded by conventions fosters many of the social functions of consumption discussed earlier (e.g., showing off levels of devotion though consumption).

Anime fans don't just buy artwork, however. Con-going and online anime fans also consume other media. For instance, both con-going and online anime fans own an average of about 3-4 anime figurines—or, measured another way, about 20-25% consider themselves to be figurine collectors. Likewise, about 15-17% of anime fans own a kigurumi costume, 12-19% own body pillows, and 4-9% have an anime-themed tattoo. In all of these examples, it's the con-going anime fans who again typically purchase more of these items, though the differences are more pronounced than they are for artwork.

As a final catch-all category, participants were asked how much they have spent on other anime-themed paraphernalia in the past year. Con-going anime fans again out-spend online anime fans—about $197 compared to $104. When asked directly how likely they would be to spend

---

[19] Interestingly, despite the stigmatizing stereotype of anime fans as perverts or sex-obsessed, con-going fans spent just $17 per year (and online fans $15 per year) on erotic artwork, though they were willing to go as high as $74 and $63 per year if they could. For comparison's sake, an annual subscription to the popular adult magazine *Playboy* costs about $60 per year, putting the average anime fan in about the same ballpark as the millions of people who have a subscription to some form of adult-themed media.

$250 on something anime related, con-going anime fans scored significantly higher than online anime fans.

By itself, these data paint a picture of anime fans as rampant consumers of fan-related merchandise. However, how do they stack up against other fandoms? Well, compared to *My Little Pony* fans, who spend an average of about $200 per year on their interest and who estimated their *total* collection of merchandise to be valued at an average of between $1,000 and $1,100 (Edwards et al., 2019), anime fans seem to be pretty much in the same ballpark, with anime fans only somewhat outspending *My Little Pony* fans in this regard. Likewise, if we assume that sport and music fans take in a live event once or twice per year along with purchasing the occasional shirt, poster, album, or piece of memorabilia, these numbers seem pretty much on-par with what we expect to find in other fandoms. In other words, anime fans do a lot of spending, but so do most other fans.

Conclusion

To summarize this chapter: Consumption is an important part of the anime fandom, but it's far from being a unique or defining part of the fandom itself. Anime fans regularly consume the source material itself, alongside a great deal of fan-made content, both of which form the backbone of the fandom's shared interest. Many anime fans choose to share their interest with other fans face-to-face at conventions, while others may prefer—or only have the means—to pursue their interests online. Most fans' consumption moves beyond simply watching the shows or reading the manga itself, with many fans purchasing art, figurines, and other memorabilia, an act which serves a number of important social psychological functions beyond simply wanting to own these objects for their own sake.

Chapter 5
Otaku

We're far from the first scholars to write about otaku. Our own work on this topic is preceded by a considerable body of research, from Azuma (2009) to Galbraith (2019). For readers looking for a deep dive into the theory or history of otaku culture, we have included citations for you to follow. We particularly like an article by Kam (2013) who describes the history of the word otaku and those who identify with it as well as describing and explaining otaku (if you are looking for a shorter read).

The main purpose of the present chapter is not to summarize all the work conducted on the subject of otaku culture, but rather to describe the results of our own studies on the subject. However, we see no reason to reinvent the wheel, especially when we've got a well-built and effective wheel to work from! As such, in this chapter we'll be following Kam's tried-and-true format, starting with a quick overview of the history of the term otaku and a review of prior scholarly work on the topic. We'll then delve into the results of our research and discuss the light it sheds on existing literature.

Otaku: A Very Brief History

The first use of the term "otaku" was in an essay published in an erotic manga by Akio Nakamori in 1983 (Ahn, 2008). Young fans who showed an extreme liking for manga, idols, computers, or trains were described as otaku. A few years later, in 1988, a serial killer named Tsutomu Miyazaki—"the otaku murderer"—was found to have a large collection of manga. In the wake of the publicity, the term otaku developed a negative connotation through its association with Miyazaki.

In the mid-1990s the term would lose some of its stigma when studio co-founder Toshio Okada taught classes on "Otakology" at prestigious universities. At around the same time, anime was growing in popularity in the U.S., where many fans adapted the term otaku to mean "a devoted fan of anime and manga" (Ahn, p. 84; for better and longer histories see Annett, 2011; Eng, 2006, 2012; Galbraith, 2019; Kaichiro & Washburn, 2013; Lamarre, 2009; Wang, 2010).

The term would further become destigmatized around 2005, when Japan began to embrace a "Cool Japan" policy aimed at promoting Japanese culture abroad, in part as a response to reports about the size and profitability of the otaku consumer market (Ho, 2018). Despite this openness to the otaku market, however, the Japanese version of otaku never quite lost its stigma, and the term remains somewhat more stigmatized in Japan than in other parts of the world.

Another perspective on otaku history ties it closely to the progress of technology. Toshio Okada suggests there have been three generations of otaku, each corresponding to a large-scale change in technology, including television being available in the home, access to personal computers, VCRs, and video games, and the advent of the internet and mobile phones (Bueno, 2016). Speaking to the importance of both VCRs and the internet to otaku culture in particular, Li (2012) states that one fairly distinct facet of otaku culture is its reliance on video sharing among fans. As such, otaku need to keep abreast of current technology as a means of both consuming and spreading their interest.[1]

Definitions of Otaku

Given the storied history of the term otaku, it should come as no surprise that its definition has both changed over time and differs across context. For example, Kaichiro and Washburn (2013) argue the best translation for otaku is "nerd" or "geek," treating the term as analogous to these words. In contrast, Azuma (2009) defines otaku as "those who indulge in forms of subculture strongly linked to anime, video games, computers, science fiction, special-effects films, anime figurines, and so on" (p. 3). In other words, according to Azuma, not all nerds or geeks are otaku—otaku refers to a subset of nerds or geeks and is defined based on those with an interest in specific *content*.

Other researchers' definition of otaku focuses not on the content of which they're a fan, but rather on their having a particular *passion*: "passionate anime fans" (Wang, 2010, p. 3), "enthusiastic fans of anime, manga, games, and related texts" (Nozawa, 2009, p. 180), and "enthusiastic collectors and manipulators of useless artifacts and information" (Grassmuck, 1990, p. 1). In a related vein, some focus their definition on *devotion* to the object of interest: "fans devoted to the worlds of anime, manga, video games, and cosplay" (Josephy-Hernández, 2017, p. 178),

---

[1] There is empirical evidence supporting this claim in particular. In a 2002 survey of English-speaking anime fans ($N = 137$), Dr. Ru Igarashi asked whether fans would consider themselves technophiles. A majority, 63%, agreed (Igarashi, 2002).

"dedicated fans, or in some cases, hyperconsumers of Japanese popular culture" (Dziesinski, 2014, p. 90), and "a dedicated, usually male, fan of manga and anime" (Hinton, 2014, p. 60).

Some researchers go one step further, focusing on a characterization of otaku as *obsessed*: "a colloquial Japanese term that refers to an obsessive, excessive, and addicted fan of certain cultural materials" (Ahn, 2008, pp. 73-74) and "people who are obsessed with something" (Burkett, 2009, p. 41).

Still others mention obsession, but pair this obsession specifically with a lack of *relationships* with others: "a group of young people who lack the ability to form meaningful relationships with others because of their intense attachment to manga and anime" (Gn, 2011, p. 592), a person who is "obsessed with anime to the detriment to all other aspects of life, such as work, family and responsibilities" (Zielinski, 2014, p. 1), and an "interest in visual media, technology and… seclusion" (Sullivan, 2005, p. 21).

Across varying conceptualizations of the term otaku, they all share in common a recognition that otaku share an intense interest in something (be it characterized as obsession, passion, or devotion). Some, however, roll obsession or a lack of social relationships into the definition itself, while others do not see these as necessary nor defining features of otaku. If we're being charitable, we can characterize definitions of otaku as, at best, fairly neutral acknowledgements of highly-motivated fans and, at worst, unflattering or outright stigmatizing.

Descriptions of Otaku

Prior descriptions of otaku behavior are typically as harsh as the definitions, although some researchers do broaden their perspectives beyond the negative to also focus on the positives. As in the previous section, we'll be including a large number of quotations to emphasize that these are descriptions written by others, and do not represent our own descriptions, which we'll get to later in this chapter as we describe our own data.

Otaku behavior, at least in Japan, is described as being "fixated on the objects of childhood" (Lamarre, 2013, p. 133) and usually has a creepy connotation. This focus on childish media is also reflected by Schodt, who describes otaku as "a new type of culture—one that blurs the world of children and adults, worships pop culture minutiae, fetishizes objects real and virtual, and at its worst spawns an almost autistic, inward-looking possessiveness" (Galbraith, 2009, p. 6).

As we saw with scholars' definitions of otaku, many descriptions of otaku behavior include or emphasize a lack of social intelligence and/or eschewing of relations with others. In the original description of otaku, Nakamori (1983) lists characteristics such as fanatical introversion, sitting alone in class, friendlessness, and having a gloomy expression. Some characterize otaku as being unable to have normal conversations outside of their object of interest (Agcaoili, 2011) and as "isolated and socially inept" (Hack, 2016, p. 41). Going one step further, a few scholars go beyond characterizations of social ineptitude, veering straight into violence, describing otaku as "stereotyped as reclusive, self-absorbed or anti-social individuals" (Jacobs, 2013, p. 25) and "antisocial, occasionally violent, obsessive fanatics who make their hobby their life" (Davis, 2008, p. 35). Taken together, many scholars characterize the social skills of otaku as somewhere between lacking social grace and violent, antisocial fanatics.

Scholars have tried to explain this perceived inability of otaku to relate to others, often appealing to immaturity, staunch individualism, or a desire to consume their interest rather than invest in real relationships. Speaking to their perceived immaturity, otaku are described as "socially inadequate with respect to girls and focusing their erotic interest on the characters within manga and anime" and as those who have generally chosen to reject adult life (Hinton, 2014, p. 60). Annett (2014, p. 116) describes the stereotype of an otaku as "single, straight, poorly dressed, and physically unattractive middle-class young man with no social skills and a childish yet prurient fascination with cartoons." In popular media, they're frequently portrayed as "awkward, overweight bespectacled nerds who play video games and watch cartoons all day, not leaving their rooms for days on end" (Josephy-Hernández, 2017, p. 179).

Otaku in Japan are also explained as being individualistic (eschewing society for their object of interest), dysfunctional, isolated, immature, and unable to communicate with others (Kinsella, 1998). Speaking to the intensity of the otaku desire to consume the object of their interests, otaku have been characterized as "immature, socially awkward males unable to distinguish between fiction and reality, who would rather indulge in fantasies with animated, ultimately inaccessible girlfriends than interact with real women" (Josephy-Hernández, 2017, p. 179). Lastly, Odell and Le Blanc (2013, p. 39) suggest that "Otaku are stereotyped as being male obsessive collector types without (real) girlfriends, a propensity for visiting 'maid bars', hanging around Akihabara (Tokyo's electronic gadget and geek magnet metropolis) and have mercurial knowledge about whatever anime/manga they love."[2]

This last description notes one key component of otaku—knowledge. Davis (2008) suggests that otaku culture is different from other subcultures of consumption in that otaku care about knowledge of their object of interest above all else. Indeed, the more obscure the knowledge is, the more valuable it becomes precisely for its scarcity. To this end, knowledge becomes a commodity within the cultural space (Eng, 2006). Otaku collect and accumulate a vast array of knowledge, and Paré (2004) suggests that characterizations of otaku as excessively informed is precisely because of this desire to possess knowledge. Viewed through this lens, Shen (2007) posits, that, rather than being isolated, otaku instead construct loosely organized communities based around sharing information and cultivating knowledge about anime. Larsen (2018) recognizes this to be the case, describing otaku as "linked to databases, social ineptitude, and closed communities; simultaneously, to creative freedom, close relationships, and passionate engagement with objects of devotion" (p. 287). In other words, the search for knowledge in a deluge of information becomes a way of life for otaku, who build relationships and entire communities around it.

Speaking to this idea, some descriptions of otaku distinguish between "normal" fans and otaku on the basis of this search for knowledge. For example, Zielinski (2014) conceptualizes different degrees of otaku-ness, from *novice* (watched one anime) to *member* (ten or more anime watched along with potential early signs of attending a convention or purchasing paraphernalia) to *saint* (a member with much more paraphernalia and

---

[2] After reading through so many of these quotes, it becomes apparent that they're all variations on the same few themes. Indeed, categorizing them can be a bit difficult, since there is so much conceptual overlap between them. Often, the differences boil down to whether authors emphasize social ineptitude, immaturity, or obsession, rather than whether these characteristics are present at all!

potentially has been staff at a convention) to *celebrity* (saint plus a following on social media or at conventions, and/or work in the industry).[3]

Zielinski's idea of otaku as differing from typical fans as a matter of degree is far from unique. Paré (2004) suggests that distinguishing an otaku from a regular collector means recognizing that regular collectors hold down jobs and social lives and collect as a hobby in their spare time while otaku collect full time and work as a means of supporting their interest. Lamarre (2006) similarly distinguishes between regular anime viewers and otaku in terms of intensity and duration of viewing, degree of interest, engagement, and passion.

Lamarre goes one step further, however, suggesting that it is impossible to measure the difference between normal fans and otaku quantitatively.[4] He notes that otaku themselves can both speed up and slow down the spread of anime as a sort of power that works both in conjunction with, but also outside of anime corporations. Lamarre views otaku as a sort of cult fandom—a fandom that lives on after the source of the material ceases (e.g., the show stops airing).

Kam (2013) speculates that one factor distinguishing fans of something from otaku is the degree of societal stigma directed toward the interest itself. In other words, being an otaku may be less about the extremeness of one's interest in something, and more about the popularity (or lack thereof) of the fan interest itself. For example, few would consider an ardent baseball fan to be otaku, in part because being a baseball fan, even an extreme one, has been normalized in society. In contrast, being a huge fan of science-fiction or anime isn't viewed as normal in mainstream society. Anime fans fall squarely into this same category and are thus viable otaku candidates.

Reysen and Shaw (2016) provide evidence for this line of reasoning with a study showing that the more a fan interest strays from the prototypical "fan" interest,[5] the more they tend to be viewed as non-normal. Kam elaborates further on this idea, stating that once a person is labeled an otaku,

---

[3] In our own work, we would conceptualize these social statuses as differing degrees of fanship, as fanship often predicts greater media consumption (and vice versa).

[4] Or, to put it another way, there is no magical number of hours of viewing which, when surpassed, makes a person an otaku. Rather, otaku is about how and why a person views just as much as it's about how much a person views.

[5] Typical, in this case, means sport to most people.

they take on the identity that comes with it, including all of the associated norms and behaviors.[6] We follow this line of reasoning throughout our own work, described later in this chapter—if a person calls themselves an otaku, we include them in the otaku category (vs. non-otaku).[7]

Prior Research

Much of the prior theorizing about otaku has been done through the lens of sociology, philosophy, media studies, anthropology, and communications. Despite their emphasis on theory and critique, however, there have been some attempts to gather data on the subject as well. Research involving content analysis and interviews, for example, has done a great deal to shed light on otaku culture, including definitions of being otaku and otaku-related descriptions and behaviors.

For example, Kam (2013) interviewed 51 students, mostly studying in Tokyo and Kyoto, about the label of otaku. A common theme in the responses was that people who follow societal rules avoid the label, while those who eschew societal rules are often considered otaku. Reinforcing many of the stereotypes already noted in scholars' definitions of otaku, Kam noted several criteria stated by participants in the labeling of a person as otaku:

(1) The reality rule: Otaku try to escape from reality or confuse reality and fantasy.

(2) The communication rule: Otaku stay at home and lack interaction or communication with others.

(3) The masculinity rule: Otaku tend to be men.

(4) The majority rule: Otaku ignore typical consumption habits and generally ignore fashion and popular trends.

Other studies have similarly interviewed anime fans about what it means to be an otaku. Spindler (2010) interviewed 18 students in a U.S. Japanese language program about anime consumption. The respondents indicated that many students in the program were there because of their interest in

---

[6] While Kam doesn't refer to it directly, this position is in line with what social psychologists call a social identity perspective, a perspective that we will return to throughout this book (e.g., Chapter 10).

[7] A notable benefit of this approach is that it eliminates the need to come up with a concrete set of criteria for categorizing people as otaku or not that most scholars would agree upon.

anime and manga. Tellingly, in line with the previously-stated stigma toward otaku, while most of the students in the program were perceived to be otaku by the participants in the study, the respondents were reluctant to use the label otaku to describe themselves.

Bloem (2014) interviewed eight English-speaking anime fans who regularly posted in online forums about their use and understanding of fanspeak. When asked whether they would self-identify as otaku, respondents instead talked about the number of anime series they had watched or the time they had spent on anime-related activities, both emphasizing the stigma of the otaku label and making explicit the connection between otaku and frequency of consumption.

Similar results have been found in other studies. Williams (2006) interviewed 10 U.S. students in a Japanese language program who either watched anime or self-identified as fans. Respondents did not consider themselves to be otaku, distinguishing themselves from otaku based on their being less obsessed or devoted than what an otaku would be. They also tended to relegate the term otaku to other fans they knew who showed deviant behavior (e.g., a student in an anime club who would growl at people), again reinforcing the notion of otaku as those showing extremely passionate, if antisocial, behavior.

Lamerichs (2016) examined 10 anime series (e.g., *Princess Jellyfish*) to examine how otaku characters are portrayed in media. Extracted themes included isolation (and a connection to poor mental health), gender differences (female otaku were interested in fan practices that were gender stereotypical such as cosplay and doujinshi, while male otaku were interested in figurines, model kits, and video games), sexuality (female otaku were portrayed as asexual or consuming boys' love, while male otaku were interested in erotic games), and violence (while mostly nonviolent, Lamerichs highlights an otaku torturing others in the *Durarara!!* manga). Overall, the analysis revealed that when anime portray otaku,[8] they do often reflect many of the unflattering stereotypes of otaku culture, but do so in a playful, humorous manner that adds levity to the stereotypes rather than condemning or attempting to correct them.

---

[8] Anime which, presumably, will be consumed at some point by otaku!

Other researchers studying otaku have moved away from the stigmatizing facet of otaku culture, choosing instead to focus on the aspect of belongingness. Wang (2010) conducted field research and interviews with Taiwanese and American anime fans.[9] For Wang, the meaning of otaku was less about having a particular identity and was more focused on one's sense of attachment and belonging to a group. Yamato (2013) interviewed 11 Malaysian anime fans, six of whom self-identified as otaku (although two of those six did not use the term explicitly) and found similar results. Participants described otaku as being proud fans who cared about the quality of the interest, and who were knowledgeable, passionate spreaders of information. Yamato (2016) later interviewed nine additional long-time anime fans in Malaysia who suggested that most fans are otaku and experience a sense of belonging with others who share the same interests.

Likewise, Eng (2006) examined descriptions of otaku online and conducted interviews with self-described otaku in the U.S. and found several positive outcomes of otakuism. Otaku were described as media literate, open to new things (early adopters), were said to form well-connected social networks, are considered custodians of knowledge, engage in critical thinking, are discriminating consumers, tend to be good with technology, produce creative works, resist pressure from mainstream culture, and generally have fun. Rather than being overly obsessive, the results suggested that most otaku were fairly normal, well-adjusted fans.

Taken together, much of the prior research has tended to buy into the negative stereotypes of otaku. Fans of anime are reluctant to self-identify as otaku, instead focusing on what makes an otaku and defining it in ways that exclude themselves. Nevertheless, studies of otaku themselves (e.g., Eng, 2006) suggest that, despite these negative conceptualizations, most otaku are normal and well-adjusted fans. Anime/manga portraying otaku strike a balance between the two perspectives, acknowledging and playing with the stereotypes themselves without aiming to correct them.

Having reviewed existing theorizing and research on otaku, we're finally ready to delve into the present studies, a psychological study of otaku. In

---

[9] As noted by the researcher, there were few differences between the two cultures with respect to consumptive practices (with the exceptions being that Taiwanese fans created more doujinshi while U.S. fans cosplayed more).

placing our findings alongside this existing body of research, however, we should make several notes. First, we concur with Kam (2013), who allowed participants to self-identify as otaku, and do the same in our own research. Second, few, if any of the participants in our study are from Japan. While some of the studies mentioned above did include predominantly American samples, and in many instances the differences observed between American and non-American participants was minimal, it is nevertheless worth keeping in mind, given that otaku is conceptualized in Japan with greater stigma than it is in the U.S.

Otaku Demographics

In our own research we presented anime fans with a variety of subgroup identities (e.g., cosplayer, weeaboo,[10] artist, writer) and asked for them to select any that applied to them. One such option was otaku. About one-third of our respondents self-identified as otaku.

Having a sizable sample of both self-identified otaku and non-otaku anime fans, we were able to test the veracity of several existing stereotypes about otaku. For instance, descriptions noted earlier in this chapter mention that otaku are seen as overwhelmingly male. However, we found no significant difference male and female fans' willingness to self-categorize as otaku. That said, there were more male (about 70%) than female otaku. Likewise, we found no evidence of a relationship between self-categorizing as otaku and sexual orientation. Otaku were younger in age to a practically negligible extent and had been anime fans only slightly longer than non-otaku (10.2 years versus 8.9 years, on average). There was also no evidence in socioeconomic status between otaku and non-otaku.[11]

We also examined whether there exists an overlap between otaku and other subgroups within the anime fandom. For example, given the fascination of weeaboos with Japanese culture and the potential for this interest to overlap with the otaku interest in anime, one facet of Japanese culture, we examined the frequency with which otaku and non-otaku fans self-categorized as a weeaboo. As shown in Table 5.1, otaku were more

---

[10] "A weeaboo is someone who worships pretty much anything that is Japanese or related to Japanese culture" (Zeng, 2018, p. 248).

[11] In terms of education, however, we did find that otaku were more likely to be fluent in Japanese, a result in-line with interview research by Carlson (2018) who suggested that many otaku attempt to learn Japanese.

likely than non-otaku to also label themselves as a weeaboo. That said, fans were far more likely to identify as otaku than they were to identify as a weeaboo.

Category	Non-Otaku	Otaku
Non-Weeaboo	1363 (1240.2)	463 (585.8)
Weeaboo	153 (275.8)	**253** (130.2)

Table 5.1. Observed (expected) chi-square analysis of otaku and weeaboo self-identification.

In a similar vein, Hoff (2012) suggested that a majority of cosplayers would also identify as otaku, given that the investment of time, money, and resources necessary for cosplay is something less likely to be undertaken by a more casual fan. Our data showed that while under half (44.9%) of otaku self-identified as cosplayers, they were proportionately more likely to cosplay than non-otaku (29.2%) (see Table 5.2).

Category	Non-Otaku	Otaku
Non-Cosplayer	1471 (1361.2)	577 (686.8)
Cosplayer	604 (713.8)	**470** (360.2)

Table 5.2. Observed (expected) chi-square analysis of otaku and cosplayer self-identification.

A more recent demographic stereotype of otaku has been suggested by Smith (2020), who argued that otaku are politically right-leaning, finding kinship with the growing alt-right movement in the West. This hypothesis is not supported by our own data, however. We asked fans to rate their political orientation on a 7-point scale from 1 = *very conservative* to 7 = *very liberal*. Otaku (4.68 on average) and non-otaku (4.59 on average) did not differ statistically significantly in their degree of political orientation, and in fact both scored above the scale's midpoint, suggesting that, in line with other anime fans (and discussed in Chapter 3), otaku tend to hold more liberal political beliefs.

As we point out in Chapter 3, political beliefs can be nuanced and complex, and there is often a need to break them down by domain. To this end, we also asked fans to rate the extent of their *economic* and *social* orientation. Once again, we found little evidence of significant political differences between otaku and non-otaku fans. With respect to economic liberalism, otaku (4.36 on average) and non-otaku (4.25 on average) were practically the same, as they were with respect to social liberalism (otaku = 5.04 and non-otaku = 4.85 on average). In short, the empirical data from our sizable sample of anime fans do not bear out Smith's suggestion that otaku tend to lean toward conservative political views.

Relationships

As noted previously in this chapter, otaku are often characterized as friendless (Nakamori, 1983), antisocial (Davis, 2008; Jacobs, 2013), and unable to form relationships with others (Hinton, 2014; Josephy-Hernández, 2017; Kinsella, 1998; Odell & Le Blanc, 2013). In short, otaku have been largely characterized with traits that would make them unlikely to form close relationships with others.

To test this conceptualization, we asked fans to indicate whether or not they were currently dating someone or single. The results showed that otaku were no more likely to be single than non-otaku. Furthermore, when asked about the number of friends they had (defined as people outside the household that they see at least once a week), otaku and non-otaku fans scored about the same (9.34 versus 9.43 on average, respectively).

One difference which did emerge in their relationships, however, was the fact that for otaku, more of their friends are anime fans themselves (5.03 on average) than is the case for non-otaku (3.89 on average). As such, while we can say that otaku and non-otaku have friendship networks of comparable size, otaku have, on average, about one more anime fan in their social network. This finding is consistent with research on other geek cultures, which show friendship networks of similar size, albeit with more fans in their network (McCain et al., 2015).

Related to the question of whether otaku have comparable social skills to non-otaku is the question of whether or not otaku are treated worse by people because of the stigma associated with being a fan. To test this, we asked otaku and non-otaku anime fans whether they feel they are treated differently (worse) when people know that they are an anime fan (1 = *strongly disagree*, 7 = *strongly agree*). Otaku did perceive slightly more stigma (3.25 on average) than non-otaku fans did (2.64 on average), although the scores on these scales were below the midpoint, suggesting that otaku, while experiencing a bit more stigma than the average anime fan, do not typically experience an overwhelming amount of it. Moreover, any stigma they may be experiencing doesn't seem to be affecting their close relationships, despite what stereotypes might otherwise suggest.

Anime Consumption

As noted, otaku are often defined by scholars and anime fans alike as obsessive, passionate, devoted, and knowledgeable consumers of their object of interest. Data from our own studies would seem to validate such characterizations of otaku consumption.

For starters, in terms of sheer amount of media owned, otaku reported owning nearly double the number of anime videos than non-otaku anime fans did (76.7 versus 40.9 on average). A similar trend was observed when it came to manga ownership (70.0 versus 41.4 on average).

Beyond ownership of media, which might be influenced by how much expendable income a person has, we also asked anime fans more simply about their engagement with anime content and with the anime fandom in their day-to-day lives. Fans were asked how frequently (from 0 = *never* to 7 = *many times each day*) they (1) watched anime, (2) read manga, (3) read news/blogs/reviews about anime, and (4) talked to friends about anime.

As shown in Figure 5.1, otaku fans were significantly more engaged than non-otaku fans across all four frequency measures. In fact, in a set of follow-up questions, we asked fans about a variety of different forms of anime-related media, and consistently found, as shown in Figure 5.2, that otaku routinely listen to more J-Pop and more soundtracks, watch more anime music videos, read more manga, visual novels, light novels, and doujinshi, and play more anime-themed games (e.g., otome, eroge).[12] In short, while some of the other stereotypes about otaku are unfounded, the stereotype of otaku as voracious consumers of anime—even among anime fans—holds water empirically.

---

[12] Another analysis broke down consumption even further, comparing differences between otaku and non-otaku with respect to their consumption of anime intended for different age groups. While the differences were slight, Otaku did score higher than non-otaku on all of the groups, including anime made for children, anime made for adults, and pornographic anime, with the largest difference being in the pornographic anime category.

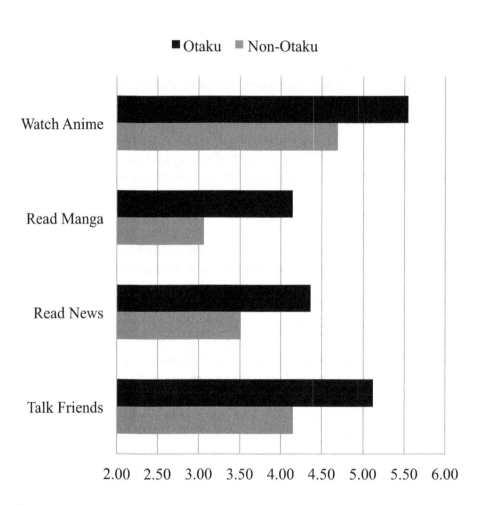

Figure 5.1. Anime fandom engagement by otaku self-identification.

118

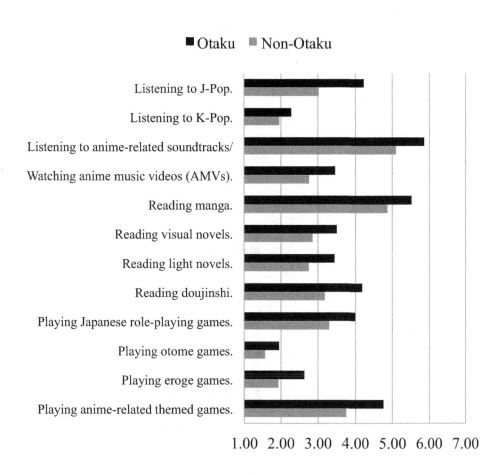

■ Otaku ■ Non-Otaku

Listening to J-Pop.
Listening to K-Pop.
Listening to anime-related soundtracks/
Watching anime music videos (AMVs).
Reading manga.
Reading visual novels.
Reading light novels.
Reading doujinshi.
Playing Japanese role-playing games.
Playing otome games.
Playing eroge games.
Playing anime-related themed games.

1.00 2.00 3.00 4.00 5.00 6.00 7.00

Figure 5.2. Consumption by otaku self-identification.

Earlier in this chapter we mentioned how one of the factors that lessened Japan's stigma toward otaku was the sheer size and purchasing power of the otaku market (Ho, 2018). While our sample was not Japanese, we did think it would be illuminating to nevertheless look at the spending habits of the average otaku and non-otaku anime fan. To this end, we asked participants to indicate how much they spent on various anime-related media and activities in the past 12 months.

As shown in Figure 5.3, otaku and non-otaku, rather surprisingly, did not differ with respect to how much money they spent on physical and digital artwork. Otaku *did* spend slightly more on erotic content and on anime-themed sponsorship pages than non-otaku fans, however, and were more likely to pay for a streaming service than non-otaku fans.[13] The biggest difference in spending by far, however, had to do with spending on conventions[14] and paraphernalia. These made up the bulk of spending for both otaku and non-otaku fans, spending which amounted to just under $500 USD per year on average for otaku. In short, not only do otaku indeed outspend non-otaku with respect to anime-related spending, but this number, when multiplied across millions of fans, represents a fairly lucrative market.

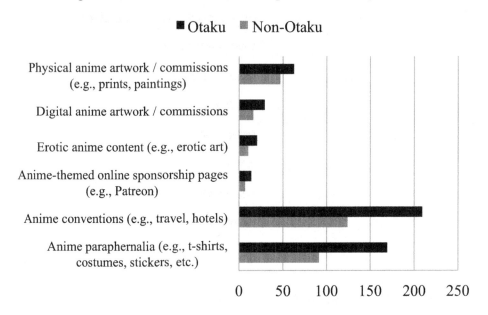

Figure 5.3. Money spent by self-categorization (USD).

---

[13] That said, otaku were also more likely to use unofficial streaming services than non-otaku fans.

[14] Indeed, far from the recluses they're often portrayed as, otaku have been to more anime conventions ($M = 5.26$) than non-otaku anime fans ($M = 3.27$)!

Given the considerable investment otaku make in their hobby, we wondered whether, as stereotypes might suggest, otaku were spending excessively, to the point of putting themselves into financial distress. In another study we asked participants to rate how frequently (from 1 = *never* to 7 = *frequently*) they experienced a variety of money-related difficulties. As Figure 5.4 shows, while otaku were, in general, significantly more likely than non-otaku to engage in excessive spending, the biggest problems tend to be spending beyond one's allocated budget and being unable to pay for commissioned work. While otaku are more likely to engage in excessive spending, it would seem that they rarely do so to the point of being unable to buy food or pay their bills.

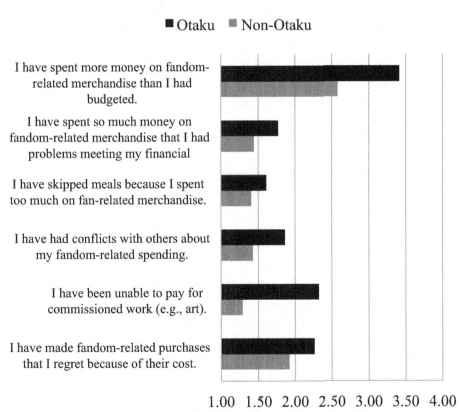

Figure 5.4. Problematic spending by otaku self-categorization.

What does Obsession Look Like?

In the previous section we alluded to the stereotype of otaku as having an obsession with anime. To this point, however, we've assessed obsession primarily in terms of excessive viewing or spending habits. Yergin (2017) notes, however, that obsession can manifest in a number of ways within the anime community.

To better understand what obsession looks like to anime fans—rather than to a bunch of scholars—we asked fans themselves to describe what it means for an anime fan to take their interests too far. The question was asked in an open-ended format, allowing fans to answer however they saw fit.

We first coded the responses to see whether fans even agreed with the premise of the question, that it was possible for a fan to take things too far. Most fans agreed that, yes, at least some fans are overly obsessive. We then scoured the responses, extracting six common themes regarding what obsession looks like. We list these six themes, as well as provide examples of participants' own words describing these themes, below.

Theme #1: Interest in anime negatively impacts one's life. To quote one participant:

"Using the same criteria of psychological diagnosis, Obsession becomes a problem when it causes distress to the individual either personally, emotionally, or between professional and personal relationships. If it does not cause distress to themselves or others, then it's fine. If it does, there is a problem. Simple as that."—Participant 408

Theme #2: Forcing one's opinions on others whether they're fans or not. This results in heated arguments and overzealous defense of one's point. As an example:

"This behavior is especially problematic when people then go online to fandom space, like Tumblr, and start attacking people who disagree with their opinions on characters like that (or any character), claim that people portray them "wrong," or otherwise try to hurt people, like by threats or trying to get them to commit suicide."—Participant 585

Theme #3: Being unable to distinguish anime from the real world. Examples include:

"seriously believing that they're an anime character"—Participant 527

122

"when they lose touch with the real world and live in the anime world"—Participant 480

"This could take subtle forms such as a guy playing too many rape themed hentai games and having it affect how he treats women in real life."—Participant 504

Theme #4: Being so consumed by anime that it is the central and defining feature of one's life. Participants noted:

"once anime, 'their most favorite thing,' becomes the defining feature of their character and personality, it goes 'too far.'"—Participant 367

"I also feel like another point is when you've become so sensitive to people criticizing shows/manga/whatever that you like to the point where it's basically attack on yourself as a person, then you also have some problems."—Participant 388

Theme #5: Unflattering or dysfunctional sexual activities and fantasies. Two examples from fans:

"When they start buying body pillows cus that shit is creepy."—Participant 602

"There are many fans who have sexual fantasies with their so called "waifus"."—Participant 369

Theme #6: In line with the defining feature of weeaboos, being overly interested in Japan in general. Quotes from participants include:

"I do believe this is possible in that setting Japanese culture as portrayed by anime on a pedestal"—Participant 403

"when they start insisting that anything Japanese is best"—Participant 527

While these findings don't refer to otaku specifically, they indirectly relate to otaku insofar as many people—scholars and fans alike—would define otaku simply as obsessive fans. More important and presently relevant, however, these findings indicate that the representation of the obsessed otaku as a person focused predominantly on obsessive consumption behavior is inaccurate both in its not aligning with the results we've presented previously in this chapter and in the fact that it doesn't take into account the various ways that fan obsession can manifest.

Fanship and Fandom as Predictors of Obsession

In line with the previous section, we aim to offer a more nuanced perspective of otaku obsession, namely a psychological approach to the topic. Specifically, we aim to not only measure and compare self-described obsession between otaku and non-otaku anime fans, but we want to look at psychological factors that could possibly predict or predispose someone to obsession.

To this end, we measured differences between otaku and non-otaku anime fans on three different scales: one measuring fanship, one measuring fandom, and one measuring obsession. Fanship refers to the extent to which one considers themselves a fan of something while fandom refers to the extent to which one identifies with a community of like-minded fans. We describe both of these constructs and how they are measured in greater detail in Chapter 10.

To measure obsession, a scale was constructed that included three items ("I spend all of my free time watching anime," "I am easily overexcited about anime," and "I can sometimes be obsessive about anime").

As shown in Figure 5.5, otaku scored well above non-otaku fans on all three dimensions, as one would predict, based on everything we've seen previously in this chapter. Moreover, whereas non-otaku fans scored around the midpoint of the fanship and fandom scales and below the midpoint for the obsession scales, otaku fans scored above the midpoint on all three scales, lending credibility to the idea that at least one of the characteristic features of otaku is a greater-than-average interest in content itself, the surrounding fandom, and engaging in more excessive fan behavior.

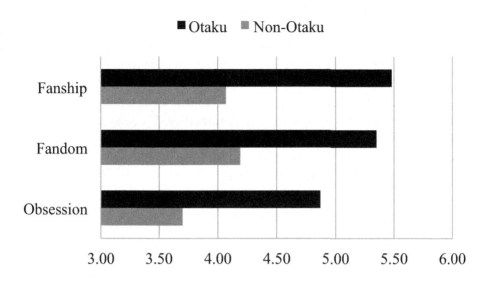

Figure 5.5. Mean levels of fanship, fandom, and obsession by otaku self-categorization (7-point scale).

We next conducted what's called a mediation analysis—a type of statistical analysis designed to test for special relationships between variables wherein one or more variables "intervenes" or "explains" the relation between two variables. In this case, given that being an otaku has been found to be associated with greater self-reported obsessive behavior, we tested whether this relation could be accounted for, at least in part, by a possible link between being an otaku and higher rates of fanship/fandom, as well as a possible link between fanship/fandom and obsession.

As shown in Figure 5.6, being otaku was associated with scoring higher on measures of fanship and fandom. Fanship and fandom were also associated with greater obsession.[15] Importantly, when we treated fandom and fanship as mediators in the model, the association between being otaku and degree of obsession was reduced. To put it in simpler terms, this means that fanship and fandom accounted for at least *some* of the link between being otaku and obsession because, when you take fanship and fandom into

---

[15] These are all examples of positive correlations, which we described in Chapter 2.

account, there is "less relation" left between otaku and obsession left that needs to be explained.[16]

One other important finding is that fanship plays a *much* stronger mediating role than fandom does when it comes to explaining otaku obsession. This suggests that the otaku obsession with anime is driven more by a deeply-felt psychological connection to anime than it is by a sense of connection with other fans in the anime community. To be sure, otaku do identify more strongly with the anime fandom than non-otaku do—it's just that this fandom association has less to do with their obsession than does their strong felt connection to anime itself.

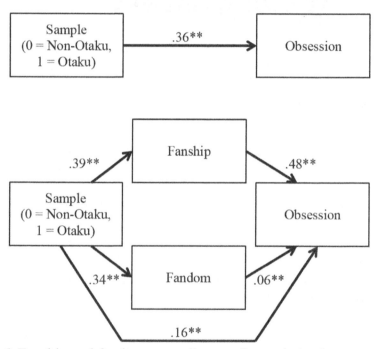

Figure 5.6. Fanship and fandom as mediators of association between sample comparison and obsession. ** *p* < .01.

---

[16] This also means that, by themselves, fanship and fandom cannot entirely explain the relation between being otaku and obsession—it's likely that dozens of other variables would be needed to fully account for this relation!

As a final note on obsession and fandom involvement, we asked participants to provide a trajectory of their involvement in the fandom in the past, present, and future (1 = *no involvement*, 7 = *very involved*). As shown in Figure 5.7, otaku (vs. non-otaku) show a greater degree of involvement across all time periods. This suggests that otaku are not only more involved than non-otaku in the anime fandom currently, but that they had a greater degree of involvement in the fandom from the very beginning, and they expect to remain involved in the fandom long into the future.

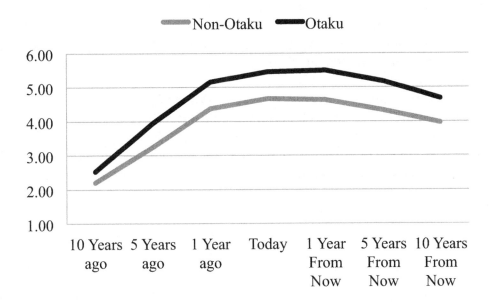

Figure 5.7. Perceived fandom involvement over time by otaku self-categorization.

Connection to Favorite Character

One stereotype of otaku put forth by Galbraith (2014, 2019) states that otaku have especially strong attachments to their favorite character(s), in particular when it comes to male otaku feeling a sense of attraction and attachment to cute female characters. Given that, as the previous section revealed, otaku show greater anime fanship, it should follow that they also feel a greater sense of connection to aspects of the content, including their favorite characters.

To this end, we asked anime fans to name their favorite character and rate the salience of the character ("How often do you think about your favorite anime character" from 1 = *sometimes* to 7 = *always*). We also asked participants to rate a number of items measuring three different facets of their felt connection to their favorite character (identification, romance, and felt similarity).

As shown Figure 5.8, compared to non-otaku fans, otaku reported thinking about their favorite characters more frequently. This, in turn, was associated with higher scores on all three facets of felt connection—identifying more with their favorite characters, being more romantically attracted to them, and feeling more similar to them.

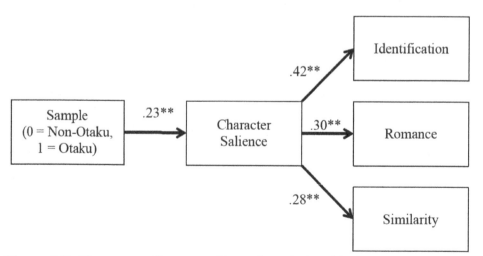

Figure 5.8. Character salience mediates the relationship between sample comparison and dimensions of connection with favorite character. Standardized betas presented, ** $p < .01$.

128

Motivation

In Chapter 14 we describe our studies about anime fan motivations in greater depth. For now, we'll briefly examine some of the results from these studies that specifically compare otaku and non-otaku anime fans with respect to what drives them to be a part of the anime community.

In particular, we asked otaku and non-otaku fans to rate ten different possible motivations that may theoretically explain their interest in the anime fandom. As shown in Figure 5.9, otaku scored significantly higher than non-otaku on all ten of these motivations. The largest differences, however, were observed for belongingness, self-esteem, and sexual attraction, results which correspond to findings and theory from the scholarly literature discussed earlier in this chapter.

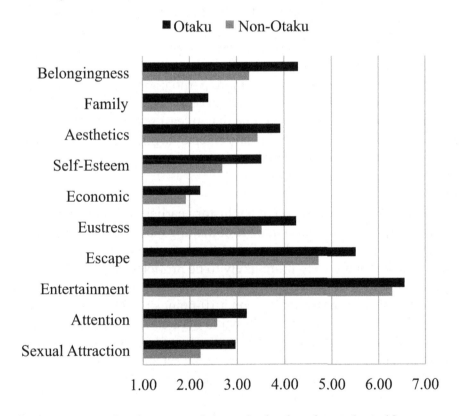

Figure 5.9. Motivation to participate in fandom by otaku self-categorization.

First, the greater belongingness motivation is related to the finding that otaku having more friends who are anime fans within their friendship network. Moreover, otaku rated their degree of fandom identification higher than non-otaku, illustrating a greater felt connection to the group. This helps contextualize the results with respect to belongingness motivation: Otaku's natural need to belong to a group of like-minded people draws them to other anime fans and may help to motivate, at least in part, their interest in anime.

Second, since the groups we belong to contribute to our sense of self-worth (i.e., self-esteem), and given the importance of fandom to otaku, it comes as no surprise that otaku also place a great degree of importance on their anime identity as a way to feel good about themselves. For example, being knowledgeable about anime can make them an admired member of their fan groups, helping them to feel a sense of value and prestige.

Third, although otaku rated sexual attraction lower than the midpoint of the measure, it was considerably higher than that of non-otaku. As noted previously, otaku do consume slightly more pornographic media and spend more on erotic art, than do non-otaku. While otaku are no less likely to be in romantic relationships, it may well be that at least some of their sexuality—including foreplay, kinks, and roleplaying activities—may be grounded in anime content, though there is no evidence to suggest that their sexuality is exclusively tied to anime.[17]

Technology

As mentioned in the section on otaku history earlier in this chapter, technology has played an important role in making otaku culture what it is today (Bueno, 2016; Li, 2012). Because of this important role, we wondered whether otaku were more likely to be proficient with technology than non-otaku anime fans. We asked fans to rate the frequency with which they use different types of technology on a 10-point scale (1 = *never* to 10 = *all the time*; Rosen et al., 2013). As shown in Figure 5.10, otaku and non-otaku are, on the one hand, comparable with respect to their use of some technology, such as watching TV on a television set and texting. On the other hand, otaku watch significantly more shows on a computer, check

---

[17] To put it another way, an otaku may be more likely to have sexual fantasies about anime characters or to incorporate hentai into their foreplay, but there is no evidence to suggest that they are unable to achieve sexual arousal in the absence of anime.

social networking sites more, and interact more online with people that they haven't met in real life. That said, these differences, while statistically significant, are small.

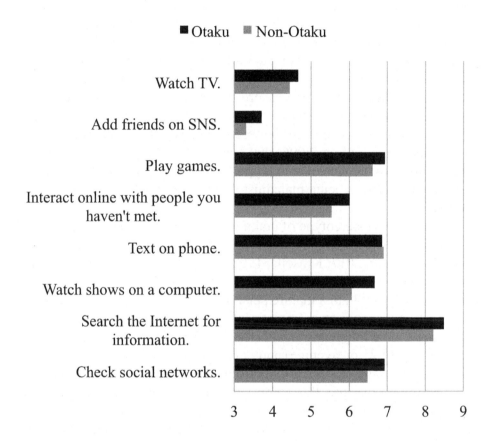

Figure 5.10. Technology usage by otaku self-categorization.

Well-Being

Xu (2016) suggests that due to the limited face-to-face contact otaku are purported to experience, they should be more likely to face challenges to their well-being.[18] We delve into this topic in far greater depth for anime fans in general in Chapter 19. Presently, however, we can briefly state that across numerous samples and using countless measures, otaku have repeatedly shown themselves to be comparable to non-otaku when it comes to well-being. Indeed, on every measure of subjective and psychological well-being we have included across our studies, there is little to no significant well-being differences between otaku and non-otaku. This fits with the conclusion by Eng (2006) that otaku are well-adjusted individuals and largely flies in the face of stereotypes of otaku specifically (and anime fans more generally) as being maladjusted (for more on this, see Part IV).

Maturity

Another frequent stereotype of otaku repeated in the academic literature discussed in this chapter is the notion that otaku are immature (e.g., Josephy-Hernández, 2017; Kinsella, 1998). To test this, we gave anime fans a short measure of self-reported maturity (Reysen & Plante, 2017) that included two items ("I am a mature person," "Other people would describe me as a mature person") on a 7-point scale, 1 = *strongly disagree* to 7 = *strongly agree*. We found no statistically significant difference between the scores of otaku (5.21 on average) and non-otaku (5.32 on average). Additionally, average scores for both groups were well above the midpoint of the measure. To be sure, this doesn't conclusively demonstrate that otaku are not immature—it may be possible, for example, that otaku are immature without realizing it (or responding in a socially desirable manner). At very least, however, it is preliminary evidence to the contrary of stereotypes, and suggests that, at very least, otaku would likely not agree with characterizations of themselves as immature.

---

[18] Primarily because humans have evolved as a social species that, by evolutionary design, rely on one another for social support. The absence of that social support, therefore, should be to the detriment of their well-being.

Flow

Flow is the psychological term for the feeling you get when you're so absorbed in something that you're doing that you're not consciously thinking about it. It has been suggested by some psychologists to be humans' optimal psychological state of functioning (Csíkeszentmihályi, 1975, 1990). Over the years, researchers have suggested numerous ways to measure flow, including feelings of control, attention focus, curiosity, intrinsic interest, time distortion, loss of self-consciousness, and having clear goals (Finneran & Zhang, 2005; Jackson & Marsh, 1996).

Despite these various dimensions, flow boils down to being highly absorbed in an activity or experience. The concept of flow has been used widely, for example examining users' experience in video games (Takatalo et al., 2010), employees' performance at work (Bakker, 2008), and consumers' online shopping experience (Koufaris, 2002). Importantly, those who report having more absorbing flow experiences more often in their lives tend to report greater self-esteem, satisfaction with life, intrinsic motivation, conscientiousness, and emotional stability (see Ullén et al., 2012). For this reason, flow is an important psychological variable to many psychologists.

With this in mind, we can consider what Kam (2013) suggests is a key facet of otaku, namely that they become immersed and lose themselves in fantasy worlds. Some suggest that otaku go beyond extremes of passion and "reach sublime immersion" (Kelts, 2006, p. 155). Haruna Anno describes otaku as people who concentrate and become totally absorbed in their interest (Galbraith, 2009). This sounds an awful lot like otaku experiencing flow states while consuming their favorite media. Since we noted that flow is related to well-being, we can speculate that otaku, who may experience more powerful flow states, may seek out more anime *because* they lead to these desirable, even beneficial flow states.

To test this possibility, we administered a single-item measure of perceived flow ("While watching anime I was so absorbed that I lost track of time and place"), which participants answered on a 7-point scale, 1 = *strongly disagree* to 7 = *strongly agree*. Anime fans also completed a single item measure of the frequency with which they consume anime ("In general, how often do you watch anime?") on an 8-point scale, 0 = *never* to 7 = *many times each day*.

We then tested a mediation model comparing differences between otaku vs. non-otaku with respect to how much anime they watch and testing whether frequency of flow experiences might explain these differences. As shown in Figure 5.11, otaku did, indeed, watch more anime than non-otaku and also experienced more flow states than non-otaku did. Most importantly, there was statistical evidence that the experience of flow partially explained the relation between being otaku and anime watching frequency. While it's a far cry from fully explaining what drives otaku to watch anime, flow experiences may at provide at least part of the explanation.

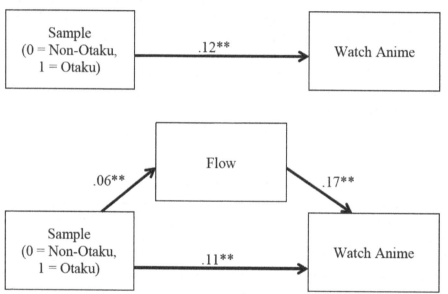

Figure 5.11. Flow mediating relationship between sample and frequency of watching anime. Standardized betas presented, ** $p < .01$.

We tested this same meditational model with respect to another potential outcome—anime-themed dreams. Dreams often contain content that reflects a person's daily activities and concerns (see Gerbasi et al., 2020 for a review). In a study of furries' dreams, for example, Gerbasi and colleagues found that furries' dreams often contained fandom-related content. As one would expect furries' lives include furry activities and consumption of furry material, and therefore this content made its way into their dreams.

We thus expected that otaku would show a similar result. In other words, otaku, being more likely than non-otaku to consume more anime, should report more anime-related dreams. Additionally, we suspect that this relationship will again be mediated by one's experience of flow while watching anime, as powerful flow experiences might make those experiences especially ripe as potential fodder for dream content.

In addition to the flow item described, we asked fans how often they have dreams about an anime world, how often anime characters are in their dreams, and the percentage of dreams they have that are anime related. We standardized[19] these measures and combined them to form a dream index. As shown in Figure 5.12, compared to non-otaku fans, otaku had more anime-related dreams. Furthermore, flow experiences seem to account for at least some of this difference, though it is likely only one of numerous variables needed to fully explain this difference. Nevertheless, flow experiences as a predictor of dream content is an interesting and fairly novel direction for future researchers to pursue.

[19] To keep it simple and avoid statistical jargon, standardizing variables is a procedure that allows researchers to compare and combine variables that use different scales (e.g., a 10-point scale and a 7-point scale).

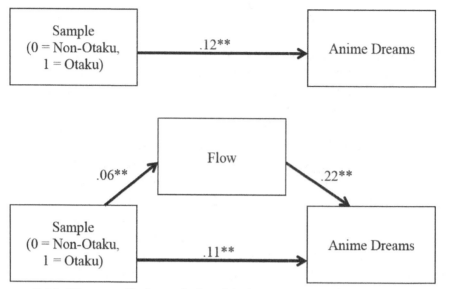

Figure 5.12. Flow mediating relationship between sample and frequency of watching anime. Standardized betas presented, ** $p < .01$.

Elitism and Gatekeeping

Lamerichs (2013) describes otaku as gatekeepers who make anime content accessible to others (e.g., translating, sharing). Inherent in this idea is the ability for otaku to influence both the content in the fandom and the potential makeup of the fandom itself (e.g., choosing what to recommend or translate based on what is deemed desirable). In fact, Lamarre (2006) notes exactly this, that otaku can increase or decrease the spread of anime internationally as influencers.

In Chapter 13 we discuss at length anime fans' degree of elitism and gatekeeping in general. However, in line with our previous gatekeeping models, we tested whether otaku are more likely to gatekeep than non-otaku, and looked at two different possible explanations for why this might be the case if they do: self-inflation (making oneself look and feel better) and other-derogation (making others look bad by comparison to oneself; see Figure 5.13).

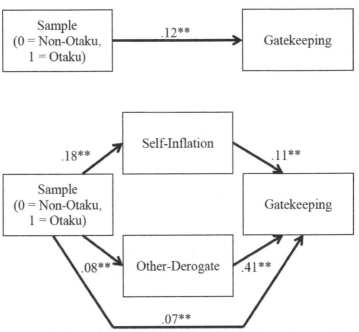

Figure 5.13. Self-inflation and other-derogation dimensions of elitism mediating association between sample comparison and gatekeeping. Standardized betas presented, ** $p < .01$.

The results of the analyses showed that otaku did, in fact, score higher on measures of gatekeeping and the elitist attitudes associated with gatekeeping behavior. More importantly, elitism seemed to partly explain the link between being otaku and gatekeeping, such that otaku were more likely to both inflate their sense of self (e.g., other people think my opinion about anime is important) and to put down other fans (e.g., other fans are ignorant and wish they knew as much as I did), both of which were linked to greater gatekeeping. The results support the notion that otaku do indeed show gatekeeping tendencies, and that these tendencies are much more strongly tied to the tendency to derogate others than they are to the tendency to inflate one's own ego.

Limitation

While we acknowledge throughout this book many of the limitations of our own work (e.g., in Chapter 2), there is one limitation in particular that we'd like to once again highlight as we end this chapter. The fans in the present research come primarily from mostly Western sources. This is important, because, as we noted in the beginning of the chapter, what it means to be otaku differs both over time and depending on where you are in the world.

For example, Condry notes that in an interview with Shinichirō Watanabe, he asked about the difference between Japanese and U.S. otaku. His response was that "otaku in Japan are kind of twisted, scary people who have issues. American otaku tend to be very cute and pure" (Davis, 2016, p. 47). Given that the U.S. version of otaku is perceived as more playful and positive, it might be unlikely to study a large number of otaku in Japan the way we have done here (Hu, 2010), in no small part because it would involve people admitting to being a member of what is a significantly stigmatized group. It may even be the case that Japanese otaku self-isolate more than non-Japanese otaku do. After all, in our own studies we have numerous fans from other countries, many of whom have described themselves as otaku. However, we do not have a large enough sample of Japanese otaku to be able to describe them. All the same, interpret the results in this chapter with caution, recognizing that participants in these studies likely self-identify with a very Western understanding of what it means to be an otaku.

Conclusion

Following a brief history and review of definitions, descriptions, and prior research on otaku culture, we looked at results from our own research on otaku. Otaku tend to be young and politically left-leaning. Otaku do heavily consume anime-related materials and identify more strongly with anime, with the anime fandom, and with their favorite characters. Otaku are more motivated fans in general, especially with respect to the desire for belongingness, self-esteem, and sexual attraction. Importantly, there were no differences between otaku and non-otaku on a variety of measures of well-being or on self-rated maturity.

In sum, based on the results of our own research, we overwhelmingly agree with the characterization of otaku put forth by Eng (2006), who argued that the majority of otaku appear to be "normal," well-adjusted fans. Otaku, if nothing else, are perhaps most remarkable for how unremarkable they are outside of their enthusiastic interest in anime.

Chapter 6
Waifus, Husbandos, and Animated Best Friends

Anime fans are often stereotyped as being detached from reality. In their drive to escape the stresses and monotony of day-to-day living, anime fans are often believed to immerse themselves so deeply into the fictional worlds that they blur the lines between fantasy and reality. To this end, anime fans as treated as being out-of-touch, obsessed, and, struggling with normal social interaction (we introduced many of these misconceptions and stereotypes in Chapter 5, and will discuss them in greater depth in Chapter 16).

It may be of some comfort to anime fans to know that, at very least, they're not alone in being stereotyped. Fans in general frequently find themselves stereotyped as obsessive, with the term "fan" itself having an unflattering origin in the word "fanatic," a person whose actions are motivated by insane, often religious devotion to a specific idea. In the case of media fans, especially those who are fans of fictional stories and characters, there is often an assumption that fans form connections with the characters in their stories that are stronger than the connections they form with people in the real world.

In this chapter we discuss whether there is any truth to these claims. We begin with fairly moderate questions about fans' favorite characters—what makes a character a favorite character, which characters are most likely to be fan favorites, and whether different fans are more likely to call different characters their favorite.

We then dive deeper into the phenomenon—from merely admiring a favorite character to feelings of connection with the character themselves. We discuss the phenomenon of forging relationships with fictional characters, relationships which range from seeing a character as a possible acquaintance or friend to a romantic (albeit one-sided) relationship with a fictional character—a waifu or husbando.

We then finish up the chapter by going the final step, considering whether and how people identify with fictional characters—not as friends or lovers, but as reflections of themselves.

Along the way, we'll be contextualizing findings from our anime research with research from other fan cultures as well. To foreshadow the chapter's conclusion, there is evidence suggesting that anime fans form parasocial relationships with the characters in their media, but anime fans are far from the first fans to do so, nor are they the most extreme or best-documented example of this happening.

For now, let's wade into the shallow end of the pool, starting with a look at fans' favorite characters and at what makes a character appealing in the first place.

Favorite Characters

The anime fandom is not organized around a single show or manga series. Illustrating this point, when we asked our 2017 sample of about 1,100 anime fans to list their favorite series and character, we ended up with a list of more than 300 different series and nearly 600 different characters![1] Reproducing both lists here in their entirety would be a horribly impractical data dump. Instead, Tables 6.1 and 6.2 feature some of the most popular responses.

Series	Number of Votes
Monogatari	32
Full Metal Alchemist	31
Naruto	26
Yuri On Ice	26
My Hero Academia	25
One Piece	24
Fate Series	23
Code Geass	22
Hunter X Hunter	22
Sailor Moon	22

Table 6.1. Favorite anime series.

---

[1] As you might imagine, coding and sorting these hundreds of different series and characters can be a herculean effort! But it's also a great way to discover new series that you may never have heard of!

Character	Number of Votes
Lelouch Lamperouge (Lelouch vi Britannia)	21
Yuri Katsuki	17
Spike Spiegel	14
Holo	13
Edward Elric	13
Naruto	13
Vash the Stampede	12
Deku (Izuku Midoriya)	11
Gintoki Sakata	11
Hachiman Hikigaya	10
Luffy	10
Saitama	10

Table 6.2. Favorite anime characters.

Several points are worth noting from these two tables. First, there is very little consensus among anime fans when it comes to favorite shows or favorite characters. To illustrate, if you wanted to meet another anime fan who, by sheer dumb luck, happens to have the same favorite series or character that you have, you would likely need to get dozens of anime fans together in the same place to do so.[2]

A second point we can take away from the tables is that anime fans are far from reaching a consensus about the sort of anime they like to watch. It's a point we discuss in greater depth in Chapter 8, but for now we can say that anime fans have eclectic tastes. As such, a myriad of different shows, genres, and characters emerge in lists of fan favorites—although there are a few series or characters that stand out as small peaks of popularity amidst a sea of choices.

Illustrating this point, Table 6.3 shows that convention-going and online anime fans have some of the same favorite anime series—though the list is

---

[2] That's assuming your favorite series or character is among the more popular ones! If it's a fairly unpopular one, you may be lucky to find one or two other attendees at a convention who share your tastes!

far from perfectly overlapping.[3] Differences in these lists may stem from demographic differences in con-going and online anime fans, such as age differences, something we discussed in Chapter 3.[4]

Rank	Online	Convention-Going
1	*Monogatari*	*Naruto*
2	*Full Metal Alchemist*	*Yuri on Ice*
3	*Code Geass*	*Dragon Ball*
4	*Fate Series*	*Sailor Moon*
5	*My Hero Academia*	*Fairy Tail*
6	*One Piece*	*Cowboy Bebop*
7	*Gintama*	*Full Metal Alchemist*
8	*Hunter X Hunter*	*Hunter X Hunter*
9	*Madoka Magica*	*One Piece*
10	*Spice and Wolf*	*Bleach*
11	*Yuri on Ice*	*My Hero Academia*

Table 6.3. Favorite anime series by online and convention-going fans.

This lack of consensus on which characters are fan favorites is far from unique to the anime fandom. In fact, other research we've done has found considerable disagreement about favorite characters even in fandoms organized around a *single* show! Take, for instance, our research on *My Little Pony* fans. Despite the fans all watching the same show, 73 different favorite characters were identified in one sample of fans. Even when fans were permitted to list as many characters as they wanted instead of just one singular "favorite" character, the most popular character among fans was still only chosen by less than half the sample (Edwards et al., 2019). Fans of

---

[3] As an interesting, but only tangentially-related note, anime fans also seem to be somewhat in agreement about which shows have the worst fanbases. While there was some contention for many of the lower ranks, the winner by far, chosen by more than 16% of participants, was the *Sword Art Online* fanbase, with the *Naruto* fanbase also being quite distinctly high in second place.

[4] The fact that con-going anime fans are typically older than online anime fans, coupled with the fact that older fans are more likely to watch older anime series, would explain why you tend to see more older anime series (e.g., *Sailor Moon, Dragon Ball, Full Metal Alchemist*) more commonly among the convention-going fans' favorite series.

142

other series similarly deliberate over which *Star Trek* captain was the best, which actor's portrayal of James Bond was their favorite, and which incarnation of The Doctor from *Doctor Who* was the greatest.[5]

Given all this variety, it might seem like there's little rhyme or reason to fans' choice of favorite character. After all, isn't it sort of like choosing whether chocolate or vanilla is better? Some people prefer the taste of one over the other, and aesthetic preferences seem fairly randomly distributed across the population. One of the benefits of doing deep dives into large datasets, however, is that it allows you hunt for fairly small, subtle effects that might otherwise go overlooked!

For example, despite the seemingly random nature of anime fans' favorite character preferences, we find that anime fans are significantly more likely to select male characters over female characters as their favorite, a tendency stronger among convention-going fans and among male fans (see Table 6.4).[6] Such responses raise questions about why this preference for male characters exists, with possibilities including the fact that there may simply be more male characters than female characters in anime in general. Research by Reysen, Katzarska-Miller et al. (2017) does suggest that male characters are overrepresented in anime compared to the population.

Group	% Choosing a Male Character
Convention-Going Fans	65.9%
Online Fans	55.5%
Male Anime Fans	61.1%
Female Anime Fans	57.9%
Intersex / Other Anime Fans*	47.1%

Table 6.4. Percentage of fans choosing a male character by category of fan. *These categories were combined because the number of participants in each separate category were too small to be able to reasonably aggregate responses.

---

[5] The answers, in the opinion of at least one of the authors, are Jean-Luc Picard, Daniel Craig, and the ninth Doctor, Christopher Eccleston, respectively.

[6] An exception to this overall preference for male characters was fans identifying as neither male nor female; 24% chose an intersex or "other" character as their favorite and 41% chose a female character as their favorite!

Of course, peoples' preferences are determined by a lot more than just their sex. As such, we looked at several character traits that may relate to fans' preferences.

For starters, we asked participants whether they would classify their favorite character's role as that of a main character, supporting character, recurring character, or an obscure background character. The results showed that the vast majority of fans—approximately 72%—chose a main character as their favorite. Supporting characters were the next-most popular at about 25%, with recurring characters at 2.5% and obscure background characters at 0.5%. This finding may not be particularly surprising, given that main characters typically receive more screen time and are typically more nuanced and thoroughly developed than other characters.[7] Psychological research may also support this explanation, as being repeatedly exposed to a person can have the effect of making us like them more through familiarity alone (Bornstein, 1989).

The same study also suggests that a character's role in the story influences what people will find attractive or endearing about that character. For example, fans report liking the personality, aspirations, values, and aesthetics of main characters precisely because they have so much exposure to these facets of the character. In contrast, when it comes to background characters, viewers rarely get much in the way of insight into the character. As such, for those who chose minor or background characters as their favorites, their decision was far more likely to be based on the character's appearance.

What about the character's personality—surely that counts for something? In general, psychologists find that, all else equal, people tend to prefer kind, likeable others (Wu et al., 2019). We should thus expect to find something similar when it comes to a favorite character. In fact, when given a large list of adjectives to choose from, the ones most frequently used to describe favorite characters were "determined," "loyal," "perseverant,"

---

[7] That said, this research question was first inspired by our research in the *My Little Pony* fandom and a fan-favorite character, Muffins, who was a background character that had a walleyed appearance due to an animation error. Fans loved the character immediately, and despite her existing almost exclusively in the background of scenes, she was the ninth-most popular character, beating out many of the show's recurring characters and beloved villains (Edwards et al., 2017).

"bold," "distinct," "kind," and "self-sacrificing"—all positive words. In contrast, the least popular words used to describe one's favorite characters were "villain," "nationalistic," "sexualized," "normal," and "morally ambiguous."[8]

Let's end this section on favorite characters by asking whether your favorite character says something about you. In short, the answer appears to be yes, to some extent. Those whose favorite character was aggressive tended to have a somewhat impulsive and aggressive streak themselves, being more prone to behaving aggressively toward others or being unwilling to consider the impact of their behavior on others before acting. Those whose favorite characters were morally ambiguous or complex or whose favorite character was sexualized were also more likely to indicate that they are regularly involved in fandom-related drama. Furthermore, those whose favorite characters have some kind of magical or supernatural ability tend to be bigger anime fans with a stronger connection to the fandom more generally than those whose favorite characters lack such abilities.

Other analyses show that those with villain favorite characters tend to not only be more hostile toward others but are even more likely to endorse ethnocentric ideas. Villain preference wasn't the only trait of a favorite character tied to ethnocentrism either: Violent, nationalistic, favorite characters who embody traditional gender norms also hint at fans who are more likely to endorse ethnocentrist views themselves.[9]

We also measured a construct known in psychology as benevolent sexism, a "soft" form of sexism. Benevolent sexism is contrasted against hostile sexism, which is sexism aimed at openly derogating someone based on their sex in a hostile manner (e.g., "Women seek power by gaining control over men"). Benevolent sexism, in contrast, involves promoting

---

[8] The moral of the story: If you want your character to be a fan favorite, you should make them likeable with a strong will and a tendency to sacrifice for others and should avoid making them morally questionable, villainous, or, perhaps, worst of all, "normal."

[9] It's important to note that we're talking about *relative* increases in aggression and ethnocentrism here! Most anime fans score well below the midpoint of these scales, so an increase in these tendencies does not mean these folks behave violently or endorse extreme nationalist beliefs, nor does it mean that this is the case for every fan whose favorite character happens to be a violent, sexist, bigoted jerk!

traditional gender stereotypes through the use of positive stereotypes (e.g., "Women, as compared to men, tend to have a more refined sense of culture and good taste;" Glick & Fiske, 1996).[10] In our study of anime fans, we found that fans whose favorite characters were kind, self-sacrificing, loyal, heroic, normal, ethnocentric, or morally ambiguous were also more likely to score higher on a measure of benevolent sexism.

Of course, all of these findings should be taken with a fairly large grain of salt, for at least two reasons. First, there are a great many reasons why someone chooses their particular favorite character. It's unlikely that a person's own attitudes toward gender stereotypes, ethnocentric beliefs, or aggressive tendencies are the only (or biggest) factor in determining who their favorite character is. Nevertheless, despite the fact that there are much bigger and more important influences on a person's favorite character (e.g., liking their personality, identifying with them, enjoying the design of the character), it can *also* be true that these other factors play a small, subtle role behind-the-scenes.[11]

The second reason to be cautious in interpreting these findings is because the correlational nature of the study does not allow us to know for sure the causal direction of these effects. As such, even though it's true that more aggressive people tend to have more aggressive favorite characters, there's no way to know whether it's because aggressive people choose more aggressive characters in the first place or whether having an aggressive favorite character causes a person to become more aggressive over time.[12]

Up to this point we've talked about the sorts of characters that anime fans prefer as their favorite and what this tells us about those fans. In the next section we'll go beyond merely liking characters, delving into the

---

[10] The reason researchers are often concerned about seemingly harmless benevolent sexism is because those who endorse benevolent sexism are also often found to endorse hostile sexism as well (Glick & Fiske, 1996).

[11] After all, a bigoted character is unlikely to be someone's favorite character if that person has strong egalitarian values, no matter how funny or charming the character is!

[12] Of course, there's also a third possibility: That neither causal direction is true, and that some third, unmeasured variable is related to both preferring an aggressive character and being an aggressive person yourself, creating the illusion of a causal relationship!

realm of parasocial relationships—forming deep and meaningful connections with characters.

Waifus / Husbandos

To begin this section, let's first define what psychologists call "parasocial relationships." In a nutshell, a parasocial relationship is a sense of connection a person forges with another person with whom they have had little to no actual contact. This occurs mainly through media—be it with a real person (e.g., a celebrity) or a fictional character (e.g., a character from an anime).

Parasocial relationships differ from typical relationships because of their one-way nature. In a parasocial relationship, viewers feel a strong attachment to a person or character who is largely unaware that the other person exists, who has had minimal interaction with the other person, or who is a non-real entity. The common feature across all of these cases is that the target of the viewer's affection cannot or does not reciprocate their affection—though this doesn't seem to put a damper on the viewer's feelings of attachment.

At first glance it's easy to trivialize parasocial relationships as an anomaly that only delusional people engage in. After all, you may find yourself thinking that you can tell the difference between fantasy and reality, and therefore couldn't imagine yourself feeling real feelings for a fictional character. The unspoken assumption of this statement, of course, is that the ability to recognize that a piece of media is fictional makes you immune to being affected by it.

Is this an assumption we can make? Both anecdotal evidence and data from scientific studies suggests otherwise! Speaking to the former point, ask yourself why people pay money to watch horror, action, comedy, or drama films? If a horror movie failed to give the viewer chills or cause them even the slightest bit of apprehension, wouldn't it be failure as a film? If a drama film failed to tug at an audience's heartstrings, it would likely be critically panned—or at least deemed boring. Wouldn't you also be disappointed if you watched an action film and left without feeling the slightest hint of exhilaration throughout the experience?

As these examples illustrate, people consume media precisely to experience emotions from them. Fans want to feel the rush of hate at a well-written villain, the sadness of unrequited lovers, or the bone-chilling terror of being hunted by a supernatural monster—and they do! What's noteworthy, however, is that fans experience these emotions *despite* being well-aware that the content of the film itself is fictional. While there may be some suspension of disbelief in the theater, if you were to pull them aside and ask them if it was real, they would all be able to tell you that what they're seeing is not real, but rather the work of skilled actors, directors, writers, and craftspeople.

So, if people can experience terror, laughter, sadness, and exhilaration from media despite its non-real status, it is conceivable that they might also experience attachment, affection, or even love toward the shows, books, movies, and video games they consume? If viewers can nominate favorite movies or stories that have had the biggest impact on the way they think, feel, and behave, then why not favorite characters that make them feel understood, appreciated, or a sense of attachment?

One especially relevant perspective from media studies on the current topic is called the "uses and gratifications" approach. In its simplest form, the theory argues that people are not simply mindless, passive consumers of media. Instead, people actively seek out and use media to satisfy psychological needs—be it a need to learn something, to be entertained, to change one's current mood, to escape or distract oneself from the real world, to forge a sense of identity, or to feel a sense of social interaction (Katz et al., 1974). This last need is the most presently relevant, as it suggests that people can use media to scratch a psychological "itch"—that need to be social and interact with other people—especially if they're currently feeling lonely and have few other ways to satisfy that need (Peplau & Perlman, 1982; Rubin & Rubin, 1985; Wang et al., 2008).

To understand how parasocial relationships with media characters can satisfy the very real psychological need for social interaction, it helps to understand our evolutionary context. Evolution, as a process, is a fairly slow, generations-long process. In contrast, modern mass-media, relatively speaking, emerged in an evolutionary blink of an eye. As a result, many of our evolutionarily-adapted quirks—quirks which made sense in an evolutionary context—are often hijacked or misfire in a media-saturated environment so different from the one where the quirks first evolved.

As an illustrative and relevant example, there is an evolutionarily-derived tendency for people to like those who we encounter more

148

frequently (Bornstein, 1989) and to become more attached to those who are frequently around us (Festinger et al., 1963). This was a helpful adaptation which allowed us to quickly bond with our tribemates and quickly recognize who was and was not a threat to us.

However, long gone are the days of our ancestors wandering the Serengeti, where the only way you could see a person's face five times a day was to have that person living in the same tribe as you. Today, thanks to the omnipresence of screen media, we're bombarded with the faces of celebrities and fictional characters all the time. A person who watches their favorite show several times a week for several years has likely seen their favorite character hundreds or even thousands of times. While they may consciously recognize that this person is an actor or a fictional character, the mechanisms in their brain which forge these attachments to those they repeatedly encounter do not make this distinction. A familiar face is a familiar face as far as this mechanism is concerned, so feelings of closeness and attachment form just as they would for a real person. Furthermore, in an era where social media enabled more seemingly "personal" interactions between celebrities or fictional characters[13] and their audiences, is it any wonder that these effects may be getting stronger?

This tendency toward forming parasocial interactions has been studied in non-anime contexts. For example, researchers have shown that sport fans can develop relationships with their favorite athletes as a result of watching them play on television, seeing their interviews on talk shows, attending games and seeing them live, and following them on social media (Basil & Brown, 2004; Brown & Basil, 1995; Brown & de Matviuk, 2010). These feelings of attachment and felt friendships with celebrities and characters can escalate into feelings of intimacy and romantic attachment (Stever, 2009, 2013; Stever & Lawson, 2013).

Unfortunately, extreme examples of these manifestations are frequently the focus of discussions about parasocial relationships, including instances of obsessive fan behavior or stalking (e.g., Hellekson, 2010; Spitzberg & Cupach, 2008). The result is that many people who express feelings of

---

[13] Speaking to this point, Batman, Homer Simpson, Darth Vader, and even Tony the Tiger—the cereal mascot—have their own Twitter accounts!

attachment to media characters are often seen in this light and branded as insane, out-of-touch, or dangerous.

Given that there has been an ongoing tendency toward the erosion of face-to-face interaction and a generational replacement of in-person relationships with online, media-mediated relationships in the past few decades (e.g., Putnam, 2000; Twenge et al., 2019), it would make sense to speculate that an increasing number of people are turning to the media as a way of gratifying unfulfilled social needs. We recognize, however, that for the vast majority of those who experience parasocial relationships, they are little more than a typical manifestation of several fairly common psychological processes, one that rarely leads to excesses like stalking or obsession.

With all of this in mind, let's turn our attention at last to anime fans and the phenomena of waifus and husbandos.

First, we should keep in mind that the phenomenon itself may often be tongue-in-cheek, with anime fans using the term as a means of making light of stereotypes about anime fans through self-deprecating humor. As such, the number of fans who report having a waifu or husbando should not necessarily be taken as an accurate gauge of the number of fans who form strong parasocial relationships with anime characters. Instead, the stats should be treated as an "upper bound" or high-ball estimate of the frequency with which this phenomenon occurs.

Indeed, without directly asking participants what, precisely, they mean when they say they have a waifu or husbando, it can be difficult to know which participants are reporting deeply-held feelings of attachment and which are simply stating "this character is cute and desirable, and so I have decided to jokingly lay claim to them in a fandom full of people who, in a similar manner, jokingly lay claim to fictional characters."

In our 2015 study we found that most anime fans did not claim to have a waifu or husbando. The number who claimed to have one was slightly higher among online fans (30.2%) than convention-going fans (25.9%). Despite this small difference, we found no evidence that online or con-going anime fans differed in their felt a sense of emotional connection or sexual attraction in this parasocial relationship, although among those who did have a waifu or a husbando, they tended to report fairly strong emotional and sexual connections to these characters (see Figure 6.1).

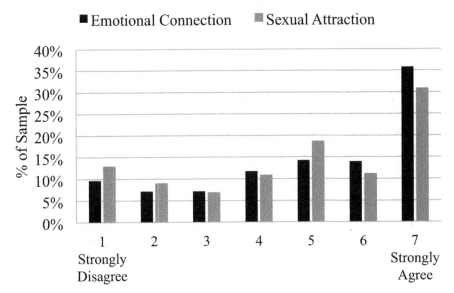

Figure 6.1. Reported emotional connection and sexual attraction of anime fans to their waifu / husbando.

To shed more light on the nature of fans' parasocial relationships with anime characters, in a 2017 study we asked anime fans to indicate the extent to which their favorite anime character represented the sort of person they could see themselves forming either a "friend" relationship with or a "romantic" relationship with.[14] Their favorite characters were significantly more likely to be described as being like a friend than being like a romantic partner or someone they were sexually attracted to, a tendency reflected in both con-going and online anime fans. In short, these findings reiterate the fact that, at least for most anime fans, having a favorite character is not the same thing as having formed a parasocial relationship with that character.

---

[14] A noteworthy flaw in these data is that it refers specifically to one's "favorite character" rather than specifically referring to one's waifu or husbando. While fans with waifus and husbandos are likely to cite these characters as being among their favorites, in the data we were not able to distinguish those with waifus / husbandos from those without them.

Also speaking to this point, we asked participants in our 2018 study whether they became jealous of their favorite character or voice actor being involved in a romantic relationship. Only 10.4% of fans indicated strong feelings of jealousy toward their favorite character being in a romantic relationship, while only 2.2% indicated feelings of jealousy over their favorite voice actor's romantic relationship.[15]

Given that only a minority of anime fans have a waifu or husbando, we can ask whether there are differences between those who do and those who do not that may help us predict which fans are most likely to have one. Across several studies, a few factors emerged as small, but predictable differences between the two groups.

We found, for example, that those who do have a waifu or husbando tend to be younger and think about their anime fan identity more frequently in their day-to-day life. In a related vein, those with a waifu / husbando are also more likely to openly display their anime identity and to be more susceptible to threats against anime fans made from non-anime fans.

Those with waifus or husbandos are also more likely to feel a greater sense of belongingness to the anime fandom, a fandom which they're also more likely to consider to be unique compared to other fandoms. This, coupled with being somewhat more likely to have lower self-esteem than anime fans without waifus or husbandos, yields one last interesting finding: those with waifus or husbandos report relying on the anime fandom to achieve a sense of optimal distinctiveness.

In a nutshell, optimal distinctiveness refers to a conflict people experience between wanting to stand out and be distinct but not wanting to do so too much—to the point of feeling alone or like a spectacle. For anime fans with a waifu or husbando, they're more likely to use the anime fandom to balance this need. It's likely that the perceived uniqueness of the anime

---

[15] An interesting phenomenon that remains for future research pertains to the conflict—if any—which arises when two different people "lay claim" to the same waifu or husbando. On the one hand, anecdotal evidence gleaned from observing fans in online forums suggests that fans are largely unbothered by other people sharing the same waifu or husbando as they do, and may even bond over their mutual interest in the same character. On the other hand, we have also observed some fans expressing displeasure or jealousy at the thought or image of their waifu or husbando with another person, especially if that person is deemed unfit or unworthy as a suitor.

fandom and their stronger identification with it helps them feel distinct from others in their day-to-day lives (e.g., coworkers, fellow students).

Putting this all together, what can we say about those with waifus or husbandos in the anime fandom—besides the fact that they tend to be in the minority? Well, for starters, they seem to be fans who more strongly embrace their identity as an anime fan and who display it more openly. The anime fandom is, to them, unique and distinct from other fan groups, something which they rely on as a source of self-esteem and well-being. If having a waifu or husbando makes them a "bigger" anime fan, they may well embrace the idea for this very purpose.

To wrap this section up, it's worth delving into whether there's evidence that anime fans struggle with forming connections to real people due to the tendency of at least some to form parasocial relationships. Several questions in our recent 2020 survey can speak to this idea, albeit somewhat indirectly.

We find, for example, that anime fans would prefer to watch shows with animated characters in them more than shows with real actors or shows with non-human animals in them. This would seem to suggest that, yes, anime fans are fans of animated characters somewhat to the exclusion of other, non-animated media. Moreover, they prefer animated characters in their media more than real characters in their media.

Is this preference for animated characters in their media an indicator of some kind of problem with interacting with people in the real world? Some preliminary evidence may hint at this possibility. Anime fans, as a group, say that they find it easier to recognize emotions in animated characters than they do in real people. A significant caveat to this finding, however, is that they have not been compared against a sample of non-anime fans. Given that animated characters are often designed with features with emotional expression in mind (e.g., large eyes), this may simply reflect a general tendency for animated characters to be easier to read the emotions of by design.

In a more direct test, we asked participants whether they had problems reading emotions in real people. The results revealed that about one-third of anime fans felt that this was the case. Again, we currently lack control data against which to compare these findings, so there's no way to know whether this number is high, low, or comparable to non-anime fans.

However, it may be the case that those who struggle with real-world interactions or who have few opportunities to have positive face-to-face interactions with people may satisfy that particular psychological need for companionship through parasocial interactions with animated characters. Future research will need to investigate whether fans who struggle with face-to-face interaction are, indeed, more likely than other anime fans to develop parasocial relationships with anime characters.

In the next, and final, section, we move beyond feelings of romantic attachment to fictional characters and instead delve into perhaps the most intimate relationship of all—identifying with these characters as representations of themselves.

Identifying with Characters

The question about whether someone identifies with another person—fictional or otherwise—is both a simple and complex one. It's fairly simple to ask a bunch of anime fans whether they identify with their favorite anime character. People generally understand what you're talking about when you ask this question—that you're asking whether they see facets of themselves reflected in this character, and not literally asking whether they have taken on the name and identity of this character.[16] As the data in Figure 6.2 reveal, anime fans differ widely in the extent to which this is the case, although the overall tendency was for fans to somewhat agree. The tendency was stronger with convention-going anime fans than online anime fans (an average score of 4.65 / 7.00 versus 4.34 / 7.00).

So, is this tendency to identify with a favorite character typical among all fans, or is it especially extreme or unique to anime fans?

Looking again at the data from Figure 6.2, we can compare data from anime fans to data from two other fandoms to see how they stack up. The

---

[16] People who blur the lines between fantasy and reality to this extent are sometimes known as "fantasy prone" people and were estimated to make up about 4% of the population (Wilson & Barber, 1983). Fantasy prone people are often studied for their susceptibility to being hypnotized and tendency to believe in paranormal, supernatural, or otherwise impossible things (Lynn & Rhue, 1988; Wilson & Barber, 1983). We would contend that anyone who genuinely blurs the lines between fantasy and reality and believes themselves to actually be a fictional character from an anime series is probably exceptionally high in fantasy proneness and does not represent a typical anime fan. As such, when describing fans identifying with characters, we are not referring to people with this particular delusion.

154

findings are generally comparable, although *My Little Pony* fans and furries were somewhat more likely to strongly identify with a favorite character than anime fans.[17] In other words, it would seem that anime fans are far from the most likely fan group to identify with their favorite characters—although a fair number of anime fans do.

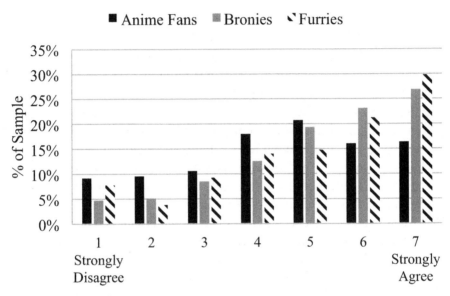

Figure 6.2. Extent to which anime fans, bronies, and furries agreed that they strongly identified with their favorite characters.

However, remember that it's fairly easy to simply ask people the extent to which they identify with their favorite characters. It's a far more complex question to dive into the nature of this identification: What does it mean to identify with one's favorite character, and what does it tell us about fans who do it? To dig down into this question, we commonly ask a variety of

---

[17] It should be pointed out that in the furry fandom more than 95% of furries creates a fursona—a furry-themed character—to represent themselves (Plante et al., 2015), while in the brony fandom it's fairly common to create one's own original character in the *My Little Pony* universe. Both of these tendencies may be a result of, or explain, the greater tendency to identify with a fictional character, for these folks, their favorite character may well be their own!

questions aimed at directly assessing different facets of identification with another character, drawing upon a variety of different research perspectives.

For starters, we can look at the extent to which fans immerse themselves into the experiences of the characters in the story: Are fans imagining themselves in the characters' shoes, seeing the story through their eyes, and reacting emotionally the same way the characters themselves do? Research suggests that those with greater levels of empathy are better able to put themselves in a character's position and, by extension, are more likely to identify with that character (Bachen et al., 2016).

Speaking to this idea, we found evidence of a significant positive correlation between the extent to which participants identified with their favorite characters and both feeling their favorite character's feelings and having the impression of living the character's story themselves. Or, to put it another way, anime fans who identified more strongly with their favorite characters were also more likely to say that they respond emotionally as their character does, and as if it were happening to them. To at least some extent, it would seem that how a fan feels toward their favorite character depends on whether they feel what their character feels.

However, there's more to identifying with a character than simply feeling what they feel. After all, you might see a person burn their hand on the stove and wince empathically, imagining how painful it would feel to do the same thing yourself. This, in and of itself, is not enough to guarantee that you would identify with this person.[18] To identify with someone, you may also need to have something in common with them—like sharing attitudes, values, and beliefs. Indeed, prior research shows that the more you share features in common with another person, the more likely you are to find them appealing and, to the extent that you find them appealing, the more strongly you should identify with them (Hogg et al., 1995).

As such, it comes as no surprise that our own study found a strong positive correlation between identifying with one's favorite character and perceiving that the character has thoughts and values similar to your own— even though there was no correlation between identifying with one's favorite character and the character coming from the same background or

---

[18] Except insofar as you both, like most people, react with displeasure at the feeling of being burned!

156

situation as you do. When it comes to identifying with a character, it's far more important whether the character believes in the same things you do than it is for the character to come from a similar background as you.

An interesting caveat to this finding also emerged during our analyses: Those whose favorite characters were background characters were the most likely to report feeling similar to their favorite characters—even more so than for those identifying with a main character. This seems a bit perplexing, given what we said earlier about more time being given to main characters to flesh out their values and beliefs compared to background characters.

We can think of two possible explanations for this finding. The first is based on the fact that, in many anime series, the main character has powers (e.g., inhuman strength, supernatural abilities) that may make them less relatable than background characters—who may be more likely to be "average people."

A second possibility is that background characters, having less-developed beliefs and values, may serve as an empty vessel into which fans can project their own beliefs and values. In other words, if a character doesn't explicitly state what their beliefs, values, or philosophical stances are, a viewer can easily interpret their behavior through their own set of beliefs and values. At the moment, whether either of these speculative explanations is correct remains to be seen in future research.

Another variable possibly driving identification with one's favorite character is that of wish fulfillment: Characters may represent an idealized version of who a person would like to become.

Psychological research has shown that role models are desirable when they reflect something a person would like to become, particularly if the model's behavior is realistically attainable (Lockwood & Kunda, 1997). A classic example of this can be found in the *Rocky* films, in which Sylvester Stallone's titular character is beloved by viewers precisely because he serves as an inspiration. His low-tech training methods, which include running upstairs, chopping wood, and jumping rope in run-down gyms suggests to the viewer that this level of fitness is something that they, too, can attain.[19]

So, is there any evidence that anime fans may be identifying with their favorite anime characters because those characters represent idealized versions of who they would like to be?

In a word: Yes. For example, there is moderately strong positive correlation between fans' identification with their favorite character and agreement that the character represents the sort of person they wish they could be. Analyses from the same studies also find that fans are more likely to identify with their favorite character the more they consider the character to be a hero and are less likely to identify with their favorite character the more they consider the character to be a villain. Fans may really enjoy a good villain in a story, but it's the heroes they aspire to become like.

When you put all of these factors together, which one is the most strongly associated with the tendency to identify with one's favorite character? Using a type of analysis called structural equation modeling, we were able to pit all of these different mechanisms against one another in a single analysis. The results showed that emotional empathy—being able to put yourself in your favorite character's shoes and feel what they feel—is the key to creating a character that fans will identify with.

We also found several additional, smaller factors that helped to predict which anime fans were the most likely to strongly identify with an anime character. For example, those who score high in fandom, that is, a felt connection to other anime fans, were more likely to also identify with a favorite character. Those who consume more anime content were, perhaps unsurprisingly, also more likely to identify with their favorite character. Finally, those who said that the majority of their fantasy activities (e.g., daydreaming, leisure time, television viewing, reading) were anime-themed were also more likely to say that they identified with their favorite anime character.

---

[19] For many, including at least one of this book's authors, Rocky's training montages and the songs which played during them were an inspiration during their training to run a half-marathon.

Conclusion

We began this chapter by considering a popular stereotype of an anime fan: An out-of-touch fanatic struggling to distinguish the fantasy world from reality,[20] one who forms unhealthy attachments to fictional characters, and who may even see themselves as an anime character. As the reviewed psychological literature, comparisons to research in other fandoms, and our own research on anime fans shows, there is little evidence to substantiate this stereotype.

It's true that anime fans frequently become attached to their favorite characters, including, in about a quarter of cases, developing romantic feelings toward a character. It's also true that many anime fans identify, at least in part, with these characters—either through empathic attachment, shared values, or seeing the character as an example of the kind of person they would like to be.

None of this behavior is, in and of itself, pathological. As we'll see in other chapters (e.g., Chapter 19), anime fans report fairly good day-to-day functioning in the real world and seem comparable to non-fans in terms of their physical and psychological well-being despite these attachments to fictional characters. If it really were the case that attachment to fictional characters led to distress and maladaptation, we would expect to see far higher rates of mental health problems or problems coping with day-to-day life in anime fans.

Nor is this behavior even all that unusual. Fans from all hobbies—from sport fans to soap opera fans, from music fans to TV fans, all form attachments to characters in the media they consume. This is, in no small part, due to the way our brains work, having evolved in a time before screen media was a thing. If anything, the attachment people feel to these characters is less the fault of the fan and more a product of their evolution-shaped brain and the talented writers who create relatable, believable, endearing characters that capitalize on our evolutionary tendencies.

Now, if you'll excuse me, I suddenly feel compelled to go for a run that ends with me running up the tallest set of stairs I find while triumphantly humming the *Rocky* theme song.

---

[20] A stereotype played for comedic effect in the computer game *Undertale*, where Undyne asks the player character "Anime's real, right?," forcing the player to choose whether to divulge to her that the anime she had seen is or is not real.

Chapter 7
Cosplayers

The word cosplay is a portmanteau of the words "costume" and "play" (Bainbridge & Norris, 2013), and refers to a person who dresses up and performs as a character from popular media (e.g., anime, video games). The origins of cosplay begin with U.S. science fiction fans, but the popularity of the term itself is often accredited to Nobuyuki Takahashi (Galbraith, 2009; McCarthy & Ashmore, 2021; Winge, 2006). As the term spread, so too did the number of people who cosplayed, especially within the anime fandom.

This means, of course, that cosplay did not begin in the anime fandom. Nevertheless, cosplay has become prevalent throughout the anime fandom, to the point where it is perhaps more strongly connected with the anime fandom than with any other fandom. In fact, cosplayers are the people we often think of when we think of anime fans. This is due, in no small part, to their increased visibility, being so visually distinct from everyday life. Chen (2007, p. 15) describes cosplayers as the "soul of an anime/manga convention" for their ability to transform the space from average to fantastical. Davis (2017) found that fans attending Anime Expo reported that watching cosplayers or cosplaying were the biggest reasons for attending the convention. Much like how otaku were once shunned but now embraced by a reluctant Japanese government, cosplayers too have found themselves embraced and promoted in the anime fandom specifically, and in Japanese culture more broadly (Ito & Crutcher, 2014).

Given the importance of cosplay to the anime fandom specifically, and to fan culture more broadly, it was only a matter of time before scholars would take note and begin to study cosplay seriously, aiming to categorize, understand, and explain the phenomenon of cosplay.

Winge (2006), for example, distinguished between four facets of cosplay: the cosplayer, social settings, character role-playing, and costume. With respect to the cosplayer themselves, Winge notes that anyone can cosplay as any character regardless of gender, age, or socioeconomic background. The only requirement is an interest in the character and the desire to dress up and act like the character. Cosplayers vary in this too, along a continuum based on just how involved they want to get in cosplay (Winge, 2006). On the high end of this continuum, some cosplayers even manage to earn a living through cosplay (Han, 2020; Ashcraft & Plunkett, 2014).

With respect to social settings, cosplay primarily takes place at fan conventions, but can include other social activities such as masquerades, panels, contests, and photo sessions. Importantly, cosplay rarely occurs in a vacuum, almost necessitating a setting in which cosplayers and spectators can socialize and interact. With the proliferation of social media, these social settings have expanded to include virtual spaces like websites, blogs, and video-sharing websites (Winge, 2006).

When it comes to characters and roleplaying, cosplayers can pick pretty much any character from the available canon or from fan-made content, with few barriers beyond one's own imagination and creativity. As Winge notes, "Role-playing is an essential skill for a cosplayer, regardless if he or she is accurate to a character, creating a parody, or just having fun" (2006, p.72). Thus, even two people cosplaying as the same character can differ dramatically, putting their own novel spin on how the character is interpreted.[1]

The final element of cosplay according to Winge—dress—refers to all of the accoutrements cosplayers use to represent their character. "Cosplay dress includes all body modifications and supplements, such as hair, makeup, costume, and accessories, including wands, staffs, and swords" (2006, p. 72). She points out that these are essential tools for the portrayal of the character, bringing the fantastical off the page or the screen and into the real world. Great time, care, and resources often go into getting the details of dress just right, with some cosplayers creating their outfits themselves and others commissioning or purchasing them through an entire cottage industry which has sprung up around cosplaying.

Other scholars have moved beyond defining and cataloging the cosplay experience, choosing instead to focus on the distinction between those fans who cosplay and those who do not. After all, just as fursuits represent a

---

[1] Among one of the authors' favorite examples of this flexibility of interpretation is the trend of crossplaying the Sailor Scouts from the anime *Sailor Moon* as large, burly men. While it's easy for this to be done lazily or mockingly in a way that veers into transphobia, when done respectfully and seriously, it is a wonderfully expectation-defying sight that marvellously demonstrates the freedom that cosplay allows for anyone to cosplay as any character.

visible minority in the furry fandom, the fursuit has nevertheless come to represent the fandom to outsiders (Plante et al., 2016); cosplayers in the anime fandom are also in the minority but have nevertheless come to represent the fandom to outsiders, too. As such, it is worth asking to what extent cosplayers truly represent typical anime fans and whether there are measurable differences between cosplaying and non-cosplaying fans.

Exploring this very question is precisely the purpose of the present chapter. We begin by describing the results of research, both coming before us as well as our own, documenting the demographics of cosplayers as well as their consumption habits and comparing them to non-cosplaying fans. We then compare cosplayers and non-cosplayers' perceived trajectory in the fandom over time as well as their motivations for participating in the fandom. After that, we examine the variables predicting the extent to which cosplayers identify with their favorite character in an analysis reminiscent of those from Chapter 6. Finally, we finish up with a series of comparisons between cosplayers and non-cosplayers with respect to a myriad of interesting psychological and fandom-related variables, including personality, entitlement, elitism, gatekeeping, involvement in fandom drama, and well-being.

Demographics

Before we begin our comparison of how cosplayers stack up against non-cosplayers demographically, it's worth taking a look at the prevalence rate of cosplayers in the anime fandom to begin with. Prior research from a 2007 study of 776 anime fans estimated that 26% of anime fans were cosplayers (Igarashi, 2007). In our own study, a decade later, we estimate that number to be 34.4%. One possible explanation is that our larger estimate represents a true increase in the number of cosplayers in the anime fandom over the past decade.[2] Another possibility is that the differences reflect differences in sampling methodology, the way the questions were asked, and random variance inherent in any sample. This interpretation suggests that the estimate will vary from study to study, with the true percentage of cosplayers in the fandom probably hovering somewhere

---

[2] Given the rise of websites like YouTube, Twitter, Instagram, and TikTok during that time, websites which allow cosplayers to reach a larger audience and which allow for more advice and support for aspiring cosplayers, this certainly seems plausible!

around 30%.[3] The reality is likely to involve both of these plausible explanations. For now, it is less important to nail down the exact proportion of cosplayers in the anime fandom and more important to note that cosplayers make up a small, but sizable minority of the anime fandom.

Armed with this knowledge, we can delve into comparisons between cosplayers and non-cosplayers with respect to demographic variables. In prior research, Okabe (2012) suggested that cosplayers in Japan tend to be women in their 20s in college who, in all other regards, lead fairly typical adult lives.

Our own research largely coincides with Okabe's work. We find, for example, that while the majority of anime fans are men (when you combine online and convention fans in our research), cosplayers are comprised of 55.2% women. In a related finding, crossplay—where an individual cosplays as a character with a different gender identity than their own (Napier, 2007)—was three times more prevalent among cosplaying women (43.1%) than among cosplaying men (13%).

Our research also supports the conclusion of Okabe that cosplayers are in their 20s. We found that cosplayers (average age 23.6 years) tend to be about two years younger than non-cosplayers (average age 25.4 years). In other words, while cosplayers do tend to be women in their 20s as Okabe stated, our own work adds some nuance to the discussion by pointing out that cosplayers are younger than non-cosplaying fans. Whether this is because newer fans are simply more likely to cosplay or because fans become less interested in cosplay as they age remains a subject for future research.

Our findings do not entirely coincide with those of Okabe, however. We find, for example, that cosplayers are actually less likely to be a student than non-cosplayers. While this doesn't mean that it can't still be true that most cosplayers are either in college or have some college experience, having college experience is actually more likely to define a non-cosplaying anime fan than a cosplaying anime fan. In fact, cosplayers, if

---

[3] We also asked cosplayers how many different characters they have cosplayed on average. The average was five characters among cosplayers, with the highest number of cosplayed characters being 84. The majority of cosplayers had played fewer than 8 different characters, suggesting that very high numbers of characters were the exception rather than the norm.

anything, were more likely than non-cosplaying fans to be currently employed in some sort of office work.[4]

To finish up this section on the demographic composition of cosplayers, we find that cosplayers are more than twice as likely as non-cosplayers to be in a current romantic relationship: 46.3% compared to 20.5%.[5] We also asked fans to indicate the extent to which they considered themselves artists and writers (1 = *absolutely not*, 7 = *completely*). Cosplayers, one might have predicted, identified more strongly than non-cosplayers as artists (3.76 versus 2.48 on average) and as writers (3.87 versus 2.90 on average).

Consumption

Given that cosplayers devote considerable time, effort, and resources to the creation of their cosplays, it would make sense that cosplaying is not something engaged in by fairly casual fans who watch only a bit of anime. To this end, one might hypothesize that cosplaying anime fans consume more anime than the average non-cosplaying anime fan.

To test this idea, we asked anime fans how often they watch different types of anime (i.e., anime aimed at different age groups) on a 7-point scale. Across all of the different types of anime, cosplayers consistently watched more anime than did non-cosplayers: they watched more anime meant for children (4.08 versus 3.65 on average), anime meant for adults that was not pornographic (6.10 versus 5.98), and pornographic anime (3.09 versus 2.63). In short, these data provide support for our prediction—cosplayers do, indeed, seem to consume more anime than do non-cosplaying anime fans.

We can assess consumption behavior in other ways beyond the amount of anime someone consumes. We find, for example, that cosplayers and non-cosplayers also spend differently. As shown in Figure 7.1, cosplayers spend considerably more money than do non-cosplayers attending anime conventions,[6] purchasing anime paraphernalia (including cosplay materials),

---

[4] A point further adding to the idea that cosplayers, outside of their fandom activities, lead fairly typical, unremarkable lives.

[5] This may owe, at least in part, to the fact that women in the anime fandom (and, indeed, in other fandoms such as the furry fandom), are more likely to be in a long-term relationship, and, as we've previously mentioned, women are more likely to be cosplayers.

[6] To this point, cosplayers attend more than double the number of conventions as non-cosplaying anime fans per year (2.35 versus 0.96 on average). They were also more likely to attend local meet-ups per year than non-cosplayers (2.03 versus 1.16 on average).

and purchasing physical artwork (which cosplayers spend more on than non-cosplayers). The two groups did not differ, however, with respect to other types of purchases (e.g., digital artwork). Together, however, the data suggest that cosplaying anime fans do tend to spend more on their fan interest, which might lead one to suggest that cosplaying anime fans are simply anime fans with more money to spend in the first place. While this is certainly a possibility, one needing to be studied in the future, we remind the reader that cosplaying anime fans also tend to be younger than non-cosplaying anime fans, which, statistically speaking, should make them less likely to have an established career and, by extension, likely to earn less per year.

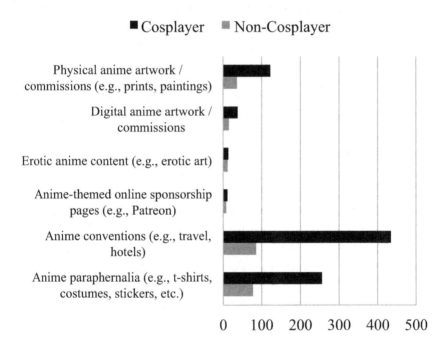

Figure 7.1. Money spent by cosplayer self-categorization.

Fandom Involvement

As noted in the prior section, cosplayers scored higher than non-cosplayers on virtually all measures of consumption—an indicator of one's fanship or identification with their interest in a topic. This result suggests that cosplayers may also be more involved or active with the fandom itself. As we saw in Chapter 5, otaku (vs. non-otaku) rated their past, current, and future involvement in the fandom higher than non-otaku. We expected to find a similar trend among cosplaying anime fans, and so we ran the same analysis comparing cosplaying and non-cosplaying fans. As shown in Figure 7.2, cosplayers are more involved than non-cosplayers, both currently and in the past, and they expect to be more involved in the fandom than in the future. In this respect, there may be some truth to the idea that cosplayers represent a core of the anime community.

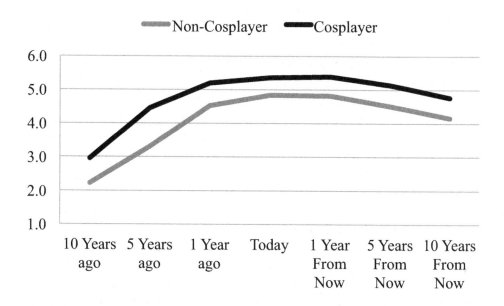

Figure 7.2. Perceived fandom involvement across time by cosplayer self-categorization.

Motivation

Considerable effort has been devoted, both in prior research and in our own research, to understanding what drives cosplayers to their unique hobby (for a great summary of 20 studies on this subject, see Reysen et al., 2018a). These studies include a range of samples from four participants to more than 1,000 participants and a range of methodologies from in-depth interviews to large surveys, and include samples from around the world.

Across all of these studies, the most commonly mentioned motivation driving anime cosplayers was a sense of belongingness.[7] This should come as no surprise as, according to Barajas (2018), cosplay itself is an inherently social activity that includes meeting to share tips on costume and prop construction, practicing, and a shared love for the activity itself. Speaking to this idea, cosplayers on Facebook point out that social media allows them to fulfill belongingness needs through checking updates on other cosplayers, making new friends, and interacting with fans (Kane, 2017). In a similar vein, Ahn (2008) interviewed cosplayers in Tokyo about what motivated them to cosplay and found that most started cosplaying to make new friends and be a part of a community. In fact, Lamerichs (2018) argues that cosplayers' main connection to the fandom is the feeling of emotional attachment they have to the community itself. It would certainly explain why cosplayers often perform together in groups or teams (Ahn, 2008).

However, belongingness is not the only motivation driving cosplayers to their craft. After all, it's unlikely that anyone would cosplay if they weren't having at least some fun with it.[8] Entertainment clocks in as the second most mentioned motivation driving cosplayers. Speaking to the importance of fun in cosplay, Rosenberg and Letamendi (2013) surveyed 198 cosplayers (mostly from the U.S.) and found that "fun" was a top-endorsed reason cited by cosplayers. Lotecki (2012) similarly surveyed 529 cosplayers and found that fun was one of the top-chosen reason for participating in cosplay. In a 2013 study interviewing Chinese cosplayers, Peirson-Smith (2013) noted that all participants mentioned having fun while doing cosplay. Another study of Chinese cosplayers by Rahman et al. (2012) similarly found that cosplayers' collection of costumes and props elicited fun and exciting memories. As participant in Langsford's (2014, p. 231) interviews with Australian cosplayers summarized it, "It is a bunch of fun people, big smiles, bright costumes having fun outside."

So, cosplayers cosplay to be among like-minded others and for fun. However, the third most mentioned motivation for cosplay adds a unique

---

[7] In fact, we could find only one study which did *not* mention this motivation!

[8] Remember, after all, that cosplay is a spinoff of a fan interest, something that, itself, is a recreational activity, something which, by definition, people do for fun or enjoyment.

twist to the story: escaping from daily life. While fun suggests doing an activity that's inherently enjoyable, escapism is different: It emphasizes the novelty of the act itself.[9] Rahman et al. (2012) note that cosplayers create imaginative worlds that they escape into to avoid the stressors and burdens of everyday life. Speaking to this very point, cosplayers in China point out that thinking about cosplay helps them get through the boring parts of their job (Peirson-Smith, 2013). Flatt (2015) also finds that cosplayers mention being able to escape from one's life for a short time without any lasting consequences. Wang (2010) mentions how one cosplayer interviewed described the stress of their job as increasing their cosplaying as a means of escaping the pressure.

Taking into account all of the above research, in our own study[10] we examined and compared the motivations of cosplayers and non-cosplaying anime fans with respect to 10 different plausible motivations (see Chapter 14 for more information, including a rationale of the 10 different motivations). We wanted to look at which motivations were listed as the most common for cosplayers and to see whether the relative importance of those motivations differed between cosplayers and non-cosplayers.

First, we found that cosplayers scored higher than non-cosplayers on all 10 of the motivations, suggesting, as we mentioned earlier in this chapter, that cosplayers may be more motivated, more active, more enthusiastic anime fans than non-cosplaying anime fans.[11] The largest differences in motivation were observed with respect to, in order, belongingness, self-esteem, family, escapism, aesthetics, and eustress. In other words, these motivations were the ones that played a significantly larger role in driving cosplayers' interest in the fandom than they did for non-cosplayers. Of note, belongingness and escapism were more important motivators for cosplayers

---

[9] As an example illustrating the distinction, imagine playing your favorite video game or watching your favorite television show. No doubt you enjoy these activities, but chances are you did not find a favorite game or show and stop there, committing yourself solely to the same piece of media for all of your spare time. As humans, we naturally seek to grow and expand, or at very least grow weary of the same old thing. Sometimes novelty, even if it's not "fun," can drive us to new pursuits.

[10] This study has been previously published, Reysen et al. (2018a).

[11] This should not be taken to mean, of course, that cosplayers are the "real" anime fans, or that non-cosplaying fans are somehow lesser fans. As in other fandoms, there are a myriad of ways one's interest can manifest, of which cosplaying is just one!

than non-cosplayers, but entertainment was not. This may suggest that the anime fandom (through cosplaying) is both a greater source of escapism and is an inherently more social activity for cosplayers than it is for non-cosplayers who, nevertheless, enjoy anime to about the same extent as cosplayers.

Going one step further, we next examined whether the fact that cosplayers also identify more strongly with the anime fandom than non-cosplayers do could be explained, at least in part, by their scoring higher on these various motivations. We tested this model, shown in Figure 7.3, which found that six different motivators in particular accounted for at least some of this difference: including belongingness, family, self-esteem, eustress, escape, and entertainment. That said, while all of these different motivations provided some explanation, the strongest predictor by far was belongingness. In other words, when explaining why cosplayers and non-cosplayers differ with respect to how strongly they identify with the anime fan community, the greater sense of belongingness experienced by cosplayers plays a sizable role.

In a second, related analysis, we shifted our focus away from motivations to be part of the fandom and instead examined the extent to which cosplayers and non-cosplayers fulfilled various psychological needs through the anime fandom. In a parallel to the previous analysis, Figure 7.4 shows that cosplayers scored higher than non-cosplayers in the tendency to fulfill their psychological needs through fandom participation. The psychological needs most strongly explaining the difference in how much cosplaying and non-cosplaying fans identified with the anime fandom were self-esteem, meaning in life, belongingness, interpersonal distinctiveness, and friendships. Many of these psychological needs (e.g., belongingness, friendships, interpersonal distinctiveness) have a distinctly social component, reinforcing what we found in our previous analysis.

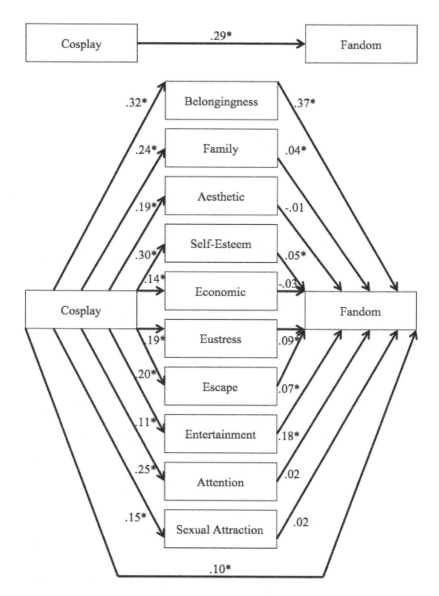

Figure 7.3. Association between comparison of whether or not anime fans participate in cosplay (0 = does not cosplay, 1 = does cosplay) and degree of identification with the anime community through different motivations. Standardized betas presented, * *p* < .05, ** *p* < .01.

Figure 7.4. Association between comparison of whether or not anime fans participate in cosplay (0 = does not cosplay, 1 = does cosplay) and degree of identification with the anime community through different psychological needs. Standardized betas presented, * $p < .05$, ** $p < .01$.

In sum, the results of these two analyses from our own research reinforce what past research has suggested about cosplayers: Their interest is driven by a number of factors, the biggest of which is the sense of and social interaction provided by the anime fandom more broadly and the cosplay community specifically.

Actual, Ideal, Ought Selves

Higgins et al. (1986) suggest that we all have multiple versions of ourselves ratting around in our mind. These include, among other self-concepts, our actual self (traits that we currently possess), our ideal self (traits we would ideally like to possess), and our ought self (traits that we feel obligated by others or by society to possess). These three selves are components of Higgins' model, called self-discrepancy theory (Higgins, 1987). In a nutshell, the model states that we experience negative emotions as the gap between our actual self and these other selves increases.

For example, we would all like to be our ideal selves (e.g., smart, funny, courageous, charming), but we don't always live up to that ideal (e.g., sometimes we do dumb things, act cowardly, or are off-putting to others). When this gap between our actual and ideal selves is seen as being large, we feel disappointment.[12] To avoid these negative emotions, people generally try to move toward their ideal or ought selves. To this end, we wondered whether the content of these different selves predicted the sorts of characters cosplayers identified with.

Before that, let's consider how psychologists understand the concept of identification. Identifying with something means feeling a psychological connection to it, be it a person, character, or group. Identifying with a favorite character represents incorporating that character into one's self-concept. For example, Klimmt et al. (2010) asked participants to either play a military first-person shooter game or a car racing game. Participants then completed measures testing the extent to which participants had incorporated the fictional character into themselves.[13] They found that while playing the games, participants were, indeed, taking traits of their played characters into themselves.

---

[12] When the gap between our actual and ought selves is salient, we experience shame.

[13] They did so using a task called the implicit-association test, which tests how readily people associate character-relevant words (in this case, words like violent or thrill-seeking) with themselves.

In a similar vein, when participants in another study were asked to create a character in a video game, Bessière et al. (2007) found that players constructed characters that more closely resembled their ideal selves than their actual selves. Furries similarly do this when they create their fursonas, imbuing them with characteristics that reflect their ideal selves (Plante et al., 2016).[14]

In this regard, anime fans' favorite characters may be comparable, representing their ideal selves. Ahn (2008) notes that cosplayers often want to become like the character they are cosplaying. They therefore choose characters that they admire to become, a way of becoming an idealized version of themselves (Atkinson, 2015; Zielinski, 2014). By acting as one's favorite character, cosplayers may in fact be practicing acting more in line with their ideal self (Lamerichs, 2018). In other words, cosplayers chose characters they idealize (Hoff, 2012; Rahman et al., 2012) or who inspire them (Rosenberg & Letamendi, 2013), which allows them to become one with an idealized persona (Hill, 2017).

We tested this idea in a now-published study (Reysen et al., 2018b) which asked anime cosplayers to rate the extent to which they identified with their favorite character (e.g., "I strongly identify with my cosplay character") and the extent to which that character represented their actual self ("This character represents who I currently am"), ideal self (e.g., "This character represents an idealized ("best") version of me"), and ought self (e.g., "This character represents the person people think I ought to be"). The results showed that cosplayers rated the characters as most strongly representing their actual ($M = 3.89$) and ideal ($M = 3.72$) selves significantly more than their ought selves ($M = 2.58$).[15]

Next, we tested a statistical model where actual, ideal, and ought selves were examined for the extent to which they predicted whether people identified with the character itself. As shown in Figure 7.5, the extent to which the character represented one's actual and ideal selves both predicted

---

[14] In fact, in a later study, it was found that the more furries' fursona reflected their ideal selves, the more strongly they identified with it (Reysen, Plante et al., 2020).

[15] Notably, however, all of the ratings were below the midpoint of the measure (i.e., 4), suggesting that while there may be some tendency to choose cosplay characters that one identifies with or idealizes to some extent, this is far from the only factor involved in the choice!

174

greater identification with cosplayers' favorite character, while the character representing one's ought self did not predict greater identification with the character.

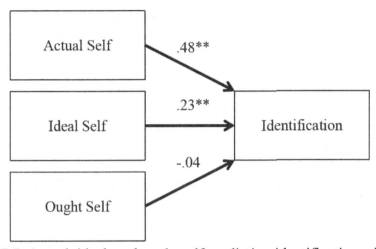

Figure 7.5. Actual, ideal, and ought self predicting identification with cosplayers' favorite character. Standardized betas, ** $p < .01$.

These results suggest that, all else equal, cosplayers may be choosing characters who are both similar to themselves while also containing idealized characteristics that the cosplayer wishes to possess. The results are in line with past research from other fandoms (Reysen, Plante et al., 2020) and also align with scholars in disciplines other than psychology (e.g., Ahn, 2008; Lamerichs, 2018; Rahman et al., 2012) who similarly suggest that cosplayers pick favorite characters due to admiration and idealization of that character. Future research may take this work one step further, examining whether cosplayers, even temporarily, take on those admired characteristics while cosplaying and, if so, how strongly and for how long. One tantalizing possibility would be to give cosplayers measures of their own traits and characteristics both during cosplay and in their day-to-day life to see whether there are differences in how cosplayers see themselves (and how others viewed them) between these settings.

Personality

In the previous section we talked about how cosplaying may lead to changes in a person's characteristics to become more like an ideal self. Scholars like Napier (2007) suggest, in fact, that engaging in cosplay allows people to become somebody else entirely, to change from an introvert to an extravert. However, despite the fact that personality can change across time and from situation to situation, it may also be the case that certain types of personalities make a person more likely to be a cosplayer in the first place. One can imagine, for example, that people who are fairly low in openness to novel experiences may be less inclined to try cosplaying. Alternatively, cosplaying in general may affect people long-term in predictable ways. Studies of U.S. (Ramirez, 2017), Filipino (Benino, 2014), and Taiwanese (Chen, 2007) cosplayers, for example, suggest that engaging in cosplay increases people's overall confidence in interacting with others.

There are numerous conceptual overlaps between cosplaying research and other areas of research which study personality theory. First, there's research showing that actors score higher in extraversion, openness to experience, agreeableness, and (slightly higher) neuroticism (emotional instability) than non-actors (Nettle, 2006). As such, if we think about a cosplayer as a type of actor, we might expect them to score in a similar manner on a personality test.

Second, Sun (2010) examined the association between the big five personality dimensions[16] and parasocial relationships. This research found higher rates of neuroticism, openness, and conscientiousness in people with stronger parasocial relationships with a favorite sport player. Maltby et al. (2004) similarly also found higher neuroticism scores for people with stronger parasocial relationships with a celebrity. Since, as noted in earlier this chapter, cosplayers tend to identify, with their favorite characters, they may show similar patterns of personality traits.[17]

---

[16] These "big five" personality dimensions underlie most modern personality research. They can be remembered with the acronym OCEAN—openness to experience, conscientiousness (attention to detail, planning, organization), extraversion, agreeableness, and neuroticism.

[17] Rain et al. (2017) similarly found that neuroticism was positively related with a tendency to become transported or highly immersed into a story. Since cosplayers both consume more anime media than non-cosplaying fans and form closer connections to the characters

Third (and finally), there is a growing body of research suggesting that both neuroticism and agreeableness are associated with more creative people (Martinsen, 2011; Maslej et al., 2017). Given the creativity involved in both playing as a fictional character and in the creation of a cosplay outfit, it comes as no surprise that cosplayers are often described consistently as creative. On these grounds, we might expect them to show similarly elevated neuroticism and agreeableness scores relative to non-cosplaying anime fans.

In light of this ample body of related research, we conducted a now-published study (Reysen et al., 2018c) comparing the personality traits of cosplaying and non-cosplaying anime fans. In this study we gave cosplayer and non-cosplayer anime fans a measure of their big five personality dimensions.

As shown in Figure 7.6, cosplayers (vs. non-cosplayers) rated themselves higher on extraversion, agreeableness, conscientiousness, and openness, and lower on emotional stability (i.e., higher in neuroticism). The greatest of these differences were on extraversion and openness. All in all, these results largely aligned with the prior research on actors, parasocial relationships, and creative people, with the exception of higher conscientiousness scores for cosplayers.[18] It is worth pointing out, however, that even though cosplayers scored higher on extraversion than non-cosplayers, they remained below the midpoint of the scale. This suggests that cosplayers are both in-line with stereotypes of anime fans as introverted (see Chapter 16) as well as in-line with both prior research and other stereotypes suggesting that, based on their engaging in an activity designed to draw attention to themselves, cosplayers are also more extraverted than the average anime fan.

---

themselves, it is conceivable that they may also show higher neuroticism scores like in line with more highly transported people.

[18] Although, with the benefit of hindsight, it might make sense that cosplayers would also score higher in conscientiousness. After all, cosplaying is a considerable undertaking, involving considerable planning, coordination, and weeks or even months of work. Being able to coordinate such an effort would surely involve at least a bit of conscientiousness!

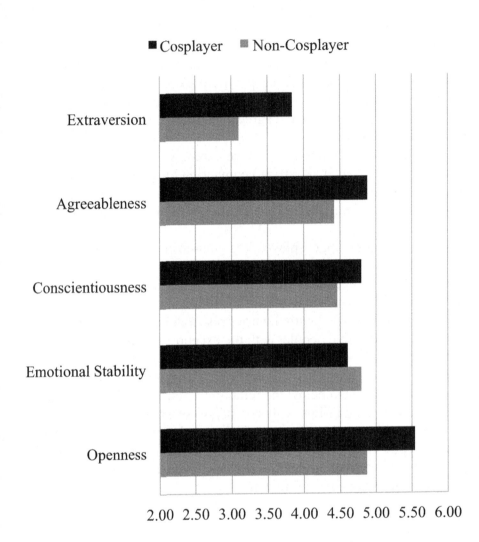

Figure 7.6. Personality by cosplayer self-categorization (7-point scale).

Fan Entitlement

Entitlement is the belief that you're owed something even though you don't necessarily deserve it (Twenge & Campbell, 2009). Much of the psychological research on entitlement has studied it from an academic perspective. For example, students may believe that because they paid tuition that deserve to receive "A's" in their classes and, if they don't, it's the professor's fault.

This research on academic entitlement has shown that students who score higher in entitlement also score higher in undesirable outcomes like academic dishonesty, using cell phones more during class, and believing that the things which happen to them are beyond their control (Reysen, Reysen et al., 2021; Sohr-Preston & Boswell, 2015). Peirone and Maticka-Tyndale (2017) found that students' entitlement didn't end in the classroom, but also carried on into other aspects of their life, like the workplace, where it is linked to job frustration, coworker abuse, perceived abuse from supervisors, organizational deviance, tension, depressed mood, and lower job satisfaction (see Jordan et al., 2017).

In short, a sizable body of research has shown that entitlement is tied to largely undesirable behaviors and that entitlement, while often studied in the classroom, can be found in other domains. With this in mind, we began incorporating measures of entitlement into our studies about the anime fandom.

Some of our earlier work (e.g., Shaw et al., 2016) tried to understand the factors that lead to entitlement in three different fandoms: furries, anime fans, and fantasy sport fans. Participants completed measures of fanship, length of time as a fan, social awkwardness (e.g., "I act awkward around non-anime fans"), extraversion, and, most importantly, fan entitlement (e.g., "If I email an artist, I expect them to email me back," "I should get special treatment from my favorite artists"). The results of this study showed that, largely across fandoms, being a bigger fan, spending more time as a fan, being more socially awkward, and being more extraverted were all associated with feeling more entitled as a fan.[19]

For the present chapter, we reexamined these predictors of fan entitlement, comparing cosplayers and non-cosplaying anime fans specifically. Our first analysis revealed that cosplayers do score higher on measures of fan entitlement than non-cosplayers (see the top of Figure 7.7).

---

[19] A follow-up analysis showed that anime fans reported significantly lower fan entitlement scores than either furries or fantasy sport fans. While entitlement certainly exists in the anime fandom, it is apparently not as prevalent among anime fans (or, an alternative explanation, is not as readily recognized by anime fans).

To try and explain this difference, we looked at the same variables as we did in Shaw et al. (2016). As Figure 7.7 reveals, at least part of the explanation for why cosplayers feel more entitled is grounded in the fact that cosplayers scored higher in most of the same measures (fanship, extraversion, and awkwardness) that, in turn, were associated with fan entitlement.[20]

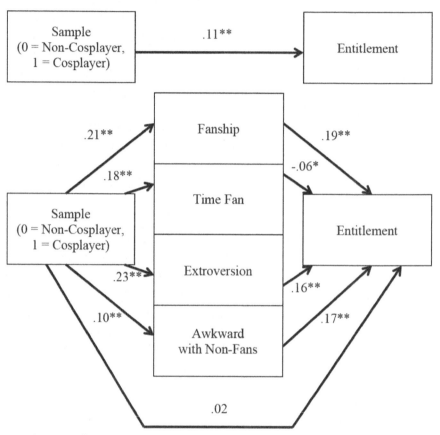

Figure 7.7. Predictors of entitlement as mediators of sample comparison and entitlement. Standardized betas, * $p < .05$, ** $p < .01$.

---

[20] One interesting caveat to this finding is that the longer cosplaying fans had been anime fans, the *less* entitled they felt, something we hadn't observed in our original study!

180

Elitism and Gatekeeping

In interviews with Tokyo cosplayers, Ahn (2008) describes cosplayers as welcoming of newcomers and the cosplay community as being one that's easy to join. We discuss the opposite of this tendency—gatekeeping and elitism—in depth in Chapter 13, but for now, we wanted to look at whether Ahn's characterization of the cosplay fandom as being low in gatekeeping and elitism held true when tested empirically.

Our first analysis, shown at the top of Figure 7.8, found that there was some truth to Ahn's statement: Compared to non-cosplaying anime fans, cosplayers scored lower in measures of gatekeeping. They were less likely to agree with statements condemning new fans or to ostracize different members of the anime fandom.

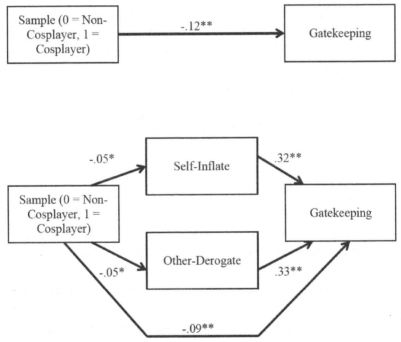

Figure 7.8. Elitism dimensions mediating association between sample comparison and gatekeeping. Standardized betas, * $p < .05$, ** $p < .01$.

In a follow-up analysis, we attempted to explain this lower rate of gatekeeping in cosplaying fans by looking at differences with respect to two dimension of elitism—the tendency to inflate one's sense of self and the tendency to look down upon other fans. As shown in Figure 7.8, cosplayers' scores were slightly lower for both types of elitism compared to non-cosplayers. Since this elitism was, itself, associated with greater support for gatekeeping, insofar as cosplayers endorsed less elitism, they were less likely to support gatekeeping.

The results are in line with Ahn (2008), who characterized cosplayers as more welcoming of newcomers. Our work suggests that this is, at least in part, due to the fact that cosplayers are less likely to look down upon other fans and less likely to think of themselves as superior.[21]

Fandom Drama

Fan groups, like any other group, inevitably experience internal conflict (DeDominicis, 2015). In this respect, the anime fandom is no exception (Dunlap & Wolf, 2010). We discuss fandom drama in more detail in Chapter 13, but for now, we'd like to briefly look at the topic of drama as it pertains to cosplayers, given that their iconic and highly-recognizable nature makes them a potential catalyst for fandom-related drama.

It's not hard to find high-profile cases of drama in the cosplay community. For example, at Anime Boston some cosplayers dressed as a character from *Hetalia* performed a Nazi salute for a photo shoot. The act sparked outrage and debate regarding the appropriateness of cosplaying as characters who embody discriminatory beliefs (Annett, 2011, 2014). In another example, Hill (2017) interviewed cosplayers and noted that there exists a social hierarchy within the cosplay community, with some cosplayers acting snobbish toward others (e.g., judging female cosplayers with sexualized costumes). Kane (2017) even suggests that some cosplayers have become renowned simply because they were the epicenter for an especially divisive or publicized incidents.

With all of this in mind, we wanted to test the hypothesis that cosplayers may be involved in more fandom drama than non-cosplayers. The

---

[21] Unexpectedly, these findings fly in the face of what one might predict based on the previous section, where we found that cosplayers feel a greater sense of entitlement. This may suggest that while cosplayers feel like they ought to have more status or special treatment, in practice they don't really see themselves as having status above others.

hypothesis is grounded on the above research, as well as on two additional premises.

First, cosplayers are especially engaged members of the anime community. As such, they have more opportunities to witness and to participate in fandom drama than someone who's only tangentially involved in fandom-related activities.

Second, as we've also noted in this chapter, cosplayers have a stronger belongingness motivation than non-cosplayers do. This includes engaging in more behavior intended to obtain this need, such as listening to others' problems (Hackenbracht & Gasper, 2013) and working together with others toward a common goal (De Cremer & Leonardelli, 2003). However, when these same people are rejected by others, the result is often a backlash of anger and aggression (Leary et al., 2006; Richman & Leary, 2009), the sort that lends itself to conflict and drama.

To test our hypothesis, we asked cosplaying and non-cosplaying anime fans to complete several measures, including how often they interacted with other fans ("This past year, how often did you talk with friends about anime"), their need to belong ("I have a strong need to belong;" Nichols & Webster, 2013), and their involvement in fandom drama (e.g., "I have been caught up in fandom drama").

The results revealed, first and foremost, that cosplayers scored higher than non-cosplayers on all of the measures, including, as shown in the top of Figure 7.9, being more likely to be caught up in fandom drama.[22] Follow-up analyses revealed that this difference is at least partly accounted for by the fact that cosplayers interact with more people and the fact that they have a stronger need to belong.

One drawback to the way we conducted this study is the fact that our question about drama was vague. As such, we had little way of knowing the role that participants were taking in the drama itself (e.g., trying to stop the drama or being a cause of it). To somewhat overcome this, we asked participants whether drama served any meaningful purpose, given that

---

[22] We should note that both cosplayers and non-cosplayers rated their degree of drama involvement well below the midpoint of the measure. This is important, because while cosplayers may engage in more drama than non-cosplayers, this is far from saying that most cosplayers are involved in drama, nor is saying that cosplayers get involved in a lot of drama.

people often find themselves embroiled in drama despite overwhelmingly stating that they dislike it in their fandom. Among cosplayers, the three highest rated functions of drama were (1) that it can be a useful tool for aggressively isolating or harming others, (2) drama can be entertaining, and (3) drama creates outgroups that fans can unite against.

Given the largely detrimental impact that drama has for those involved (e.g., may leave the fandom), and given the frequency with which conversations within fandoms turn to the subject of drama, future research should aim to extend these findings and provide a more complete picture of what drama looks like within fandoms like the anime fandom and, more importantly, how fans can best go about reducing drama when it does arise.

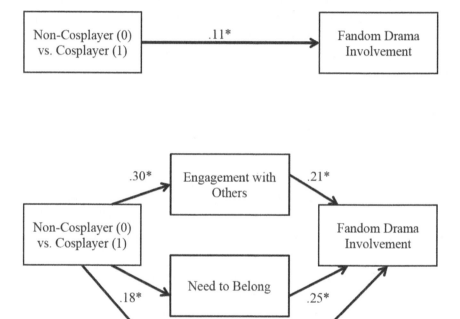

Figure 7.9. Engagement with others and need to belong mediating relationship between sample comparison and fandom drama involvement. Standardized betas, * $p < .05$.

Disclosure and Well-Being

As we discuss in Chapter 17, anime fans are a fairly stigmatized group, one that experiences its fair share of bullying and mockery due, in no small part, to the unflattering stereotypes attached to anime fans.

However, being an anime fan is a concealable identity. In other words, to avoid negative stereotypes and judgment, an anime fan can strategically choose to hide the fact that they're an anime fan in certain contexts. For example, Ahn (2008) interviewed Japanese cosplayers and found that about half did not mention cosplaying to others outside the community for fear of being found out to be an otaku. Chen (2003) suggests that cosplaying is similarly stigmatized in Taiwan, while in the U.S., Lotecki (2012) noted that conventions are often the only places where cosplayers feel like they can be themselves without fear of negative repercussions (Taylor, 2009).

As a general rule, being a member of a stigmatized group is harmful to one's well-being (Schmitt et al., 2014). There are obvious reasons why, such as being targeted by attacks because you belong to a particular group. Less obvious, however, is the fact that members of stigmatized groups who are able to conceal their identity often find that doing so takes a great deal of work and mental effort, something which is, itself, associated with reduced psychological and physical health (Meyer, 2003).[23] To this end, being able to freely disclose one's stigmatized identity to others often results in better well-being in the long run (Mock et al., 2013; Quinn & Chaudoir, 2009; Quinn & Earnshaw, 2013).

With this in mind, we asked cosplaying and non-cosplaying anime fans to complete scales asking them whether they are able to disclose their anime fan identity to non-fans on a 7-point scale (1 = *strongly disagree* to 7 = *strongly agree*), as well as measures of their overall well-being.

As shown in Figure 7.10, cosplayers are more likely than non-cosplaying fans to disclose their interest in anime to others. Even when disclosure was below the midpoint (e.g., telling peers or new acquaintances), cosplayers

---

[23] To see why, imagine having to conceal being gay from your coworkers. This involves constantly monitoring your word use (e.g., "partner" instead of "girlfriend" or "boyfriend"), frequently having to come up with excuses or change the subject (e.g., expectations that you'll bring a partner to an office party), and living in constant anxiety about your coworkers finding out and repercussions thereof (e.g., looking around to make sure none of your coworkers see you with your partner at the grocery store).

were still more likely to disclose their identity in anime, a stigmatized group. This is understandable for a number of reasons, including the fact that cosplayers are more involved in the fandom (which may make it hard to cover up all of their activities), report higher fanship and fandom identification (and may be prouder to be a fan, as well as having more social support), and may simply find it harder to avoid being seen at fan events (e.g., photos of them cosplaying at events or online). For these reasons, cosplayers may well be more likely to disclose their fan interest to others, in line with what we've found in other fandoms (e.g., Chadborn et al., 2017; Mock et al., 2013; Reysen, Plante, & Chadborn, 2017).

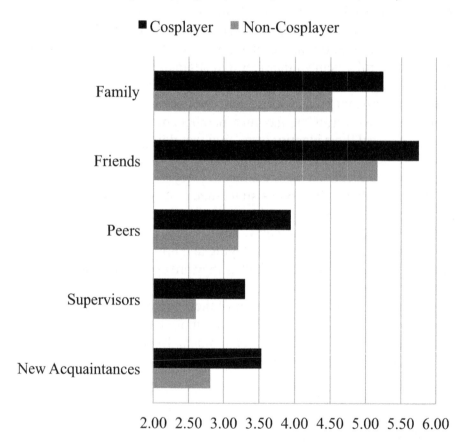

Figure 7.10. Fan identity disclosure by cosplayer self-categorization.

However, does this increased disclosure translate into better overall well-being for cosplaying fans? We tested this in another analysis that combined measures of life satisfaction, self-esteem, and depression (reversed) into an index of well-being. As shown in the top of Figure 7.11, cosplayers did score slightly higher than non-cosplayers on measures of well-being. More importantly, this difference was explained, in part, by the fact that cosplayers are also more likely to tell others about their fan identity. We suspect that disclosing one's identity not only reduces the stress of concealing a stigmatized identity, but also makes it easier to find and meet other friends in the anime fandom, something also associated with improved well-being (see Chapter 19).

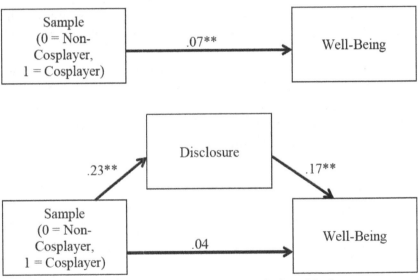

Figure 7.11. Disclosure to others mediating relationship between sample and well-being. Standardized betas, ** $p < .01$.

In a follow-up study we examined this idea that friendships contribute to one's well-being. As we found earlier in this chapter, cosplaying is an inherently a social activity, with the belongingness that it provides proving to be an important motivator for many cosplayers. It may well be the friendships that cosplayers make and maintain through cosplaying accounts for their greater well-being. Importantly, we want to make a distinction between online and face-to-face friendships. Psychological evidence on the subject of face-to-face versus online friendships and how they relate to well-being is mixed at the moment. Some studies show that online friends lead to better well-being (Grieve et al., 2013), some say that online friends have no effect on well-being (Smahel et al., 2012), and others show that online friends predict worse well-being (Lee et al., 2011; Shen & Williams, 2011).

To put all of these ideas together, we asked cosplaying and non-cosplaying anime fans to answer questions about their online friends (e.g., "Being an anime fan helps me establish new friendships online," "Being an anime fans provides me the opportunity to maintain meaningful social relationships online"), their face-to-face friends (e.g., "Being an anime fan helps me establish new friendships face-to-face," "Being an anime fan provides me the opportunity to maintain meaningful social relationships face-to-face"), and a measure of well-being (Kinderman et al., 2011).

The top of Figure 7.12 again shows that cosplayers report greater well-being than do non-cosplayers. More importantly, this difference is explained in part by the fact that cosplaying fans have more face-to-face friendships. In fact, while cosplayers also tend to have more online friendships than do non-cosplaying fans, these friendships are unrelated to their overall well-being.

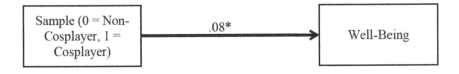

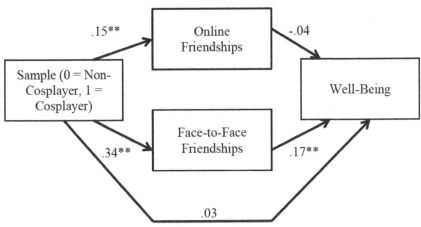

Figure 7.12. Online and face-to-face friendships as mediators of association between sample comparison and well-being. Standardized betas, * *p* < .05, ** *p* < .01.

Conclusion

Cosplayers have willingly or unwillingly become sort of mascots for the anime fandom. As a group, cosplayers tend to be young, working women who were more likely than non-cosplayers to be in relationships and to be writers and artists. Cosplayers are, all-around more active and involved when it comes to anime, watching more, spending more money on it, and attending more conventions. This may reflect the fact that cosplayers are more motivated fans in general, especially by the profound sense of belongingness the fandom provides them with. Cosplayers often choose favorite characters that are similar to them, but also contain characteristics they idealize. Personality-wise, cosplayers are similar to highly creative

189

people and people with strong parasocial connections, suggesting that their personality is hardly a unique or distinguishing factor in what makes them cosplayers (as opposed to artists or avid fans of something else). Although cosplayers are slightly entitled, they are less elitist and less likely than non-cosplaying fans to gatekeep other fans. Cosplayers do find themselves embroiled more often in fandom drama, possibly because they simply find themselves more involved in the fandom because of their powerful need to belong. Despite misconceptions about cosplayers as awkward or dysfunctional, most report higher well-being than non-cosplaying fans, in no small part because of their ability to be who they are and surround themselves with like-minded others.

In short, while cosplayers have become the faces of the anime fandom, their passion doesn't seem to undermine their ability to function in day-to-day life. One could hardly find a better representative for the fandom than that!

Chapter 8
Anime Genres and Preference

Schuster (2010) argued that the reason for anime's worldwide significance stems from the fact that anime taps countless different topics and themes. After all, with the vastness of all the anime ever produced, each story can be seen at face value (e.g., giant robots battling otherworldly monsters) and symbolically[1] (e.g., adversity, discovering identity, etc.: Fennell et al., 2013; Napier, 2005, 2007), anyone can reasonably expect to find at least one series that resonates with their own values, beliefs, and concerns. This is why it's so important to understand anime not as a single, homogenous body of content, but as a loose mix of genres and sub-types (see Table 8.1 for a list of just some of the various genres). By analyzing these different genres, we can get a better understanding of the different communities one finds in the anime fandom and the underlying motivations that draw them to anime in the first place.

Fully understanding the psychology of fans means understanding such subdivisions. In this chapter we do exactly that, splitting off from prior chapters which have, until now, largely treated "anime" as a single body of content, with the goal of breaking this content down into subgenres and the fan groups which form around them. After all, in a fandom that includes fans of fantasy, mecha, slice of life, and action, we should probably expect at least a few differences to emerge.

Top Genres

It's one thing to argue that there are at least 40 distinct genres of anime out there, but it's another entirely to show that these are meaningful genres that anime fans actually distinguish among them. We can imagine, for example, an ice cream shop which claims to have ten different varieties of chocolate. While this may sound appealing at first glance, if customers can't distinguish any meaningful differences among the ten flavors, then what the ice cream shop really has is one flavor—chocolate.

---

[1] It's precisely because of this complex layering that it can often be difficult to classify genres of anime: Do you base such classifications on complexity? Story arcs? Characters? Setting? Pacing? (Poitras, 2001).

Genre	Examples
Action	*Bleach, One Piece, Freezing*
Adventure	*Kino no Tabi, Fullmetal Alchemist, Pokémon*
Bishounen	*Ouran High School Host Club, Fruits Basket*
Comedy	*Sayonara Zetsubou Sensei, Full Metal Panic*
Demons	*Inuyasha, Yu Yu Hakusho, Ichiban Ushiro no Daimaou*
Drama	*Darker than Black, Death Note, Monster*
Ecchi	*Elfen Leid, Freezing, Zero no Tsukaima, Futari Ecchi*
Fantasy	*Fairy Tail, Fullmetal Alchemist, Inuyasha*
Game	*Yu-Gi-Oh, Duel Masters, Bakugan*
Harem	*Da Capo, Love Hina, School Days*
Hentai	*Bible Black, Mistreated Bride*
Historical	*Rurouni Kenshin, Baccano, Shigurui*
Horror	*Mnemosyne, Higurashi no Naku Koro ni*
Josei	*Paradise Kiss, Honey, Clover*
Kids	*Digimon, Pokémon*
Love/Romance	*Love Hina, Ai Yori Aoshi, Clannad*
Magic	*Da Capo, Twin Angel*
Martial Arts	*Historys Strongest Disciple Kenshi, Hajime no Ippo*
Mecha	*Mobile Suit Gundam, Neon Genesis Evangelion*
Military	*Ghost in the Shell, 07-Ghost*
Music	*NANA, Nodame Cantabile*
Mystery	*Death Note, Monster, Darker than Black*
Psychological	*Death Note, Monster, Code Geass*
Samurai	*Blade of the Immortal, Rurouni Kenshin*
School	*The Melanchony of Haruhi Suzumiya, Beelzebub*
Sci-Fi	*Level E, Tengen Toppa Gurren Lagann, Zoids*
Seinen	*Cowboy Bebop, Futari Ecchiand, Rainbow*
Shoujo	*NANA, Lovely Complex, Kare Kano, Vampire Knight*
Shoujo-ai	*Candy Boy, Simoun, Ga-Rei: Zero*
Shounen	*Chobits, Bleach, Bamboo Blade*
Shounen-ai	*Junjo Romantic, Sekaiichi Hatsukoi*
Slice of Life	*Kino no Tabi, School Rumble, Ai Yori Aoshi*
Space	*Planetes, Cowboy Bebop, Mobile Suit Gundam*
Sport	*Major S1, Hajime no Ippo, Prince of Tennis*
Super Power	*Dragonball Z, Naruto*
Supernatural	*Natsume Yuujinchou San, Ao no Excorsist*
Vampire	*Hellsing, Rosario + Vampire, Trinity Blood*
Yaoi	*Love Stage, Tyrant Falls in Love*
Yuri	*Sakura Trick, Aoi Hana, Sasameki Koto*
Live Action	*Over Flowers, Goong, Playful Kiss*

Table 8.1. List of genres studied.

In our 2016 study we provided anime fans with a list of 40 different genres and asked them to indicate the extent to which they had a positive (or negative) preference toward each. As Figure 8.1 shows, fans certainly made distinctions between the different genres, with the range of favorability ratings varying from 20% to 85% depending on the genre. Or, to continue with our chocolate analogy, while every flavor was chocolate (anime), fans tasted differences between the different types, making them meaningful distinctions.

In this format, however, the data are rather unwieldy. With 40 different genres, it's hard to reach any sort of consensus about fan preferences. On one hand, shows that seem like clear examples of the action genre (i.e., *Dragonball, Naruto, Sword Art Online*) sometimes throw us for a loop with the occasional slice of life episode or with a long story arc that features dramatic events and moral dilemmas. Poitras (2001) makes this argument eloquently with *Gundam 0080*, which is a mecha anime in the same way that *War and Peace* is a novel about combat: Both transcend the surface themes and trappings of their genre. And, when a series involves fantasy elements with demons (e.g., *Yu Yu Hakusho*) that could realistically be combined with other fantasy action anime like *Full Metal Alchemist: Brotherhood*, technological series with strong action elements like *Ghost in the Shell* or *Cowboy Bebop*, or historical anime such as *Rurouni Kenshin*, all of which contain events classifying them as action, drama, and the occasional slice of life episode, you can see how muddled the problem gets.

In an effort to simplify the results, we strove to find a middle-ground approach between scholars like Poitras (2001), who consider dozens of different genres in a largely unwieldy fashion, and authors like Schuster who primarily focus on a single genre. In short, we wanted a model that acknowledged the variety of anime genres without becoming little more than a list of different anime series that doesn't recognize any commonalities among them.

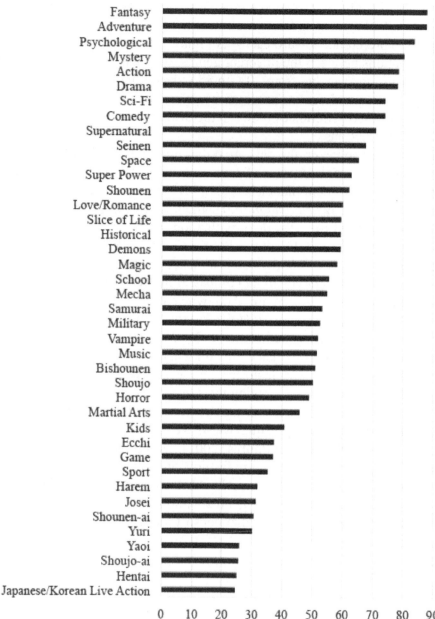

Figure 8.1. Percentage of anime fans with preference for viewing each genre studied.

In the end, we settled on five core genres of anime based on both their similarities and also how fans in our previous studies classify their favorite anime.[2] By doing so, we can meaningfully compare a manageable number of subgroups on the basis of whether their favorite series falls primarily within the category of action, drama, slice of life, mecha, or hentai.[3]

Action

This category represents series in which conflict or combat is part of its overarching plot and features prominently into most episodes. While drama and development may underlie the ongoing story, the action is front and center, with the main characters fighting antagonists regularly. Anime in this category would include fantasy and sci-fi series such as *Dragonball*, *Inu-Yasha*, *Naruto*, *Sword Art Online* and *Record of Lodoss War*. While these series all have very different plots, characters, and settings they are similar in the action-oriented focus of their plots and themes.

Drama

Like the action category, drama encapsulates several subgenres under a larger umbrella. For anime classified as drama, action scenes may be occasionally present, though the main driving force is typically drama-oriented plot. These series also often involve themes of romance, such as those seen within the anime *Maison Ikkoku*, or character development driven story arcs set in a more realistic world such as *Kimi no Na wa* or *Shigatsu wa Kimi no Uso*.[4]

Slice of Life

Slice of life represents a category of anime largely absent of the intense action, drama, mystery, or complex romantic plots seen in other genres. Instead, enjoyment comes from seeing typical characters navigate a realistic world, with an emphasis on quality writing and believable character development. Even when these other elements are present, they tend to be grounded in reality (mostly, as anime such as *Fruits Basket* while adding

---

[2] It is very important to note that these factors were developed statistically to more easily and accurately test fans' genre preferences and other variables. There can and is a lot of nuance and overlap in anime genres.

[3] For more information on the subject of anime with predominantly pornographic elements, see Chapter 9.

[4] This holds despite the fact that *Kimi no Na wa* involves some fantasy/supernatural elements such as body swapping.

some supernatural, revolves around school and everyday life). Anime such as *Free!*, *Great Teacher Onizuka,* and *Byousoku 5 Centimeter* can be noted as examples of this genre.

Mecha

Poitras (2001) argues that any anime that involves someone controlling a mechanical object (from giant robots to even the simplest of machinery) could be considered a mecha anime.[5] For our purpose, we consider in this category any series where the focus is on giant robots or fighting vehicles and the pilots who find themselves in the grip of war and strife. Examples from the genres include one of the most famous anime series of all time, *Neon Genesis Evangelion,* along with notable others such as *Gurren Lagann* and *Mobile Suit Gundam*, the latter of which has been prolific in spawning dozens of series and spinoffs. Unlike our other categories, which tend to be far broader, mecha is in its own category, distinct from action, drama, or slice of life aspects, since fans themselves frequently distinguish these series from those in other genres.

Hentai

Adult themes are hardly rare in anime, but to fall into the category of hentai, a series typically needs to include fairly dominant sexual themes. While nearly any anime series could be made to fall into this category with the addition of considerable explicit content, hentai is a classification on its own because it is so categorically different from the other genres with respect to its preference, acceptability, and the behavior of fans who favor it over others. While there is far more to be said on the subject beyond this brief description, we will save that for our discussion in Chapter 9.

A Second Look at Preference Data

With these new categories in mind, we can re-examine the data from Figure 8.1. The results paint a much clearer picture of anime genre preference (see Figure 8.2). The most universally beloved anime genres were those from the action and drama genres, while the least-enjoyed anime

---

[5] While we agree with the broader sentiment, technically speaking, their suggestion would mean that a young boy using an electric beard trimmer would constitute a mecha anime. For our purposes, we're typically thinking more along the lines of anthropomorphic fighting suits.

series typically involved the hentai genre.[6] Importantly, these results remained consistent when we separated our samples into convention-going and online anime fans, suggesting the resilience of these categories and their relative popularity.

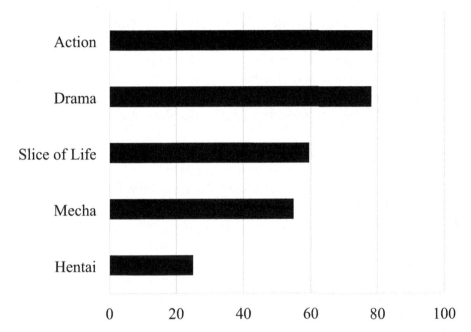

Figure 8.2. Percentage of preference ratings of five different anime genre dimensions.

As we continue through this chapter, we will describe additional findings regarding genre preference by primarily focusing on these five core clusters and what they say about the fans who prefer them. We will occasionally offer insight with respect to specific subgenres from the more elaborate 40-genre model, but only when it is especially relevant. We do this primarily to keep this chapter manageable in length and to put the

---

[6] This may be due to the stigmatization of pornography, often associated with the negative stereotypes of anime fans (see Chapter 16).

emphasis on commonalities across numerous subgenres rather than getting lost in the idiosyncrasies of fans of a specific series or niche subgenres.

What Your Preferred Genre May Say About You

While it's easy to point at the findings in the rest of this chapter and make broad, sweeping claims about certain anime fans, like saying that stereotypes about *Sword Art Online* fans are valid, it's important to interpret the results of this chapter (like the rest of this book) with caution. To be sure, in the following sections we find evidence that being a fan of a particular genre can predict a number of interesting psychological variables. However, these correlations by themselves do not take into account the vast array of other environmental and personality factors, nor are they sufficient to make causal claims that watching a particular show makes a person a certain way.[7]

The Mecha and Hentai Standouts

One of the most consistent results we find based on genre is that there is a bit of a rift between fans of mecha anime and fans of all other anime genres. One possible reason is that, on average, mecha fans tend to be older fans compared to fans of other genres. As we point out in earlier chapters (e.g., Chapter 3), an age difference may underlie numerous other notable differences, including the fact that mecha fans also attend more conventions and have been in the anime fandom for longer on average.

Mecha fans also stand out as distinct from the other four genre categories in other ways. For example, mecha fans were the only ones for whom their fan identity was not related with a measure of hostility, something else which could be explained by the fact that aggression tends to decrease with age (Rushton et al., 1986). Mecha fans are also the only one of the five categories to not perceive stigma toward themselves and other anime fans in relation to their own genre preference.[8]

---

[7] We feel compelled to emphasize this precisely because we anticipate some anime fans (or non-anime fans) using these findings to justify treating fans of specific series or genres in a less-than-kind manner.

[8] To put it another way: For all other categories, the more strongly someone was a fan of that genre, the more they perceived themselves and other anime fans to be the targets of outside stigma. This may be due to mecha anime being older and more established in mainstream culture than more recent anime popularized by younger fans. Maturity could also be playing a factor, with older mecha fans simply caring less about what others think about their interests.

Mecha fans, score higher on measures of elitism than non-mecha fans, something which may coincide with the fact that, as older fans, they feel a sense of superiority or elitism over other fans.[9] Mecha is also the only genre where preferring it was not associated with more engagement in fantasy activities in one's day-to-day life, something which, again, may be a product of mecha fans' older age.

Fans who rated hentai as their preferred genre also showed significant differences compared to the other genre preferences. Whereas mecha fans stand out predominantly when it comes to their age, hentai fans generally consume more anime content in general than do fans of other genres (including buying merchandise). To this end, it should come as no surprise that hentai fans also report buying more anime-themed figurines, body pillows, and tattoos. Furthermore, while mecha fans tended to be more elitist and feel a greater sense of entitlement, hentai fans were significantly more likely to gatekeep against new fans.[10] While it's currently unknown why fans interested in the most stigmatized genre of anime would also be the most critical of other fans and gatekeep the most, we speculate on the topic in Chapter 9.

Politics

While we touched on the political views of anime fans in Chapter 3, it's worth noting some political differences that emerge when it comes to anime fans' genre preferences. Recall that, generally speaking, anime fans tend to be slightly on the liberal side of the political scale. In prior research, however, we've found that a fan community's values and beliefs may reflect the norms and values of their favorite show (Plante, Chadborn, Groves, & Reysen, 2018). To this end, we do see some slight shifts in political orientation with respect to two genres in particular. Mecha fans tend to be slightly more conservative than typical anime fans,[11] while hentai and slice of life fans tend to be more liberal than the average anime fan.

---

[9] See Chapter 13 on elitism for more on this topic.

[10] Adding stipulations and barriers to being considered a true fan. For more on this, see Chapter 13.

[11] It's important to note, however, that being "more conservative" does not mean "being conservative." Mecha fans, in fact, tend to be almost perfectly centrist on average, compared to the slight liberal leaning of the rest of the anime fandom as a whole.

Paranormal Beliefs

Given the prominence of paranormal occurrences in many anime series (e.g., ghosts, demons, supernatural powers), one might expect anime fans in general to be especially prone to believe in the paranormal.[12] After all, we know from abundant psychological research that the media we consume influences the way we think and behave (Potter, 2011), ranging from aggression (Anderson et al., 2010) to support for gun control (Dowler, 2002) to the fear of death (Schiappa et al., 2004).

As such, Reysen and colleagues (2017a) compared anime fans with a sample of similarly-aged college students. They assessed the groups' endorsement of seven different types of paranormal beliefs, adapted from Tobacyk's (2004) revised paranormal belief scale. These seven types of paranormal beliefs were religious, psi (e.g., mind reading is possible), witchcraft, superstitions, spiritualism (e.g., communicating with ghosts or the dead), extraordinary life forms (e.g., the existence of cryptids), and precognition (e.g., predicting the future). The results showed that for four of the seven types of paranormal beliefs, anime fans scored significantly lower than non-fan college students.

Are paranormal beliefs (or lack thereof) evenly distributed among all anime fans, or are there some fans who are more likely to endorse paranormal beliefs than others? As Table 8.2 reveals, put simply, there are small genre differences. Being a fan of slice of life and action, for example, was associated with stronger religious beliefs, while slice of life, action, and hentai preferences were all similarly associated with higher spiritualism.

Belief	Action	Drama	Slice	Mecha	Hentai
Religious Belief	.18*	< .01	.12*	.04	.02
Psi	.26*	.12*	.18*	.13*	.28*
Witchcraft	.19*	.14*	.19*	.02	.19*
Superstitions	.19*	.08*	.16*	.13*	.20*
Spiritualism	.20*	.13*	.15*	.02	.24*
Ext. Lifeforms	.22*	.11*	.13*	.10*	.31*
Precognition	.22*	.14*	.18*	.08	.25*

Table 8.2. Paranormal endorsement by genre, * $p < .05$.

---

[12] It's worth noting that a sizable number of Americans in general believe in paranormal phenomena, so it can hardly be said to be unique to anime fans (Moore, 2005).

With respect to witchcraft, precognition, and superstition, all of the different genre preferences were positively associated with these beliefs except for one: In the case of witchcraft and precognition, mecha preference was the only genre not associated with this belief, while drama preference was the only genre preference not associated with superstitious thinking.

Finally, when it comes to belief in psi and otherworldly lifeforms, all genres showed a positive relationship with belief.

In short, while anime fans are generally less likely than non-fans to endorse paranormal beliefs in general, one's preferred genre does say a bit about their willingness to hold certain supernatural beliefs.[13]

Sexism

No group wants to be associated with negative labels like racist, bigot, or, presently relevant, "sexist." Not only does this lead to backlash from those who receive such labels, but it can also lead to people throwing the term around or labeling entire groups of people with the label.

With this caution in mind, we sought to test whether endorsement of sexist ideals is more prominent among those who prefer particular genres of anime. Importantly, in Chapter 6 we made the distinction between hostile sexism and the far more subtle form of sexism: benevolent sexism. To reiterate, hostile sexism is what most people think of when they think of sexism: it's overt, undoubtedly negative views toward others on the basis of their sex (e.g., "women seek to gain power by getting control over men"). Benevolent sexism, on the other hand, is far more subtle and often flies under the radar, namely because individuals high on this measure appear to be positive on the face, masking the fact that, under the surface, they presume something more negative. For example, the statement "men should protect women" sounds positive on its face—after all, who wouldn't want to be protected? On the other hand, the unspoken assumption baked into the statement is that women are weak and vulnerable and need to be

---

[13] Of course, whether or not being a fan of an anime series influences one's belief or whether one's belief makes one more or less likely to be a fan of a particular genre remains to be seen. While it is true that we are influenced by the media we consume, it does also make sense that a person who does not believe in, say, ghosts, might find it difficult to enjoy an anime series whose premise is based upon the existence of ghosts.

protected—a statement which, if stated out loud, would be considered hostile sexism.

With respect to the 40 original specific genres (not the five clusters), we do find evidence that some, in particular, are more associated with sexism. Fans of "games," "fantasy," and "hentai" genres are more likely to endorse benevolent sexism, with those who support the fantasy and hentai genres in particular being more likely to also endorse hostile sexist beliefs.[14] On the other hand, fans of "sci-fi" anime scored lower on measures of hostile and benevolent sexism.[15]

When we collapse the original 40 categories into our five big clusters (these five genres include 15 from the original 40), other patterns emerge: Being a bigger fan of all of the clusters (with the exception of drama) is associated with higher hostile and benevolent sexism scores (see Table 8.3). While the association seems to be weaker for slice-of-life and mecha fans, a surprising trend emerges for action and hentai fans: Hentai fans are far more likely to be in-your-face with overt, hostile sexism than with benevolent sexism, while the reverse is true for action fans, who reveal considerably more benevolent sexism than hostile sexism.

Belief	Action	Drama	Slice	Mecha	Hentai
Hostile Sexism	.16*	.01	.12*	.12*	.26*
Benevolent Sexism	.23*	.01	.17*	.19*	.16*
Narcissism	.04	.06	.01	.01	.07
Psychopathy	.02	.11*	.02	.09*	.18*
Machiavellianism	.04	.10*	.04	.09*	.12*
Maturity	.14*	.14*	.06	.13*	.05
Hostility	.13*	.09*	.09*	.03	.12*

Table 8.3. Genre correlations with other variables, * $p < .05$.

---

[14] These effects are fairly small, and should not be taken to mean that all, or even most fans of these genres are sexist—being "more sexist" than a group already fairly low in sexism does not mean "very sexist." For instance, overall scores on a 7-point scale for the anime fandom in general were well below the scales' midpoints (hostile sexism average = 2.99, benevolent sexism average = 3.07).

[15] This trend is largely in-line with the more progressive ideals of the science fiction fandom in general which, for decades, has been fairly ahead of the curve with respect to gender equality and LGBTQ+ rights.

Critical readers may, at this point, notice a possible drawback to these measures: Being sexist is, generally speaking, undesirable. As such, fans may feel compelled to lie and downplay the extent to which they actually endorse sexist beliefs in order to make themselves look more desirable to the researchers.

This is an entirely fair criticism with implications for how we analyze the data. On the one hand, it suggests that our estimates of the prevalence of sexism in the anime fandom is likely an underestimate, since it's far more likely that fans are understating their sexist beliefs than it is that they are overstating their sexist beliefs.

On the other hand, we note that fans did admit to at least *some* endorsement of sexist beliefs in the first place, suggesting at least some willingness to admit to the attitudes they have. Given that the survey itself was anonymous, there is little reason for fans to feel compelled to lie—after all, the researchers will never be able to tie their responses to them. Plus, it's worth noting that this same problem exists for other samples which have used the same measure—meaning, despite the flaws in the instrument, we can still compare across groups using the same imperfect measure. For example, when compared to both university students and a sample of the general public, anime fans' sexism scores were, on average, significantly lower (Reysen, Katzarska-Miller et al., 2017).

Taken together, the data suggest that sexism, while still present in the anime fandom, and more prevalent among some subgenres within the anime fandom, may not be as rampant as what one finds in the general population. Future research would do well to build on this subject, including assessing whether questions about equal representation of gender, sexist content, and sexist tropes in anime contribute to these sorts of beliefs, the consequences of these attitudes in the fandom, and whether targeted interventions or policies may undermine sexism when it does arise.

Dark Triad

While sexism tends to be more readily recognized and denied by some in the anime fandom, people tend to be more open and honest when it comes to acknowledging their own undesirable personality traits. The dark triad is a measure of three of these traits in particular: narcissism, psychopathy, and Machiavellianism. Narcissism represents a lack of empathy, a heightened sense of pride, grandiose thoughts, and a strong need be reassured about one's own value. Psychopathy represents feelings of remorselessness, a lack of emotion, selfishness, and general anti-social behavior.[16] Finally, Machiavellianism is a personality trait characterized by a lack of morals, self-interest, and, most importantly, manipulating and exploiting others for one's own purpose. Taken together, these three traits represent the "darker" side of human nature.

Once again, we should note that, like sexism scores, anime fans' average scores on these three measures are all relatively low, with average scores ranging from 2.9 to 3.5 out of 7—well below the midpoints.

However, despite these low averages, we do find differences in genre preference with respect to the dark triad traits (see Table 8.3). With respect to narcissism, no relationships were found between genre preference and the dark triad traits. This doesn't mean that fans scored super low in narcissism, but rather that one's preferred genre didn't predict who scored higher and who scored lower on the scale.

The same cannot be said for psychopathy and Machiavellianism. Specifically, while slice-of-life and action preference was unrelated to these traits, mecha, drama, and especially hentai preference were associated with higher psychopathy and Machiavellianism scores.[17]

Some Other Interesting Findings

Before wrapping up this chapter, we wanted to review a few final results, results which don't warrant their own full sections but which we nevertheless consider interesting and worth consideration. Some of these can be found in Table 8.3.

When asked about their level of maturity, fans with a stronger preference for drama, mecha, and action rated themselves as more mature, while hentai and slice-of-life preference was unrelated to maturity.[18]

---

[16] Anti-social in this regard does not mean wanting to avoid social activity, but engagement in behavior that largely disregards the well-being of others.

[17] Given that personality traits are treated as fairly stable, long-term patterns of behavior, it seems unlikely that watching a show would fully account for these traits. Instead, it is far more likely that people who already have these traits would be more drawn to these particular genres and the themes therein.

[18] There are numerous problems with asking a person to report on their own maturity, including the fact that an immature person might not be aware of what it means to be mature in the first place, or may lack the self-knowledge to be able to accurately assess

When it comes to hostility, we've already mentioned how the maturity and age of mecha fans may explain why they were unique among the genres in not being associated with hostile feelings in general (Barefoot et al., 1993). For the other fans, it may be the case that whatever personality traits or experiences lead to a person being more passionate about something may also make anime fans specifically more likely to be hostile.

Conclusion

While many of our findings offer some insight into how genre preferences might shape individual fans, overall, it is difficult to pin down any sort of causal direction for these relationships. In many ways, we're left with a chicken-or-egg scenario, not knowing whether certain types of people are drawn to specific genres or if consuming certain genres shapes people to become a certain way.

Regardless, we can say that genre preferences do reflect, in small, subtle ways, various facets of a person's personality, beliefs, and behavior. Even the mecha genre, which stands out among the other genres, perhaps because of its age, can tell us a lot about those who are fans of it. As we continue to discuss the relationship between anime and these various personality, belief, and behavior outcomes, it's worth keeping in mind that there will be variability in the results because of factors as small and seemingly trivial as a person's favorite anime series.

Before we move on, we'd like to make one detour with respect to genre, and that's to talk about hentai. Given the stigma associated with hentai content and the unwillingness in some circles (especially in academia) to address hentai, it behooves us to shed a bit of additional light on this genre in particular. Unlike some other fandoms, where discussions of lewd works and the subversion of original IPs[19] into a transformed pornographic medium are common, hentai is often treated as shadowy and behind-the-scenes. So, while discussion of rule 34[20] and the transformation of

---

their maturity. Nevertheless, this represents a first attempt to measure something as abstract as maturity, and it remains for future research to attempt to replicate this finding.

[19] Intellectual property.

[20] A "rule of the internet" stating if it exists there is porn of it. It is usually used to describe popular work which has been transformed into porn by others. This is in contrast to hentai, in which there is often original characters and plot written from the start to be erotic in

characters has been discussed in relation to other fandoms (see Edwards et al., 2019; Chapter 11), hentai is genre unto itself deserving of the deeper dive we give it in the next chapter.

---

nature. As an illustrative example, rule 34 art depicting sex between *Dragonball Z* characters is categorically different from an original hentai series such as *La Blue Girl*.

Chapter 9
Hentai: Anime? Pornography? or Something In Between?

In the previous chapter, we noted that hentai was the genre of anime rated by anime fans to be the least appealing and the least preferred. On the surface, this would seem to suggest that hentai is neither a popular nor accepted part of the anime fandom.

A brief internet search offers a competing narrative, however. McLelland (2005) noted that a Yahoo search for "hentai" netted over 7 million hits, more than twice that for popular elements of Japanese culture, including samurai, geisha, or sushi. Replicating his findings on Google in 2020, the results were 393 million hits for hentai and 226 and 77.5 million for samurai and geisha respectively.[1] Of course, there are a myriad of problems with using search results as the sole indicator of something's popularity, especially when comparing something as distinct as "hentai" and "samurai." The point McLelland was making is that hentai is a large and growing presence online, something that seems like a bit of a contradiction, being the least-preferred genre of anime.

The same contradiction is reflected in the scholarly literature on anime, where hentai, despite its prevalence and widespread consumption, is also one of the least discussed in terms of research. To reconcile this oversight, this chapter aims to delve into the hentai genre and its place in the anime community. We offer preliminary explanations for why this contradiction of popularity and lack of preference might exist among fans and explore our findings on both anime fans who do prefer hentai and how the fandom as a whole interacts with hentai-related topics.

Hentai as a Genre, a Subgenre, and its Cross-Cultural Complexities

Before we begin our deep dive into the topic of hentai, it's useful to define the term in the first place. While we did so briefly in Chapter 8, it's

---

[1] Surprisingly, sushi netted a whopping 1.5 billion results, apparently moving up in popularity in Western culture. Also notable was the fact that popular anime series like *Sword Art Online*, *Dragon Ball Z*, and *Naruto* yielded around 300 million hits on their own, making clear that these single series are almost as popular as all of the hentai on the internet, at least based on this particular metric.

worth taking a moment to consider not just the content of hentai, but everything else that comes along with it. How would you define the term?[2]

Your answer to this question will depend on a number of variables, including whether you're approaching the question as an academic, an anime outsider, a typical anime fan, or an otaku. Your experience, preconceptions, and biases may lead you to a definition that's rather off the mark.[3]

The term hentai, which meant something unusual or abnormal, first appeared in mainstream Western culture in the 1894 translation of Kraft-Ebing's *Psychopathia Sexualis*.[4] The term appeared as *Hentai seiyoku shinrigaku*, translated as the psychology of perverse sexual desire. While the word itself is far older than that, its popular use connoting anything associated with unusual sexual behavior is argued to have begun around this time (Saito, 2004).

In an extensive discussion of the history of hentai, McLelland (2005) notes that among producers of hentai, the work they create is not categorically different from anime, it just is anime. More specifically, many creators consider hentai to be a subset of ecchi[5] that range from the most vanilla of soft-core of pornographic scenes to what others would consider to be the "real" definition of hentai, pornography involving monsters, aliens, or taboo topics (e.g., underaged participants, incest, etc.)[6] However, where the nuance and distinction between hentai, ecchi, and other anime is deliberated and debated in Japan, in the West, the term hentai typically exists as a blanket term for any and all sexually-themed anime.

Complex Themes, Plot, and Some Elephants in the Room

Whether describing it under the Western omnibus term hentai or incorporating the nuance of Japanese ecchi, these terms describe something

---

[2] Go ahead, we'll wait!

[3] While researching this topic, one of the authors of this chapter discovered that he was way off when he compared his own definition of hentai to the Japanese history of the term.

[4] The book itself is essentially an attempt to catalogue all of the paraphilias, or atypical sexual practices. It's noteworthy that the book itself had a sort of medical connotation, viewing these paraphilias as evidence of mental illness or dysfunction and as something needing to be cured or corrected. Suffice it to say, it hasn't aged well.

[5] Ecchi defines sexually themed manga and anime, regardless of content.

[6] In this latter case, this subgenre of ecchi or "H," lives up to its original definition of "hentai seiyoku" or unusual/perverse sexual desire!

far from one-size-fits-all. Napier (2005) describes hentai as pornographic anime, recognizing hentai as being capable of being "both thematically wide ranging and narratively complex." In other words, just as there is no one type of anime, there is also no single type of ecchi or hentai.

One of the biggest sources of division between a Japanese and Western understanding of hentai specifically—and anime in general—stems from the censorship of plot, themes, and other content. Examples of this abound, ranging from the Sailor Scouts being "just friends" to the overuse of tentacles to sidestep censorship laws that prohibit the showing genitals.[7] For anime in general there's a tendency to Westernize the content when it is being localized, such as when the character Brock from *Pokémon* refers to rice balls as "jelly filled doughnuts." This can create disconnects between the characters, their actions, and the situations they find themselves in.[8] And, while the lolicon[9] genre of ecchi/hentai has been argued to tap into teenage anxieties about the adult world (Hinton, 2014), they are often prone to this sort of modification or rationalizations when localized in the West due to legal issues (e.g., illegal to own in some countries).

While these issues are just a drop in the bucket when it comes to discussing the complexity of perceptions, modifications, censorship, and cultural differences in perceptions of hentai, they set the stage for a genre of anime that's different depending on where you are in the world. It's also important to consider that hentai is both an idiosyncrasy of the anime fandom—given the complexity of scope, plot, and themes of the content, which can stand on its own as a genre—but also is somewhat akin to erotic fanfiction communities in other fandoms.

Pornography in Other Fandoms

While writing a chapter on fan pornography for another book about fans (Edwards et al., 2019), one of the authors stumbled down the rabbit hole of pornography's history, a history worth considering in order to properly contextualize hentai within the anime fandom.

---

[7] This last factor, in particular, may have had of the biggest impact on questions surrounding, among other things, how women are portrayed in anime.

[8] Don't get us started on 10,000 year old immortals depicted in the bodies of preteen girls.

[9] Derived from Lolita (Nabokov's 1955 book), referencing erotic stories featuring young girls, similar to, but distinct from, shotacon, which involves young boys.

First and foremost, pornography has a long and storied history, existing in one form or another for centuries across cultures. The Romans for instance, have the tintinnabulum, a famous sculpture of a flying two-legged phallus, perhaps akin, at least in renown and cultural impact, to Hokusai's Tako to Ama (1814), a famous piece of Japanese artwork depicting a woman having sex with an octopus.

Unlike the rise of transformative works in the U.S. (e.g., the Tijuana Bibles of the 1960s), pulp magazines in Japan would feature erotic content alongside discussions with researchers, readers, and fans (McLelland, 2015). These works would push boundaries by discussing issues that were highly stigmatized at the time in the U.S., issues like homosexuality, BDSM, and fetishes. While slash fiction[10] would eventually rise to prominence in other fan communities (e.g., the *Star Trek* fandom in the 1970s), these same ideas were being raised far earlier and far more openly in Japanese hentai.

In contemporary fan culture, fans often consider erotic fanfiction and rule 34[11] content to be something categorically distinct from hentai. For fans of fanfiction and rule 34, there is the understanding previously-existing content is being riffed upon and changed (i.e., it's transformative content), something which may seem far less valid or acceptable to fans. If, for example, you are a huge fan of the characters Naruto or Goku, you may be uncomfortable seeing them portrayed in lewd situations,[12] not only because you are unaccustomed to seeing them this way, but also because many of these situations are decidedly non-canon. For fans of hentai, on the other hand, these characters exist in a world where lewd situations are both in character and canon. For these folks, hentai is a category distinct from fanfiction and fan erotica precisely because of its non-derivative nature.

It's worth noting some of the implications this has for research on hentai. First, it may suggest that hentai, while perhaps not the most popular genre of anime, may be more popular than erotic content from other fandoms, in part because it's less likely to infringe upon preexisting characters that fans have developed connections with. Second, it is difficult to equate hentai to

---

[10] Fanfiction focusing typically on non-canon same-sex romantic or sexual relations between fictional characters in a series.

[11] Presently, we use "rule 34" to refer to fan-made art that sexualizes otherwise non-sexual characters, sometimes, though not always, as an act of parody.

[12] Or not, who are we to judge?

the pornography one often sees in other fandoms because whereas in other fandoms, porn often exists to parody or transform existing work, rarely standing on its own, hentai really is just another genre of anime which happens to focus on sexual content. Finally, it's a bit harder to make broad, sweeping claims about hentai in the way one can about pornography in other fandoms given that hentai often contains complex plots, characters, and settings, making it a distinctly more complex and nuanced medium.

With these implications in mind, we're properly armed with the context needed to fully appreciate and begin explaining some of the results of our psychological studies of hentai fans.

Hentai: The Disliked, but Popular Kid
The Basics

To start, let's go back to the beginning of this chapter, where our Google search results revealed that hentai, as a genre, is at least as popular, if not more popular that most mainstream anime series. Despite this apparent popularity online, our own data suggest that most anime fans do not consider themselves to be fans of the hentai genre.

For example, as seen in Figure 9.1, only 34.3% of fans rate hentai as being at least somewhat favorable and something that they are a fan of.[13] Even more telling, only 4.3% of anime fans rated hentai as their favorite anime category (as compared to the mecha, action, drama, and slice-of-life genres).[14] Even though there are a number of original hentai series with their own complex plots, characters, and settings, and even though it's common for characters and settings from other genres to be placed in fan-made erotic contexts, just as we've seen in previous fan research, anime fans really aren't in it for the hentai.[15]

---

[13] This should read as not immediately disapproving of it.

[14] It's worth noting that non-hentai anime series which include lewd scenes, nudity, sexual activity, or scantily-clad characters are not likely to be considered hentai by all or even most fans. Hentai, to many fans, may refer specifically to the most explicit of explicit content.

[15] This actually helps to dispel one popular stereotype of anime fans as little more than "people with an anime fetish," a stereotype akin to other fandoms (e.g., bronies as people with a "My Little Pony" fetish, or furries as "people with a fursuit fetish"). It's noteworthy that these stereotypes similarly hold little water for members of these other fandoms.

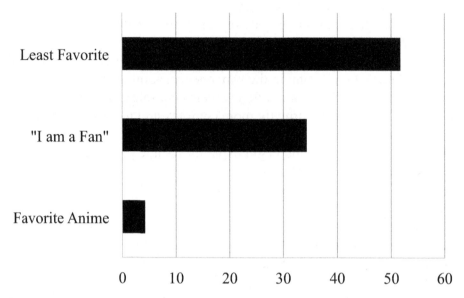

Figure 9.1. Percentage of hentai favorability amongst anime fans.

Conventions and Spending

While it may not be most fans' favorite genre, there is considerable variability in the extent to which anime fans hold favorable attitudes toward hentai. However, what can we tell about a fan just from the knowledge that they view hentai in a more positive light, beyond the fact that they enjoy hentai content and hold fewer stigmatizing views toward it or other people who enjoy it?

As seen in Figure 9.2 convention-going fans are more likely than online fans to have a favorable attitude toward hentai content. Despite this difference, however, con-going and online anime fans had spent about the same amount of money purchasing erotic art in the past 12 months (see Figure 9.3).[16] This leaves us with a similarly perplexing question as the one we started with: If hentai is so disliked and disapproved of, why do so many

---

[16] These numbers should be tempered by other numbers, reported elsewhere in this book, that hentai fans are far more willing to drop big bucks on merchandise like body pillows.

anime fans engage with it, including buying erotic content to about the same extent as hentai fans?[17]

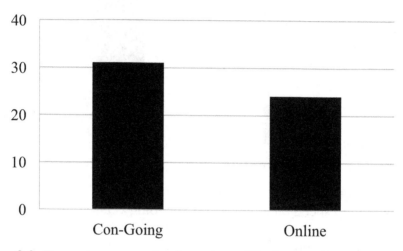

Figure 9.2. Percentage reporting hentai as a liked genre in online and con-going fans.

---

[17] True, erotic content of one's favorite non-hentai series is not the same thing as being interested in a hentai series specifically, but you have to admit that there may be at least a kernel of hypocrisy in viewing hentai unfavorably while simultaneously purchasing erotic artwork of characters from one's favorite series!

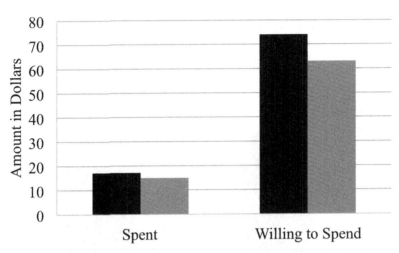

Figure 9.3. Average amount of money spent in the last 12 months and amount willing to spend on erotic art for congoing versus online fans.

What Predicts Viewing?

Whenever we study a fan community, one question we commonly ask is "what leads someone to become a member of this fan community?" Elsewhere in this book we discuss the factors which predict a person identifying as an anime fan (e.g., Chapter 10), a cosplayer (Chapter 8), or an otaku (Chapter 5). Here, we take the same approach with respect to hentai fans, asking what factors predict an anime fan's being more likely to view pornographic content.

Demographic Variables

In one of our first analyses, we found that the longer someone is a fan of anime, the more likely it is that they rate hentai as something they are a fan of. One possible explanation stems from the fact that many anime fans get into the fandom at a younger age, sometime in their early-to-mid teens (see Chapter 3). As such, many younger fans may not have access or be permitted to view hentai content until they have been in the fandom itself for several years. Another possible explanation needing to be tested in future research stems from the concept of familiarity, a concept we introduced in Chapter 6. In a nutshell, the more someone sees something, the more familiar they become with it, which can increase their felt level of comfort with it. As such, while pornographic content may once have unsettled or weirded out anime fans early on, seeing it regularly through their time in the fandom may help them to warm up to it, and perhaps even stumble across some that they enjoy.

Another demographic variable tied to hentai-viewing is gender: Men are more likely to view hentai than are women. This is hardly a trend unique to hentai, as men in general are significantly more likely to watch and seek out pornography in general. Speaking rather humorously to this idea, in one study, researchers had difficulty finding any men in their 20s to be a participant in their "never exposed to porn" group (University of Montreal, 2009). In fact, of all of the predictors of hentai consumption looked at, being a man was the factor most strongly tied to hentai consumption.[18]

Motivation for Consumption

One of the least surprising results from our analyses of those with a strong preference for hentai was the fact that, among other things driving their interest in anime in general, hentai fans were especially interested in anime because of significant sexual attraction to the content. Other motivating factors what were significant, but smaller in magnitude, included sense of belongingness and escapism.

While belongingness with the anime community might not seem conducive to hentai consumption, as we describe in the following section, fandom identification is associated with being a fan of hentai, meaning that hentai fans, like other anime fans, are motivated, at least in part, by being part of a like-minded community—perhaps in this case, a fan of other hentai enthusiasts.

As for the link between escapism and hentai use, we can turn to other research on non-animated pornography. Specifically, prior work suggests that people sometimes turn to porn as a coping mechanism in response to other unfulfilled needs (Hesse & Floyd, 2019). This might suggest that fans who are unable to fulfill certain psychological desires (e.g., sex) may be turning to porn for gratification. These results are contradicted, however, by

---

[18] It's worth noting that in studies of porn consumption in the general population, gender differences can also be found, though the magnitude of the effect is significantly smaller.

an analysis showing that hentai fans were actually somewhat more likely to be in a relationship than single. One possibility is that a third variable, being older, is associated with both being more likely to be in a relationship and being more likely to look at hentai, creating the appearance of a direct relationship where none exists.

Other Psychological Variables

Besides the demographic predictors, a number of psychological factors were also found to predict hentai viewership.

While discussed in greater depth in Chapter 10, the concepts of fandom (i.e., identifying with a fan community) and fanship (i.e., identifying with a particular interest) both positively predict hentai viewership. This makes sense when coupled alongside the aforementioned age data, since those who have been an anime fan for longer are also more likely to identify more strongly as an anime fan and to be more involved in the anime community. As such, these factors may directly be tied to hentai viewership, or they may be related to viewership only insofar as they are associated with the amount of time one has been an anime fan.[19]

Two additional psychological factors found to predict being a hentai fan are hostility and negative fantasy engagement—the tendency to excessively engage in fantasy or for fantasy to be causing problems in one's own life. The reasons for this are a bit tricky to pin down. One possibility is grounded in the fact that hentai titles may be more likely than other anime to contain more extreme titles and plotlines (e.g., rape in *La Blue Girl*). This could make these series off-putting to people who are fairly low in aggression or hostility, or to people who are less comfortable with engaging in fantasies that feature such extreme content. Future studies may thus benefit from examining differences in attitudes between "hentai," which contains more graphic, extreme content, and the tamer term ecchi.

One final variable found to predict hentai consumption is an anime fan's political leanings. In our study, we asked participants to indicate both their political party identification as well as their political leanings on a 7-point Likert-type scale ranging from conservative to liberal. The results found

---

[19] As we discussed in Chapter 2, this is an example of third variables explaining a correlation!

that more conservative participants were, in fact, more likely to rate their hentai consumption higher.

At first glance, this is a bit perplexing, given that conservativism is often associated with religiousness and religiousness, in turn, is often associated with sexual inhibition. However, there have been studies with results in line with our findings, showing that in places with higher conservative and religious populations, more pornography is consumed (Perry & Whitehead, 2020).[20]

Prior research on the subject is more complex than an all-or-nothing, simple relationship between religion, political orientation, and pornography use. For instance, people with higher religiosity and conservativism, while more likely to consume porn, state that they are less likely to have recently consumed porn (Perry & Whitehead, 2020). Ultimately, results like these suggest that when interpreting our own findings, we should take care to avoid overly simplistic blanket statements about conservatives or religious people and hentai and recognize that the link between hentai use and one's deeply-held beliefs likely require a nuanced understanding.[21] Speaking to how nuanced these points can get, while social conservatism (e.g., opposition to gay marriage, LGBTQ+ rights, and policies supporting racial equality) is associated with pornography consumption in our studies, economic conservativism (e.g., opposition to minimum wage laws, privatizing health care) was unrelated to pornography consumption.

What Does Hentai Viewing Predict?

Sexism and Prejudice

To this point, we've discussed several factors that are conceptually thought to precede and predict hentai-viewing.[22] However, what does a preference for hentai content actually tell us about those who consume it?

---

[20] Their findings showed that states with more evangelicals, theists, Biblical literalists, and higher church attendance had more total internet searches for porn.

[21] It's also worth keeping in mind that these findings are do not say that liberals don't consume porn at all!

[22] While factors like years in fandom, fantasy tendencies, hostility, and political leanings are only *correlated* with hentai viewing, we are inferring a causal direction on the grounds that these factors are thought to come *before* one's interest in hentai. In other words, it seems more likely to us that a person's attitudes toward hentai are formed after they've made their minds up about their political leanings, and not the other way around (that, as a result of viewing hentai, they have decided their political beliefs). To be fair, several of the

217

To be clear from the outset, the answer is "not a lot." Of all the variables we examined with respect to hentai preference, only two significant variables emerged: a tendency toward more sexism and less prejudice. Those who had a stronger preference for hentai tended to score the highest on measures of sexism and lower on measures of prejudice toward LGBTQ+ people.

Let's start by trying to understand the sexism data. Research on pornography consumption and sexism has shown that pornographic content in general (not necessarily anime-themed) can have a persistent impact on a person's sexism. For example, Hegarty et al. (2018) show that viewing erotic magazines can normalize sexist attitudes and beliefs in young men. In other study, Hald et al. (2010) noted that increased viewing of pornography was linked to lower beliefs in gender egalitarianism and higher endorsement of sexist ideas.

That said, not all research has shown a link between pornography and sexism. For example, Kohut et al. (2016), McKee (2007), and Miller et al. (2020) all found no association between pornography and sex, including violent and humiliation-based pornography.[23,24] Miller and colleagues (2020) propose that this discrepancy is the result of sexism increasing only for measures of sexism with respect to sexuality (and not for sexist beliefs in general). Miller and colleagues also suggest that the relationship between porn and sexism may only be present for people who believe that pornographic depictions are accurate representations of reality.

What about research showing lower prejudice among hentai fans toward groups like the LGBTQ+ population? Studies suggest that this is hardly unique to hentai consumption. Billard (2019), for example, found that watching porn featuring transgender performers increased positive attitudes toward transgender people.[25] Wright and Bae (2013) similarly found that

---

authors believe these effects to be bidirectional, meaning that hentai-viewing can both be affected by and affect these variables.

[23] That said, some of these studies did observe an increase in tolerance of violence against women associated with violent pornography use.

[24] We do not know what specific titles or types of hentai participants watched, a factor that is often measured and controlled for in pornography research.

[25] Billard did, however, find that for participants who felt a lot of shame from watching, porn viewing was associated with higher prejudice, illustrating the importance of considering nuance and additional variables when trying to interpret these findings.

porn consumption was related to more positive attitudes toward homosexuality.[26] With respect to anime fans specifically, hentai preferers rated members of other stigmatized fandoms (e.g., furries, bronies) more positively.

One possible explanation for these findings is that those who prefer hentai represent a stigmatized subgroup within the anime fandom. Having this stigmatized identity, they may be more sympathetic and less judgmental of other stigmatized groups as a result.[27] It remains a topic for future research to explore.

Other Outcomes

Those with a greater preference for hentai are also more likely to engage with anime content more frequently, including binge-watching anime more, reading more manga, and talking to their friends about anime. They are also more likely to own more anime-themed merchandise (figurines, kigurumi costumes, body pillows, and tattoos). In fact, these spending results are notable, as additional studies have shown that being a bigger fan of hentai content is also associated with reporting more problems when it comes to controlling one's own spending. This "impulse control" variable would not only explain a tendency to spend more on merchandise and to consume more anime, but also explain why a person may consume more pornography and one of our earlier findings, that hentai fans are also more likely to engage in excessive fantasy—or in fantasies that cause problems with close others around them.[28]

All of these findings could be explained by the fact that older fans, who also happen to identify more strongly as fans, may simply be more likely to spend more time engaging in the consumption of anime content *and* also hold more positive attitudes toward all genres of anime—including hentai.

---

[26] Measured through questions on moral judgments of gay people and views towards same-sex marriage.

[27] While this sounds like a plausible-sounding hypothesis, it is somewhat contradicted by results from the last chapter showing that higher rates of hentai preference were associated with more dark triad traits (e.g., Machiavellianism, psychopathy) and with more entitlement and gatekeeping behavior.

[28] It is important to note that these are correlations, meaning that the direction could go either way. Problems with impulse control could lead to more pornography-viewing, pornography-viewing could lead to reduced impulse control, or perhaps both!

Comparisons to Other Fandoms

In a previous section of this chapter, we suggested that hentai may differ from other fandom pornography, specifically rule 34 content, since hentai is generally more likely to represent original work while rule 34 content and fanfiction tends to be derivative or transformative, placing preexisting characters in pornographic situations. For anime fans, both of these types of pornographic content are likely to exist, meaning that when we ask "are you a fan of hentai?," participants may have trouble distinguishing between established hentai series and fan-made fiction or rule 34 artwork, a problem less likely to occur in other fan communities.

Nevertheless, it is informative to compare attitudes toward pornographic content in other fandoms relative to the anime fandom to find parallels and differences that may offer insights into our understanding of what is novel about hentai versus what is typical of pornography in any fan group.

Love them or hate them as a fan community, bronies, or the fans of *My Little Pony: Friendship is Magic,* have been researched by the authors of this book for almost as long as the anime fandom,[29] including conducting studies on the subject of pornography in the brony fandom (Edwards et al., 2019). In general, while anime fans tend to be more fairly divided with respect to their tendency to consume only fandom-themed pornography (relative to non-fandom pornography, see Figure 9.4), bronies are overwhelmingly likely to say that the majority of the pornography they consume is not limited to fandom-related content (see Figure 9.5).[30] Specifically, while anime fans' responses tend to follow a u-shaped pattern, suggesting a very all-or-nothing pattern of responses, the distribution of data for bronies tends to be fairly skewed, with a pretty strong "strongly disagree" response and a fairly weak "strongly agree" response by comparison.

---

[29] That said, the anime fandom has, for sure, existed for longer than the brony fandom, and it has been studied outside of the psychological literature for a much, much longer time.

[30] Lest you believe that this is because there is simply no *My Little Pony* related pornography, rest assured that it is both plentiful and highly contentious among *My Little Pony* fans. We apologize if this has put images into readers' heads that they would rather not have. As they say, it's impossible to put the toothpaste back into the tube.

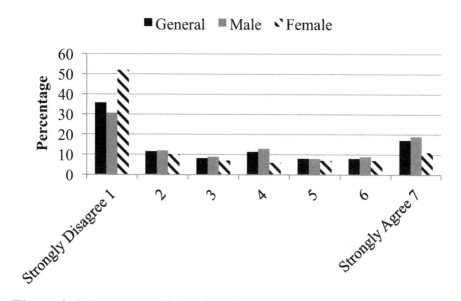

Figure 9.4. Extent to which anime fans' pornography consumption is limited to anime-themed pornography/hentai.

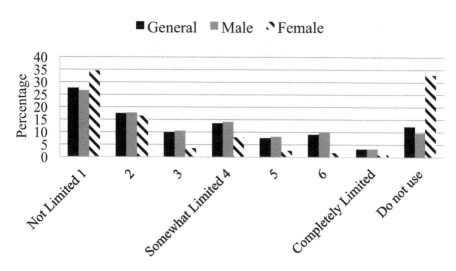

Figure 9.5. Extent to which bronies' pornography consumption is limited to *MLP*-themed content.

One final point worth comparing is the extent to which fans were brought into the respective fandoms by explicit content itself. As Figure 9.6 makes clear, neither anime fans nor bronies were drawn to their respective fandoms solely based on the pornography on offer.[31] That said, bronies were almost twice as likely to strongly disagree with this assertion than anime fans, who were far more likely than bronies to agree somewhat or completely with this statement.

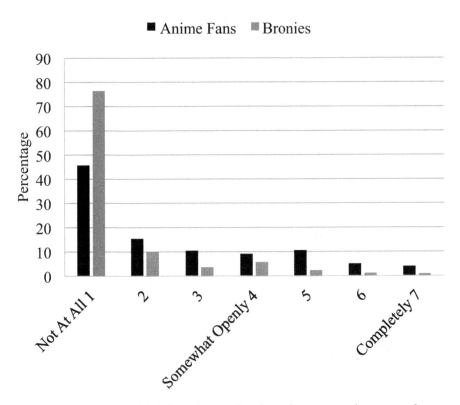

Figure 9.6. Extent to which bronies and anime fans were drawn to the fandom through fan related pornographic content (e.g., hentai/rule-34).

---

[31] Once again, with so much porn available, a niche subgenre like rule 34 or hentai may not be sought out unless one has a specific interest to begin with (i.e., anime in general or a specific title).

Conclusion

As you made your way through this chapter, you have no doubt been developing your own beliefs about what hentai is, what it your attitudes toward it are, and how you feel about those who consume it. Before you reach a final decision on the subject, it's worth keeping in mind a study by Daspe and colleagues (2018), who found that in the past six months, 98% of men and 73% of women watched porn; in the past week, those numbers were 80% and 26% respectively.

Put simply, the overwhelming majority of people, anime fans or otherwise, consume pornographic material—albeit to varying degrees and looking at dramatically different content. Given that this is the case, what should we conclude about those who admit to watching anime-themed pornography? Or those who acknowledge or even prefer hentai as a genre? Research on the predictors and consequences of pornography-viewing is fairly divided in its findings (see Miller et al.'s, 2020 discussion and conclusions), and so it should come as no surprise that peoples' beliefs about hentai and its role in the anime fandom is similarly divided.

We advise you to interpret this chapter's findings with caution, as neither tacitly promoting hentai nor as demonizing it or its fans. If nothing else, we hope that the discussion itself has made you more aware of the nuances and complexities of studying a subject like hentai, including how difficult it is to parse out the effects of the media on fans or the role that personality and other individual differences plays in driving fans to consume hentai. It may even warrant some rethinking about your own attitudes about the subject and consideration of your own consumption behavior one way or another.

Chapter 10
Fanship and Fandom

When we talk about fans, our first impulse is to imagine a person passionately watching their favorite show, listening to their favorite band, or cheering for their favorite team. We imagine their connection to the media, celebrities, or athletes manifesting through a variety of behaviors, including cheering, wearing the regalia of fans, or re-enacting the scene themselves. Importantly, in these examples we often find ourselves focusing on individual fans.

As any fan will tell you, however, they often feel just as strong a sense of psychological connection to other fans as they do the fan interest itself. It's true, for example, that anime fans love watching their favorite series or reading their favorite manga. It's also true that many love talking about their passion with other fans online or attending conventions to be around other fans just as much.

Just which one is the essence of "real fans," and how do we know this?

In this chapter we delve into some of the basic, central concepts necessary to underlying the psychology of fans. We begin by discussing a classic paper on fans and their felt connection to an object of interest. Next, we review social identity theory and self-categorization theory, two theories that will come up again and again throughout the rest of this book because of their applicability to understanding the concept of fan identity and explaining fan behavior. Finally, we return to where this chapter began, explaining the difference between fanship—a felt connection to an interest—and fandom—a felt connection to other fans of that interest—and showing how important these factors are to understanding many of the fan-related variables we've studied over the years.

BIRGing

In the earliest days of fan research in psychology, a group or researchers set out to demonstrate and explain a phenomenon they called "basking in reflected glory" or BIRGing (Cialdini et al., 1976). It's a phenomenon you're probably intuitively familiar with, even if you didn't realize there was a name for it! In a nutshell, BIRGing is when people latch onto the success of their own group's accomplishments, wearing them proudly as their own accomplishments despite having little to nothing to do with the achievement itself. As an illustrative example of this, recall how people from your country behaved during the last Olympic games. Chances are, after an athlete from your country did well and won a medal, people felt compelled to celebrate the win as though it was also theirs (e.g., "we won!").[1] They feel a sense of collective achievement despite the fact that they had nothing to do with the win. Unless they were the athlete or the coach in question, they probably had minimal impact on the victory itself. Nevertheless, that athlete's win puts a smile on their face, and for the rest of the day they get to feel like a winner. That's BIRGing.

So how do you study BIRGing scientifically? Well, in their first study, the researchers measured the number of students who wore university-themed apparel (e.g., hoodies, hats) at seven universities on a given day. Of interest to the researchers, however, was the number of students who did so after the school's football team either won or lost their most recent game. The results showed that, in general, students were more likely to wear university apparel after a win than after a loss. In other words, just like people who buy their country's Olympic apparel after a recent victory, these college students wanted to publicly bask in the victory of their school's football team.[2]

In a later study, the researchers called a sample of randomly-selected students, ostensibly as an out-of-state research center conducting a survey about campus issues.[3] During the survey, participants were given a small set of questions testing their knowledge of various subjects. They were then told one of two things at random: Some were told that they either did really well on the test, while the others were told they had done poorly on the test. This was done to either boost or bruise the students' self-esteem.

Next, the researchers did a second manipulation: They asked participants to describe, in half the cases, a university football game in which their team

---

[1] In Canada, where two of the authors are from, this is always the case whenever Canadians win a gold medal in hockey.

[2] Again, it should be emphasized that these were not students who were *on* the football team itself! In theory, these students had no reason to feel any sense of pride or accomplishment, since the victory was not their own doing!

[3] This was a lie. Researchers often construct cover stories like this to mask the true intention of the study, since participants often change their responses if they know what the study is about—sometimes to help the researcher, other times to try and disprove whatever the researcher is trying to test.

won, while in the other half of cases they were asked to describe a university football game in which their team had lost. Importantly, the researchers paid attention to whether the participants used the word "we" to describe the outcome of the game (e.g., "we won").

So, what did they find? First, participants were more likely to use we when describing a game where their school's team won than they were to describe a game where their team lost (e.g., "we won" versus "they lost"). This is a beautiful demonstration of BIRGing, feeling a sense of connection with a team that makes you look and feel good.

They also found a second result: The BIRGing effect was stronger when participants were told that they had done poorly on the test beforehand. In other words, after a personal failure, participants felt a stronger need to BIRG and connect themselves with the winning university team. In short, the study not only showed evidence of BIRGing, but also suggested a reason why it happens: To preserve and bolster one's self-esteem.[4]

The Social Identity Approach

BIRGing and CORFing are interesting phenomena in their own right. However, by themselves their usefulness is fairly specific and limited. Without a broader theoretical framework within which to understand BIRGing and CORFing, we can really only use them to tell us something about winning sport teams. As psychologists, we'd prefer to take what we've learned about BIRGing and CORFing and use it to better understand something broader and more fundamental about what makes people tick.

So, what sort of broader theoretical framework are we talking about, exactly? Well, in the 1970s, Henri Tajfel and his graduate student John Turner at the University of Bristol ran a series of experiments which culminated in the proposition of social identity theory (Tajfel & Turner, 1979) and later, after Tajfel's death in 1982 (Hogg & Williams, 2000), self-categorization theory (Turner et al., 1987). These two theories explain what happens when we think of ourselves as group members and when we're

---

[4] We should note that in a footnote to this classic paper, the researchers state that the reverse can also be true, distancing from an unpopular or unattractive group. This effect would later be called CORFing or cutting off reflected failure (see Snyder et al., 1986; Wann & Branscombe, 1990).

most likely to do so, respectively.[5] Together, they not only shed light on BIRGing and CORFing specifically, but they also form the backbone of much of the psychological research on fan behavior.[6]

Social Identity Theory

Social identity theory (Tajfel & Turner, 1979) starts with a very simple premise: People can think of themselves as individuals (based on personal characteristics that make us different from others) or as group members (based on characteristics we share with others).[7]

Okay, so what's the big deal? Why does it matter whether Joe thinks of himself as "Joe the strangely tall guy" instead of "Joe the American?"

The reason it matters is because whether we're thinking about ourselves as individuals or as groups affects the way we see others, what we believe about them, how we feel about them, and ultimately how we behave toward them.

As an example: When the group that we're a part of (called our "ingroup") is on our mind, we tend to recognize the diversity within our own group, but view people who are part of a different group (called "outgroup members") as being very similar to one another.[8] We also tend to show ingroup bias: We paint people from our own groups in a positive light, downplaying their bad sides and focusing on their upsides, while failing to extend the same courtesy to people in the outgroup. This tendency to make biased comparisons leads to us believing that our ingroup is generally better than other groups.[9]

Another key assumption of social identity theory is that we generally want to feel good about ourselves. To do this, we try to belong to positive groups that are fairly distinct (e.g., that stand out from other groups).

---

[5] Today, although the two theories are distinct, researchers tend to merge them together and refer to them as the social identity approach (Hornsey, 2008).

[6] Not to mention a great deal of the research done today on business, conflict, prejudice, and intergroup dynamics!

[7] A different way of saying this would be to think of yourself either as an individual who's distinct from others or as part of a group that's distinct from other groups.

[8] This is called "outgroup homogeneity," and it's one of the reasons why people say things like "Asian people all look the same" or "Conservatives all act the same way!"

[9] For examples of this, think of all the people who believe that their country is the best one to live in, that their political party is the best one, or that their sport team is the best team to root for.

Comparing our own groups to other groups is how we learn whether or not we belong to positive, distinct groups.[10] These groups are a big part of who we are.[11] As such, belonging to positive groups becomes an important part of our self-esteem: When we belong to positive groups that are exclusive or hard to get into, we feel pretty good about ourselves.

Because of the importance of groups for maintaining our self-esteem, members of really positive groups (e.g., high status, viewed positively by others) will be motivated to preserve that group's distinctive quality. They do this in a number of ways, including justifying their status and prestige as legitimate and trying their best to keep their group from being infiltrated by low-quality group members.

What about members of low-status groups? The theory argues that they have different strategies available to them, which will depend on some of their group's characteristics. This includes whether the group is one they can leave (permeability), whether their low status is legitimate or valid, and whether the low status is seen as something that is likely to change in the future or not. One can imagine, for example, that if one is part of a low-status group whose status is unlikely to change and which they can leave at any time, they're likely to jump ship and find another group to belong to.[12] In contrast, if one belongs to a low-status group, but the legitimacy of that lower status is questionable and may one day change, they may instead choose to stand and fight to defend that group and improve its perceived status.[13]

By now, the power of social identity theory to explain a wide range of group phenomena should be apparent. Now let's look at a second, related theory, to see what additional light it can shed on how we think about ourselves and the groups we belong to.

---

[10] Which, more often than not, we do, thanks to the biases we just described!

[11] To see this in action, think about how you'd describe yourself in a biography. Chances are, you'd mention your citizenship, the schools you attended, your political affiliation, your race, gender, and sexual orientation—these are all groups that you're a part of!

[12] Think, for example, about being a fan of a struggling, underfunded sport team that's unlikely to ever win. Meanwhile, there's a winning sport team nearby that you could easily see yourself cheering for.

[13] In this case, think about a member of a racialized group. You can't simply stop being a part of that group. If the stigma directed toward it is considered illegitimate and could be changed, you may work, instead, to dismantle the stigma, perhaps through activism.

Self-Categorization Theory

Self-categorization theory (Turner et al., 1987) argues that all of our different identities exist at differing levels of abstraction or specificity. At the lowest, most specific level, we have our personal identity, the things that make us a unique individual. At a level above that, a more abstract, inclusive level, we have our social identity, describing ourselves in terms of the groups that we belong to. One level above that is the highest level of identity, human identity, which is all the things we have in common with every other person.

According to self-categorization theory, when we think of ourselves at any given level, it affects who we compare ourselves to. For personal identity, the comparison is with other ingroup members; for social identity, the comparison is with outgroup members; for human identity, the comparison is with other non-human things (i.e., plants, animals). At any given time, based on what the situation necessitates, we can switch effortlessly between these different levels of identity. This will, in turn, affect whether we see ourselves (and others) in terms of what makes us unique or as a stereotypical member of our own group.[14]

Together, social identity theory and self-categorization theories form a unified perspective that can be used to understand all sorts of fan behavior from a psychological perspective. We'll see just some of the applications of this unified social identity perspective to understanding the behavior of anime fans throughout the rest of this chapter including, as we'll see in a couple of sections, BIRGing and CORFing.

Identification

One variable critical to the social identity approach is the extent of one's identification (e.g., with a group). Tajfel noted that at extremely high levels of group identification, people entirely internalize the group. From a self-categorization view, when the group is salient, people stop thinking about what makes them distinct and instead take on the group's prototypical traits—again, becoming the group.

---

[14] For example: When Jane is in her home country, Canada, she may think about personal identity—things that make her distinct from other Canadians. But when she's in another country, Australia, she may think about her social identity. This will activate thoughts and concepts related to being Canadian, causing her to think and behave more stereotypically Canadian, all while she distinguishes herself from the Australians around her.

At the moment, this sounds extremely vague and abstract, so let's see what this looks like in laboratory study. In a reaction time study, Smith and Henry (1996) had participants respond (with a yes or no) about whether a variety of different characteristics (e.g., cheerful, sympathetic) described themselves. These were words that were stereotypical of either their ingroup or an outgroup. The researchers found that people were quicker to connect the ingroup's characteristics to themselves. A later study found the same effect after they replaced "characteristics" with different attitudes, as well as finding that the effect was stronger for people who more strongly identified with the ingroup in the first place (Coats et al., 2000).

In the context of fans, this means that fans very much *become* their fan interests and their fan groups, meaning that when one's fan interest is threatened, they, themselves, are threatened. This is highlighted in a study that was done on basketball fans. Participants were randomly assigned to watch their favorite team win or lose a game (Hirt et al., 1992). Fans who watched their team lose (vs. win) reported a more negative and less positive mood, as you might expect. More surprising, however, they also experienced lower self-esteem and estimated their own ability to perform on a variety of tasks as being significantly lower. Just as with other groups, when fans' teams lost, it was felt as a blow to themselves due to their identification with that interest.

That's all well and good, but how do psychologists set about studying something as abstract as "identification" in the first place?

As it turns out, this is a question whose answer has a rich and varied history. Early researchers (e.g., Hinkle et al., 1989; Karasawa, 1991) constructed measures that consisted of three parts which reflected Tajfel's definition of social identity: (1) do you consider yourself to be a member of the group, (2) do you see the group as having value, and (3) how positively do you feel toward the group?[15] In the years since, researchers have proposed other measures. For example, some ask about the importance of the group to the self, how attached they feel to the group, or how embedded the group is in the person's everyday life (see Ashmore et al., 2004).

---

[15] The idea was that if people called themselves members of a group (self-categorization), saw the group in a positive light (evaluation), and felt good about the group (emotional significance), it was pretty compelling evidence that they felt a sense of connection to the group, and could thus be said to identify with it.

At this point you might be wondering "Why beat around the bush? If you want to study group identity, why not just ask if they identify with the group?"

As it turns out, sometimes the simplest answers are best. Despite the complexity of the field and the multitude of measures within it, researchers have shown that you really can measure identification—a person's sense of psychological connection with something—just by asking them the extent to which they agree (1 = *strongly disagree*, 7 = *strongly agree*) with the statement "I strongly identify with [*insert group*]" (Reysen et al., 2013).

Which brings us to the question of what any of this has to do with measuring identification within fan groups.

One of the earliest measures of fan identification was developed by Wann and Branscombe (1990), who were looking to measure sport team identification (also see Wann & Branscombe, 1993). The measure consists of eight items such as "How important is being a fan of [insert team] to you?" Later, more complex measures would follow, such as in Trail et al. (2003), who asked about sports fans' identification with the players, team, coach, community, specific sport (e.g., football), university, and with sport in general. Heere and James (2007), on the other hand, measured even more factors: private evaluation (e.g., "I am proud to think of myself as a fan of my college football team"), public evaluation (e.g., "In general, others respect the college football team I am a fan of"), importance of team to self (e.g., "Being a fan of my college football team is important to me"), felt interconnection with team (e.g., "I have a strong attachment to my college football team"), felt interdependence with team (e.g., "My destiny is tied to the destiny of the college football team"), embeddedness (e.g., "Being a fan of my college football team is an important part of my social life"), behavioral involvement (e.g., "I am actively involved in team-related activities"), and cognitive awareness ("I am aware of the tradition and history of my college football team").[16]

In addition to being rather long and unwieldy, all of these measures were designed specifically for sport fans.[17] Of course, given that fans can be

---

[16] All of these measures highlight the idea that a person can feel psychologically connected to various aspects of an interest.

[17] In fact, up until the past couple of decades, nearly all of the psychological research on fans had been done almost exclusively on sport fans.

enthusiastic supporters of other, non-sport interests, Reysen and Branscombe (2010) developed a fandom non-specific measure of the extent to which people identify with a fan interest (i.e., fanship). Other measures were adapted from prior social identity research, which measured identification with the group of other fans who are also interested in the same fan interest (i.e., fandom). Together, these constructs of fanship, and to a lesser extent, fandom are used in psychological fan research and have proven themselves to be fairly versatile in their application and useful in predicting a variety of fan behaviors, as we'll mention in a later section.

Identification and Fans

So, we've seen the importance of group identification and the various ways that identification has been studied in the context of other groups. However, we're here to study fan groups, specifically anime fans. So, how do researchers apply the study of identification to fan groups?

To begin, let's take a moment to return to Cialdini and colleagues' (1976) research on BIRGing, which we can now reassess with a fuller theoretical understanding. Recall that social identity theory argues that people want to maintain positive and distinct social identities. If, after an intergroup comparison, one's ingroup is deemed low status and the boundary between groups is permeable, people will leave the group for a higher-status group.

However, what about fans who famously continue to follow poorly-performing teams?[18] Wann and Branscombe (1990) asked university basketball fans who were either low, moderate, or highly-identified with their team how much enjoyment they felt when their team won and when their team lost. Highly-identified fans were significantly more likely to BIRG and less likely to CORF than low-identified fans. In other words, highly identified fans felt greater enjoyment because the team is a reflection on themselves. They were also more likely to stick by their team after a loss.[19]

---

[18] Long-suffering fans of the Chicago Cubs baseball team come to mind, who waited through a 108-year drought for their team to win the World Series!

[19] This may also explain the insistence of die-hard fans that "bandwagon" or "fair-weather" fans, those who only appear when something is popular (e.g., a team is doing well) and who abandon the interest at the first sign of trouble, are not *real* fans.

Moving beyond BIRGing and CORFing, identifying with a team is associated with a slew of other variables. Those who more strongly identify with a team, for example, score higher on measures of psychological well-being (e.g., lower depression, fewer feelings of alienation; Branscombe & Wann, 1991), and feel a greater sense of trust in others (Wann & Polk, 2007). Highly-identified fans also tend to have more favorable attitudes toward a team's sponsors (Gwinner & Swanson, 2003) and a greater willingness to purchase team-licensed merchandise (Kwon et al., 2007).

In terms of fan behaviors, being a more highly-identified fan predicts greater attendance at team events, more sport television viewing, listening to sport radio, searching for team-related information on the internet, discussing sports with others (Parry et al., 2014), and feeling more knowledge about sport (Wann et al., 1997).

However, higher team identification isn't always a good thing. Team identification is also related to fans' willingness to anonymously injure an opposing team's player and coach (Wann, Peterson et al., 1999) and a greater willingness to commit illegal actions (e.g., drugging an opposing team's water) to help their favorite team (Wann, Hunter et al., 2001). All in all, however, the take-away message is that, far from being a trivial or pedantic distinction, knowing how strongly a fan identifies with their interest can tell us a lot about that fan's attitudes, behaviors, emotions, and well-being.

Fanship versus Fandom

The bulk of the research on fan identification has focused on sport fans' identification with their favorite team and understanding this relationship from a social identity perspective. However, some might argue that identifying with a team isn't necessarily a group identity. After all, simply being a fan of a team doesn't mean that one is part of the community of fans who support the team.[20]

To this end, in our own work we distinguish between fanship (e.g., team identification) as an individual's connection with a thing (e.g., team), while fandom (e.g., identification with a community of fans) is one's connection with the group who shares an interest in that thing (i.e., ingroup

---

[20] One can imagine, for instance, being a fan who cheers for their favorite team while watching every game by themselves in their home.

identification; Reysen & Branscombe, 2010). Another way of saying this is that fanship is more similar to personal identity, while fandom is a collective identity from a social identity perspective. Indeed, studies show that there are plenty of people who wouldn't call themselves sport fans (fanship) but who nevertheless enjoy the social connections they've formed while watching sports with other fans (fandom; van Driel et al., 2019). Much of the psychological research on sport fans largely omits this distinction, leaving out fandom entirely.

The sport fan research which *does* include fandom identification measures illustrates the importance of fandom, like fanship, in predicting important fan behaviors. Hedlund (2014), for example, found in a study of American football fans that their fandom was positively correlated with self-reported participation in fan activities, and intention to attend games, purchase team merchandise, and spread word-of-mouth positivity about the team to others. Others (Gordon et al., 2019; Yoshida, Gordon et al., 2015; Yoshida, Heere et al., 2015) have similarly studied fandom among Japanese soccer and baseball fans and found, rather comparably, that fandom was positively correlated with positive attitudes toward the team, pride in the team (e.g., logo, stadium, fight songs, history), purchasing and wearing team apparel, creating fan-made products, a felt sense of duty to new fans, spreading positive word of mouth, and attendance frequency. Indeed, Yoshida, Heere et al. (2015) showed that fandom is a better predictor of game attendance than fanship in a longitudinal study.

To this point, we've spoken about fanship and fandom as two distinct constructs, but it should be noted that they are fairly highly correlated. After all, people who are a fan of a particular interest are also fairly likely to want to hang out with like-minded fans, and vice versa. However, despite this high correlation, fanship and fandom are not quite the same thing (Reysen & Branscombe, 2010).

We can demonstrate the importance of distinguishing the two from one another in prior research on the brony fandom (Edwards et al., 2019), where the researchers measured both fanship and fandom and found that they were differently associated with different fan-related variables. For example, fandom (but not fanship), predicted more consumption of fan-made content, talking to friends about *My Little Pony*, purchasing fan-made products, creating fan-made content, attending conventions and meetups, and watching re-runs. On the other hand, fanship (but not fandom) predicted purchasing official merchandise, displaying fan symbols (e.g., wearing a *My Little Pony* t-shirt), and identification with a favorite character. In short, fanship was a stronger predictor of consuming officially licensed products and showing off one's liking of the show, while fandom was related to the more interpersonal aspects of the fandom.

More importantly, these results illustrate the importance of considering fanship and fandom as separate, but related, constructs when assessing the impact of fan identification on fan-related thoughts, feelings, and behaviors. With this in mind, we turn to the present research on the anime fandom and how fanship and fandom differently predict important facets of anime fan behavior.

Purchasing

As shown in Table 10.1, anime fans' fanship scores were, in most instances, more strongly associated with fan purchases than were fandom scores. For example, fans' fanship scores more strongly predicted owning more videos (e.g., DVDs), books, figurines, physical art, paraphernalia, and both official and unofficial merchandise, while fandom scores were more strongly associated with getting a tattoo.[21] Tellingly, fandom scores were also more strongly associated with spending money to attend a convention, an activity which, itself, has a fairly strong social component to it. These findings are in-line with the previously-mentioned research from the brony fandom, which similarly found that fanship was more strongly associated with fan-related material purchases and fandom was more strongly associated with interpersonal aspects of one's fan interest.

---

[21] One possible explanation for the unexpected direction of tattoos has to do with a possible social function of tattoos. Unlike videos, books, and figurines, which one often stores, views, and keeps at home, a tattoo is something a person brings everywhere with them, and which may serve a number of social functions, including permanently signaling one's group membership to other fans.

236

Variable	Fanship	Fandom
Number of Videos	.06*	< .01
Number of Books	.06*	.02
Number Figurines	.15**	.05
Number Kigurumi	.08	.06
Number Body Pillows	.06	.02
Number Tattoos	.03	.11*
$ Physical Art	.08*	.03
$ Digital Art	.03	.01
$ Erotic Art	.06	-.01
$ Sponsor Sites	.04	.03
$ Convention	.03	.14**
$ Paraphernalia	.12**	-.01
Collect Official Merch	.37**	.04
Collecting Unofficial Merch	.25**	.09**

Table 10.1. Regressions predicting purchasing, standardized betas presented, * $p < .05$, ** $p < .01$.

Consumption

As shown in Table 10.2, and in-line with the previous section, participants' fandom scores (but not their fanship scores) were positively correlated with the number of conventions and local meetups they attended. This provides important context for fandoms' positive relationship with greater convention spending and suggests that, yes, this greater spending is associated with frequenting more conventions in general (and not with, say, purchasing more fan merchandise at a convention).

Variable	Fanship	Fandom
Number of Cons	-.04	.26**
Number of Meetups	-.01	.21**
Watch Anime	.25**	.11*
Loot at Fan Art	.18**	.04
Read Fanfiction	.06	.17**
Read News/Reviews	.35**	-.12*
Talk w/Fans Online	.10*	.14**
Talk w/Fans Offline	.08	.28**
Talk w/nonFans Online	.10*	.20**
Talk w/nonFans Offline	.07	.24**
Watch with Friends	-.08	.24**
Talk about Anime w/Friends	.13**	.25**
Read Forums	.14**	.18**
Post in Forums	.05*	.24**
Consume Theorycrafting/Reviews	.14**	.25**
Produce Theorycrafting/Reviews	.07*	.12**
Play Anime-Related Games	.27**	.06*
Play Eroge Games	.19**	.02
Play Otome Games	.15**	.03
Play Japanese Role-Playing Games	.21**	-.08**
Read Doujinshi	.23**	.03
Read Light Novels	.19**	.09**
Read Visual Novels	.17**	.10**
Reading Manga	.19**	.09**
Watch Anime Music Videos (AMVs)	.18**	.20**
Listen to Soundtracks/Theme Songs	.33**	.13**
Listen to K-Pop	.08**	.09**
Listen to J-Pop	.28**	.06*

Table 10.2. Regressions predicting consumption, standardized betas presented, * $p < .05$, ** $p < .01$.

The importance of the connection between fandom and social activities is further evidenced by fandom predicting social activities such as talking with fans and non-fans both online and offline and watching and talking about anime with friends. While fanship and fandom both predicted greater reading of anime-related forums, fandom was a stronger predictor of actually posting in these forums. Fandom also more strongly predicted consuming and producing theorycrafting/reviews, where fans discuss and speculate about their favorite anime.

Also in line with previous research linking fanship to purchasing and consumption, anime fans' fanship scores were a stronger predictor of consuming anime content (watching anime, looking at fan art, reading news/reviews) than their fandom scores were.[22] Fanship was also tied to playing anime-related games (including eroge and otome games), consuming written works (e.g., doujinshi, light novels), listening to soundtracks/theme songs, and listening to J-Pop (Japanese Pop).[23] One notable exception to this was watching anime music videos (AMVs), which were tied to both fanship and fandom.[24]

Relationships and Obsession

Table 10.3 shows the results our studies which, among other things, looked at a number of important social outcomes for anime fans.

Fandom was more strongly associated with having more anime fans within one's friendship network, as well as seeing the anime fandom as a place to make new friends and maintain existing friendships—although both fanship and fandom predicted using the fandom to make and maintain friendships online specifically. This difference between online and face-to-face friendships may be related to two other variables: Fandom predicts less shyness, while fanship predicts greater shyness and feeling awkward around non-fans. Both of these factors may hint at a possible third

---

[22] Surprisingly, fandom, but not fanship, was more strongly tied to reading fanfiction. We suspect this may have to do with the fact that fanfiction is both created by other fans and is more likely to be spread to other fans via word-of-mouth than, say, new anime series released by big studios and advertised on Crunchyroll or Netflix.

[23] Despite fanship being much more strongly tied to J-Pop than fandom, the same could not be said for K-Pop (Korean Pop), where fanship and fandom were far more weakly tied to its consumption. This result may suggest that there is relatively little conceptual or functional overlap between J-Pop and K-Pop consumption among anime fans.

[24] Similar to fanfiction, AMVs are fan-produced and may be similarly tied up in social interaction between fans via word-of-mouth.

variable—lacking social skills,[25] which may account for both preferring to interact with other fans online instead of in-person and a person's tendency to identify less strongly with the fan community in general.

Variable	Fanship	Fandom
Number Anime Friends	-.02	.16**
Face-to-Face Friendships	.13**	.40**
Online Friendships	.21**	.18**
Shyness	.18**	-.17**
Awkward with Non-Fans	.27**	.01
Correct Japanese	.24**	-.02
Harmony in Discussion	.14**	.30**
Obsession	.53**	.08**
Identity Importance	.65**	.13**
Jealous Favorite Character	.18**	.02
Jealous Voice Actor	.11**	.03
Controllable Identity	-.22**	.05
Biological Essentialism	.19**	.06
Personal Stigma	.24**	-.16**
Private Collective Self-Esteem	< .01	.59**
Public Collective Self-Esteem	-.06	.41**
Identity Disclosure	.04	.28**

Table 10.3. Predicting friendships, obsession, stigma, disclosure, standardized betas presented, * $p < .05$, ** $p < .01$.

While fandom was more strongly tied to more frequent and harmonious social engagement, fanship tended to be more strongly tied to obsessive tendencies with respect to anime. For example, fanship strongly predicted the extent to which anime was considered to be an important part of one's identity. And, while this, by itself, doesn't speak to obsession, fanship, but not fandom, was also related to considering anime to be something one had little control over and could not stop (i.e., biological essentialism). Fanship

---

[25] Speaking further to this idea, fanship was associated with a stronger tendency to correct others' Japanese, something which may be seen as rude or inappropriate in some contexts, while fandom was associated more strongly with seeking harmony in discussions about anime.

240

also predicted feelings of jealousy when one's favorite character was in a romantic relationship with a different character, as well as when one's favorite voice actor was in a romantic relationship with another person. Taken together, fanship, at least for those who are rather high on it (and perhaps without being tempered by comparatively high scores in fandom) are associated with some less-flattering, socially awkward fan behaviors.

For this reason, it comes as little surprise that fanship is positively related to feeling personally stigmatized for being a fan, whereas fandom is negatively related to felt stigma. Fandom, but not fanship, predicts feeling a sense of self-esteem, both privately and publicly, about the anime fandom, and as such, people higher in fandom are also more likely to disclose their anime fan identity to others.

Immersion, Fantasy, Dreams

Anime fans in one of our studies were asked a number of questions about their fantasy engagement and the way in which they experienced anime content. As shown in Table 10.4, fanship was positively associated with all of the measures in this section, including fantasy engagement, immersion into anime while consuming it (i.e., getting sucked into the world, feeling like you're really there, losing track of time and space while watching), and having more anime-related dreams.

Variable	Fanship	Fandom
Negative Fantasy	.19**	-.04
Positive Fantasy	.41**	.20**
Time Fantasy	.40**	.10*
Immersion	.31**	.13**
Engagement	.31**	.14**
Transportation	.27**	.07*
Flow	.22**	.15**
Presence	.24**	.18**
Dreams in Anime World	.28**	.05
Dreams with Anime Characters	.27**	.04
Dreams Anime-Related	.28**	.04

Table 10.4. Predicting fantasy, immersion, dreams, standardized betas presented, * $p < .05$, ** $p < .01$.

On the one hand, these findings may suggest exactly why some fans become especially strong fans of anime. After all, relative to people who find it difficult to "get into" an anime series or who struggle to let their minds go and engage in fantasy, people who find anime to be incredibly immersive and who have especially active imaginations may be particularly drawn to anime and, thus, consider themselves to be especially big fans of anime content.

On the other hand, the results also speak to our earlier findings showing that anime fans may be more obsessive or engage in more concerning behavior. For instance, negative fantasy engagement refers to fantasy activities which are excessive or lead to problems with day-to-day functioning (e.g., family and friends being concerned about you). These scores are fairly robustly associated with fanship scores, providing converging evidence for the notion that especially high fanship may be a predictor of dysfunction or other problems among particular anime fans.[26]

Well-Being

We'll finish this chapter with a final set of findings, shown in Table 10.5. Across every measure of well-being we've assessed, we find that fanship is associated consistently with more well-being problems (e.g., depression, anxiety, stress) and lower well-being in general (physical, psychological, relationships). These findings are consistent with research from other fandoms (e.g., bronies) as well as with our prior findings suggesting that excessive fanship may be associated with obsession, excessive fantasy, and other worrisome beliefs and behavior. Fandom, on the other hand tends to be associated with positive well-being. This is likely due to social support from others in face-to-face friendships.

---

[26] This may well be the inspiration for stereotypes about anime fans as maladjusted, obsessive, or dysfunctional.

Variable	Fanship	Fandom
Depression	.13**	-.18**
Anxiety	.16**	-.15**
Stress	.14**	-.10**
Physical Well-Being	-.09	.18**
Psychological Well-Being	-.19**	.35**
Positive Relationships	-.19**	.32**
Self-Esteem	-.19**	.29**
Loneliness	.26**	-.31**
Satisfaction with Life	-.02	.19**

Table 10.5. Predicting well-being, standardized betas presented, $* p < .05$, $** p < .01$.

Conclusion

In this chapter we reviewed two psychological theories, social identity theory and self-categorization theory, which have been used by researchers to better understand fan behavior ranging from BIRGing and CORFing to fan loyalty, spending, and consumption behavior. We reviewed findings from both our own research and research by other scholars showing that fan identity should be considered in terms of both fanship and fandom since, despite being conceptually related to one another, they are differently associated with important fan-related outcomes. Fanship tends to predict greater consumption of anime and more purchasing of merchandise, more obsessive and socially unskilled behavior, and reduced well-being, whereas fandom tends to be associated with the social components of fandom (e.g., convention attendance) and with better well-being overall.

Chapter 11
Socialization: What We Learn from Being Anime Fans

In the previous chapter we looked what it means to identify as a fan and at how identifying with fan groups (or with any group, really) is linked to a number of fan-related thoughts and behaviors. We also briefly hinted at the idea that people are both aware of, and internalize, the norms and values[1] of their groups: We learn what's important to our groups and, wanting to be good, valued members of those groups, we change ourselves to align with those norms and values.[2] In short, the groups we're a part of shape the way we think, feel, and behave.

With this in mind, the present chapter aims to build upon the previous chapter by first considering the different roads into the anime fandom itself. We also consider several ways that the fandom affects people once they find themselves steeped in it. We then discuss whether there are differences in how people learn about and internalize the fandom's norms and values— for example, whether fans learn the same thing about the anime fandom if they primarily interact with it online versus in-person at conventions. Finally, we consider the practical impact of these socialization processes on fan behavior—whether the way we behave as fans is changed by the groups we're a part of.

The Path to Fandom

An ancient proverb states that "all roads lead to Rome." Setting aside the modern falseness of that statement, we can ask ourselves a thought-provoking follow-up question to this adage, are all of the roads to Rome the same?

That's the idea behind this first section of the chapter: To ask whether fans, despite being part of the same fandom, all arrived there in the same way. We know, for example, that members of different fandoms often find their respective fan communities in different ways. Whereas bronies

---

[1] Norms refer to what is seen as typical or average behavior in a group (e.g., there is a norm that people keep quiet while in a library). Values refer to the things that a group considers to be important (e.g., Americans value personal liberty and freedom of speech, treating these things as an important part of what it means to be American).

[2] Or, if we disagree with them, we may fragment off and start our own group, or leave to find another group that we're a better fit for.

typically joined the *My Little Pony* fandom through memes and friends convincing them to watch an episode ironically (only to later discover that they liked it; Edwards et al., 2019), older fandoms, like the *Star Trek* fandom, drew fans in through clubs, conventions, and fanfiction-writing circles (Mazar, 2006).

If you find yourself wondering "who cares *how* they became fans, what matters is the fact that they're fans *now*," know that you're not alone. In fact, until recently, few psychologists had focused their efforts on understanding how fans made their way into their respective fandoms (Hills, 2014). This isn't surprising, given that much of the psychological research has tended to focus on mainstream fan communities (e.g., sport fans). Because this content can be found everywhere in society, no one can reasonably claim that they know for sure the specific influence that nudged them toward their mainstream fan interest.[3] The same can't be said for smaller, non-mainstream communities. In some communities, like furries and bronies, fans can often pinpoint the precise moment they began their path into the fandom, often because it corresponds with the moment they first discovered it by accident or the moment a friend introduced them to it (Edwards et al., 2019; Reysen, Plante, Roberts, Gerbasi, Schroy et al., 2017).

So, where do anime fans fall? Do they tend to become fans purely by cultural osmosis, like sport fans, or, like members of smaller fandoms, do anime fans need to stumble upon it themselves or be shown the way?

The answer is "a little of both."[4] In some of our own studies, we've asked anime fans and furries to report how the source of introduction to the fandom (see Figure 11.1). The results show that stumbling upon anime online or being introduced to it through their friends were both bigger influences on anime fans' induction into the anime fandom than simply being exposed to anime through mainstream media, though not quite to the same extent as was the case for furries. We do see, however, that having

---

[3] Keeping with our sport fan example, sport fans' initial interest is typically the culmination of seeing them on TV, hearing about them in the news, watching people on the street wearing jerseys, playing sports in schools or in video games, or hearing their friends and families talk about them (e.g., Smith et al., 1981; Wann, Melnick et al., 2001).

[4] Not surprising, given that the popularity of anime is somewhat less than the global popularity of sports and the relative obscurity of small fandoms like the brony fandom.

access to a local anime club (e.g., at one's school) was just as impactful to anime fans' becoming fans as seeing anime in mainstream media.[5] These results offer quantitative support for some of the interview data by Napier (2007), who found that while many anime fans gained an initial interest in anime by seeing it on television, they made their way into the fandom itself through school clubs and the internet.

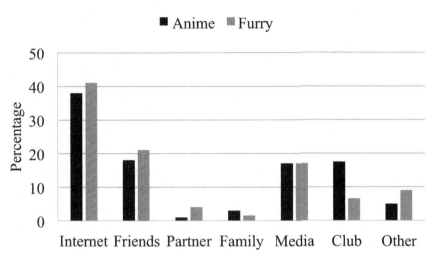

Figure 11.1. Fans' pathways to the fandom through various sources for anime fans and furries.

Socialization: Comparing Convention-Going and Online Fans

As Jenkins (1992) described, fans are far from passive consumers of their interests. While it's true that anime fans do consume a great deal of anime and have been known to spend a few dollars on their hobby from time to time (see Chapter 4), anime fans are far from mindless, passive consumers. Decades of interviews and ethnographic study of anime fan communities reveals, quite to the contrary, that fans interact with one

---

[5] In contrast, given how relatively rare furries are by comparison, there typically are no "furry clubs" in schools; state or provincial furry clubs are lucky to get a few dozen to a few hundred members, depending on how populous the region is.

another to discuss, debate, challenge, deconstruct, remix, and riff off of their hobby.

Anime fans, like most modern fan communities, have developed a very active following online, primarily as a means of seeking out new titles and interacting with the global fan community. However, it also has its origins in fans sharing recorded and translated recordings, manga, fanfiction, and fan artwork with one another face-to-face and at local meetups. This blend means that at least some anime fans will primarily engage with other fans through face-to-face interactions (e.g., attending fan conventions, meet-ups, etc.) while others will do so on forums, fan sites, and through social media. While research suggests that both groups satisfy similar psychological needs through similar psychological processes, there are notable differences in the way fans think and behave between these groups (Chadborn et al., 2018).

Interacting with Others

To be clear from the start, fans interact with one another both online and through face-to-face interaction. Few would deny that it's entirely possible to forge lifelong friends and important social support networks online just as one can do in person through clubs and fan conventions. For example, in our own studies, while convention-going fans were more likely to say that being an anime fan helps them make more face-to-face friends, online fans said that being an anime fan made them more likely to make online friends (see Figure 11.2).[6] These results paint a picture of social engagement occurring regardless of where it's taking place.

However, other results do suggest at least some differences between fans based on the modality with which they interact with the fandom. Fans who engage in more face-to-face interaction, for example, are more likely to also attend meetups, to have more friends in general, and to roleplay more, both online and in-person. Convention-going fans are also more likely to try and discuss anime with non-fans. Findings such as these may be explained by convention-going fans being more extraverted and having a greater tendency to seek out social situations (for more on extraversion in the anime fandom see Chapter 15).

---

[6] Unlike con-going fans, however, who say that being an anime fan also helps them make online friends, online friends do not report that being an anime fan helps them make face-to-face friends.

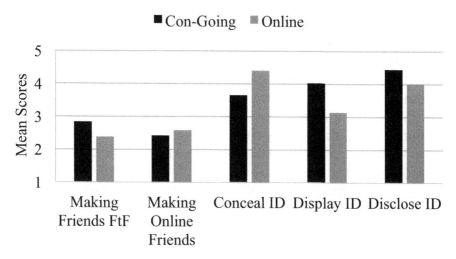

Figure 11.2. How being an anime fan helps with socialization, FtF = face-to-face.

Perception of Others

Perceiving stigma from the world around you can play a significant role in your own willingness to openly disclose being a fan of something. For example, prior research on the brony fandom shows that many bronies see themselves as violating gender norms by liking a show commonly seen as being made for young girls (Edwards et al., 2019). For these bronies, the stigma they expect to receive makes it harder for them to not only attend conventions and meetups, but even just to admit their interest around others.

It's likely that most anime fans can recall a time in which they chose to hide or outright deny their interest in anime out of fear that a boss, parent, or peer would judge them negatively for it.[7] Such expectations might explain why online fans may limit their interaction with other fans or even

---

[7] There's even an anime-themed name for this phenomenon, referred to as "hiding your power level," itself a reference to the series *Dragonball Z.*

their own consumption habits by restricting their purchase of DVDs, figures and other products: In Figure 11.2, we see that convention-going anime fans are more likely to disclose and outwardly display signs of their anime interests, while online anime fans are more likely to conceal it. This represents an example of how social pressures and perceived stigma from others leads to divisions in the way con-going and online anime fans engage with both anime content and with other fans.

Function of Anime for Fans

In this final section comparing convention-going anime fans and online anime fans with respect to the psychological functions that the fandom fulfills for both groups (see Figure 11.3). Across the various functions, convention-going fans routinely cited the anime fandom as being more useful in fulfilling that function than was the case for online anime fans. Put simply, for con-going anime fans, the anime fandom is a more functional, useful part of their life than it is for online anime fans, for whom it may be more likely to be "just a hobby."[8]

---

[8] Anecdotally speaking, we've observed fans in other fandoms occasionally making the distinction between "lifestyles" and "casual fans." While we haven't heard the term used often among anime fans, the distinction may get at the difference noted here, between fans for whom the fandom is integrated into many facets of their life (fulfilling many purposes) as opposed to fans for whom anime is simply a leisurely pastime.

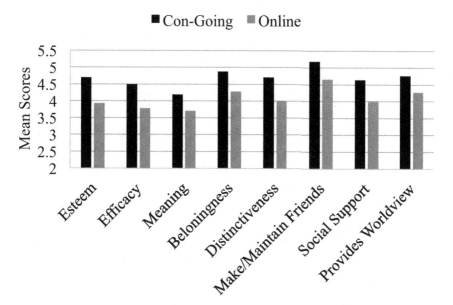

Figure 11.3. Function of fandom for anime fans.

Instead of delving into all of these different functions now (something we do in Chapter 14), for now we'll focus our attention on just a single function, fulfilling the need for belongingness.

Fans of all types likely to feel some sense of belonging to their fan community, something boosted by the presence of other fans. One can imagine that being at a fan convention, surrounded in-person by thousands of other fans, attending panels and events related to your interests, and being bombarded by the fan-related merchandise, the feeling of being immersed in one's fan community is at its peak.

Beyond the core functions of fandom already mentioned, convention attendees (vs. online) also report higher agreement that anime provides them with a worldview and further validates their existing worldviews. This may be because being in an environment where you're surrounded by anime content and anime fans can help make the norms and values of the community more salient to you as well, something that may provide you with a stronger sense of how the world works, what's important, and what is right or wrong. Research on the topic of group polarization, for example, shows that as like-minded people spend time together, their thoughts and beliefs begin to converge and become stronger, reinforcing and strengthening the group's initial beliefs (Stoner, 1968). While it might be a bit extreme to suggest that a person's religious or moral beliefs derive from the anime they consume, as we'll see in later chapters (e.g., Chapter 12), components of one's worldview can certainly be influenced by, or at least reinforced, by being among those who share the same view—something more likely to happen in-person to convention-going anime fans than online ones.

To this point, we have catalogued some of the associations between how fans socialize with the anime fandom (e.g., predominantly online versus in-person at conventions) and psychological or fan-relevant variables of interest. We have also speculated on some of the reasons why these associations may exist, including the important role of identity salience in bringing our groups' norms and values to the front of our mind. These norms and values, in turn, can both shape our worldview and the way we behave,[9] something we discuss in the next section.

Socialization Through Normative Learning

Research in social psychology has long established the connection between a person's social identity, the norms of their groups, and their own behavior (Hogg & Reid, 2006; Chadborn et al., 2016). Norms represent the rules of a group, spoken or unspoken, that govern the group's behavior, and they thus have the power to impact the members of that group, even when their group identity is not salient (Cialdini & Trost, 1998).[10] When groups accept or reject certain behaviors, ideas, or beliefs, we too accept or reject them the more strongly we identify with the group (Christensen et al., 2004).

Of course, groups need not explicitly state a belief or rule in order for us recognize and internalize them. For instance, research makes a clear distinction between what are called injunctive norms and descriptive norms (Cialdini et al., 1990). Injunctive norms represent a group's stated values

---

[9] The logic being that if fans see specific behaviors or aspects of worldview as routinely being considered acceptable and normal in their fan community, they, as members of that community, will start to endorse those behaviors and engage in them more.

[10] Or, as self-help book author Dr. Steve Maraboli (2013) suggested, those who hang out with chickens are going to cluck while those who associate with eagles fly.

and expected responses of behavior. As an example, a group might espouse the importance of acceptance and tolerance and a willingness to punish those who behave in an intolerant way. Descriptive norms, in contrast, are how group members actually behave, regardless of injunctive norms. So, even though there may be an official policy of tolerance in a group, if group members ignore this policy and routinely behave in bigoted ways, it says something powerful about fans' actual beliefs and what is normal in the group.[11] Moreover, if other group members are following the norms and are in close proximity to you (i.e., they have the ability to inflict consequences on you), there is considerable pressure on you to fall in line with, and internalize, the group's norms.

With all of this in mind, we can talk about the norms which exist in the anime community, both for better and for worse, as well as factors that may influence a fan's willingness to internalize these norms.

Anime Fans and Contradictory Norms

In a community as broad in both geographical reach and in terms of content as the anime fandom, one might expect that the fandom's norms may be difficult to pin down—if there can even be said to be a consistent set of norms across the fandom as a whole.

For example, anime fans across our studies frequently indicate the importance of acceptance and inclusivity within the fandom, emphasizing the need for fans to accept one another for who they are. Despite this stated norm, however, some fans demonstrate considerable willingness to look down upon other fans for their preferred genre or interests in the anime fandom, illustrating both elitist attitudes and gatekeeping behavior that runs counter to the fandom's stated norms of tolerance and acceptance. While anime fans express a general disregard for traditional sex roles within their community, there is also a positive relationship between identifying more strongly as an anime fan and sexist beliefs. Likewise, while the fandom itself purports to be opposed to ethnocentrism and prejudice, one can still

---

[11] Another common example of this distinction involves a no littering sign (injunctive) surrounded by a bunch of litter on the ground (descriptive). Seeing this tells you something about peoples' regard for the laws and willingness to ignore them in these parts, and may influence your willingness to litter as well.

find support for authoritarianism and acceptance of ethnocentric ideas in some corners of the fandom.[12]

Contradictions like these illustrate the distinction between the fandom's injunctive norms (tolerance and acceptance) and descriptive norms (pockets of fans and places where these norms are mocked or disregarded). They also raise questions of how such contradictions arise, and whether we can predict when they're more likely to arise. One plausible candidate, based on our prior discussion, may be the extent to which one's fan identity is made salient, something which is more likely to occur in-person at meet-ups and conventions and, which may help fans better internalize the fandom's injunctive norms of tolerance and acceptance.

Speaking to this idea, we turn to data looking at sexism in the fandom. Our studies show, for example, that convention-going fans are less likely to endorse traditional gender roles than are online fans—something which may owe to the fact that convention-going fans are also more likely to be women than is the case among online fans (see Chapter 3 for more on this). However, convention-going fans also scored slightly higher on measures of sexism (see Figure 11.4).[13] One possible explanation for this finding is that sexism may be reinforced through activities which take place more at conventions but not online (e.g., cosplay). Another possibility is that content and discussion of genres more closely tied to sexist beliefs (e.g., hentai, see Chapter 9) may be present at conventions. Regardless of the reason, the data seem to be suggesting that, if anything, having a more salient anime fan identity seems to be associated with increased endorsement of values and beliefs that run counter to the fandom's stated injunctive norms of acceptance and tolerance, and may speak to power of witnessing first-hand descriptive norms which violate the fandom's injunctive norms (e.g., witnessing sexism in-person at a convention).[14] Further research is needed to disentangle these results.

---

[12] At least for groups in the majority.

[13] It is worth keeping in mind, as we've stated elsewhere in this book, that fans still scored well below the midpoint of both scales. Also, these differences are not large (but they are there).

[14] This is just speculation, for now. Future research is needed to test this hypothesis.

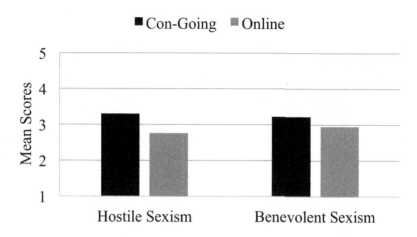

Figure 11.4. Online and con-going anime fan differences on sexism.

Positive Norms Within the Community

While the previous section demonstrated a negative norm rearing its ugly head with respect to increased fan identity salience (e.g., being a con-going fan), it's certainly not all bad. Let's finish up on a positive note, shall we?

Recall that one of the distinguishing features of the anime fandom is its global reach, representing a global fandom.[15] As such, it should come as no surprise that many anime fans see the anime fandom as strengthened by its cosmopolitan atmosphere, leading to a norm which encourages open-mindedness to people from other cultures and a willingness to think of oneself as part of a global community, including the need to look out for and support people across the globe as one would show care and compassion to their neighbor.

As seen in Figure 11.5, when we asked participants in our studies about their agreement with global citizenship ideas (a topic we discuss at length in Chapter 12), they largely scored above the midpoint on the scale.

---

[15] This should be especially salient to Western fans in particular, who are, themselves, fans of Japanese media by definition!

Importantly, these scores were higher for convention-going fans than they were for online fans. Moreover, these same fans were both willing to give and to receive help from others in the fandom (at least as indicated in our surveys), in line with these values of helping one another out as part of a global community. Taken together, these findings reinforce the idea that having a stronger and more salient fan identity is associated with greater endorsement of prosocial norms and values, including, among other things, a greater concern for social justice, valuing of diversity, and a greater sense of responsibility and desire to help those in need, wherever they may be from.

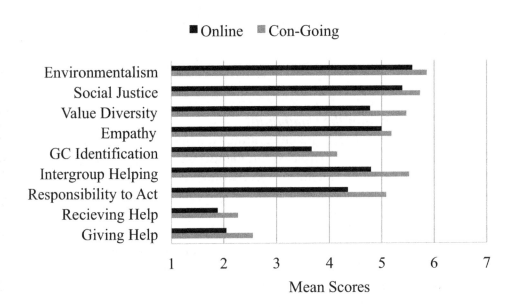

Figure 11.5. Online and con-going anime fan differences in prosocial factors and global citizenship (see Chapter 12).

Conclusion

Throughout this chapter we've seen numerous examples of how fan communities are associated with fans' norms and values, including the extent to which they socialize with the fandom in ways that make their group identity more salient to them (e.g., face-to-face at conventions versus online). We discussed how the path fans take into the community may influence the way they engage with their community, which in turn may have downstream effects on how influenced they are by the fandom and to what extent they internalize the group's norms. For better and for worse, fans internalize both the injunctive and descriptive norms of their communities, an important counterpoint to those who trivialize fan activities as frivolous, pointless, or as little more than mindless consumption of content. As this chapter has shown, anime fans, like other fan groups, are far from passive consumers, and actively influence—and are influenced by—the communities which spring up around their interests.

Chapter 12
Global Citizenship

Technically speaking, anime fans who don't live in Japan are consumers of media content from a foreign culture. Or, to put it in scholarly speak, anime is *transcultural* (Annett, 2014). The fact that anime is transcultural is far from trivial or a mere coincidence: For some fans, the differing societal norms that are baked into anime are a big part of its appeal![1]

This raises an interesting question for media scholars: If we're all influenced by the media we consume,[2] what are the effects of regularly consuming media that prominently features characters, settings, norms, and values of other cultures?

Brenner (2007) suggests that anime fans, as consumers of products from another culture, should, as a result of this consumption, develop a better understanding not just of Japanese culture, but of global culture. This is, in part, because exposure to other cultures helps fans to think critically about their own culture. In this respect, consuming anime expands fans' global awareness, or understanding that there are other cultures in the world filled with people who think and behave differently than they do.

With theory suggesting that anime should have this important, paradigm-shifting effect on the way anime fans see themselves and the world around them, the present chapter explores the concept of global citizenship in the anime fandom. Specifically, we examine aspects of anime content and the anime fandom itself to see whether there is any evidence that anime consumption impacts a person's likelihood of identifying as a global citizen and what practical, real-world impact this may have. We begin by first reviewing the theory behind global citizenship identification, along with prior research on the subject, before delving into the results of the present research on global citizenship within the anime fandom.

---

[1] Consider the vast number of young travelers who cite anime as their initial, or even primary reason to want to travel to Japan!

[2] Media consumers often have a knee-jerk response to this statement, denying that media have any discernable impact on the way they think, feel, and behave. Decades of psychological research suggests otherwise (e.g., Plante et al., 2019).

A Model of Global Citizenship Identification

Before we begin, let's make sure we have a solid definition of what global citizenship is. Global citizenship is defined by scholars "as global awareness, caring, embracing cultural diversity, promoting social justice and sustainability, and a sense of responsibility to act" (Reysen et al., 2012, p. 29). In other words, global citizenship is the recognition that we are part of a global community, which carries with it both the benefits of diverse cultural products, art, and ideas, but also the responsibilities of needing to help others around the world and be mindful of our impact on them.

The concept of global citizenship has been exponentially growing in academic circles (see Reysen & Katzarska-Miller, 2018), but it also is slowly working its way into common usage (e.g., Global Citizen music festival). Perhaps the largest area of growth has been in scholarly work focusing on education. For example, there has been a considerable push among K-12 teachers and administrators to include more global curriculum in classes. Likewise, universities are increasingly working to recruit international students, encourage exchange programs, and forge international partnerships, recognizing the benefits for students and faculty alike.

In short, while the general public may only just becoming aware of the importance of global citizenship, educators have increasingly been aware of the need to expand society's worldview. We'll describe these myriad benefits later in this chapter when we describe the outcomes of viewing the self as a member of a global community. However, for now, having defined what global citizenship is, let's next turn our attention to the question of what causes someone to identify as a global citizen in the first place.

Predictors of Global Citizenship Identification

To get an understanding of the causes and outcomes of global citizenship, we turn to a model proposed by Reysen and Katzarska-Miller (2013). Within this model, they propose that identifying as a global citizenship means feeling a sense of psychological connection to the label "global citizen." As we discussed in Chapter 10, a social identity perspective (Tajfel & Turner, 1979; Turner et al., 1987) on this self-labeling would argue that identifying as a global citizen means seeing yourself as part of a group of like-minded global citizens, including being attached to other ingroup members and taking on their norms and values as your own.

Reysen and Katzarska-Miller go on to argue that two major factors predict a person's tendency to identify as a global citizen: norms in their environment and global awareness. They based this on work by Richard Shweder (1990), who argued that we all live in a world filled with meaning that was constructed by people who came before us.[3] And, whether intentionally or unintentionally, the worlds they created for us shape us, since we tend to internalize their norms and values and reproduce them in the world.[4] As a bit of a silly example, if someone grows up in a culture where wearing trucker hats is cool, they are likely to don a trucker hat themselves, something which others will see and also pick up.[5]

With all of this in mind, let's consider what happens as the world becomes an increasingly globalized place. One effect is that people have more groups they can identify with (along with their associated norms and values). For example, if anime was not transported from Japan to the world, being an anime fan would not be an identity available (or even on the radar) for most people around the world. A globalized world thus provides people with access to social identities primarily available in other countries.[6] It also provides us with a novel identity: that of a global citizen, an identity that transcends international borders.

We can find evidence for this reciprocal relationship, where culture shapes people and people shape culture, in a study by Miyamoto et al. (2006). The researchers took pictures of streets in small, medium, and large cities in the U.S. and Japan. They noted that city streets in Japan (vs. U.S.) tend to be filled with more objects (i.e., they were busier, more complex).

---

[3] It's not hard to look around and see examples of this for yourself. You walk along streets named by other people, pay with money adorned with those that our society considers to be important, sit in classes, work, and vote in systems organized by people who are not us, and pass by historical monuments dedicated to those who lived well before your time.

[4] Not everyone does, of course; some people reject these norms and values, or twist/modify them and put back into the world. But this tends to be the exception rather than the rule.

[5] In line with our above footnote, some will choose not wear a trucker hat, hoping to kill the fad, or they may wear a trucker hat in a novel way that creates a new trend (if others do the same).

[6] It also provides a useful model to help us understand the spread of certain shows, memes, and products.

They then showed these images to undergraduate students in the U.S. and in Japan, and then asked the students to complete a change-blindness task.[7]

In general, Japanese participants tended to notice changes to background or distant objects more than U.S. participants. However, *both* U.S. and Japanese participants could be made to notice more contextual changes if they were previously looking at Japanese (vs. U.S.) streets. In other words, the city streets themselves are constructed in ways that impact the way people who live in those environments see the world—a demonstration of how our culture shapes us. Viewing those streets impacted one's perception of the world (even in a short laboratory experiment). What's more, the researchers note that when Japanese people are asked to take photographs or draw scenes, they tend to include more context and deemphasize the focal object.[8] In other words, Japanese people are not only shaped by their culture (e.g., how busy their streets are), but they reproduce this perceptual tendency in the works they create, perpetuating that tendency.

This is part of the backbone of the global citizenship model, the idea that one's culture shapes their identity. In the case of global citizenship, the extent to which a person sees global citizenship as the norm (e.g., being valued by others) indicates to them whether being a global citizen is desirable. This can include everything from seeing billboards advertising media from other countries to role models who idealize global citizenship (e.g., teachers encouraging students to consider the perspectives of other countries and the presence of world maps in classrooms).

A second factor that predicts global citizenship is one's perceived knowledge of the world and how connected they feel with others in the world. Importantly, we describe "perceived knowledge" rather than "objective knowledge," since it may be more important that a person simply feels knowledgeable about the world than it is that they are actually

---

[7] In a change blindness task, participants watch a picture as it slowly transforms into a very similar, but slightly different picture. For example, in a picture of a city street, the height of a pole might change or an airplane might appear gradually in the sky over the course of one minute. The researchers then ask if participants noticed the changes.

[8] Think of a travel photo: The person is the focal point and the landmark they're standing in front of is the background. Japanese people tend to take pictures where the person is smaller relative to the background behind them (as compared to U.S. people).

knowledgeable about it in the case of seeing oneself as a global citizen.[9] Related to this perceived knowledge about the world is one's felt sense of interconnectedness with others, which reflects an understanding of the globalized world we live in today (e.g., the fact that most of the products we consume are produced in other countries).

Ultimately, the extent to which our culture endorses global citizenship norms and our own perceived knowledge and awareness of the globalized world are related to one another. If we see others around us encouraging a global citizen identity, we too will be more likely to perceive ourselves as globally aware. When the cultures around us promote seeing yourself as a global citizen and promote knowledge about the world, we are more likely to take on the identity of a global citizen.

Identification and Outcomes

Okay, so people, as a result of the culture around them, may be more likely to label themselves as global citizens. What does this mean?

Well, as we've noted before, according to the social identity perspective (Tajfel & Turner, 1979; Turner et al., 1987), salient identities lead to stronger adherence to the norms of that identity. In other words, the more strongly we belong to a group and the more the group is on our minds, the more we take on the beliefs, behaviors, and values of that group.

So, what norms or values are tied to global citizenship? Researchers suggest at least six clusters of prosocial values:

(1) Intergroup empathy: concern for others outside of one's ingroup.

(2) Valuing diversity: an interest and appreciation for other cultures.

(3) Social justice: the endorsement of human rights and the equitable treatment of all people.

(4) Environmental sustainability: a desire to protect the natural environment through environmentally responsible actions.

(5) Intergroup helping: a desire to aid people outside one's ingroup.

(6) A felt responsibility to act: a moral duty or obligation to act for the betterment of the world.

In effect, viewing oneself as a global citizen is associated with beliefs and behaviors that aid others and the natural environment. Given this, and

---

[9] That said, it's often the case that if one knows a lot of facts about the world, they also probably perceive themselves to be knowledgeable.

since most people will agree that most, if not all of these values are fairly desirable, it should be apparent why global citizenship has gained traction in schools, academia, and activist organizations.

Anime Fans and Global Citizenship

Having established what global citizenship is, what predicts it, and what sorts of outcomes it's associated with, we can now turn to global citizenship in the anime fandom.

First, to examine the association between fan groups in general and global citizenship, Plante and colleagues (2014) conducted a study comparing samples of furries and U.S. community members on measures of the antecedents of global citizenship, global citizenship identification, and the outcomes of global citizenship. Since the furry fandom has norms that revolve around accepting others, valuing diversity, and environmental sustainability (especially protecting natural wildlife), the researchers suggested that being a furry may predict greater global citizenship identification as compared to a sample of U.S. community members.

Furries (vs. non-furries) reported that their normative environments (e.g., friends, family, and the people around them) valued global citizenship more and they also reported having a stronger sense of global awareness (antecedents to global citizenship identification). Furries were also more likely to identify themselves as global citizens. The comparison (furry vs. non-furry) also had an indirect effect on the endorsement of the six prosocial outcomes mentioned above. In other words, being a furry, surrounded by other furries who value global citizenship, has a downstream influence not only on their identification as global citizens, but also on their endorsement of prosocial values and beliefs.

So, what about anime fans?

As noted in Chapter 11, scoring higher on fandom identification tends to be associated with more interpersonal fan activities (e.g., face-to-face meetups, conventions, watching anime together). Given this, it would seem that more strongly-identified anime fans would be more likely to interact with other anime fans who, potentially having stronger norms in support of global citizenship (given that anime itself comes from another country), might lead fans themselves to more strongly identify as global citizens. As such, we measured anime fans' fandom identification, along with measures of the antecedents (normative environment and global awareness) of global citizenship, identification as a global citizen, and the outcomes of global citizenship—similar to the study of furries above.

The first difference we observed was striking: Unlike furries, anime fans showed levels of global citizenship that were comparable, not greater than, those observed in studies of U.S. undergraduate college students. In other words, just being an anime fan isn't enough to make a person more likely to identify as a global citizen.[10]

This wasn't the entire story, however. Other aspects of the fandom play an important role, as we'll see in a moment.

Despite anime fans not scoring higher than non-fans on global citizenship, stronger anime fandom identification did nevertheless predict scores on the antecedents of global citizenship, which turn predicted global citizenship identification and prosocial outcomes (see Figure 12.1). Specifically, the more anime fans felt psychologically connected with other fans, the more likely they were to view those around them as prescribing a global citizen identity and the more they perceived themselves as globally aware, which led to more global citizenship identification and all the prosocial values that come with it.

The results suggest that simply being an anime fan might not be associated with global citizenship and prosocial values, but that specifically identifying more strongly with the anime fandom is.

Cosplayers

Given that previous chapters have noted differences between various subgroups within the anime fandom, we sought to compare cosplayers to non-cosplayers with respect to global citizenship. After all, cosplayers tend to differ from non-cosplaying anime fans on dimensions that may make them more likely to be global citizens. For example, cosplayers score higher on measures of openness to new experiences (see Chapter 7), something which has been found to be related to global citizenship in prior research (Jenkins et al., 2012). Cosplayers also tend to score fairly high on measures of fandom (see Chapter 7), meaning that they should be

---

[10] It's important to note that other studies suggest that younger people tend to hold more of the prosocial values that are reflected in the outcomes of global citizenship (Norris, 2000). This may also be the reason anime fans as a whole did not differ from college students, as both groups tend to be higher on global citizenship values, if for different reasons (anime fans being younger, college students being educated in fairly progressive institutions).

especially likely to internalize any global citizenship norms present in the anime fandom. As shown in Figure 12.2, cosplayers, compared to non-cosplaying anime fans, did score higher on the predictors of global citizenship (greater normative environment and global awareness) which, in turn, predicted greater global citizen identification and stronger endorsement of prosocial values.

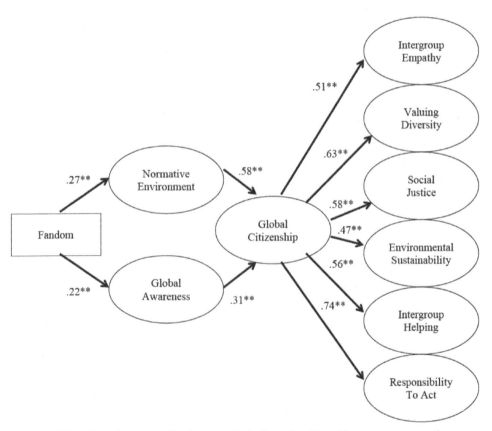

Figure 12.1. Fandom predicting model. Standardized betas presented, ** $p < .01$.

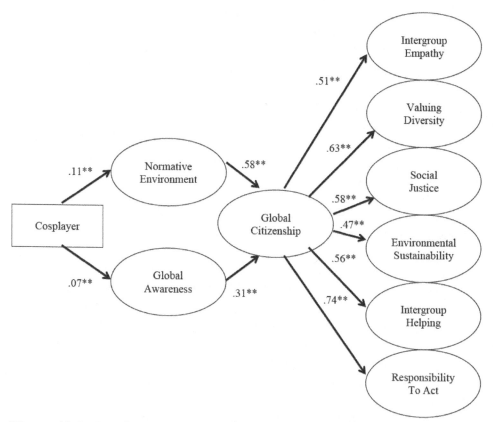

Figure 12.2. Cosplayer (vs. non-cosplayer) predicting model. Standardized betas presented, ** $p < .01$.

Sources of Influence in the Community

Reysen, Katzarska-Miller, and colleagues (2020) also examined four potential sources within the anime fandom that may promote global citizenship:

(1) Anime content: Prosocial themes involving helping others, social justice, empathy, cooperating with others, and environmental

sustainability (Napier, 2007).[11] The meanings and messages portrayed in anime content may encourage fans to endorse global citizenship.

(2) Anime creators: Many fans read interviews with and follow creators on social media. If creators express opinions supportive of global citizenship, fans may take note and change their attitudes and behaviors to match.

(3) Voice actors: Like creators, voice actors hold a prominent place within the fandom and are often the public face of the shows they voice (e.g., holding press announcements and attending conventions; Clements & McCarthy, 2015). Similar to anime creators, they may serve as role models for prosocial values.

(4) Other fans: As pointed out in Plante et al. (2014), other fans may normalize global citizenship. If an anime fan believes that other fans view global citizenship positively, they may align themselves more closely to this norm.

To test whether these four sources contribute to global citizenship among anime fans, Reysen, Katzarska-Miller et al. (2020) asked anime fans about the extent to which they saw each of these sources as promoting global citizenship, along with measures of the predictors of, identification with, and outcomes of global citizenship. As shown in Figure 12.3, the anime content and other fans specifically predicted the predictors of global citizenship. Voice actors only predicted perceptions of global citizenship norms in one's normative environment, but not global awareness, while anime creators were not associated with either of the predictors of global citizenship. In short, while anime fandom is associated with global citizenship, there is no clear, single explanation for why this is the case.

---

[11] For example, Hayao Miyazaki films often contain themes endorsing environmental sustainability (Napier, 2006).

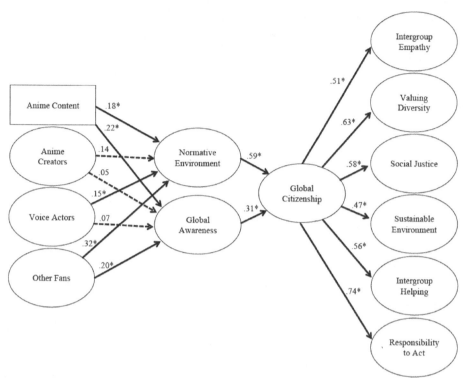

Figure 12.3. Aspects of anime fandom predicting model. Standardized betas presented, ** *p* < .01.

Conclusion

Following the publication of the global citizenship model, researchers have sought to examine various psychological variables that can help predict a person's likelihood of becoming a global citizen (see Reysen & Katzarska-Miller, 2018). In the present chapter, after reviewing the model, we explored various facets of the anime fandom (identification with the anime community, being a cosplayer, anime content and other anime fans) that are associated with the predictors of global citizenship. While anime fans, as a group, do not differ from college students when it comes to their average levels of global citizenship, the results suggest that this is because there is no single relationship between anime fandom and global citizenship. All anime fans are different, interacting with some facets of anime fanship and fandom more than others, and this variability may explain why only some anime fans score higher than the typical undergraduate student.

Chapter 13
Elitism, Entitlement, Gatekeeping, and Drama

Human beings are an inherently social species—owing, in no small part, to the tribal nature of our primate ancestors. We naturally organize ourselves and the world around us into groups and pay a great deal of attention to who falls into our group and who doesn't. As we discussed at length in previous chapters (e.g., Chapter 10), part of our reason for doing so is to ensure that we belong to groups that are both distinct and desirable (e.g., Jetten et al., 1996; Tajfel & Turner, 1979). To this end, our self-esteem is based, at least in part, on whether we belong to groups that reflect positively on us, and so we aim to be positive, high-ranking members of our groups while cultivating those groups to be as exclusive and desirable as possible.

The present chapter considers several topics related to these ideas of becoming high-ranking members of our groups and shaping our groups to be exclusive and desirable. We begin by taking a look at psychological research on the concept of elitism—when one sees themselves as being better than others—in fan groups. We then look at one downstream consequence of elitism, gatekeeping—feeling like you're entitled to decide who should or shouldn't be allowed in your group. Next, we take a step back and look at other manifestations of that feeling of entitlement in fans, including measuring how prevalent feelings of entitlement are among fans and some of the variables that predict fan entitlement. Finally, since elitism, gatekeeping, and entitlement are likely to be a source of conflict in fandoms, we finish this chapter by discussing the scientific study of fandom drama.

Elitism

The drive to improve ourselves and test our skills is a fairly fundamental one in humans (Deci & Ryan, 2000). We can see this across the full range of human abilities: athletes competing to be the strongest or fastest, scholars pursuing the boundaries of human understanding, artists pushing themselves to become greater at their craft, and yes, most presently relevant, in fans who want to distinguish themselves among other fans.

What does it mean to excel as a fan and become an "elite" fan? As it turns out, that differs from fandom to fandom and from person to person.

For some, being an elite fan means knowing more fandom-related trivia.[1] For others, being an elite fan means devoting more time and effort than others to their fan interest.[2] A few fans might even limit being an elite fan to being part of the select few who have the ability to influence the fandom's content itself—being a content creator or having access to renowned content creators.

When we think about fan elitism, we intuitively treat it like a singular concept, as something you have more or less of. A closer look at the concept of elitism, however, suggests that it may actually be comprised of two distinct, but related concepts: self-inflation and other-derogation.

Self-inflation is the process of focusing on all the things that make you great and which elevate you above other people. The gamer who marvels at the number of hours they've put into their favorite game or the furry who obsesses over how much their fursuit cost is engaging in self-inflation.[3]

Other-derogation, on the other hand, involves making downward comparisons toward other fans, emphasizing the ways that they're not as good as you. For instance, a *Star Trek* fan may revel in the fact that other fans don't know an obscure fact or background detail. Or, as a real example, cosplayers and fanfiction writers sometimes spend time seeking out examples of bad or cringe-inducing cosplay or fanfiction online[4] (e.g., Zubernis & Larsen, 2012) or, in some noteworthy examples, in-person (Matthias, 2018).

The dual processes of self-inflation and other-derogation are hardly unique to anime or science fiction fans. For example, as we mentioned in Chapter 10, people often bask in the glory of their own achievements and in

---

[1] Imagine *Star Trek* fans arguing over who knows more about the technical details of fictional spaceships.

[2] Gamers often brag about the thousands of hours they put into their favorite games and furries frequently brag about how many thousands of dollars they spent on their fursuit.

[3] Of course, self-inflation doesn't *have* to be malicious or mean-spirited. There's certainly nothing wrong with feeling pride in one's accomplishments! After all, many people are legitimately elites in their craft and, in and of itself, this isn't a problem!

[4] This, by the way, is absolutely a thing. There are, for instance, numerous social media pages and websites dedicated to mocking fanfiction writers or cosplayers who are deemed to be cringe-worthy or unskilled. Regardless of any high-minded rhetoric about wanting to motivate these creators to improve themselves through shaming, few can deny that the appeal of these sites is to take glee in the embarrassment of others.

the achievements of ingroup members to feel better about themselves, an example of self-inflation (Cialdini et al., 1976). Research is also full of examples showing that people often compare themselves to others who are doing worse than they are, including sick people who bolster their spirits by comparing themselves to sicker people (e.g., Buunk et al., 2002). In short, psychologists have long known that people naturally compare themselves to others in ways chosen to make them look better.

With this in mind, we recently published a series of psychological studies looking at elitism in several fandoms, including the anime fandom (Plante, Reysen, Chadborn et al., 2020). The results from the furry fandom and the *My Little Pony* fandom both showed that both self-inflation and other-derogation were present among these fans—although self-inflating attitudes are somewhat more prevalent than other-derogating attitudes.[5] Follow-up analyses revealed that a sense of fanship—identifying strongly as a fan of particular content—was positively correlated with both self-inflation and other-derogation tendencies, and that self-inflation was positively correlated with other-derogation. In other words, the more one considers themselves to be a fan of something, the more likely they are to engage in *both* self-inflation and other-derogation. Moreover, self-inflation and other-derogation seem to go hand-in-hand: People who self-inflate are more likely to other-derogate than people who do not, and vice versa.

What about the anime fandom? Do anime fans similarly self-enhance and other-derogate?

In a word, yes. We found the same general pattern of results among anime fans, with anime fanship being positively correlated with self-inflation, but not with other-derogation. In contrast, identifying more with the anime fandom—that is, with other anime fans—was far less strongly associated with self-inflation—and was even associated with significantly *lower* other-derogation.[6]

---

[5] This could be because people are less likely to look down on others than they are to puff themselves up. It could also be because it's less socially acceptable to derogate others, and participants in our study were unwilling to admit to looking down on other fans.

[6] It's pretty hard to look down on other fans and see them in a negative light when you strongly identify with those other fans!

Moving beyond the analyses of the anime fans in that one article, let's look at some additional datasets and follow-up analyses to see what else we can learn about elitism in the anime fandom.

For one thing, when we asked specifically about the extent to which anime fans felt like they had higher status than others in the anime fandom, con-going and online anime fans did not differ significantly from one another; most fans in both groups tended to see themselves as comparable in status than other fans (see Figure 13.1). As such, it seems that elitism—at least with respect to seeing oneself as better than other fans, is less common than one might expect to find in the anime fandom.[7]

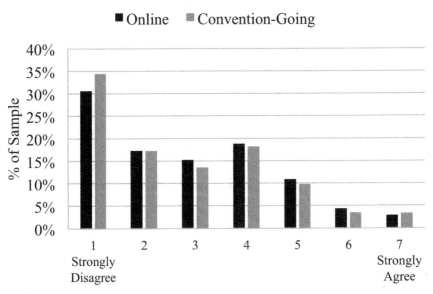

Figure 13.1. Extent to which online and convention-going anime fans felt that they were higher status than the average anime fan.

---

[7] We say "less common than one might expect" because, in theory, if everyone was perfectly aware of their status then, in theory, half of all anime fans should be higher in status than the average anime fan as a matter of mathematical principle. Instead, only about 40% of anime fans feel their status is higher than average, suggesting that, if anything, many anime fans are *underestimating* their status!

Other analyses of anime fans found ways to predict which fans would score higher on measures of elitism. For example, those who consider the fandom to be deeply significant and meaningful for them were also more likely to hold elitist attitudes.[8] This may play into the distinction fans sometimes make between "casual fans" and "lifestylers" whose interest permeates every facet of their life. It's not hard to imagine a person who takes anime that seriously being annoyed by those who say they just like the way anime looks or who only watch the occasional episode.

Related to this idea, analyses also revealed that those who watch the most anime, spend the most time reading anime-related news, post the most on anime-related forums, and who spend more time talking about anime with other people also tend to view themselves as more elite than other fans. Of course, few would argue that if there was such a thing as an "objective ranking" of how big of an anime fan was, those who consume the most anime would probably rank high on this list. Nevertheless, as we see in the next section, elitist attitudes are tied to negative behaviors. As such, fans should consider some of the downsides that come about from excessively consuming anime, including, among other things, its effects on the way they may treat other fans.

Finally, we found a scattered set of other variables that predict elitism in the anime fandom. For example, politically conservative anime fans are more likely than liberal fans to adopt elitist views.[9] We also found that hentai fans were also more likely than non-hentai fans to hold elitist attitudes.

Taken together, we found evidence that anime fans are just like any other group when it comes to the very-human tendency to want to see oneself in a positive light by inflating oneself and looking down upon others. This tendency is especially pronounced in those who identify with their interest in anime (high fanship), but not necessarily with other anime fans (low fandom).

---

[8] For example, fans who say that anime gives them a sense of meaning in their life or fans who use anime to help them grow as a person or to guide their day-to-day actions.

[9] This finding is actually in-line with political psychology research on right-wing views which shows that those with conservative ideologies are more likely to see the world in terms of hierarchies (e.g., Morrison & Ybarra, 2009).

Okay, but so what? Is it necessarily a bad thing to think of yourself as better than other fans? We'll address this question in the following sections, starting with a look at gatekeeping behavior.

Gatekeeping

Gatekeepers are like the bouncers at a nightclub: They determine who gets in and who stays outside. Bouncers help preserve the exclusivity and safety of the club by keeping out undesirables and potential threats. Gatekeepers try to do the same thing, tasking themselves with preserving the integrity of the fandom, protecting those within it, and keeping out potential sources of drama.[10]

How did anime fans score on a scale of gatekeeping? In one of our recent studies of anime fans, we found that they scored an average of 2.65 / 7.00 on a gatekeeping scale—well below the scale's midpoint. In other words, anime fans were largely against pro-gatekeeping attitudes. Online anime fans did score significantly higher—about half a point higher (2.72 vs. 2.31)—than convention-going fans. As Figure 13.2 shows, this difference was predominantly driven by the fact that convention-going fans were about twice as likely as online fans to score at the very bottom of the scale, while online fans were more likely to score at around the midpoint of the scale. In general, remarkably few fans from either group scored above the scale's midpoint.

Gatekeeping is hardly unique to anime fans, and can be found across fan cultures, though the extent and formality of these efforts varies. For example, some fandoms decry or outright deny the membership of superficial or shallow members (Zubernis & Larsen, 2012), like gamers and the stigmatization of "fake gamer girls"[11] and casual gamers.[12] In both

---

[10] Or, to paraphrase Dunlap and Wolf (2010), gatekeepers are fans who insist that other fans don't belong by accusing them of making the fandom look bad.

[11] This refers to the stereotype of a girl that surrounds herself with the trappings of gamer culture for attention without actually becoming knowledgeable about gaming or understanding and respecting the norms of gamer culture (Scott, 2019).

[12] Some gaming communities have pushed back against adding an "easy mode" to difficult games like *Dark Souls*, arguing that an easy experience is inauthentic and that including it to improve the game's accessibility would cheapen the accomplishment of beating the game and compromise the integrity of the game's fanbase (e.g., Sterling, 2019; Wynne, 2017).

cases, fans are trying to prevent the dilution of their devoted fanbase with casual or non-committed fans that may not endorse the fandom's norms.

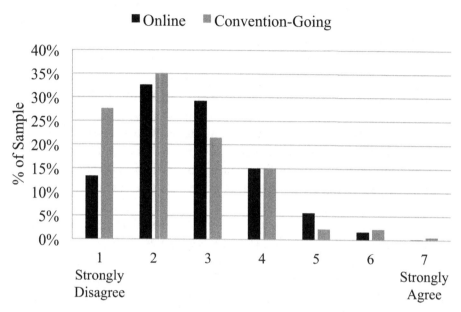

Figure 13.2. Extent to which online and convention-going anime fans endorsed pro-gatekeeping attitudes.

In other contexts, however, gatekeeping is more about protecting the image of the fandom or avoiding the corruption of the fandom's core norms and values. In the furry fandom, for example, gatekeeping efforts aim to distinguish "furry art"—art featuring anthropomorphized animal characters—from art portraying acts of bestiality—sexual acts with non-human animals—and, in some cases, have led to banning the sharing of images that could be construed as bestiality or zoophilia (e.g., FurryLife Online, 2020). Similar discussions have emerged in the anime fandom with respect to the banning of sexualized portrayals of prepubescent characters (e.g., lolicon / shotacon; u/Impressive-Pin, 2019).

Existing research supports the idea that gatekeeping has a number of functions. For example, if our self-esteem is tied to the groups we belong to, we should be motivated to make sure the group is a positive, desirable one

(Tajfel & Turner, 1979). As such, group members should want to exclude those who would undermine the group's ability to make us look good (e.g., Eidelman & Biernat, 2002; Ojala & Nesdale, 2004).

Others have suggested that the act of gatekeeping itself helps to forge and solidify a fan group's sense of identity by rallying it against an external, undesirable group (e.g., Shirky, 2003). In other words, by rallying against particular groups, fans can define themselves by what they are against just as much as they can define themselves by what they are in support of.

Intuitively, gatekeeping and elitism seem to go hand-in-hand. After all, if you're going to judge another fan as "unworthy" or "undesirable," you're assuming that you are knowledgeable enough and have enough status within the fandom to make that sort of judgment.[13] Furthermore, if you plan on those judgments to call for the removal or exclusion of other fans from the fandom, you require enough status to be able to override the desires of other fans.

Data from our studies of various fan groups—including anime fans – seem to agree with this intuition (Plante, Reysen et al., 2020). For example, in a 2020 study, we found that elitism—especially the tendency to derogate other fans—was correlated positively with pro-gatekeeping attitudes.[14] In other words, fans who hold themselves in high regard *and* those who tend to look down on other fans are the most likely to support pro-gatekeeping attitudes.[15]

---

[13] To see what we mean, imagine being completely new to a fandom and going to your first local meetup. Most fans couldn't imagine walking in and immediately insisting that certain people be kicked out of the meetup. Why? Because anyone with a sense of humility recognizes that being new to the group means they lack knowledge about the group's norms and existing social dynamics. You need to know at least a bit about a group before you can start reasonably making those sorts of judgments—although how much you need is certainly debatable.

[14] This was measured by asking participants to what extent they agreed with items such as "You can't call yourself an anime fan unless you've been in the fandom for a while," "The anime fandom would be better if it were less accepting of new members," and "I'm not shy about telling certain people that they don't belong in the anime fandom."

[15] A weakness of these studies is that they ask about pro-gatekeeping attitudes but not about gatekeeping behavior. In future studies we want to ask participants whether they actually engage in gatekeeping behavior or give them a chance to actually do so.

It's important to note, however, that this link is strongest for the "other derogation" part of elitism. Insofar as consuming more anime increases this tendency to look down upon other fans (e.g., as being less of a fan, for having not watched the same shows or watching to the same extent), anime consumption itself is also associated with greater gatekeeping tendencies.

Other factors predict lower gatekeeping tendencies, however. For example, global citizenship identification (see Chapter 12) was associated with less gatekeeping behavior, more acceptance of LGBTQ+ people in the anime fandom, and being more welcoming to new fans. This is a promising finding, especially in Western cultures, since exposure to anime (content from other countries) contributes to a person's sense of global citizenship. This is also especially likely if anime fans see the anime fandom as a community that values global citizenship norms (Plante et al., 2014).

Before we move on, it's worth briefly touching on why gatekeeping behavior, in and of itself, may be undesirable. After all, from what we've reviewed, it seems like gatekeeping serves a number of potentially important functions, like preserving the self-esteem boosting function of the fandom and solidifying the fan group's identity by rallying members around a common cause.

Despite these benefits, however, gatekeeping also has its share of drawbacks. For example, if the criteria one is using to justify gatekeeping are invalid, immoral, or grounded in falsehoods or fallacious reasoning, gatekeeping may lead to the exclusion of positive, productive, desirable members from the community, as well as leading to a narrowing of perspective and a lack of diversity within the fandom (e.g., Thorson & Wells, 2015). Put simply, when a group makes it clear that different attitudes, beliefs, or members are not welcome in their group, others will be less interested in trying to become members of that group (Gunderson et al., 2012). While this may be desirable when those potential members are troublesome, if the exclusion criteria are based on inaccurate stereotypes, mere aesthetic preference (e.g., "I just don't like that style of art"), or simply being new (e.g., "You don't belong here you filthy casual"), then gatekeeping may do more harm than good to a fan community.

Entitlement

While not quite the same thing as elitism and gatekeeping, fan entitlement is certainly in the same vein as these concepts. In past research we've defined fan entitlement as a fan's belief that they deserve special treatment from others (e.g., celebrities, content creators) or should otherwise be held in high regard (Shaw et al., 2016).[16] In general, when we refer to "entitlement" in this context, we're largely talking about unearned or narcissistic entitlement—a feeling of deserving resources, success, or special treatment that is largely unearned or which is disproportionate to one's achievements.[17]

It's not hard to find examples of fans feeling entitled to special treatment. One of the most famous classical examples of this involved Sir Arthur Conan Doyle's most famous character, Sherlock Holmes. Doyle had initially killed off Holmes in 1893 when, in a scuffle with his rival, Professor Moriarty, the two fell into a waterfall and were presumed dead. After nearly a decade of pressure from fans, however, Doyle somewhat reluctantly resurrected the beloved character, with Holmes himself explaining that his death had been faked. Other, less prominent examples of entitlement include fans feeling owed face-time and individual attention from their favorite celebrities in exchange for their admiration (e.g., "Emma's Pen," 2013), fans demanding that movie studios cast their favorite characters to play certain roles (e.g., Mendelson, 2013), and fans insisting on getting refunds at sporting events when their team loses (Smith, 2014).

It's not hard to imagine how the elitist attitudes we've discussed may contribute—or indeed be a product of—feelings of entitlement. In a non-fan context, investing time and effort into something makes people feel that they deserve special consideration when it comes time to make decisions in that domain (Kelly et al., 2002). In a fan context, fans who identify strongly

---

[16] We are far from the first to study the broader concept of entitlement (Plaschke, 2005; Twenge, 2006; Twenge & Campbell, 2009). For example, this work has largely been studied in the context of students' feelings of academic entitlement: Students who feel that they are owed good grades in school despite putting in minimal effort (e.g., Chowning & Campbell, 2009).

[17] For example, we wouldn't describe a nutritionist as being "entitled" to tell their patients what they should eat because they have gone to school to become an expert in this field. Likewise, an artist who has dedicated their life to honing their skills and becoming the best at their craft has likely earned the praise and fame they have achieved.

with their fan interest (e.g., die-hard fans[18] or lifestylers) may feel they are more deserving of special treatment than less-strongly identified fans (Wenzel, 2001).[19]

It's not a stretch to imagine entitled fans feeling like they have the right to decide who is and isn't worthy of inclusion in their fandom. After all, if fans feel entitled to tell content creators what they should create, what's stopping them from dictating which fans should and shouldn't be allowed into the fandom?

With all of this in mind, our 2016 paper (Shaw et al.) set out to measure rates of fan entitlement across several different fandoms and to assess psychological variables that might help us to better predict which fans are the most entitled. The study itself surveyed more than 4,400 participants, including more than 3,100 anime fans, 900 furries, and 385 fantasy sport fans. It assessed fan entitlement by asking participants to indicate the extent to which they agreed with items like:

(1) [Artists / Players] should make sure they are able to meet me in person.

(2) I think that [artists / players] are obligated to go above and beyond expectations to fulfill their fans' requests.

(3) If I email an [artist / player], I expect them to email me back.

(4) The [artists/players] that I am a fan of should make special accommodations for me, or other fans, because we are devoted.

The results of the study found that fans from all three groups scored fairly low in entitlement,[20] as all three fan groups scored below the midpoint of the scale. That said, of the three groups, anime fans scored the lowest, with an average score of just 2.67 / 7.00 compared to fantasy sport fans' 2.98 and furries' 3.24. The distribution of anime fans' entitlement scores, shown in Figure 13.3, also makes it clear that while most anime fans

---

[18] That is, fans who are fans no matter what. We're not referring to fans of the beloved Christmas action film starring Bruce Willis.

[19] For example, imagine a lifelong sport fan being upset if a one-on-one meet-and-greet with their favorite player was given to a bandwagon or fair-weather fan instead.

[20] Or, at very least, were not willing to openly admit to being entitled. We recognize that these estimates are fairly conservative, since it's not particularly flattering to come across as entitled. Actual rates of entitlement are likely somewhat higher than what we have measured in this study.

feel some low-level feelings of entitlement, very few go beyond that into the realm of being highly-entitled fans.

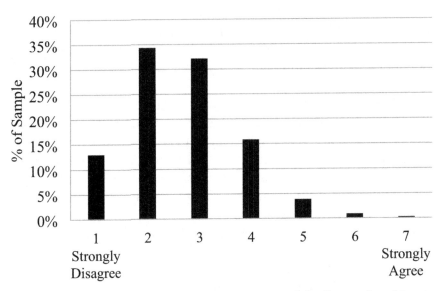

Figure 13.3. Extent to which anime fans expressed feelings of entitlement in the Shaw et al. 2016 study.

Having said that, 20% of anime fans do agree at least somewhat with entitlement-related attitudes.[21] As such, it's worth diving a bit more into the psyche of these more highly-entitled fans and the variables that help us predict them.

In the 2016 paper, for example, we found, as one might expect, that highly-identified fans who spent more time on their fan interest tended to show greater signs of entitlement. In other words, the self-described "biggest fans" and those who put the most time into their interest are the ones showing this sense of entitlement.[22]

---

[21] In this case, an average score of 4 or higher on the scale.
[22] The question of whether this entitlement is deserved or not is debatable. Ultimately, it's a value judgment more than a scientific one, so we leave the answer to that one up to the reader: Are fans who devote themselves to their hobby right to expect special treatment from artists, content creators, and other fans as a result of their devotion?

Follow-up analyses from the same study revealed additional predictors of entitlement. For instance, one of the strongest predictors of fan entitlement is identifying with *other fans* in the anime fandom. This result merits a bit of discussion, since we saw earlier that fandom scores are *negatively* associated with elitism and gatekeeping. One possible explanation may be that fandom is simply tapping into how big of a fan you are (since the two largely go hand-in-hand). This possibility is somewhat diminished, however, by the fact that we can control for time spent in the fandom (another measure of how big a fan someone is), and still find the relationship between fandom identification and entitlement.

A second possibility is that fans who score high on fandom may feel a sense of *collective entitlement*. That is, rather than feeling that they, themselves, are owed special treatment, they may feel like the fandom as a whole deserves special treatment. This may have been at play in the aforementioned case of Sherlock Holmes, whose fans may have felt that the fandom as a whole was owed more stories of their favorite character. Collective action on behalf of fans—such as working to get a show put back on the air (e.g., *Futurama*) or petitioning to add or change fan-favorite characters (e.g., *My Little Pony* fans and the case of the fan-favorite character Muffins) speak to this possibility (Edwards et al., 2019).

A final predictor of fan entitlement is a felt sense of stigma. Put simply, the more anime fans feels like they suffer because of stigma directed toward anime fans (more on this in Chapter 17), the more likely they are to feel entitled to special treatment. This may be another angle on a point we made earlier. Recall that more devoted fans feel like they've earned the right to special treatment. Those who feel they've suffered for being an anime fan (e.g., bullying) may feel like they've shown their devotion to anime, and are thus entitled to special treatment as a result.[23]

As an interesting final analysis, in a 2018 study we assessed one facet of fan entitlement among anime fans: The extent to which they felt they could

---

[23] As an analogy, imagine a fan of a celebrity camping out in the rain for hours outside of a studio in the hope of meeting the celebrity. Because of their dedication and willingness to suffer, they may feel like it's reasonable to expect the celebrity to talk to them for a minute out of respect for their devotion. In fact, the fan may feel "owed" a moment of the celebrity's time precisely because of how much the fan suffered, despite the fan's actions being unsolicited.

influence the behavior of the anime industry. Specifically, we asked participants whether they felt that fans could pressure companies to change the direction of a storyline, whether they could influence what the anime industry produces, and whether they, personally, felt they had an influence on the behavior of the anime industry. The study revealed that online anime fans were significantly more likely than convention-going fans to agree with items like these.

As Figure 13.4 illustrates, however, anime fans were hardly of a single mind on the topic. With respect to the first two questions, one could argue that, at a very literal level, anime fans do have the ability to impact the industry through their purchasing decisions. A large-scale boycott, petitioning to have a series adopted by a mainstream network, or word-of-mouth spreading of a particular anime series can impact its success and the likelihood that a studio will continue to make the series. It's a bit less clear, however, whether fans have the same impact on specific storylines or decisions about characters within established storylines. This isn't to say that it's impossible for fans to have an impact, and there have certainly been instances where this has happened. However, it is unlikely that fans are able to have the sort of impact on specific characters or storylines that they'd hope to have.[24]

What about the belief that an individual fan has the ability to personally impact the anime industry? It's telling that nearly half of anime fans somewhat agreed with this idea (and about 5-10% of anime fans agreed fairly strongly with this sentiment). Whether these fans are, indeed, employees in the anime industry or whether they simply feel that, as devoted fans, their voices have the power to influence the industry itself is something to be determined by future studies.

---

[24] As an example of this, see all of the *Star Wars* fans who were displeased with the direction of the prequel (or sequel) films and the way those films eradicated decades of fan-created lore.

284

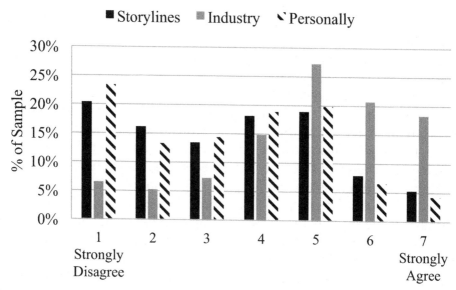

Figure 13.4. Extent to which anime fans felt they could influence anime storylines, influence what the anime industry produces, and felt personally able to influence the anime industry.

Drama

The topics covered in this chapter—elitism, gatekeeping, and entitlement—are all manifestations of the broader concept of "fandom drama." To the best of our knowledge, there is no consensus among psychologists about what constitutes "drama" in fandoms, although fans themselves are confident that they can recognize drama when they see it.[25]

In a 2017 study, we attempted to derive a data-driven, bottom-up definition of fandom drama based on open-ended input from nearly 300

---

[25] This, of course, is a reference to Supreme Court Justice Potter Stewart's discussion of what constitutes obscenity in the 1964 case Jacobellis v. Ohio, when he famously stated that he would not attempt to define the term "hard-core pornography," but instead stated "I know it when I see it." (Stewart, 1964).

furries who were asked to define the term drama for us (Plante, Roberts et al., 2020). After coding and condensing the responses, three common themes emerged:[26]

(1) Drama involves interpersonal conflict.

(2) Drama involves a disproportionate escalation or overreaction to that conflict.

(3) Drama needlessly involves the public (in-person or online) in a conflict between individuals.

Based on this conceptualization of drama, it's easy to see how elitism, gatekeeping, and entitlement among fans contribute to drama, given that all are potential sources of conflict, the type which escalates needlessly and which, in many instances, can be fairly trivial in nature. For example, disagreements between fans over perceived status, questions about who is the bigger fan, or distaste about the posturing of specific fans may lead to arguments in local fan groups. With respect to gatekeeping, a fan's insistence that certain members of the fan group do not belong—such as an anime fan claiming that furries have no place in the anime fandom—may spark conflict over whether this is fair and whether anyone has the authority to gatekeep this way. Finally, feelings of entitlement may lead fans to engage in tactless or selfish behavior—like an anime fan insisting that an artist owes them special treatment since they have commissioned the artist or are friends with the artist.

Of course, elitism, gatekeeping, and entitlement are far from the only potential causes of drama in a fandom. Indeed, any time you get people from all walks of life (e.g., different religious, political, ethnic, generational, and socioeconomic backgrounds) together in the same place, you've got yourself a situation that's primed and ready for interpersonal conflict.

---

[26] It's important to note that these three criteria can be thought of as necessary but not sufficient for drama to occur. In other words, just because interpersonal conflict arises and escalates in a public setting does not guarantee that it will become a source of fandom drama. Moreover, not all interpersonal conflict is considered by fans to be drama. For example, if there is a serious, legitimate grievance between two parties (e.g., involving a criminal act), then a severe response may be warranted and would likely not be considered "drama"—namely because the conflict is not escalated disproportionately. Thus, one should be careful about trivializing all conflict in fandom spaces as "mere drama."

Nevertheless, it's worth keeping these factors in mind as background contributors to drama in the anime fandom.

In a 2017 study we asked anime fans a series of questions about the extent to which they had been personally affected by or involved with drama in the anime fandom (e.g., "I have been caught up in fandom drama," "I can't seem to avoid drama in the anime fandom") and the extent to which they saw drama as a problem in the anime fandom (e.g., "There is too much drama in the anime fandom," "Drama in the anime fandom is undesirable"). As shown in Figure 13.5, most anime fans believed that drama is a problem in the fandom itself and many reported at least some involvement with fandom-related drama.

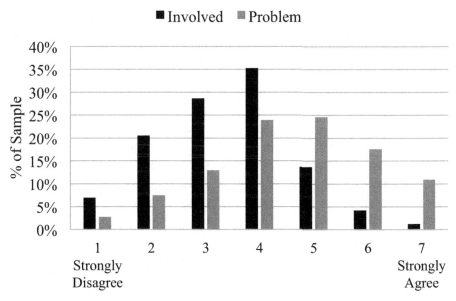

Figure 13.5. Extent to which anime fans were affected by drama and saw drama as a problem in the anime fandom.

Follow-up analyses reveal that con-going fans are especially likely to experience drama—likely owing to the fact that more face-to-face interaction with fans creates more opportunities for drama to spark in the first place. Despite con-going fans experiencing more drama, however, both online and con-going fans agreed that drama was an undesirable force in the anime fandom.

Related to the idea that con-going fans experience greater fandom drama, those who scored higher in fandom—that is, identification with the anime fan community—were more likely to have experienced drama first-hand. This would seem to align with stereotypes of anime fans as quarrelsome and critical. Greater interaction with anime fans in closer proximity may create friction that sparks the sort of conflict that ultimately leads to drama.

Despite this intuitive hypothesis, however, those highest in fandom and fanship—the tendency to identify as a fan of anime content—were also the *least* likely to see drama as a problem in the anime fandom. Interpreting this finding can be a bit tricky. On the one hand, we may be seeing desensitization, where anime fans who see the most drama learn to "tune it out" compared to a person new to the fandom or someone who's watching from the outside. Alternatively, those for whom the anime fandom is most important may see all the benefits of the fandom as a whole, which makes the drawback of occasional drama seem relatively small in comparison. Ultimately, future research is needed to tease apart these possibilities.

Before we wrap up this chapter, let's take a look at one last, recent study on the subject of drama within the anime fandom—specifically, a study looking at the potential function of fandom-related drama. The idea behind this study is that if drama were entirely functionless and negative, people would, presumably, choose not to participate in it and would work to actively stamp it out. Nevertheless, drama persists in fan cultures—not just the anime fandom—hinting at the idea that people must get some kind of benefit from it.[27]

To this end, in our 2020 study we gave anime fans a list of 14 possible functions of drama in the anime fandom, functions which ranged from providing personal benefits (e.g., "it's entertaining") to group-level benefits (e.g., "it creates outgroups that fans can unite against"). Fans were asked to indicate the extent to which they believed that fandom-related drama served that particular function. The results are shown in Table 13.1.

---

[27] This way of thinking is analogous to the arguments made by evolutionary biologists, who argue that if an organism evolved with some kind of feature, that feature likely (though not always) serves some kind of function, otherwise it would have been evolved out of existence.

288

Proposed Function of Fandom Drama	% of Fans Agreeing with the Function
Can be entertaining.	68.5%
Can be a useful tool for aggressively isolating or harming others.	62.5%
Creates outgroups that fans can unite against.	54.7%
Satisfying to see people get what's coming to them because of drama.	52.0%
Teaches people important lessons about what to avoid doing themselves.	50.9%
Help a group recognize important threats within the group.	47.2%
Forces people to be accountable for their actions.	44.0%
Builds a sense of community with a shared interests and common information.	41.1%
Improves our understanding of the fandom.	40.4%
Helps a group improve itself by getting rid of undesirable elements within it.	37.8%
Allows a fandom to make it clear what its moral boundaries are.	37.7%
If one does not keep up with fandom drama, they might be seen as less of a fan.	34.7%
Allows group members to compare notes on which potential mates / friends are better than others.	32.3%
Provides a way for fans to share information about the group.	30.2%

Table 13.1. Perceived function of drama in the anime fandom as rated by anime fans, sorted by most-to-least agreed-upon.

The results reveal that the most agreed-upon function of fandom-related drama is as a means of entertainment. Put simply, more than two-thirds of anime fans agreed that there's at least some fun to be had in watching drama unfold. After all, drama involves conflict, and conflict, itself, is novel and interesting to watch.[28] Insofar as drama provides fans with a way to observe conflict from a safe distance, it may well prove to be

---

[28] The novelty and excitement of conflict is the reason why people are drawn to violence-filled action films and video games, which wouldn't be nearly as interesting if everyone got along and played nice with one another!

entertaining, which may prevent fans from doing more to step in to stop it when it happens.

The second-most common function of drama is that of a weapon to be used against others. When coupled with the next most popular functions (creating outgroups, giving people what's coming to them), it seems clear that drama may be tied to elitism, gatekeeping, and entitlement. After all, if drama is a way to create outgroups and exclude people, it's a useful tool for gatekeeping. Alternatively, the schadenfreude[29] associated with watching a smug, self-important fan getting put down by a celebrity, content creator, or by a significant portion of the fandom carries with it a certain guilty pleasure and illustrates the connection between some of these functions— including, as half of anime fans mention, being a teachable moment for new fans about the sorts of behaviors that they should avoid.

It's rather notable that several "fandom-improving" elements of drama— including helping to build a community around common information or helping purge a group of undesirable elements, are far less endorsed by the average anime fan. In other words, drama is a guilty pleasure or something undesirable that fans simply can't help participating in[30] far more than a tool with which to improve the fandom. This is supported by the fact that anime fans, despite having personally been involved in, or affected by, drama, nevertheless see it as a largely undesirable force.

Conclusion

To finish up this chapter, we began with a look at how fandoms—like any social group—serve a number of important social psychological functions. Chief among these functions is the fandom's ability to boost the self-esteem of its members. We've reviewed some of the ways people seek to bolster this esteem-boosting function, including inflating themselves while putting down others, keeping undesirable others out of the group, and deriving a sense of entitlement from one's devotion to the fandom. We've also discussed some of the downsides of these tendencies—what happens when these tendencies go awry or are taken to excess. We finished by taking a look at drama—a fairly divisive topic in the fandom despite its

---

[29] A German word referring to the pleasure a person experiences upon witnessing the misfortune of another person.

[30] Just as drivers are often unable to resist the allure of slowing down to watch the aftermath of a car crash on the side of the highway.

prevalence, and its connection to gatekeeping, elitism, and entitlement. Taken together, this chapter finds that anime fans are far from unique in experiencing these undesirable elements, though it should not prevent fans from working against these forces to improve their fandom for the better.

Chapter 14
Motivations and Values

Psychology is the scientific study of behavior. Just as important to psychologists as studying behavior itself is understanding the causes of a given behavior, what drives someone to do the things they do.

Psychologists recognize at least two answers to this question: motivation and values. Motivation is defined as "a driving force that initiates and directs behavior" (Stangor, 2010, p. 521), while values are the ideals and principles we consider important and desirable, which shape and guide our behavior (Schwartz & Sortheix, 2018).[1]

In the present chapter we examine both motivations and values in anime fans to better understand what drives them to do the things they do. We'll explore not only what anime fans get out of being anime fans, but also what we can learn about individual anime fans based on their motivations and values.

Wann's Motivations

Daniel Wann is the most-renowned fan psychologist in the world, having worked in the field for more than 25 years. Despite the fact that his research focuses primarily on sport fans, his work remains relevant and has been applied in one form another to nearly all fandoms that have been studied from a psychological perspective.

In a 1995 paper studying the motivations of sport fans, Wann suggested that fans were driven by a combination of eight different motivations:

(1) Belongingness: feelings of connectedness with other fans.

(2) Family: the desire to spend time and connect with one's family.

(3) Aesthetics: enjoying the beauty and creativity of one's fan interest.

(4) Self-esteem: wanting to see oneself in a positive light.

(5) Economics: including gambling or benefitting financially from the fandom.

(6) Eustress: experiencing positive, enjoyable forms of stress.[2]

---

[1] Another way to put it is to say that motivations compel us to do a certain behavior and values are the principles and ideals that are important to us which can, themselves, motivate behavior.

[2] An example of eustress in sport fans would be watching a game and feeling the thrill of not knowing whether your team is going to win or not. For media fans, this might include

(7) Escape: wanting to forget or distract oneself from daily life hassles.

(8) Entertainment: the desire to experience enjoyment.

In his initial study on the subject, sport fans scored the highest on entertainment, eustress, belongingness, and self-esteem, meaning that these were the most prominent motivations driving sport fans. These same variables, in turn, were strongly correlated with fanship (team identification)—that is, feeling a sense of psychological connection to one's fan interest.[3]

In later studies, Wann, Schrader, and Wilson (1999) tested whether the motivations driving fans differed from sport to sport. Participants indicated whether they were fans of team-based sports (e.g., football, basketball) or individual sports (e.g., tennis, boxing). They also indicated whether their preferred sports were aggressive (e.g., hockey, football) or nonaggressive (e.g., basketball, baseball).

The results of the study showed that fans who preferred individual sports were more likely than those who preferred team sports to be motivated by aesthetics and were less likely to be motivated by eustress and escapism. Fans with a preference for nonaggressive sports were similarly more motivated by aesthetics than fans of aggressive sports, who were more motivated by economic factors. A later study, much larger and on a sample of U.S. college students similarly found differences in the motivations of fans of different sports (e.g., figure skating, boxing; Wann, Grieve et al., 2008). The results again showed that fans of different sports had varied motivations.

For now, we'll avoid delving too deep into all of the specific reasons why particular motivations are more prevalent for fans of different sports. For our purposes, it's enough just to say that past research shows that fans with different motivations prefer different sports, suggesting that different sports may "scratch different itches" for fans, making them more or less appealing depending on what the fan is hoping to get out of their hobby.

As an illustrative example of one fan motivation and its impact on fan-related behavior, let's consider escapism. In a 2004 study, Wann and

---

watching a movie or show and enjoying the thrill of not knowing whether or not the hero is going to prevail.

[3] In the case of sport fans, this means a felt connection to their favorite team. An analogous comparison for anime fans would be a connection to a series or to anime itself.

colleagues (2004) took note of sport fans who were significantly motivated by escapism. Two-thirds of these fans used sport as a way to escape life's hassles, while about a third used sport as a way to escape boredom. Escapism's prevalence is not limited to sport fans either. For example, Chadborn et al. (2017) asked a sample of undergraduate students to list a fan interest they had and then complete measures of various motivations for participating in that interest. They found that escapism was the highest-rated motivator across the different fan groups. While escapism hasn't been previously studied from a psychological perspective within anime fans specifically, scholars from other disciplines have pointed to escapism as a primary motivator of anime fans (Eng, 2006; Napier, 2007).

So, what does motivate anime fans, and is escapism the largest of these motivations? To test this, we looked at anime fans' motivations using a measure based on Wann's (1995) eight primary motivations (Schroy et al., 2016). We also included two motivations that were not part of Wann's measure: attention (e.g., participating in the fandom to get attention) and sexual attraction (e.g., participating in the fandom because you are sexually attracted to the content). Finally, we included measures of fanship and fandom to test the link between various motivations and participants' felt connection to the content itself and to the community of fans, respectively (see Chapter 10 for more information on fanship and fandom).

As shown in Figure 14.1, escapism was among the most prevalent motivators driving fans, second only to entertainment. The remaining motivations all fell below the midpoint of the scale. In other words, while individual anime fans certainly have their own reasons for being anime fans, on average, anime fans are primarily driven by its entertainment value and by the opportunity anime provides for fans to escape from life's daily hassles.

In a follow-up analysis, we wanted to see which of the motivations was most strongly tied to fandom.[4] As shown in Figure 14.2, it wasn't entertainment, but belongingness which most strongly predicted the extent to which fans identified with the anime fandom. In other words, while most anime fans consider anime to be an enjoyable escape from reality, it's the

---

[4] After all, it's likely that most anime fans watch anime because it's fun. But is this entertainment factor what separates those who interact with the fandom from those who distance themselves from the fandom?

fans who are looking for a place to belong that are most likely to connect with other fans and actively participate in fandom activities.

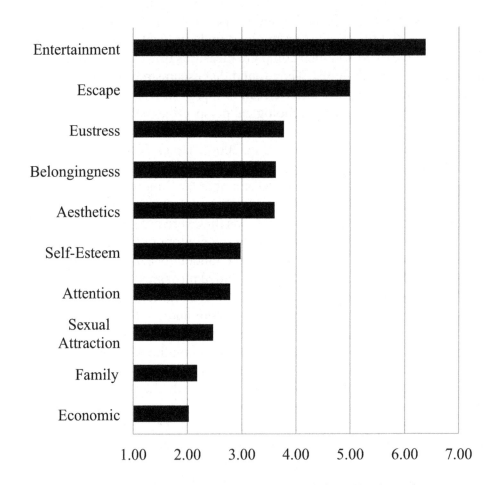

Figure 14.1. Mean ratings of motivations to participate in the anime fandom.

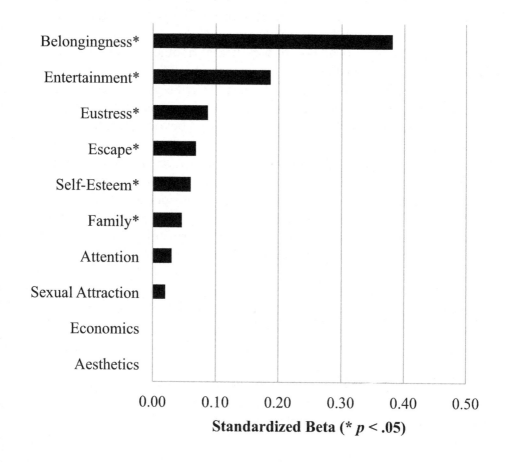

Figure 14.2. Motivations predicting fandom identification.

As a final note on the prevalence of escapism in the famine fandom, it's worth noting research showing that one's motivation can tell us a lot about their overall well-being (Reysen, Plante, & Chadborn, 2017).[5] As such, we

---

[5] For example, in a study of bronies we found that people who were more motivated by escapism were also less likely to experience positive feelings in their day-to-day life, perhaps suggesting that these fans may have the greatest need to escape in the first place (Edwards et al., 2019).

examined whether the different motivations predicted anime fans' well-being. Fans whose motives were entertainment, family and aesthetics had better psychological well-being, while those who were motivated by escapism ad self-esteem had poorer well-being. In other words, relying on anime as a form of escape and leaning on it too hard for one's sense of self-worth is a possible sign of lower well-being. Taken together, findings like these illustrate how knowing what drives fans can tell us a lot about the way they think, feel, and behave, both within and beyond their fan interest.

Psychological Needs

In the previous section we looked at what motivates fans to seek out anime and considered a number of different motivations. Another way to understand motivation is to flip it on its head—considering what psychological needs a person may be fulfilling by engaging in an activity.[6] In other words, motivation can be thought of in terms of the needs we are currently seeking to fulfill and our desire to engage in behaviors that will satiate those needs.

As we've discussed in previous chapters (e.g., Chapter 10), humans are a social species, particularly driven to belong to groups. This is due, in no small part, to the fact that groups satisfy a number of basic psychological needs. To understand some of these needs and test whether the anime fandom fulfills these needs, we scoured the psychological literature to come up with a list of 11 possible benefits that groups provide.[7] We then asked anime fans to indicate the extent that the anime fandom provided them with each of those 11 benefits on a 7-point scale ranging from 1 = *strongly disagree* to 7 = *strongly agree*.

---

[6] Psychological needs, while perhaps not as essential to survival as more basic needs (e.g., food, water), are nevertheless essential for optimal functioning and thriving. Most folks are probably familiar with need hierarchies that place more basic, biological needs at the bottom of the hierarchy and psychological needs like social interaction and self-esteem at a higher level. According to such hierarchies, we typically need to satisfy our more basic needs before we tend to worry about higher-order needs. But in order to self-actualize, or function at our peak, we eventually need to take care of all these needs!

[7] Many of these items were adapted from Vignoles et al. (2006).

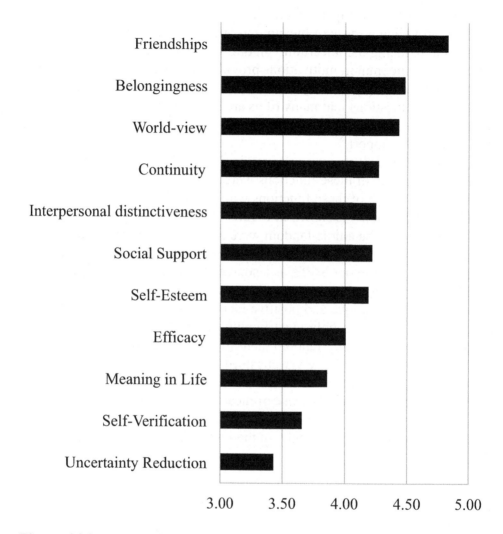

Figure 14.3. Mean ratings of psychological needs met through fandom participation.

As shown in Figure 14.3, the functions most strongly provided by the anime fandom were friendships, a sense of belongingness, and a consistent worldview. Other motivations, such as a feeling of continuity in one's life, a sense of interpersonal distinctiveness, social support, self-esteem, and

299

feeling competent and capable (self-efficacy) were also important. In contrast, providing a sense of meaning in one's life, feeling validated by others, and reducing the uncertainty in one's life seemed to be relatively infrequent or uncommon motivations provided by the anime fandom itself. In short, while the fandom may not necessarily be answering the big philosophical questions that many of us are seeking answers to, fans do at least get a sense of connection to others and an overall sense of comfort, well-being, and support.[8]

Similar to the analysis we conducted in the previous section, in addition to measuring which of these functions were most fulfilled by the fandom, we also asked which of these functions was most strongly associated with fandom identification. As shown in Figure 14.4, the strongest predictors of identification with the anime fandom were relying on the fandom as a source of self-esteem, as a means of attaining interpersonal distinctiveness, for greater meaning in one's life, as a source of friendships, and to feel a sense of belongingness. In other words, those for whom the fandom provides a sense of unique and positive identity, meaning, and friendships are the most likely to strongly identify with the fandom.

In addition to predicting fandom identification, we also looked at whether those who meet these various needs through the fandom differ with respect to other fan-related outcomes. For example, those for whom the fandom provides them with a sense of meaning in their lives are much more likely to attend conventions, consume more anime, and to think more about being an anime fan, shedding light on the importance and centrality of anime in their lives.

---

[8] This makes sense when you consider that humans are a social species primarily because our social groups provide us with support and are an essential resource for our survival. One can imagine, for example, that if you were to break your leg or struggle to find food for a few days in the wild, you would surely perish. Having others take care of you until you can support yourself, however, helps not only you to survive, but also helps the species as a whole to bolster its numbers and thrive.

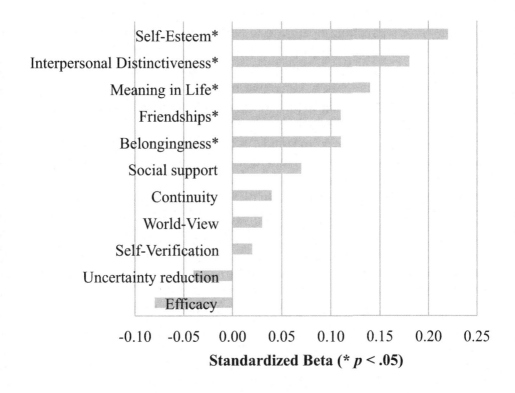

Figure 14.4. Regression of psychological needs predicting fandom identification.

As another example, the extent to which the fandom satisfied one's need for interpersonal distinctiveness and self-esteem was associated with wearing clothes bearing anime-related content. It would seem that for some fans, participating in the fandom helps them gain a sense of uniqueness from others, something which helps them feel positive about themselves. This would explain the desire to wear clothing that helps them to stand out from others in their day-to-day lives. We investigate this need in greater detail in the following section.

Optimal Distinctiveness

In Chapter 10 we described the social identity perspective, which argues that people have a psychological need to belong to groups that reflect positively on them. As an offshoot to this theory, Marilynn Brewer (1991) proposed what she called a model of optimal distinctiveness. This theory posits that people struggle to balance two opposing needs. On the one hand, people have a need to belong to positive groups that reflect well on them and provide them with security and a positive sense of self. On the other hand, people also have a need to stand out and distinguish themselves as unique in their personal accomplishments, to not lose their sense of identity entirely within their groups.[9]

According to the theory, people can differ in what they consider to be the optimal balance between these two needs,[10] and will choose to identify with groups that represent what they consider to be the optimal balance between the needs. In other words, people choose to belong to groups that let them stand out from others, but also allow them to not feel *too* unique and risk being shunned or ostracized for being different.[11]

Optimal distinctiveness theory has been applied to numerous group contexts, including fan groups. Andrijiw and Hyatt (2009), for example, interviewed 20 Canadian hockey fans who were fans of a team from a different city than the one in which they currently lived. These fans reported feeling both connected to the group of fans while also feeling fairly unique, since they stood out from other fans in their city. In other

---

[9] It's worth noting that optimal distinctiveness theory is far from a fringe theory; it's received a great deal of empirical validation over the years (Leonardelli et al., 2010).

[10] You can probably think of examples of people who differ considerably in their desired balance between these needs. Some people, like celebrities, seem to demand the spotlight, having a high need for uniqueness and relatively little felt need to belong. Others shy away from drawing attention to themselves and would prefer to disappear into a crowd. Most of us fall somewhere between these two extremes, and, indeed, one's own level of optimal distinctiveness may vary from situation to situation!

[11] As a real-world demonstration, imagine a person choosing to cosplay. Doing so alone in the middle of a crowded city street would likely make most people feel fairly uncomfortable with how much they stand out. However, doing so with a group of a few friends makes the prospect sound a lot more fun, since it allows you to stand out from the average people in the street while still feeling *too* ostracized, since you're part of a group.

words, part of the appeal of being a fan of a distant team is that it can provide fans with an optimal level of distinctiveness.

In a similar vein, Abrams (2009) examined the music preferences of young adults in the United Kingdom. Participants indicated their top three preferences of music (e.g., pop/rock, disco/dance) and how they followed that style of music (e.g., attending concerts, buying CDs, wearing clothes related to that style of music). The results showed that fans of music that was in the mid-range of popularity consumed the most music, relative to fans of very popular or unpopular music genres, possibly suggesting (through their consumer behavior) that they might identify more strongly as fans.

In a study with furries, Reysen, Plante, Roberts, and Gerbasi (2016) similarly found that furries' perception of the furry fandom as distinct from other fandoms and provided a sense of belongingness predicted greater identification with the furry community as a whole. In other words, insofar as the furry fandom may provide furries with a way to obtain that optimal level of distinctiveness, they seem to more strongly identify with the fandom itself.

What about anime fans—does anime provide fans with a sense of belongingness while also being distinct enough from other hobbies that it lets fans feel distinct? Non-psychological scholarly work certainly suggests this may be the case. Napier (2007) proposes that fans participate in the fandom in part because they are surrounded by a culture that's different from the one anime provides. Or, to put it another way, anime fans participate in anime culture precisely because of the ways it differs from mainstream culture.

We've assessed optimal distinctiveness within our own research on anime fans. For example, in one study we tested whether distinctiveness and belongingness predicted fandom identification in a sample of anime fans (Reysen et al., 2017b).[12] The results showed that fans who scored highest on measures of both felt belongingness and perceived distinctiveness of the anime fandom were also the ones who most strongly identified with the anime fandom (see Figure 14.5).

---

[12] Belongingness was measured with questions like "I feel included and well-integrated into the anime community", while distinctiveness was measured with questions like "The anime community is different and distinct compared to non-anime groups."

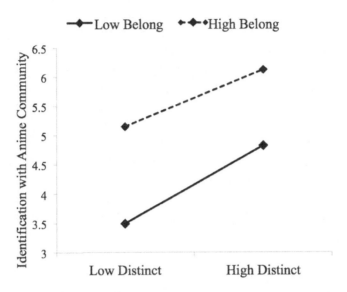

Figure 14.5. Interaction between inclusion (belongingness) and differentiation (intergroup distinctiveness) predicting identification with the anime community. From Reysen et al. (2017b).

Schwartz's 10 Universal Values

Up to this point, we've been discussing motivations and needs as drivers of anime fan identity, identifying with the anime fandom, and fan-related behavior. For now, let's shift gears a bit and consider something else which may drive fan behavior—not the satisfaction of any particular need, but a fan's deeply-held values and their desire to seek out activities that coincide with these values.

Shalom Schwartz (1992) proposed 10 distinct values that are largely considered to be universal—that is, you can find these values to some extent across all cultures.[13]

(1) Benevolence: the importance of caring for the welfare of others.
(2) Universalism: appreciating diversity and the natural environment.
(3) Self-direction: the importance of independent thought and action.
(4) Stimulation: appreciating novelty, excitement, and challenge.
(5) Hedonism: things that bring pleasure and gratification.
(6) Achievement: appreciating personal success and accomplishment.
(7) Power: desiring prestige and dominance.
(8) Security: the importance of safety and stability.
(9) Conformity: seeking harmonious relations and following societal norms.
(10) Tradition: the importance of respecting customs and religious norms.

By themselves, these values tell us a bit about a person (e.g., whether they value power over benevolence or hedonism over achievement). What makes them so important, both practically and theoretically, is that these values predict behavior. After all, knowing that a person values power over benevolence would be meaningless if this didn't also predict, say, their power-seeking behavior or a lack of stepping in to help others in need. For this reason, social scientists have extensively tested what these values predict, and have discovered correlations between these universal values and other theoretically important variables such as well-being, environmentalism, social behavior, and political orientation.

For example, Bobowik et al. (2011) tested whether these values were related to psychological well-being in a large sample of Europeans. They found that well-being was higher in people who valued hedonism and self-direction and was lower in people who valued security. Other studies have shown that people experience greater well-being when they achieve goals that align with the values they deem important, such as a person who values power achieving greater prestige (Schwartz & Sortheix, 2018).

---

[13] It's important to note that not everyone will have these different values to the same extent. Chances are, as you read through this list, you'll consider some of these values to be more important than others. Across cultures, however, you can typically find people who endorse all of these different values to varying degrees.

Researchers in marketing and business have similarly shown that values can predict consumer orientation, employee attitudes, and environmental beliefs. In a study of employees at a large bank in Israel, for example, employee attitudes and behaviors were linked to the values of conformity,[14] benevolence, and universalism (Cohen, 2009). In other studies, valuing universalism was associated with the belief that corporations should be held accountable for environmental irresponsibility and socially irresponsible behavior (e.g., unfair labor practices: Fukukawa et al., 2007).

In short, the reviewed research shows that a person's values reveal a lot about their everyday beliefs and behaviors (e.g., politics, work). With this in mind, we can look at the values of anime fans and what they tell us about their attitudes, beliefs, and behaviors.

To examine anime fans' values, we measured Schwartz's (1992) 10 universal values alongside a measure of fandom identification. As shown in Figure 14.6, the highest-rated values among anime fans were universalism, self-direction, benevolence, hedonism, and security.[15]

---

[14] One can imagine, for example, that an employee who doesn't value conformity might not follow instructions or work well alongside co-workers, at least in an environment that values uniformity and structure rather than freedom and self-expression.

[15] The fact that universalism was the value most strongly endorsed by anime fans coincides with research from Chapter 12, which suggests that anime fans also tend to score fairly high on measures of global citizenship, a construct which emphasizes concern for the environment, a global perspective, and appreciation of diversity. While this should hardly be surprising, this is a nice demonstration of the validity of the findings (or, as we sometimes call it, a "sanity check," to make sure our findings agree with one another).

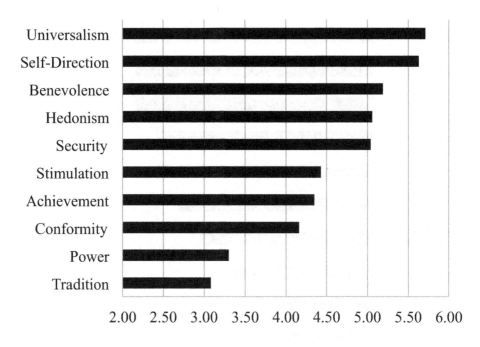

Figure 14.6. Mean ratings of 10 universal values (7-point scale).

As we mentioned in Chapter 10, according to the social identity perspective, people tend to internalize the values of their groups, especially if they happen to be more strongly identified with that group. In other words, I will start to value and believe the things that my group believes if that group is important to me. To test this idea, we examined whether anime fans' values were associated with the extent to which they identified with the anime community. Sure enough, the many of the values that were most strongly endorsed by the anime fandom as a whole (e.g., universalism, benevolence, hedonism) were also the most strongly endorsed by the most highly-identified fans, just as one would predict from a social identity perspective (see Figure 14.7).

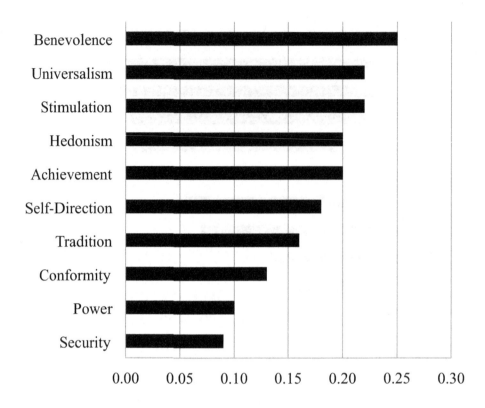

Figure 14.7. Correlations between values and identification with the fandom.

Given the importance of universalism as a value for anime fans, we wanted to test whether the associated acceptance and embracing of diversity would manifest with respect to the LGBTQ+ population, a group which frequently finds itself stigmatized in mainstream culture. To this end, we asked anime fans to rate how accepting they were toward people from the LGBTQ+ community ("Asexual," "Bisexual," "Gay/lesbian/homosexual," "Transgender/non-conforming") on a 7-point scale. They were also asked to estimate how accepting the anime fandom as a whole would be.

As shown in Figure 14.8, anime fans reported being overwhelmingly supportive of the LGBTQ+ population, coinciding with our expectations for a fandom that values universalism. Having said that, it's notable that anime fans also expressed some reservations about other anime fans, seeing them as largely accepting of LGBTQ+ people, albeit to considerably less of an extent.

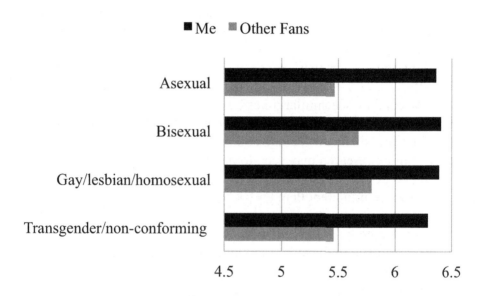

Figure 14.8. Mean ratings of acceptance of diverse others in fandom for self and perception of other fans.

One possible explanation for this discrepancy stems from the concern to look desirable. Participants may want to present themselves as an accepting, tolerant person to researchers, and may thus portray themselves as more accepting than they actually are toward the LGBTQ+ population.

A second explanation is based on a quirk of how our memory works. Put simply, we tend to remember things that are surprising, shocking, or emotionally charged more than more neutral content. As such, we're more likely to remember a particularly bigoted social media post or a single anime fan behaving in a transphobic manner than we are to remember the hundreds of more mundane interactions. Because these negative instances of behavior spring to mind more readily, fans may overestimate how often these incidents occur in the fandom, causing them to overestimate bigotry within the fandom.[16]

A third explanation is grounded in what psychologists call pluralist ignorance. In a nutshell, pluralistic ignorance is when people think that their own beliefs are different from others, even when their beliefs/behaviors are the same (Prentice & Miller, 1993).[17] When applied to the present data, we can see that the anime fandom seems to be supportive of LGBTQ+ people, but believe other fans are not nearly as supportive. This may be because fans may engage in homophobic or transphobic behavior (e.g., derogatory jokes), telling themselves that they're only doing it as a joke, and that it doesn't reflect bigotry. However, they may not extend that same courtesy to other fans when they see similar jokes being told.

If nothing else, these findings suggest that there is a mismatch between how fans interpret their own beliefs and how they interpret the beliefs of other fans. Future research may seek to better explain this mismatch, while also hinting at the possibility that fans' own beliefs/behaviors may be perceived as more intolerant than they might assume.

Conclusion

Any given anime fan will have their own reasons for why they consume anime and participate in the anime fandom. Nevertheless, when you look across anime fans as a group, we can find similarities and trends in what drives their interests. Anime fans are especially motivated by the need for belongingness, entertainment, eustress, and escapism. The fandom itself also satisfies a number of important social psychological needs, including self-esteem, distinctiveness, meaning in life, friendships, and a group to belong to. In fact, according to optimal distinctiveness theory, an important function of the fandom for many fans is providing fans with an opportunity

---

[16] The technical name for this cognitive bias is the availability heuristic.

[17] A classic example of this is college drinking. College students often drink a lot at parties. When asked why, they say that they don't actually support excessive drinking, and that they're doing it simply to fit in. However, when asked why they think *other* college students are drinking, they don't offer that same explanation: Instead, they assume that the average college student just likes drinking a lot. This leads to the belief that binge drinking is the norm and that college students enjoy doing it, when in reality, most people who do it may be doing it because they believe this norm.

to both stand out among others while having the social support and reassurance of a like-minded group of others at their back.

Anime fans also tend to share a number of similar values, a finding which coincides with a social identity perspective. These values include universalism, self-direction, benevolence, and hedonic pleasure, and many of these values themselves predict which anime fans identify the most strongly with the anime fandom. One possible outcome of these values is fans' attitudes toward subgroups within the fandom, including fairly positive attitudes of inclusion and acceptance of LGBTQ+ people within the fandom, although fans tend to see themselves as even more accepting than the fandom itself, for reasons that will need to be studied in future research.

Chapter 15
Personality

Intuitively, most people have a basic idea of what personality is. For example, we might describe someone as having a lot of personality,[1] or say that we really like someone for their personality. However, what exactly are we talking about when we describe a person's personality?

In a nutshell, when we talk about a person's personality, we're talking about a person's stable traits, aspects of their way of thinking, feeling, and behaving that distinguish them from others.[2] Or, as psychologists would say, personality is "an individual's characteristic patterns of thought, emotion, and behavior" (Funder & Fast, 2010, p. 669).

Of course, when you think about all the different ways that people can differ from one another, it's not hard to generate a list of hundreds, or even thousands of differences. These range from differences in how much people to go out on a Friday night to differences in how willing people are to try a new dish. Early psychologists ran into this very problem, generating lists of thousands of traits that could be used to describe people.[3] They realized that such lists were too large and unwieldy to be practical, not to mention the fact that they were often terribly redundant.[4]

Over many decades, personality psychologists worked to whittle down these lists of personality traits until they arrived at a set of five which we today call the "big five" personality dimensions (Goldberg, 1990; John, 1990). These dimensions exist as a set of mostly independent continua onto

---

[1] Or, in the case of a boring person, as having no personality.

[2] This distinctiveness component is often overlooked: Describing something that's fairly universal to humans does not make it a personality trait. For instance, the fact that someone eats food is not a personality trait because all humans need to eat. What *can* differ from person to person, however, is how much they pay attention to what they eat, or their manners while eating, both of which can vary considerably from person to person.

[3] In fact, one methodology—the lexical approach—involved going through the dictionary and pulling out all the adjectives that could be used to describe people!

[4] For example, you could describe someone as hostile, surly, sour, bitter, cranky, cantankerous, short-tempered, and crochety—but these are all tapping into the same idea— an argumentative or unpleasant person!

which everyone falls—typically somewhere between two extremes. These five dimensions are:[5]

(1) Extraversion versus introversion.

(2) Agreeableness versus antagonism.

(3) Conscientiousness versus irresponsibility.

(4) Neuroticism versus emotional stability.

(5) Openness to new experiences versus closed to new experiences.

We devote the first half of this chapter to the big five model of personality, in no small part because it's currently the most widely-used personality model in the field of psychology (Gosling et al., 2003).[6] After a brief review of some of the research tied to each of the big five traits, we report on what these traits can tell us about the behavior of anime fans. In the latter half of the chapter, we shift our focus to other, less-studied, more specific personality traits, traits which seem especially relevant to anime fans. As we proceed through the chapter, remember that we're painting a picture, in broad strokes, of what a "typical" anime fan is like personality-wise: What traits do they share in common with other fans and what traits distinguish them from non-fans?

Defining the Big Five Traits

Extraversion

Extraversion "refers to the degree to which an individual is outgoing, is energetic, and experiences positive emotion" (Funder & Fast, 2010, p. 679).[7] Extraversion, like the other big five traits, can tell us a lot about a person's thoughts, feelings, and behavior. Specifically, extraverts are defined by being especially social, engaging in a variety of positive, high-energy behaviors.

---

[5] The big five can be remembered easily with the naval acronyms "OCEAN" or "CANOE."

[6] Pick a topic in psychology, any topic. Chances are, there's probably a published study on the relationship between the big five personality traits and that topic. For example, an Italian study found that the big five trait of introversion was correlated with being an early adopter of the *Pokémon Go* mobile phone game (Tabacchi et al., 2017)!

[7] Laypersons often erroneously define extraversion as the extent to which people like being around others. In fact, extraversion is more precisely thought of as the extent to which one is energized by being around others. Introverts still typically enjoy the company of others, but may find it draining and require more time alone than extraverts, who may consider time spent with others to be the way that they unwind and relax.

314

For example, extraverts value stimulation more than introverts do (Roccas et al., 2002), and so it's no surprise that they also show a greater preference for upbeat and energetic music (Rentfrow & Gosling, 2003) and for greater physical activity (Rhodes & Smith, 2006).[8] Extraverts also show less perfectionist concerns and therefore get less bogged down and stressed about imperfections (Stricker et al., 2019). Extraverts surround themselves with more extraverted friends (Feiler & Kleinbaum, 2015) and tend to feel a stronger connection with their local community (Lounsbury et al., 2003). For this reason, extraverts also are more likely to experience better subjective well-being, more gratitude, greater felt inspiration in their lives, and to volunteer their time to help others (Ozer & Benet-Martínez, 2006). They're more resilient (Oshio et al., 2018) and generally better able to handle stress, since extraverts typically seek help from others when problem-solving (Connor-Smith & Flachsbart, 2007).

However, this desire to be around others can have some downsides as well.[9] For example, while extraverted people use social networking websites more (Kim et al., 2017), they are also more likely to be compulsive users and consumers (Aiken et al., 2018). Extraverts also engage in more risky sexual behavior (Allen & Walter, 2018) and are more likely to believe in false rumors (Lai et al., 2020).

Agreeableness

Agreeableness "refers to the degree to which an individual is cooperative, warm, and gets along well with others" (Funder & Fast, 2010, p. 679). In short, agreeable people empathize with others and get along well with them—something that, conceptually, seems to overlap a bit with extraversion.

Illustrating this point, like with extraverts, agreeable people prefer upbeat and energetic music (Rentfrow & Gosling, 2003), score higher on measures of resilience (Oshio et al., 2018), and are less worried about perfectionism (Stricker et al., 2019). Agreeable people also tend to score

---

[8] While we talk about "extraverts" and "introverts," note that people don't fall neatly into one box or another—this is simply shorthand for "people who score higher / lower on measures of extraversion."

[9] Indeed, a recurring theme throughout the big five personality traits should be that more is not always better. The most well-adjusted people are typically somewhere between the two extremes of any given dimension.

higher in measures of gratitude, forgiveness, humor, empathy, and volunteerism (Ozer & Benet-Martínez, 2006). As you might imagine, agreeable people tend to make good relationship partners, being unlikely to engage in sexual infidelity (Allen & Walter, 2018) and scoring higher on marital satisfaction (Sayehmiri et al., 2020).

Speaking to facets of agreeableness that differ from extraversion, agreeable people value benevolence and tradition more, tending to avoid rocking the boat or bucking social norms (Roccas et al., 2002). They also tend to report greater religiosity (Saroglou, 2002). Agreeable individuals also report greater pro-environmental behaviors (Pavalache-Ilie & Cazan, 2018). Furthermore, unlike people who score higher in extraversion, agreeable people are less likely to become addicted to social media or to their smartphones (Erdem & Uzun, 2020).

Conscientiousness

Conscientiousness is "the degree to which an individual is dependable, organized, and punctual" (Funder & Fast, 2010, p. 679). Conscientious people can be thought of as epitomizing the "ideal" student or employee: studious, organized, hard-working, and rule following.

Speaking to this idea, conscientiousness is correlated positively with academic effort, perceived academic ability, college grade point average (Noftle & Robins, 2007), and with caring more about achievement (Roccas et al., 2002). Conscientious people are also more motivated to perform well at work (Judge & Ilies, 2002) and to concern themselves with getting their work done perfectly (Stricker et al., 2019). By virtue of their tendency to like and to follow rules, including having stronger religious beliefs (Saroglou, 2002), conscientious people tend to engage in less criminality and commit fewer antisocial behaviors (Ozer & Benet-Martínez, 2006). They also tend to live longer, healthier lives, due to a combination of mindfulness (Giluk, 2009), resilience (Oshio et al., 2018), physical activity (Rhodes & Smith, 2006), and taking fewer risks (Ozer & Benet-Martinez, 2006).

Conscientiousness does have its downsides, however. Conscientious people, focused on rules and perfectionism, do find it more difficult to get absorbed or immersed in an activity (e.g., while playing a video game: Soutter & Hitchens, 2016). Despite their rule following tendencies, highly conscientious people are more likely to engage in sexual infidelity and sexually aggressive behaviors (Allen & Walter, 2018; Moors et al., 2017).

Neuroticism (Emotional Stability)

Neuroticism describes "the degree to which an individual worries, is reactive to stress, and experiences negative emotion" (Funder & Fast, 2010, p. 679). In effect, individuals scoring higher on neuroticism have difficulty coping with stress and with the ups and downs of interpersonal relationships.

In general, neuroticism is linked to negative outcomes, sort of the opposite of the previously described traits. For example, neuroticism is negatively associated with work performance (Judge & Ilies, 2002), mindfulness (Giluk, 2009), resilience (Oshio et al., 2018), physical activity (Rhodes & Smith, 2006), and marital satisfaction (Sayehmiri et al., 2020).

Neuroticism isn't just associated with a lack of thriving and doing well, however—it's also associated with more severe problems, such as personality disorders, antisocial behavior, and lower scores on well-being measures (Ozer & Benet-Martínez, 2006). Neurotic people engage in more wishful thinking and often cope with problems through escapism (Connor-Smith & Flachsbart, 2007) and excessive or dysfunctional fantasizing (Reyes et al., 2017). Highly neurotic people also deal with a host of other issues ranging from sexual dissatisfaction and dysfunction (Allen & Walter, 2018) to dissatisfaction with their body (Allen & Robson, 2020), and from smart phone addiction (Erdem & Uzun, 2020) to a tendency to believe in false rumors and conspiracies (Lai et al., 2020).

Openness

The final big five trait, openness to experience, can be thought of as "the degree to which an individual is creative, open minded, and aesthetic" (Funder & Fast, 2010, p. 679). Of the big five traits, openness is probably the most intuitive and easy to understand, with people scoring high in openness being generally characterized as intelligent and willing to learn, creative, and eager to seek out new people and new situations.

Those who score higher on measures of openness tend to score higher in forgiveness, inspiration, and artistic interests (Ozer & Benet-Martínez, 2006), as well as in their tendency to engage in more intense flights of fantasy (Reyes et al., 2017) and more frequent lucid dreaming (Hess et al., 2017). They also tend to reflect attitudes in support of lifelong learning, including scoring high in cultural intelligence (Ang et al., 2006) and in college exam (SAT) scores (Noftle & Robins, 2007), and preferring more reflective and complex music (Rentfrow & Gosling, 2003). People more open to experience hold more progressive ideas, including liberal sexual attitudes (Allen & Walter, 2018), a greater willingness to engage in consensual non-monogamy (Moors et al., 2017), and more pro-environmental behaviors (Pavalache-Ilie & Cazan, 2018). They also tend to cope better with setbacks (Oshio et al., 2018).

Comparing the Big Five Traits Across Fandoms

Having briefly reviewed what the big five personality traits are and shown that they can play a significant role in predicting the way people think, feel, and behave, we can now turn to question of how anime fans score on these big five traits.

Of course, knowing the score of the average anime fan on each of these five traits would be useless in isolation. Without numbers to compare them to, they're just scores. As such, we compared anime fans, furries, and fantasy sport fans on the big five traits in one of our largest studies. As shown in Figure 15.1, anime fans scored significantly lower in extraversion, agreeableness, and conscientiousness than the other two fan groups. In contrast, with respect to emotional stability and openness to experience, anime fans fell between the other two groups.

It's worth considering the implications of these findings. For example, anime fans tended to be more introverted. These Western anime fans live in a society that's generally constructed to favor extraverts (Cain, 2012).[10] This can be a blow to the well-being of introverts, who may feel like there is something wrong with them for preferring solitary hobbies like artistic endeavors or watching their favorite animated shows (Lawn et al., 2019). Such feelings may contribute to feelings of stigma among anime fans (see Chapter 17) and could explain, at least in part, the sense of kinship they feel among other, like-minded fans, who share not only their hobby, but also be comparable in their personality.

---

[10] Despite the fact that this same research suggests that introverts are more empathic, creative, and do better at school.

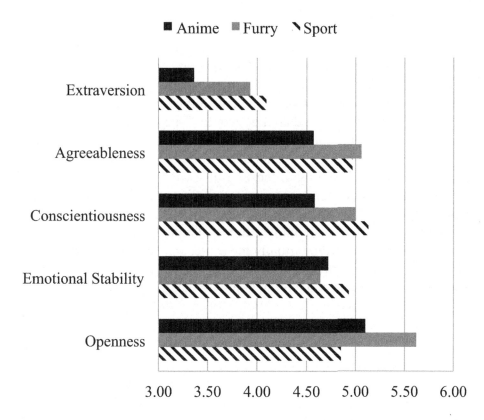

Figure 15.1. Mean ratings of personality for anime, furry, and fantasy sport fans (7-point scale).

Personality Traits in Different Contexts

As Napier (2007) suggests, fan conventions are a place where fans can escape from the burdens of work and school and be one's true self. This is exemplified by a response from a Malaysian fan in a qualitative study of anime fans, who pointed out that while she is typically an introvert in everyday life, in certain situations (like being at an anime-event) she becomes an extravert (Yamato, 2016). Given that fan conventions are set up to encourage interactions and possible new friendships, it's possible that the conventions themselves can potentially lead to more interactions and extraversion among anime fans.[11]

To test this idea, we asked anime fans to complete a measure of the big five personality dimensions. As shown in Figure 15.2, in line with prior research on anime fans, those sampled at an anime convention scored significantly higher on extraversion than those sampled online.[12] One possibility for this finding is that anime fans felt more extraverted while filling out the survey at a con than they would if they were to complete the survey while sitting at home. Another possibility is that more extraverted people are simply more likely to attend an anime convention.[13]

As a test of the replicability of these results, we conducted a similar study nearly five years later, looking at two different conventions (AnimeFest in the U.S. and anime fans sampled at ComicCon in London, ON, Canada) compared to an online sample of anime fans. As shown in Figure 15.3, the results were virtually the same, and can therefore not be chalked up to being a weird quirk of a single sample at a single point in time or due to one anime convention being especially likely to have extraverted participants.

---

[11] This idea also builds upon the social identity perspective (see Chapter 10), with Reynolds et al. (2012) arguing that our personalities change depending on which of our social identities are on our mind. As a demonstration, researchers had Australian participants think about either their national identity, their identity as a student, their identity as non-Aboriginal people before completing a measure of the big five. The results showed that participants' neuroticism differed depending on which social identity was on their mind (also see Reysen et al., 2015a).

[12] In fact, they scored significantly higher in all of the personality dimensions except emotional stability.

[13] Likewise, people more open to new experiences, more agreeable / sociable, and who have the foresight and conscientiousness to plan for a convention may also be more likely to attend a fan convention.

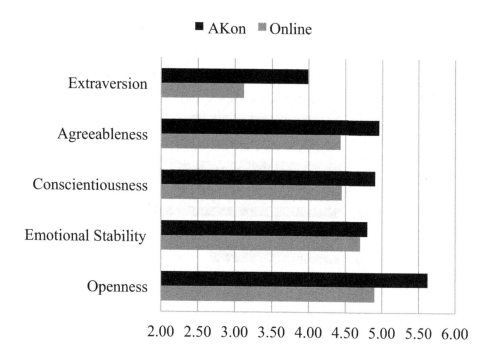

Figure 15.2. Mean ratings of personality for fans completing the survey online compared to at a convention, A-Kon (7-point scale).

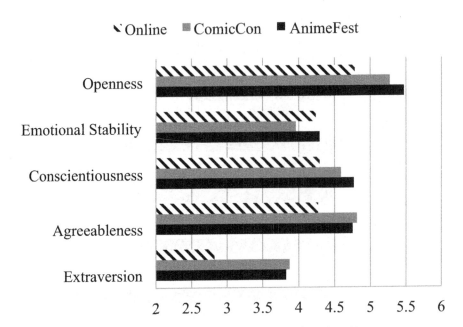

Figure 15.3. Mean ratings of personality completed online versus at conventions (7-point scale).

The Big Five Traits and their Relation to Other Variables

Having shown that the personality of anime fans differs somewhat from that of other fan groups, and, having shown that convention-going and online anime fans differ in their personality scores, it's worth asking what, if anything, knowing about these personality traits can tell us about anime fans and their beliefs and behavior.

To this end, in addition to asking anime fans to complete measures of their personality traits, we also asked fans to complete a number of other psychologically interesting variables, the results of which are shown in Table 15.1.

Variable	E	A	C	ES	O
Well-Being	.34**	.13**	.27**	.46**	.17**
Awkward with Non-Fans	-.25**	-.02	-.14**	-.25**	-.12**
Fanship	.06**	.10**	.07**	-.04*	.11**
Fandom	.15**	.17**	.10**	.02	.20**
Disclose to Close	.09**	.13**	.05**	.02	.12**
Disclose to Distant	.22**	.10**	.08**	.05**	.20**
Obsession	.01	< .01	-.06**	-.09**	< .01
Consume Media	-.11**	-.03	< .01	.13**	-.05
Positive Fantasy	.01	.13**	-.04	.01	.15**
Negative Fantasy	.05	-.04	-.10**	-.13**	-.10**

Table 15.1. Correlations between big five dimensions and assessed variables, E = extraversion, A = agreeableness, C = conscientiousness, ES = emotional stability (low on neuroticism), O = openness, $*p < .05$, $** p < .01$.

In short, the table reveals that many important fan-related variables, from fanship and fandom to consumer behavior and the fan's overall sense of well-being, were all tied to fans' personality traits. Without delving into each link—which could be a chapter in itself, we'll briefly touch on some of the more interesting observations.

Extraversion was strongly associated with well-being, a finding consistent with research we reviewed earlier in this chapter showing that extraverts tend to have better interpersonal relationships. Speaking to this idea, extraverts also tend to score lower on social awkwardness—suggesting they have better social skills—and score higher on measures of identification with others in the anime fan community. Extraverts are also more likely to be able to disclose their anime fan identity to others, suggesting that they may have more friends who are also anime fans.

We also find that emotional stability—the opposite pole of neuroticism—is associated with more consumption, but also with less obsessive consumption of anime in general. It was also less associated with negative, dysfunctional forms of fantasy engagement. In other words, it would seem that more neurotic fans, while not necessarily consuming more anime in general, are more obsessive about the anime that they do consume. They're also more likely to engage in that consumption in more

323

troublesome ways (e.g., blurring the lines between fantasy and reality, or doing so in ways that make other people uncomfortable).

Finally, we note that all of the personality traits assessed were positively correlated with fans' overall sense of well-being, suggesting that these traits, despite being differently associated with different elements of fan behavior, are all tied in some way to a person's overall degree of functioning. This is an important demonstration of the importance of personality when putting together models of anime fans' thoughts, feelings, behaviors, and other outcomes of interest.

The Dark Side of Personality

While the big five personality traits represent the most frequently-used model of personality in psychological research, they're far from the only game in town. Paulhus and Williams (2002), for example, suggest a triad of personality traits that are important for understanding troublesome or disliked aspects of human behavior. These three traits include Machiavellianism (being manipulative for one's own gain), narcissism (entitlement, felt superiority over others, egotism), and psychopathy (low empathy, impulsiveness, and antisocial behavior). In general, those who score higher score on this dark triad are also more likely to engage in counterproductive behavior, cheating in school, bullying, and criminal activity (Furnham et al., 2013).

Given the stigma sometimes associated with anime fans (see Chapter 17), we sought to test whether they scored higher than the average person on the dark triad. We gave the "dirty dozen," a 12-item measure of the dark triad (Jonason & Webster, 2010), to anime fans, comparing them to a general population sample of 309 U.S. participants recruited online. As shown in Figure 15.2, anime fans did score significantly lower on measures of narcissism and Machiavellianism but scored higher on psychopathy.[14]

While this analysis shows that anime fans are not especially high on the dark triad traits, there was variability in anime fans' scores, with some scoring much higher or much lower on each of these traits. As such, we next examined whether anime fans' scores on the dark triad traits could tell

---

[14] That said, the means on all these scales were below the midpoint of the measure (4.00 / 7.00). In other words, while anime fans scored higher in psychopathy, this is a far cry from saying that anime fans, are a group, are remorseless psychopaths.

us anything meaningful about other facets of their fan-related activities (Table 15.3).

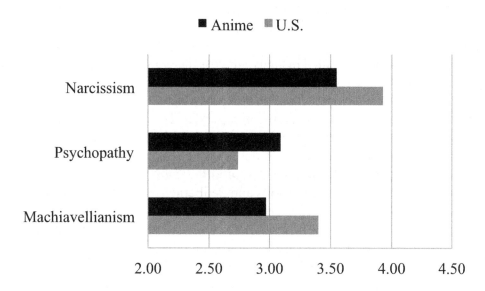

Figure 15.2. Mean ratings of dark triad for anime fans and U.S. community sample (7-point scale).

Variable	N	P	M
Time Fan (Years)	-.02	-.03	-.03
Watch Anime	-.14**	.02	-.01
Read Manga	-.04	.02	< .01
Read News/Blogs	.03	.05	.04
Talk with Friends	.02	.02	.06
Fanship	.11**	.01	.02
Fandom	.07*	-.04	< .01
Negative Fantasy	.13**	.19**	.19**
Positive Fantasy	.16**	.06	.08*

Table 15.3. Correlations between dark triad and fandom related variables (N = neuroticism, P = psychopathy, M = Machiavellianism), * $p < .05$, ** $p < .01$.

For the most part, dark triad scores said relatively little about anime fans' behavior. Narcissism was associated with watching less anime and was more associated with fanship, suggesting somehow that narcissists, despite consuming less anime, nevertheless feel more strongly like anime fans. More importantly, however, the dark triad traits were all associated with greater fantasy engagement. This may suggest that something about engaging in fantasy activities that are excessive or which disturb others may be, at least in part, associated with personality traits that also predict someone's generally being dislikable as a person. To better understand these results with respect to fantasy engagement, this last part of the chapter dives a bit into some of the research on fantasy engagement as a trait.

Fantasy Engagement: A Specific Personality Trait

Fantasy is defined "as a conscious and deliberate suspension of disbelief in nonreality" (Plante et al., 2017, p. 127).[15] Much of the psychological research on fantasy focuses on child-like activities like playing pretend or having imaginary friends. This is despite the fact that fantasizing is a common facet of everyday life in adulthood—playing video games, reading books, daydreaming, or watching movies, as just a few examples.

To better understand the dual nature of fantasy as both something with immature, dysfunctional elements (e.g., losing touch with reality, immaturity) and as something that's a positive facet of most peoples' day-to-day life, Plante et al. (2017) constructed a short measure of fantasy engagement that assesses these two dimensions, describing them as negative fantasy engagement (e.g., "My fantasies about anime have interfered with my relationships") and positive fantasy engagement (e.g., "Fantasizing about anime makes me more creative"), respectively. In prior studies, we found that positive fantasy engagement is related to more frequent fantasy engagement, being able to picture things more vividly, and becoming more immersed in fantasy worlds. In contrast, negative fantasy engagement is related to lower well-being, maladaptive ways of coping with setbacks, losing touch with reality, and drug use.

As shown in Table 15.4, fantasy engagement was generally associated with virtually every facet of anime fan behavior. Positive fantasy

---

[15] It's important to note that fantasy, as defined here, refers specifically to acts that a person deliberately engages in. A person who's hallucinating, or someone who is dreaming and doesn't realize that they're dreaming, is not engaging in fantasy.

engagement was generally associated with more consumption behavior, with stronger identification as an anime fan and with other anime fans, and with greater well-being. This is akin to what many anime fans picture when they imagine a very devoted, high-functioning anime fan.

Variable	Positive	Negative
Watch Anime	.22**	.04
Read Manga	.16**	.07
Read News/Blogs	.17**	.09*
Talk with Friends	.29**	.09**
Fanship	.53**	.06*
Fandom	.48**	.01
Number Figurines	.12**	.14**
Number Kigurumi	.09**	.26**
Number Body Pillows	.10**	.29**
Number Anime Tattoos	.08*	.30**
Satisfaction with Life	.16**	-.08*
Self-Esteem	.12**	-.17**

Table 15.4. Regressions with fantasy engagement predicting fandom related variables, standardized betas presented, $* p < .05, ** p < .01$.

In contrast, negative fantasy engagement paints a less flattering picture of anime fans, one characterized by reduced well-being and less of a tendency to involve themselves in the anime fandom. Surprisingly, while negative fantasy engagement was only minimally associated with one's fanship score and was unrelated entirely to a person's tendency to watch anime or read manga, negative fantasy engagement did fairly strongly predict the purchasing of kigurumi, body pillows, and anime tattoos. Given this pattern of associations, one could possibly make the argument that the consumption of these items specifically, coupled with a lack of being especially connected to the broader anime community, may be a potential red flag for a person who is struggling with respect to their overall well-being.

Conclusion

In the present chapter we reviewed the big five dimensions of personality. Anime fans tended to report being fairly introverted as a group, and also scored relatively low in agreeableness and conscientiousness relative to other fans. However, anime fans should not be thought of as all being the same, as we presented evidence supporting the idea that context matters: Convention-going anime fans seem to differ in their personality traits—for example, being more outgoing—than online anime fans.

When we assessed measures of undesirable personality traits, anime fans scored fairly low, especially on the traits of narcissism and Machiavellianism, suggesting a relatively low level of dysfunctionality, at least in terms of personality. And, with respect to the nature of their fantasy engagement, we found that positive fantasy engagement is considerably more tied to most facets of anime fan consumption and identification, while the more troublesome negative fantasy engagement seems to be more limited to specific types of consumption habits (e.g., collecting body pillows and kigurumi).

Given that, to this point in the book, we've alluded to connections between various facets of being an anime fan and well-being, it's about time we turned our attention to the question of how well anime fans in general are functioning and the various factors contributing to their ability to function in day-to-day life.

Chapter 16
Anime Stereotypes

As a social species, we humans spend a lot of time comparing ourselves to others. And why shouldn't we? According to social identity theory (Chapter 10), our sense of self-esteem is built upon belonging to the best groups and being the best members of those groups that we can be. How can we know whether we're part of the best group if we don't compare ourselves to other groups from time to time?

So, it comes as no surprise—to psychologists or to fans alike—that fan groups get compared to one another all the time.[1] As a general rule, when trying to make up our minds about a particular fan group, our go-to move is to compare the group to a standard or prototypical fan. For most folks, this means comparing other fan groups to sport fans, since sport is undoubtedly the most mainstream of fan groups, what with having entire television networks and news segments dedicated to their coverage.

As the "default" fans, sport fans tend to be portrayed in a generally positive manner,[2] including being treated as both popular and normal, despite the inherent weirdness of sport itself (End et al., 2003). By extension, this means that non-sport fans, like anime fans, are considered unpopular, abnormal, or downright deviant by comparison (Reysen & Shaw, 2016). While some non-sport fandoms are gaining in popularity (e.g., music and TV fans), they largely remain stigmatized compared to sport fans, with people often associating negative stereotypes with these groups (e.g., furries, bronies).

Anime fans, in this regard, find themselves in a particularly precarious position. On the one hand, they exist on the fringe of mainstream fan culture, and so most people know what anime is. However, most people also know very little about anime itself or about who anime fans are. Stereotypes exist to fill in the gaps of this ignorance, and this is precisely what researchers such as ourselves investigate. After all, prior research on

---

[1] Fans and non-fans are guilty of doing this!

[2] True, not all stereotypes of sport fans are flattering (e.g., the beer-swilling, aggressive football fan, riots at soccer games), but it's hard to deny that sport fans, with their mainstream presence, are treated as more positive than negative.

the stereotypes of other groups generally shows that while some stereotypes contain a kernel of truth, many are inaccurate (Jussim et al., 1996; Ryan, 2002). With all of this in mind, in this chapter we examine the stereotypes commonly attributed to anime fans and test whether there's any truth to be found in any of them.

Why Stereotypes Matter

Before we delve into the stereotypes of anime fans, it's worth asking why we should care in the first place about stereotypes. After all, if many stereotypes have at least a kernel of truth to them, is it really a bad thing to believe them? Even if a stereotype exists, one can simply choose to ignore it, can't they? After all, a lot of people claim that they judge people on their own merits, regardless of the stereotypes one might otherwise endorse. So, what's the harm in assuming a few things about a group as a whole?

Well, for one thing, whether we realize it or not, stereotypes affect the way we perceive members of those groups. Even if we're consciously trying to look past stereotypes or don't feel like we're affected by them, the reality is that stereotypes affect the way we look at people at a fundamental level. We know, for example, that people are more likely to remember stereotype-consistent information about someone than they are to remember stereotype-inconsistent information (Fyock & Stangor, 1994). Or, to put it another way, if someone believes the stereotype that anime fans are socially awkward, they're more likely to notice and remember socially awkward anime fans and to forget about charismatic anime fans. We don't choose what we do or don't remember—this tendency is simply a product of how our minds work.

Stereotypes can also influence the way people behave, whether they realize it or not. In one notable study, Bargh and colleagues (1996) put the idea of "elderly" into their participants' heads. Later, as the participants were leaving the study, they walked toward the elevator more slowly, in-line with the stereotype of elderly people.[3] In short, simply having the stereotype of a group on one's mind can affect our behavior in ways we're not consciously aware of. After all, it's unlikely that no one in the previous study consciously thought "well, now that I'm thinking about older people,

---

[3] A future research idea may be to see if priming anime fans as a social category may prompt a "Naruto" run in a follow-up task? We should note that Bargh et al.'s (1996) study has been criticized after other researchers have been unable to replicate their results.

who stereotypes say are slow and frail, I'm going to decide to walk slowly, because that idea is now on my mind." These processes operate largely outside of our own awareness and, as such, we can't just take people at their word when they say that they don't think their behavior is affected by these stereotypes.

Stereotypes can also alter the way group members see themselves. For example, in studies of basketball players, researchers found that racial stereotypes (e.g., Black people are better at basketball) not only influence the viewer's interpretation of a player's performance (Stone et al., 1997), but these same stereotypes also influenced how the players saw themselves (Stone et al., 1999). In fact, researchers have discovered a phenomenon known as stereotype threat, in which stereotypes can hurt the performance of people who feel like they are being judged by others, leading to the sorts of stereotypical underperforming that people expect to see (e.g., worrying about stereotypes that women are bad at math can undermine women's performance on math exams: Steele & Aronson, 1995).

Ultimately, stereotypes are embedded within in our culture and influence us in subtle ways, regardless of whether we even believe the stereotypes ourselves (Adams et al., 2008). They become mental shortcut that help us make decisions and interact with others quickly and easily (Hilton & von Hippel, 1996; Schneider, 2005) and which allow non-fans to assume knowledge about anime fans without having to spend the hours necessary to become familiar with the fandom and its norms. For outsiders, this can mean approving or disapproving of anime based on the one or two fans they know or what they have heard about anime fans from the media. As it turns out, "disapproving" is the more likely outcome, given that many of the stereotypes of anime fans are far from flattering.

The Stereotypical Anime Fan

If you do a Google autocomplete search for the term "why are anime fans," the top suggestions include completions like "so weird," "so ugly," and "losers." Likewise, the phrase "anime fans are…" yields completions like "disgusting," "cancer," "cringe," "creepy," "annoying," and "the worst."

Yikes!

This exercise, while crude, certainly makes clear that the average Google user tends to endorse some pretty unflattering stereotypes about anime fans.

Scholarly literature outside of the field of psychology, while less extreme, tends to paint a similarly negative picture of anime fans. Napier (2001), for example, notes that anime fans are often stereotyped as consumers of violent and pornographic cartoons. Dinnie (2012) notes that fans are seen as adults who are obsessed with anime and who avoid the outdoors; Mycella (2012) focused on stereotypes of anime fans using anime to escape from life while also having no life themselves, with anime consumption (especially hentai) taking up most of their time.[4]

In our own published research (i.e., Reysen, Plante, Roberts, Gerbasi, Mohebpour, & Gamboa, 2016), we asked a sample of non-fans to indicate the extent to which they endorsed a number of stereotypes about the anime fandom. Table 16.1 shows the results, as well as whether or not there was evidence to support the stereotype from our research (also see Reysen, Plante, Roberts, Gerbasi, & Shaw, 2016).

As the table shows, anime fans are indeed stereotyped by non-fans as being an introverted, creative, socially awkward nerds who are detached from reality and escape life through consumption of anime and manga. Some of these findings overlap with the non-psychology research, such as social awkwardness, spending large amounts of time watching anime, watching lots of cartoons, using anime as an escape, and anime fans being nerds and geeks. While some of these stereotypes are true, the evidence for many of them are mixed at best when held up to empirical scrutiny, a topic we'll explore in greater depth later in this chapter. Before then, however, let's briefly detour to look a bit closer at where these stereotypes come from and how unique they are to anime fans.

---

[4] Anime fans also experience many of the same stereotypes that plague other geek and nerd communities (Fu, 2013), including being treated as mindless (Manion, 2005), socially awkward, and having poor hygiene (Dunbar, 2011).

Stereotype	Empirically Supported?
Introverted	Supported
Open to new experiences	Not supported
Spend most time with Anime	Supported
Overweight	Not supported
Pale	Partial support
Wear glasses	Supported
Geeks / Nerds	Supported
Asian	Not supported
Overly excited about anime	Supported
Detached from real life	Not supported
Only look at porn	Not supported
Computer geeks	Partial support
Own body pillows	Not supported
Play too many games	Supported
Sexual perverts	Not supported
Lack social skills	Not supported
Anti-social	Not supported
Socially awkward	Not supported
Immature	Not supported
Bad hygiene	Partial support
Have no friends	Not supported
Obsessed with anime	Supported
Social outcasts	Not supported
Young	Supported
Not very religious	Supported
Not athletic	Not supported
Don't play sports	Not supported
Motive: Self-Esteem	Supported
Motive: Belonging	Supported
Motive: Aesthetic	Supported
Motive: Not Economics	Supported
Motive: Escape	Supported
Motive: Eustress	Supported
Motive: Entertainment	Supported
Are cosplayers	Partial Support

Table 16.1. Anime fan stereotypes, and whether there was empirical evidence supporting the stereotype.

Stereotype Comparisons

As we mentioned earlier, some of the stereotypes attributable to anime fans are tied to "geek" and "nerd" culture more broadly, a culture which, itself, is plagued with a number of unflattering stereotypes. Because of this, it's hard to know which of the stereotypes outlined in Table 16.1 are distinctly about anime fans.

To address this problem, we ran a study asking non-fans to estimate the personality traits of an average anime fan, eSport fan (professional gamer), and renaissance fair performer. As seen in Figure 16.1 (7-point scale), anime fans were perceived as comparable to the other fan groups personality-wise, with one notable exception: introversion. Anime fans were seen as distinctly introverted compared to the other fans and were, in fact, the only group that was rated as being below the midpoint on the extraversion scale. This perception of anime fans as introverted fits the stereotype of anime fans as shy and socially awkward.[5]

---

[5] And while renaissance fair performers were rated fairly high on all of the traits, eSports enthusiasts were notable in being lower in agreeableness. If you know anything about *Overwatch* or *League of Legends* and some of the toxicity present in player banter, it's not hard to see why this is the case.

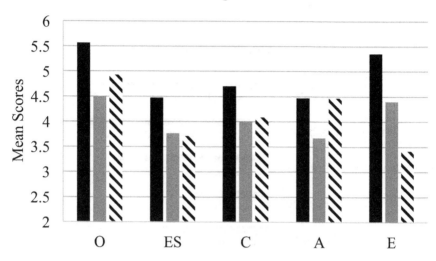

Figure 16.1. Non-fans' perception of personality traits in anime fans, eSport fans, and Renaissance faire performers, O = openness, ES = emotional stability, C = conscientiousness, A = agreeableness, E = extraversion.

Moving beyond the perceived personality of anime fans compared to other fan groups, we also compared the perceptions of the three groups on a number of the stereotypes shown in Table 16.1. As Figure 16.2 reveals, anime fans stood out in being especially geeky, being easily overexcited by their hobby, and lacking in social skills.[6] The latter point reinforces what we found in our first analysis, showing in another way that anime fans are seen as being introverted, perhaps in part, because of a lack of social skills. While most of these stereotypes were only somewhat endorsed by people (with many falling below the scale's midpoint of 4), it is notable that none of the stereotypes were wholly denied or opposed by participants (e.g., the belief that anime fans—and geeks in general—have poor hygiene).

---

[6] Strongely, aииие fans were also rated the highest, albeit not statistically significantly so, to excessively play video games. This is a pretty impressive feat, considering they were being compared against eSport enthusiasts who, by definition, watch and play video games as a hobby.

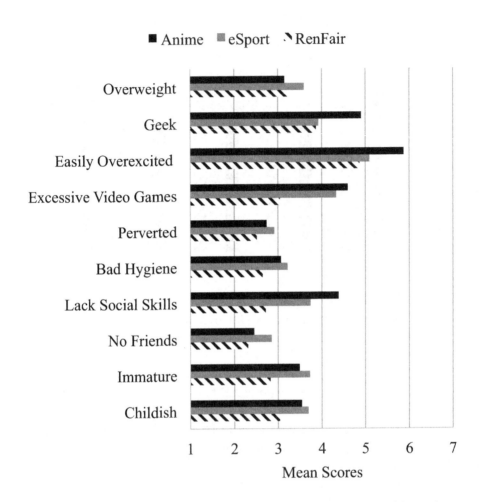

Figure 16.2. Stereotyped traits in anime fans, eSport fans, and Renaissance faire performers (7-point scale).

As a final analysis from the same study, we asked the same participants to rate members of the three different fan groups with respect to what they believe motivates these fans. As seen in Figure 16.3, anime fans were seen as fairly comparable with the other fan groups with respect to most of the motivations, although they were seen as significantly less motivated by family or economic benefits than members of the other two groups. That aside, the three groups were rated as the most motivated by entertainment, belongingness, and escapism, numbers which map onto the actual motivations of anime fans fairly well (see Chapter 14). As a final point, anime fans were the only one of the three groups rated above the midpoint of the scale with respect to being seen as motivated by sexual attraction to fan-related content.

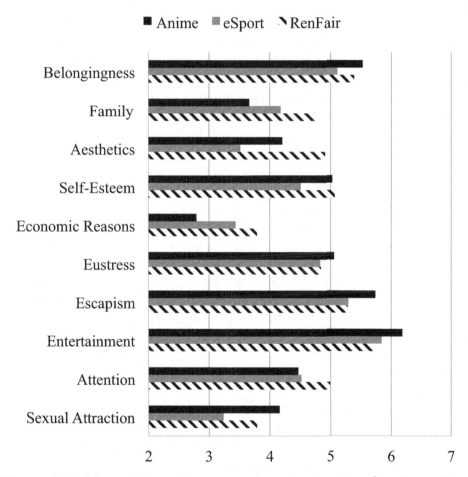

Figure 16.3. Mean ratings of stereotyped motivations in anime fans, eSport fans, and Renaissance faire performers (7-point scale).

In conclusion, our own research has shown that anime fans are the subject of a number of unflattering stereotypes—some specific to anime fans, others directed to geek and nerd fandoms more broadly.

As scientists, however, we're not content to merely document the existence of these stereotypes. One of the questions we're routinely asked is whether these stereotypes hold any water empirically. After all, while many of these stereotypes are undoubtedly born from ignorance or the memorability of extreme examples, a look at some of the existing literature on anime fans suggest there may be at least some merit to some of the stereotypes. As such, we examine these stereotypes and how they hold up to seven years of concerted research on the anime fandom.

A Critical Look at Anime Fan Stereotypes

The story of anime fans throughout this book (e.g., Chapter 12, Chapter 19) has been one of people with an unusual hobby who, nevertheless, benefit from belonging to the anime community. Of course, we temper these conclusions with the caveat that, in many cases, these findings are correlational in nature[7] and are aggregated across thousands of anime fans—meaning they don't preclude the existence of extreme or dysfunctional fans. Even so, our conclusion is largely that anime fans seem to be, on average, normal, well-adjusted people with a non-mainstream hobby.

As such, we need to reconcile the discrepancy between our own findings about anime fans with the negative stereotypes we raised earlier in this chapter in Table 16.1. What follows is the documentation of our attempts to empirically test many of these stereotypes when possible, allowing us to contextualize the good of the anime fandom with the drawbacks of the fandom while also dispelling inaccurate or misleading misconceptions about anime fans along the way.

What do we know about anime fans, as a group? In our earliest studies we found that anime fans, while leaning a bit more toward introversion than the average person (see Chapter 15), are not, as the stereotype would suggest, extremely introverted and socially awkward.[8] However, on average

---

[7] And remember, as we pointed out in Chapter 2, correlation does not equal causation!

[8] They do, however, play fewer sports than other fan groups we've studied, playing into another stereotype associated with geeks.

anime fans do lean toward introversion. We do note that anime fans identify as nerds (although not necessarily as geeks), a term which, traditionally, has been associated with social awkwardness. However, when we consider fan scholarship outside of psychology, it becomes clear that geek identification is increasingly common amongst fan communities (e.g., "comic book geeks"), as fans have worked to embrace and removed the stigma associated with the term[9] (Jenkins, 2007; Kohnen, 2014).

Also, in line with stereotypes about nerds, stereotypes suggest that anime fans spend a great deal of money on, and get exceedingly enthusiastic about, their interest. Our data suggest that this is largely the case (Chapter 4). This finding is again unsurprising when compared to fans in general, who tend to be defined by having a considerably higher passion for an interest than is typical (Wann et al., 2000), although, even among other fan groups (e.g., fantasy sport fans), anime fans seem to spend a considerable amount of time on their interest compared to fantasy sport fans (see Figure 16.4).[10]

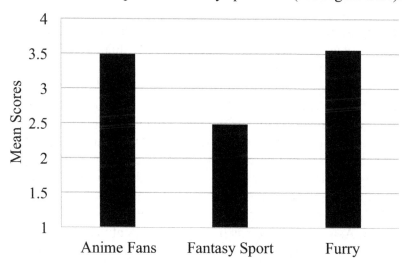

Figure 16.4. Time spent on fan activities between anime fans, fantasy sport fans, and furries (7-point scale).

---

[9] Among many fans, the term "geek" today is interchangeable with the term "fan."
[10] We consider this stereotype to be only partly supported, since these same data shows that other fan groups, like furries, spend even *more* time engaging with fan-related content. At very least, we can say that anime fans are far from the worst offenders.

As mentioned in previous chapters (e.g., Chapter 14), we've found that one of the primary motivations driving anime fans is to escape reality through anime and manga, something in-line with stereotypes of anime fans as seeking escapism or, in a less-flattering framing, being out-of-touch. This seeking of escapism is hardly unique to anime fans, however, as even sport fans report using their interest as a cathartic release from day-to-day stressors (Wann et al., 2004). It's hardly done to a dysfunctional extent, however, as research on negative fantasy engagement discussed in Chapter 15 makes clear: Anime fans have especially active imaginations and fantasy lives, but rarely to a dysfunctional extent.

While some of the common stereotypes about anime fans were mixed or only partially substantiated, other stereotypes of anime fans seem to be fairly spot-on. For example, non-fans accurately described the primary motivator of anime fans as being for entertainment, escape, and self-esteem, while also correctly pointing out that the least-motivating drives were money and family.[11]

Other substantiated stereotypes about anime fans include the stereotype that anime fans are not especially religious or spiritual, something we noted was true in Chapter 3, both for anime fans but also for younger fan communities and young people in general (see Edwards et al., 2019 on bronies). While anime fans may not be quite as young as stereotypes might suggest, they are, statistically speaking, younger than other fan groups we've studied, if only by a year or so on average. Furthermore, while there are plenty of religious anime fans, studies generally find that each new generation is less and less likely to be associated with organized religion.[12]

Other stereotypes about anime fans missed the mark by a fair bit. For example, one stereotype about anime fans is that most fans are "non-White," with Asian being seen as the most prevalent racial group in the fandom. This stereotype makes sense intuitively, given that anime itself is Japanese. However, given that we were asking participants from mainly Western countries about the anime fandom, their estimates were fairly off.

---

[11] Given what we've said already about anime fans' consumption habits, it's hardly surprising that anime, as an interest, is hardly a profitable endeavor for most fans.
[12] It also doesn't help that anime may receive stigma from religious communities because of its content. A notable exception to this is Beneath the Tangles (a group that seeks to bridge the gap between anime fans and Christianity: beneaththetangles.com).

Most American anime fans (nearly 70%) are White, while only around 16% are Asian. This would seem to suggest that non-fans are using what little knowledge they have of anime (e.g., that it's made primarily in Japan) to draw statistical conclusions about the Western anime fandom that are largely incorrect.[13]

Non-fans also largely endorsed the stereotype that sex was among the biggest motivators driving anime fans' interest (second only to entertainment). As previously discussed in Chapter 9, hentai, as a genre, is not especially popular with anime fans. Moreover, other motivating factors, like belongingness and entertainment, play a much bigger role in driving anime fans' behavior. This misconception may be grounded in the availability heuristic—the tendency for people to remember things that are emotionally shocking or jarring to them. In this case, seeing hentai content (e.g., tentacle porn) may be especially surprising for non-fans, sticking out in their mind as a particularly poignant and salient example of anime content. This, in turn, could lead non-fans to assume that hentai content makes up the bulk of what anime fans consume, which could lead to the stereotype that most anime fans are motivated by sex.

As seen in Figure 16.5, non-fans predicted slightly higher number of male versus female anime fans. As a final, fairly significant misconception of anime fans, stereotypes suggest that as many as two-thirds of anime fans engage in cosplay. In reality, the actual number is about half of that.[14] It suggests that non-fans are extrapolating what little they know about anime fans to the anime fandom as a whole. Most people probably know that cosplay is a thing that some anime fans do (given how visually iconic cosplay is as part of the anime fandom). As such, they paint most anime fans with the same brush, and assume that they all engage in this particular activity. It's an excellent demonstration of how people erroneously apply

---

[13] Although it is worth noting that there is a higher proportion of Asian people in the anime fandom than one finds in the general American population, this is a far cry from saying that most Western anime fans are Asian.

[14] This misconception is tellingly similar to the common misperception that most furries wear full-body, mascot-style fursuits. In reality, only about one-quarter of furries owns one, in part because of the sheer cost of buying one and the difficulty in making one for oneself.

stereotypes and how they can, in some cases, lead to entirely inaccurate conclusions about anime fans.

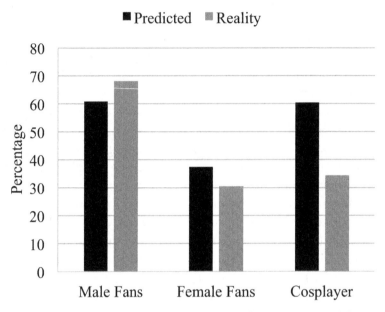

Figure 16.5. Non-Fan predictions of gender and percentage of fans who cosplay.

Conclusion

Throughout this chapter, we've seen examples of how non-fans assume certain things to be true about the anime fandom—assumptions based on stereotypical beliefs about anime fans. Many of these stereotypes are unflattering, to say the least, and owe, at least in part, to the fact that anime, while almost mainstream in its appeal, is nevertheless distinct from, and less popular than, sport fans, marking it as a "deviant" fan interest. From this, assumptions about anime fans as dysfunctional, excessive, or undesirable take hold and shape peoples' perceptions about, and behavior toward, anime fans (something we'll discuss in Chapter 17 and Chapter 18).

Some of the stereotypes people hold about the anime fandom are true, some are somewhat mixed in their accuracy, and some are outright wrong. Stereotypes grounded in the fact that anime fans are geeks tend to hold a bit of water, such as anime fans being more introverted and having an especially strong passion for their interest. Others are somewhat more mixed—such as stereotypes that anime fans, as a group, are fairly young. Others are wrong entirely, such as the stereotype that Western anime fans are predominantly Asian and engage in cosplay.

As we move forward, let's keep these stereotypes in mind, along with the idea that stereotypes themselves can affect the way we think about and behave toward others, whether we realize it or not. It is essential to understand that point if we're to have any chance of understanding how largely negative stereotypes about anime fans can lead to the stigmatization, ostracism, and outright bullying of anime fans.

Chapter 17
Stigma and the Anime Fandom

A stigma is an identity that's judged negatively by others (Major & O'Brien, 2005). The term is typically used to describe marginalized groups including, but not limited to, racially or ethnically marginalized communities (e.g., Black, Indigenous, Mixed People of Color), incarcerated people (e.g., prison inmates), people of lower socioeconomic status (e.g., people living in poverty, uneducated people), people with illnesses or maladies (e.g., people with HIV/AIDS), sexual or gender-diverse folks (e.g., LGBTQ+ people), and people with visible and invisible disabilities.

Since the publication of Erving Goffman's (1963) seminal work on stigma, scholars across disciplines have studied the concept, in no small part because of the detrimental impact it has on the lives of stigmatized people. For example, studies have shown that stigmatized people experience lower well-being (Schmitt et al., 2014), poorer academic performance, economic disadvantage (Major & O'Brien, 2005), and social exclusion (Major & Eccleston, 2004)—to name just a few of stigma's negative effects.

Knowing well that stigma has an impact on stigmatized people, the present chapter asks whether anime fans, as members of a minority group (both as fans themselves and as fans of a non-mainstream fan interest), experience stigma.[1] To test this idea, we assess whether there exists a link between the stereotypes non-fans have of anime fans and those same non-fans' desire to keep their distance from anime fans. We then ask whether anime fans themselves can accurately perceive the extent of any prejudice directed toward them. Finally, we address some of the ways fans have learned to cope with any experienced stigma.

---

[1] The question is important not just because it allows us to better understand stigma for anime fans specifically but also for fan groups more generally. Much of the research on stigma tends to focus on groups that people belong to through no choice of their own (e.g., racial groups). In contrast, there has been far less research looking at the extent to which people experience stigma for volitional group membership—that is, belonging to a group that they have chosen to belong to.

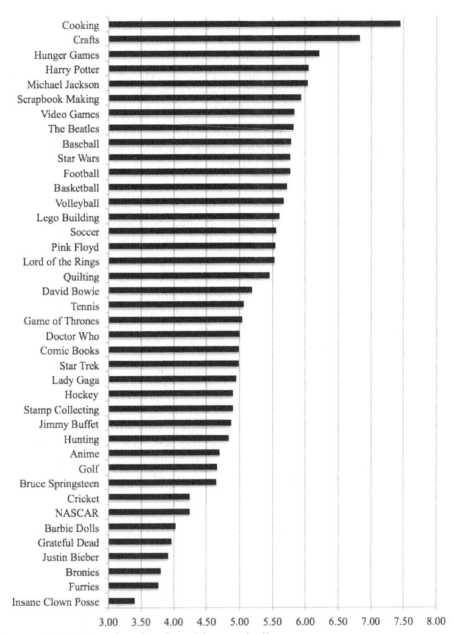

Figure 17.1. Mean levels of positive prejudice.

Are Anime Fans Stigmatized?

In previous chapters (e.g., Chapter 16) we addressed some of the negative stereotypes that exist about anime fans. However, while negative stereotypes are related to stigma, they are not necessarily the same thing as stigma. To assess stigma, one would, ideally, ask people directly how positively or negatively they felt about the group in question.

Which is precisely what we did. We asked 236 U.S. undergraduate students[2] to rate their attitudes toward fans of 40 different popular leisure activities. The measure ranged from 1 = *cold* to 10 = *warm*, with a value of 5.5 representing the midpoint of the scale. Higher scores indicate positive attitudes toward a group while lower scores indicate prejudice toward a group.

As shown in Figure 17.1, anime fans showed a mean of 4.70, below the midpoint of the scale. This suggests that people have a somewhat negative attitude toward anime fans, one exemplified further by the fact that anime fans were rated in the bottom quarter or so of the different fan interests.[3]

To understand why this stigma exists toward some fans, take a look again at the fan groups held in the most positive regard and the most stigmatized fan groups. What do the positively-regarded fans have in common, and what makes them different from the stigmatized fans?

We can answer this question with a bit of psychology! Research has shown that things which deviate from what is considered normal or prototypical are often viewed unfavorably. For example, studies show that when you ask Americans to describe a typical "American," they usually describe a White person. In fact, the more a group differs from this White prototypical American, the more they tend to be viewed as less American (Devos & Banaji, 2005). In a similar vein, the prototype of "sex" has been

---

[2] It's worth noting that looking for stigma in a population of fairly progressive college students is a fairly conservative (no pun intended) test. In a more representative population, one would likely expect to find higher levels of stereotyping, intolerance, and, by extension, stigma directed toward others.

[3] It appears that cooking is the most beloved of the interests studied, which would probably explain the seemingly endless barrage of cooking shoes on television and, more recently, on YouTube. Furries and bronies, on the other hand, two groups we have studied extensively and which anime fans are compared to throughout this book, fare far worse, near the bottom of the list behind only juggalos, self-identified fans of the hip hop duo, *Insane Clown Posse*.

shown to be heterosexual vaginal intercourse (i.e., missionary) for most people. As such, people who engage in other, less-frequently practiced sexual activities are stigmatized because of this deviation (Reysen, Shaw, & Brooks, 2015).[4]

The list goes on and on: single people (i.e., not in a relationship) and left-handed people report lower self-esteem when they compare themselves to people in a relationship or to right-handed people (Hegarty & Bruckmüller, 2013), in part because of the discrimination they face for being different (Devos & Mohamed, 2014).[5] As if that weren't enough, people in non-prototypical groups are also faced with the additional burden of having to explain why they are different from the default group (something that, for instance, heterosexual people, right-handed people, or people in a relationship don't have to explain; Hegarty & Bruckmüller, 2013). Unfortunately, higher-status, prototypical group members often conjure up unsavory explanations to legitimize the stigma directed at non-prototypical group members while also conveniently legitimizing their own elevated status (Sibley, 2010).

To put it simply, the more different a group is, the more its members tend to be stigmatized.

In a follow-up study to the one mentioned earlier, we asked 264 U.S. undergraduate students to describe what they thought of as a typical fan, and then rated how normal (i.e., prototypical) the 40 fan interests from Figure 17.1 were. Participants also again listed how positive or negative they felt toward the groups.

The results showed, first and foremost, that sport fans were what most people thought of as the prototypical fan (50.8% of participants spontaneously mentioned sport fans). Follow-up analyses of their ratings of the 40 groups showed that anime fans were, again, rated below the

---

[4] Relevant to the present topic of anime, this same study found that people who own body pillows, engage in yaoi role-play, and watch tentacle erotica are seen as both statistically rare (deviant from the prototypical person) and significantly stigmatized.

[5] The case of left-handed people is especially telling, since, as far as traits go, being left-handed or having red hair (vs. brown hair) is about as innocuous as a trait can be. And yet, by virtue of simply being different, members of these groups frequently experience stigma just for being different.

midpoint of the prejudice measure, suggesting a moderate amount of stigma toward anime fans as a group.

Most importantly, however, an analysis of all 40 groups revealed that the most prototypical groups were the ones that were seen the most positively. In other words, among fan groups, just like other groups (e.g., racial groups, sexual orientation), deviating from what's normal or prototypical is linked to stigma. The results thus show that, yes, anime fans are stigmatized, if for no other reason than for simply liking something that's different from what most people like.[6]

Distancing from Anime Fans

As with most things in life, stigma is not completely black-and-white—it exists on a scale. As such, rather than thinking about anime fans as either falling into a "stigmatized" or "non-stigmatized" box, we can instead ask the more sophisticated question: To what extent are anime fans stigmatized?

To answer this question, we can ask how far non-anime fans would prefer to distance themselves from anime fans. This "social distancing" approach was first developed by Bogardus (1928, 1933) to study racism in the U.S., based on the idea that racists would go out of their way to avoid going to school with, working with, and living near racially diverse people. The measure has been adapted numerous times since then and has been used to measure stigma directed at other groups (e.g., mentally ill people, people with HIV).

The scale was given to non-anime fans, who completed the 12 items (Biernat & Crandall, 1999) that asked them about their desire to be around a typical anime fan, eSport fan, or renaissance fair performer on a 7-point scale (1 = *strongly disagree* to 7 = *strongly agree*).[7] As shown in Figure 17.2, both eSport and renaissance fair performers were at about the midpoint of the measure, suggesting a moderate amount of social distancing.

---

[6] We don't wish to argue, of course, that this is the *only* reason for stigma toward anime fans. Media portrayals of anime fans that play into negative stereotypes and the ability to share extreme instances of anime fan behavior on social media likely contribute to this stigma. But it can't be denied that, even in the absence of these other factors, anime fans would almost certainly continue to be stigmatized just for being different.

[7] Questions asked, for example, to what extent they would want to marry, be friends with, or work alongside an anime fan.

In contrast, anime fans were significantly below the scale's midpoint, suggesting that people, on average, have at least some desire to distance themselves from anime fans—a practical demonstration of stigma.

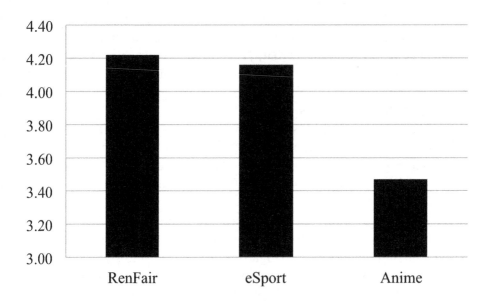

Figure 17.2. Mean level of social distance.

We can break the analysis down further by looking at how the stigma toward anime fans manifests at differing degrees of intimacy. As shown in Figure 17.3, non-fans are more accepting of an anime fan as a neighbor, work peer, or the owner of a restaurant that they're eating at. The stigma really shows itself with the prospect of having an anime fan living in close proximity (e.g., as a roommate), having an anime fan in a position of power (e.g., President of the U.S.), and, strongest of all, as a romantic partner. In short, non-fans are fine with anime fans as long as they keep their distance and as long as they don't have to actually see, interact with, or be impacted by anime fans.

A later study shed light on one possible reason for peoples' desire to avoid anime fans: the stereotype that anime fans are immature (Reysen & Plante, 2017). To put it simply, the more immature someone imagines anime fans to be as a group, the less likely they are to want to interact with that person—for example, to date them. Studies like these shed light on the possible mechanisms underlying the stigma felt toward anime fans, a subject we now turn to in greater detail.

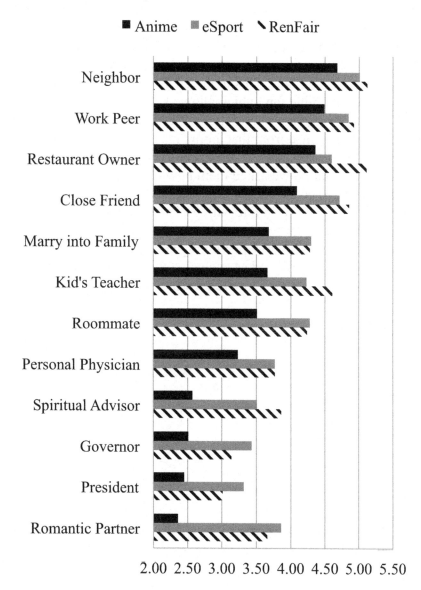

Figure 17.3. Degree of social distance per item.

Why is there Stigma toward Anime Fans?

People aren't monsters;[8] most people wouldn't consider themselves to be a bigot. Nevertheless, negative stereotypes, prejudice, and stigma exist.

One possible reason for this apparent contradiction stems from the fact that people often justify the stigmatization of others, making their prejudices toward them seem valid (Major & O'Brien, 2005). To test this, we examined whether there were potential reasons for why non-fans were prejudiced against anime fans. This involved asking undergraduate students to describe a typical anime fan, which allowed us to see whether they spontaneously used negative stereotypes to describe anime fans. We then rated their desired distance from that anime fan (i.e., prejudice). Next, we asked participants to rate whether they agreed with a set of stereotypes about anime fans. Finally, we asked them how cold or warm they felt toward anime fans (a second measure of prejudice).

As shown in Figure 17.4, in line with previous findings, negative stereotypes about anime fans are associated with greater prejudice felt toward anime fans. For example, perceiving anime fans as detached from reality, as socially awkward, and as exclusively liking things from Japan all predicted a greater degree of stigma felt toward anime fans.

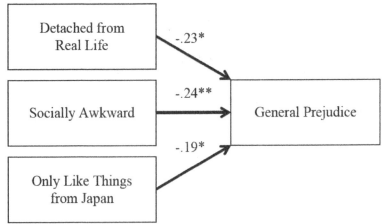

Figure 17.4. Non-fans' perceptions of a typical anime fan as predictors of desire to distance the self from that person.

---

[8] Unfortunately, we don't actually have a psychological test for this, so you'll have to take our word on it!

Figure 17.5 summarizes the results of a follow-up analysis showing the practical implications of this prejudice: people's willingness to get close to anime fans. Those who agreed with the stereotype of anime fans as introverted and who assumed that anime fans interact with others is in an introverted way predicted a greater desire to maintain their distance from that imagined typical anime fan. In contrast, those who believed more flattering stereotypes of anime fans (e.g., that they were creative) were more okay with getting closer to anime fans. This suggests that the stereotypes people have about anime fans are linked to the prejudice and stigma they feel toward anime fans, illustrating that this stigma is likely to have practical, real-world implications for anime fans.[9]

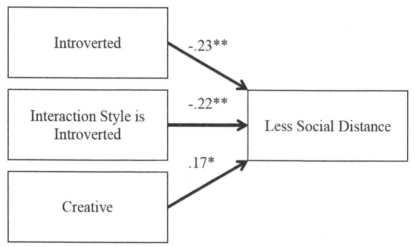

Figure 17.5. Non-fans' perceptions of a typical anime fan as predictors of less desire to distance the self from that person.

---

[9] The results also suggest that not all stereotyping leads to bad outcomes. Positive stereotypes about anime fans may, in fact, make people more willing to interact with anime fans. Of course, positive stereotypes may not always be a good thing either: They might lead to unrealistic expectations and disappoint when anime fans don't live up to those expectations (e.g., anime fans who are not creative).

With all of this in mind, there is a social psychological theory that can shed additional light on the stigma directed at anime fans. The stereotype content model (Fiske et al., 2002) and its various corollaries (e.g., Cuddy et al., 2007, 2008) suggest that how we interact with members of a group is determined by our stereotypes toward that group and how the group makes us feel. Specifically, the theory argues that stereotypes inform us what to expect about how emotionally warm and how competent members of a group are. This, in turn, affects how we feel about those group members (an emotional response), which ultimately directs how we'll behave toward them.

For example, groups that are seen as being emotionally warm (e.g., kind) and highly competent (e.g., smart, mature) make us feel positively about the group, which will cause us to want to interact with members of that group. In contrast, groups that are seen as low in emotional warmth (e.g., cold, rude, cruel) or low in competence (e.g., ignorant, immature) tend to lead to negative feelings toward the group and, by extension, a desire to, at best, take pity on the group and, at worst, avoid or even lash out at the group.

Our own data from Chapter 16 suggest that stereotypes of anime fans put them fairly low on emotional warmth (e.g., introverted, lacking social skills, socially awkward) and somewhere in the middle with respect to competence (e.g., geeky and intelligent, creative, but also immature). As such, it comes as no surprise that non-fans would be okay with working alongside anime fans (e.g., relying somewhat on their competence), but otherwise have no interest in being emotionally close to them (e.g., not wanting to date them).[10] In other words, according to this model, we might more precisely say that anime fans face a particularly ambiguous style of stigma, one in which people aren't actively seeking to harm them, but would also prefer to avoid them.

To test whether there is merit to this idea that anime fans are specifically stereotyped as somewhat low in warmth and moderately higher on competence, we asked U.S. undergraduate students ($N = 236$) to rate anime fans' warmth (i.e., "good natured, sincere, trustworthy, friendly") on a 7-point scale (1 = *not warm*, 7 = *very warm*). We also asked them to rate

---

[10] Funnily enough, Cuddy et al. (2007) also find this pattern of stereotypes and responses for Asian people, while Grigoryev et al. (2019) observed it for Japanese people specifically.

anime fans' competence (i.e., "intelligent, smart, efficient, capable, confident") on a 7-point scale (1 = *not competent*, 7 = *very competent*). As shown in Figure 17.6, warmth fell just above the midpoint of the measure, while competence was significantly above the midpoint. The results largely support the idea that anime fans are seen as somewhat low[11] in emotional warmth and higher in competence, in line with prevailing stereotypes. Taken together, in conjunction with the results of the social distancing measure (i.e., non-fans fine with obligatory contact, but shun close relationships with anime fans) the results support the ambiguous style of stigma predicted by the stereotype content model (Cuddy et al., 2007, 2008; Fiske et al., 2002).

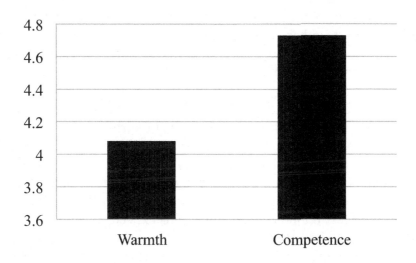

Figure 17.6. Mean level of perceived warmth and competence of anime fans.

Prejudice Accuracy

To this point, we've hopefully convinced you that anime fans are, indeed, stigmatized. From this premise, however, a more interesting question arises: To what extent do anime fans know about and accurately perceive this stigma? It's a classic question from psychology, one that delves into

---

[11] Or, at very least, middling.

our ability to accurately assess what others are seeing, thinking, and feeling (Jussim, 2012). While we can be reasonably sure that most anime fans are at least somewhat aware of the stereotypes that exist about their fandom,[12] we don't know to what extent anime fans are accurate in predicting the extent of the stigma directed toward them. They may, for example, overestimate the stigma directed toward them, seeing anime fans as more attacked and as a more visible target than they actually are.[13] In contrast, anime fans may underestimate the stigma directed toward them, being blissfully unaware that the stigma being directed toward them is more than just some gentle ribbing.[14]

To test these possibilities, we asked furries and anime fans to think about how other fans would rate their own group (e.g., how furries would rate anime fans: Reysen et al., 2017c). Participants then rated their own prejudice toward the other group (e.g., how would, you, an anime fan, rate furries) on a scale from 0 = *extremely negative* to 100 = *extremely positive*. In our analyses, we reversed these scales so that higher scores would mean more stigma.

As shown in Figure 17.7, furries—another heavily-stigmatized fan group—thought that anime fans would rate them fairly negatively (just below the midpoint). They were fairly accurate in this regard, as anime fans did, in fact, rate furries relatively negatively (just above the midpoint of the measure). On the flip side, anime fans thought that furries would perceive them negatively (but still below the midpoint); in reality, furries rated anime fans with less prejudice than anime fans expected.

In short, furries underestimated prejudice from anime fans while anime fans overestimated prejudice from furries. Of course, the test is far from ideal. One of the biggest reasons is the fact that around 44% of furries are anime fans (Plante et al., 2016), while only about 6% of anime fans are

---

[12] Otherwise, they wouldn't be able to embrace and parody those stereotypes as they commonly do at conventions and in online forums.

[13] This is related to a psychological phenomenon called "the spotlight effect," where people overestimate the extent to which others notice and judge them.

[14] This may arise from anime fans surrounding themselves with like-minded fans, preventing them from being exposed to non-fans and causing them to overestimate how many other people think and feel as they do—something psychologists call a "false consensus."

356

furries. As such, many furries are anime fans themselves, and would thus likely hold the fandom in fairly high regard. This means that anime fans' tendency to underestimate the stigma directed toward them may be an artifact of our using a group that is more likely to hold anime fans in high regard. This study represents only an initial look at the question, and future studies will want to replicate this study by collecting data on how other fan groups—namely those who don't have a sizable overlap with anime fans— or non-fans entirely judge anime fans.

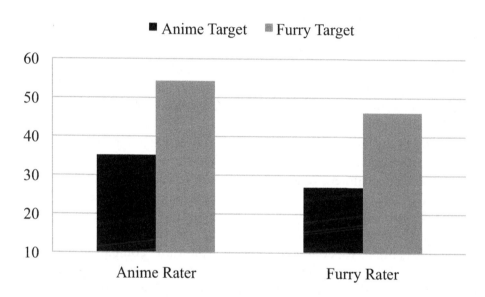

Figure 17.7. Mean level of prejudice.

Coping and Disclosure

Earlier in this chapter we mentioned that some group identities are volitional—something we can choose or not (e.g., belonging to a fan group versus our race). In the present section we introduce another distinction: The distinction between visible stigmas (e.g., scars, physical disabilities) and invisible stigmas (e.g., sexual orientation, being a fan of something).

Invisible stigmas allow people to strategically conceal their stigmatized identity to avoid the fallout that comes from being a member of a stigmatized group. For example, if a person is gay and is concerned about being judged negatively because of it, they could choose to conceal this part of themselves from others.

On its surface, concealing a stigmatized identity might seem like an ideal way to avoid the detrimental effects that come from being part of a stigmatized group. However, as we have noted previously in this book, this concealment carries with it a fairly steep toll: In the long run, identity concealment is related to poorer well-being, including anxiety, depression, hostility, and demoralization (Pachankis, 2007). This is because concealing a part of one's identity is inherently stressful. To continue with our previous example, trying to avoid revealing that you're gay to your coworkers involves being constantly vigilant about slipping up (e.g., mentioning your partner's name) or being detected outside of work (e.g., walking with your partner at the grocery store). This vigilance leads to anxiety about being detected, which, in turn, is associated with a myriad of physical and psychological problems.

Speaking to this point, in a study of furries it was found that many furries hide their identity from others: from their friends, family, and co-workers. This concealment was associated with lower overall well-being (Mock et al., 2013). In short, while identity concealment might help someone occasionally skirt a thorny or difficult social situation, in the long run it's a poor strategy for coping with societal stigma.

With this is mind, we conducted a large-scale study comparing anime fans, furries, and fantasy sport fans on the extent to which they openly disclosed their fan identity to family, friends, work peers, work supervisor(s), and to strangers or new acquaintances (1 = *strongly disagree* to 7 = *strongly agree*). As shown in Figure 17.8, anime and fantasy sport fans were both fairly likely to tell their families that they are fans, as compared to furries. All three fan groups indicated that they would be the most likely to tell their friends, with anime being the highest of these groups.[15]

Participants' likelihood of disclosing their fan interest falls below the midpoint of the scale when it comes to other groups. While anime fans do

---

[15] This is unsurprising, given that many fans, and especially anime fans, have friends who are, themselves, anime fans!

frequently disclose their interest in anime to friends and family, they look a lot more like furries than they do fantasy sport fans when it comes to disclosing to peers, supervisors, and new acquaintances. In follow-up analyses of this data, we found, just as was shown by Mock et al. (2013), that anime fans experienced greater well-being if they were more able to disclosure their anime fan identity to others.

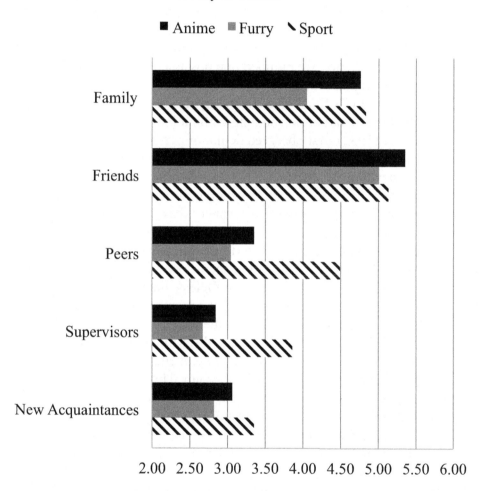

Figure 17.8. Mean level of disclosure of fan identity.

Two pieces of advice may stem from this research. On the one hand, we might suggest that one should, whenever possible, be proud about being a fan and not give into the fear of telling others. On the other hand, a more conservative interpretation might be to not necessarily be "loud and proud" about your fan identity, but rather surround yourself with people who accept you for who you are, so you have more opportunities to be open and genuine about your interest in your day-to-day life.

Coping and Denial of Personal Discrimination

In the previous section we outlined one possible strategy for anime fans to cope with the stigma they face. However, it's far from the only strategy available to them. Let's finish this chapter by discussing one additional strategy called the denial of personal discrimination.

Faye Crosby (1984) first observed denial of personal discrimination when studying people in a Boston suburb. The survey asked questions about work grievances that they had personally experienced and about work grievances experienced by women in general. Surprisingly, men and women did not differ in how many grievances they had personally experienced. This was despite the fact that Crosby knew that women in the study were facing measurable sex discrimination at work (e.g., lower pay for same work). Moreover, nearly all of the respondents agreed that women are treated worse in the workplace. Nevertheless, the women reported being just as satisfied as the men, reporting that the women in the study didn't feel the discrimination was happening to them.

This, in a nutshell, is denial of personal discrimination, the belief that one's group is discriminated against, but they, themselves, have not been discriminated against as a member of the group. This phenomenon has been observed across a variety of stigmatized groups, both visible (e.g., race) and invisible (e.g., religion: Dion & Kawakami, 1996).

To assess whether stigmatized fan groups—including anime fans—engage in this denial of personal discrimination, we asked furries, bronies, and anime fans—all stigmatized fan groups—to rate the extent to which their group is discriminated against (i.e., "Anime fans are discriminated against"), as well as the extent to which they personally have experienced discrimination (i.e., "I have felt discriminated against because I am an

360

anime fan") on a scale from 1 = *strongly disagree* to 7 = *strongly agree* (Leshner et al., 2018).

As shown in Figure 17.9, all three groups felt that their fandom did, indeed, experience some degree of discrimination. More importantly, however, members of all three fan groups felt that their group was discriminated against more than they were themselves. In fact, in a follow-up study of undergraduate college students, we found that, regardless of their particular fan interest (sport, music, media, hobby), participants felt that their own fan community was discriminated against significantly more than they personally were.

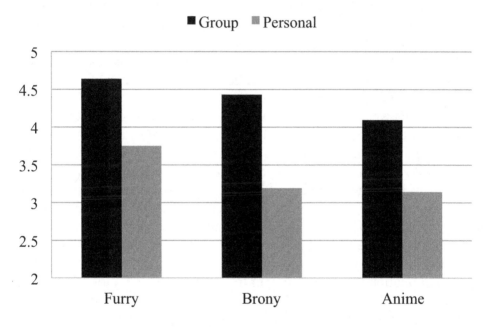

Figure 17.9. Mean level of perceived discrimination.

Taken together, members of stigmatized fan groups fans are aware that they are part of a group that experiences stigma—even if they are unaware—or in denial—about its effects on themselves. This could be chalked up to people legitimately not experiencing discrimination.[16] Alternatively, it may be a way to preserving one's self-esteem by pretending that one's stigmatized group identity has not, and does not, continue to adversely affect them. Related to this idea, it's possible that fans may be conjuring up extreme examples of discrimination toward specific members of their own fandom and, treating those extreme cases as "typical," conclude that they, themselves, have had things fairly easy by comparison.

Conclusion

Throughout this chapter we've seen that anime fans experience a moderate degree of stigma—somewhere between the more extreme stigma experienced by other fan groups (e.g., furries and bronies) and the lack of stigma experienced by more mainstream fan groups (e.g., sport fans). This is likely due, at least in part, to the stereotypes associated with anime fans, coupled with the fact that, by virtue of being non-prototypical fans, people will tend to see them as somewhat deviant.

Anime fans were found to somewhat overestimate the degree of prejudice directed toward them, at least from other, more stigmatized fan groups (e.g., furries). Nevertheless, the stigma is real, as non-fans consistently report a greater desire to distance themselves from anime fans. Anime fans, like other stigmatized groups, may turn to maladaptive ways of coping with this stigma, including strategically choosing to conceal their identity and outright denying the discrimination they may have personally faced. Neither of these strategies is likely to be viable long-term, and the data suggest that the best way to minimize the potential consequences of this discrimination is not to deny it or to conceal one's identity, but rather to craft one's social life in a way that allows them to be open about their fan interest and genuine in who they are as often as possible.

---

[16] It would be an unlikely coincidence, given both objective measures showing that stigmatized groups do get treated unfairly and given the number of different groups the phenomenon has been observed in.

Chapter 18
Bullying in the Anime Fandom

In the previous chapter we discussed stigma toward the anime fandom and provided evidence that anime fans, while not the most stigmatized fan group we've studied, are nevertheless stigmatized. This is largely because anime fans differ from other, more mainstream fan groups, coupled with the existence of a number of unflattering stereotypes about anime fans.

In the last chapter we primarily focused on the existence of stigma, where it stemmed from, and anime fans' perception and reaction to it. What was largely absent from that discussion was a look into the real-world implications of being a member of a stigmatized group, including negative treatment at the hands of others because of that stigma.

What was missing was a discussion about bullying.

Prior Research on Bullying

Scholars have been increasingly recognizing the significant harm— physical, mental, and emotional—that bullying can do to people of varying ages (Hamburger et al., 2011). To perhaps no one's great surprise, studies have shown that suicide, the third leading cause of death in adolescents, increases as one becomes involved with bullying, regardless of whether they're the bully themselves or the bullied (e.g., Baldry & Winkel, 2003; Carney, 2000; Hinduja & Patchin, 2010; Kim & Leventhal, 2008; Mills et al., 2004). Of course, you don't have to be a psychologist to turn on the news and find stories about the most severe consequences of bullying (e.g., Bender, 2014).

Scientific research on bullying and its causes and effects has been steadily growing since the 1970s and 1980s (Smith & Gross, 2006) and shows no sign of slowing down or being any less important (Berger, 2007). In fact, the impact of bullying has become so concerning that it's now considered to be a major public health issue (Hertz et al., 2013), given all of the potential damage it can do to a person's healthy, normal development (Nansel et al., 2001). Some studies have focused directly on these detrimental effects (e.g., Ponzo, 2013; Sharp, 1995), while others have focused on understanding the origins of bullying and when it's more likely to occur (e.g., Gini, 2006; Guerra et al., 2011; Spriggs et al., 2007).

How prevalent is bullying? As it turns out, it's a harder question to answer than you might think. Studies which have tried to answer this question vary considerably in their estimates: Cook et al. (2010) puts the number at 10-30% of children and adolescence, while Nansel et al. (2001) suggest that 11% of adolescents were bullied, 13% identify as bullies, and 6% identify as both. Hertz et al. (2013) puts the numbers even higher, suggesting that 20-56% of young people are involved, in some way, with bullying. Some studies report that bullying happens most in elementary school and dissipates in high schools (e.g., Smith et al., 1999), while other research argues that the prevalence of bullying remains steady from childhood to adolescence (e.g., Smith & Gross, 2006).

At least part of the reason why scientists can't seem to get consistent numbers about bullying is the range of methodologies used to study bullying. Studies have looked at bullying with surveys and through longitudinal studies, they've looked at current circumstances and at retrospective recall (e.g., asking adults about their childhood), and they've looked at varying types and degrees of bullying (Smith & Gross, 2006).[1] As such, comparing data across studies can be tricky and should be done with great caution.

The Current Study

Taken together, the existing research makes it clear that more research is needed to help us better understand the many nuances and complexities related to bullying and its outcomes (Berger, 2007). In that spirit, the rest of this chapter documents our own research on bullying, exploring its intricacies and manifestations for anime fans, a group at higher risk for bullying due to the stigma surrounding the fandom. The studies were intended to be an initial foray into the bullying experiences of anime fans with some loose comparisons between anime fans and another heavily-stigmatized fan group we've previously studied, furries. The data we'll review came from two particular studies—a 2015 study of nearly 1,000

---

[1] See Hamburger et al. (2011) for a good overview of the factors one must consider when measuring bullying. These can include, for example, whether you measure the medium of the bullying (e.g., in-person or cyber), the type of harm done (direct or indirect), and whether you focus solely on the bullied or the bullies (e.g., Nansel et al., 2001; Schäfer et al., 2004).

online and convention-going anime fans and a 2012 study on several hundred convention-going furries.[2]

Bullying Prevalence

We began by asking participants some basic global questions about the experience of bullying in childhood. Specifically, we asked three questions, which participants responded to on a 5-point scale ranging from 1 = *almost never* to 5 = *very often*:

(1) When you were a child, do you recall another kid, even a brother or sister, picking on you by chasing you, grabbing your hair or clothes or by making you do something you did not want to do?

(2) When you were a child, do you recall getting scared or feeling really bad because kids were calling you names, saying mean things to you, or saying they didn't want you around?

(3) When you were a child do you recall any kid, even a brother or sister, hitting you? This may have been at home, at school, out playing, in a store, anywhere?

The data from Figure 18.1 show that anime fans' experienced bullying was, on average, just below or at the midpoint of the scale, suggesting that anime fans sometimes faced childhood bullying. Follow-up analyses also reveal that the three types of bullying are fairly strongly positively correlated with one another, meaning that when someone experiences one type of bullying, they're likely to experience the other types of bullying as well. Finally, analyses show that convention-going fans experienced more childhood bullying than online fans did. Given that the scores were relatively close to one another, however, in all later analyses we merge the online and convention fans to keep the presentation of the data manageable.

---

[2] We readily acknowledge the numerous flaws and limitations of these datasets, including the fact that we are trying to make claims about anime fans as a group from a limited sample of online and convention-going fans. As always, we advise caution when interpreting the results. Nevertheless, these studies are an initial foray into understanding bullying in the anime fandom and are some of the only available data available on the subject.

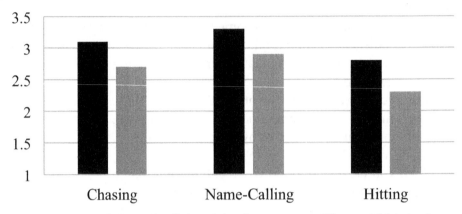

Figure 18.1. Childhood bullying (chasing, name calling, and hitting) reported by participants at anime convention and online.

Since prior research has revealed that those who are bullies often experience many of the same negative outcomes as those who are the victims of bullies,[3] we also asked participants about their experiences of being bullied, witnessing bullying, and being the bully themselves for the ages of 4-10 and 11-18 using same 1-5 scale described above:

Please think back through your past including your various educational experiences. You may have seen some bullying, and you may have been involved in some way. For each of your age groups below indicate how frequently you experienced each of the following, using the scale provided.

The data shown in Figure 18.2 reveal that anime fans were significantly more likely to report having been bullied by others than to have been bullies themselves.[4] Follow-up analyses also revealed that both being a

---

[3] We should note that this doesn't mean that the act of bullying someone *causes* the bully to experience worse well-being. Rather, it's likely the case that people who are struggling or experiencing developmental difficulties are, themselves, more likely to bully.

[4] It's worth noting that only about 16% of anime fans scored a 3 or higher when it came to being a bully themselves. One interpretation is that anime fans simply weren't bullies growing up. Another possibility is that anime fans may have engaged in bullying behavior,

victim of bullying and witnessing bullying actually *increased* from childhood and adolescence, something in line with prior research, which suggests that bullying doesn't decrease as one gets into high school (e.g., Smith & Gross, 2006).[5] Later analyses also revealed a small, but significant positive correlation among the three bullying statuses, meaning that those who are bullied are also somewhat more likely to be bullies themselves and to have witnessed others being bullied.[6]

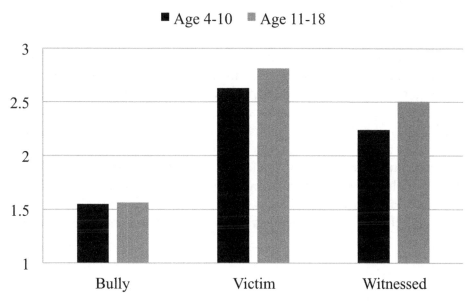

Figure 18.2. Reports of bullying at different ages.

but simply didn't consider what they did to be bullying. A third possibility is that anime fans may have engaged in bullying in their youth but are denying it on the survey to avoid looking bad to the researchers.

[5] In fact, Smith and Gross (2006) found only that bullying levels remained stable over time, but the present results point to a significant *increase* in bullying over time for anime fans.

[6] In light with a previous comment, this does not mean that someone who is bullied is necessarily a bully themselves, but rather they are at a greater risk of being a bully.

Different types of Bullying Behavior

In the research we reviewed earlier in this chapter, we mentioned that scholars often take into account differences between different types of bullying. To this end, we asked anime fans to indicate, using the same five-point scale as before, the extent to which they experienced six different types of bullying within three categories, being physically, verbally, or indirectly[7] bullied:

(1) Being hit, punched or kicked (Physical)
(2) Being stolen from (Physical)
(3) Being called nasty names (Verbal)
(4) Being threatened (Verbal)
(5) Having lies or nasty rumors spread or told about you (Indirect)
(6) Being deliberately excluded from social groups (Indirect)

As Figure 18.3 shows, the most prevalent form of bullying is name-calling, followed closely by deliberate exclusion, although none of the specific types of bullying score above the midpoint of the scale. Beyond this, the data reveal, in line with our previous findings, that bullying is experienced to a greater extent as kids get older compared to when they are younger (with the exception of being hit, punched, or kicked, which did not differ statistically with age). This is even more evidence in support of the claim that bullying seems to *worsen* between childhood and adolescence for anime fans.

---

[7] The indirect bullying items are also known as "social aggression" to aggression researchers. They involve attacking another person through their relationships with others.

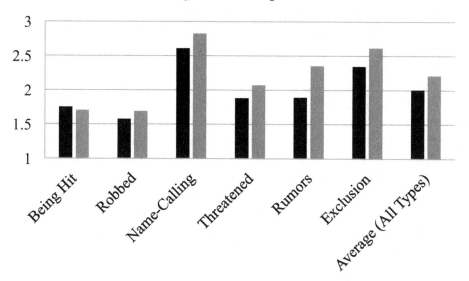

Figure 18.3. Various types of bullying experiences reported by participants.

Comparing Bullying in Anime Fans and Other Groups

To this point, our data paint a picture of anime fans having, on average, experienced some bullying in their adolescence, and the amount of bullying they suffered typically increased in their high school years relative to their elementary school years. However, by themselves, these data cannot tell us one way or another whether anime fans experience any more bullying than others.[8]

To address this issue, in this section we loosely compare anime fans to other samples which have used the same measures of bullying.[9] For

---

[8] Or, to put it another way: Naysayers may argue that "most kids get bullied—how are anime fans any different?"

[9] We emphasize "loose comparisons" here. While we used the same scale in our anime study as was used in other studies, the results were calculated somewhat differently between the studies. For example, in the Schäfer et al. (2004) study, participants were asked about *both* the frequency and intensity with which they experienced bullying, and did so on the same five-point scale we used. Due to space constraints, however, we only

example, in Schäfer et al.'s (2004) article, they examined 884 participants who were average people drawn from three different countries: Germany, Spain, and the UK. This allows us to compare anime fans to average non-anime fans from around the world.[10] We also drew upon our own past research on furries, which allows us to compare the bullying experienced by anime fans to the bullying experienced by another significantly stigmatized fan community.[11]

Figure 18.4 illustrates the results across three different samples. Perhaps the most glaring difference between the groups can be found with respect to the "total bullied" category, where we see that anime fans fall somewhere between furries and non-fans with respect to how prevalent a history of bullying there is. This is in line with our prior findings on stigma (see Chapter 17), which similarly suggests that anime fans, while stigmatized, are not as stigmatized as other, more fringe fandoms. Insofar as stigma may be a cause of bullying, it would seem to follow that anime fans are less likely to be bullied than anime fans, but more likely to be bullied than non-fans (who carry none of the stigma associated with being a fan).

---

asked about the frequency with which participants experienced bullying. As a result, when participants were categorized as either having been bullied or not, our own data were based solely on frequency, while the Schäfer et al. (2004) data were based on frequency and intensity data. As such, interpret the results with caution.

[10] The participants in these studies were not asked directly whether or not they were anime fans. It is conceivable that at least some of them were anime fans by luck alone. However, the sample was not chosen specifically because it was full of anime fans, and so it is unlikely to be comprised entirely—or even mostly—of anime fans, allowing it to serve as a "general population" comparison group.

[11] Data from the furry study should also be compared to anime fans with caution. In the furry study, participants were asked to answer "yes" or "no" to whether they had been bullied in each of the categories. In the anime sample, we transformed the scale data (the 1-to-5 response) into a yes or no by turning 3s, 4s, and 5s into a "yes" and the 1s and 2s into a "no." Because of these differences, we do not attempt to make direct statistical comparisons between these studies, and rely only on cautiously interpreting the averages.

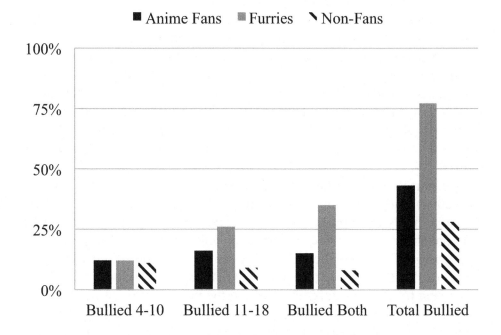

Figure 18.4. Percentage of anime fans, furries, and non-fans bullied in primary school, secondary school, both, and overall.

It's illuminating to move beyond the overall prevalence data, however. For example, if we look just as the people who were only bullied from the age of 4-10, it would seem that all three groups were comparable in the extent to which they were bullied, with differences only starting to emerge in their teenage years. However, as the data from people who were bullied in both categories indicate, a significant proportion of people who were bullied in their younger years were also bullied when they were older. Even so, among people who were bulled only at one point in time, members of the two fan groups were more likely to be bullied in their older years than in their younger years—a trend that was not reflected in the non-fan data. Or, to put it another way: Bullying may get worse for fans as they get older, whereas for non-fans, the opposite may be true.

Bullying, Anime, and Additional Stigma

To this point, we've argued that the stigma one experiences for being an anime fan is related to a number of negative outcomes including, among other things, being more susceptible to bullying. But if you recall our discussion about social identity in Chapter 10, we argued that people are a complex patchwork of different group identities (e.g., student, American, fan, White, woman, etc.). Given that this is the case, it's worth asking whether people may experience additional stigma—and by extension, additional bullying—as the result of being part of multiple stigmatized groups?[12]

Let's start with the topic of gender. If you delve deeper into the Schäfer et al. (2004) study in the previous section, you find that girls in the study were more likely to be bullied than boys. This, however, flies in the face of a national study of American adolescence, which found that boys were actually *more* likely to be both the bullies and the victims of bullying (Nansel et al., 2001). More recent studies that recognize transgender youth suggest that transgender folks may have it the worst, with upwards of 86% experiencing some form of bullying (Norris & Orchowski, 2020). Put simply, based on the existing literature, we can't take for granted the idea that all anime fans will equally experience bullying.

In our own study, we found that females were bullied more than males[13] both in childhood and in adolescence (see Figure 18.5). However, transgender and non-binary[14] participants were considerably more likely than both groups to have experienced bullying, both in their childhood and in their adolescence. All three groups—in line with what was observed in our prior findings—experienced an increase in bullying as they got older,

---

[12] Or, to put it another way, would a Black anime fan experience more bullying than a White anime fan? What about a transgender anime fan compared to a woman who was an anime fan?

[13] The study, several years old, asked participants to indicate their identification with a number of terms, including "male" and "female," which refer to sex rather than gender. This is an artifact of an outdated way of thinking about the topic, and were we to run the study again, we would use the terms "man" and "woman" instead.

[14] For the purpose of this study, self-identified transgender and non-binary participants were condensed into a single category, as the number of participants in each separate category would be quite small and make averaging the data tricky, since it would be more susceptible to being swayed by a single extreme value.

though the effect was the most pronounced for transgender and non-binary anime fans.

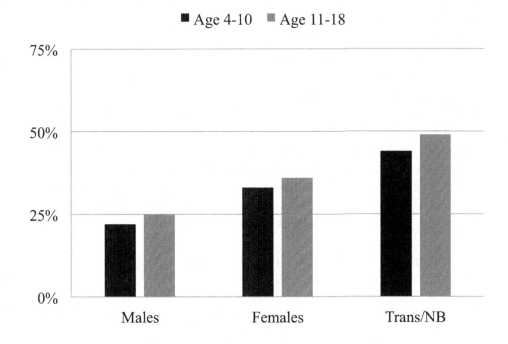

Figure 18.5. Percentage of each sex / gender category experiencing bullying in childhood and adolescence.

In a follow-up analysis we calculated the average change in participants' reported bullying from childhood to adolescence for anime fans and for furries, separating the results by gender. The results revealed that for anime fans and furries alike, bullying tended to get worse as they got older, regardless of gender—although the effect was largest for transgender and non-binary fans and furries, in general, experienced more bullying than did anime fans.

As previously mentioned, stigma can come from numerous group identitics, not just one's gender. One of the most frequently-studied categories of stigmatized groups is that of racialized folks. While the Western anime fandom is comprised of a majority of White people, it would be wholly inappropriate—both for statistical reasons and for ethical reasons[15]—to treat anime fans as a racially homogeneous group. To this end, we examined whether the bullying data we've observed to this point differ based on a person's self-identified race.[16]

Figure 18.6 shows that, for the most part, Black and White anime fans were more likely to experience bullying than fans from other racial groups—with Black fans being slightly more likely than White fans to experience to experience the most bullying.[17] In contrast, Asian anime fans were the least likely to experience bullying. This could be attributed, at least in part, to the fact that anime has its origins in Japanese culture, which would make an Asian anime fan seem expected, rather than atypical. This explanation does not, however, explain why Hispanic people and member of other racial groups score similarly lower in bullying, although, unlike Asian fans, whose bullying decreased as they got older, members of these racial groups, like White and Black anime fans, all reported greater bullying as they got older.

The data in this section (much like findings throughout this book) should not be taken as the final word on this topic. If nothing else, delving into the nuances of how a stigmatized fan identity may interact with other facets of one's identity reveals just how complex the question of stigma and bullying can get. Future research will certainly be needed to help disentangle and explain these findings. We can, however, confidently state from the present

---

[15] The history of social research is rife with examples of painting over or ignoring the lived experiences of disadvantaged groups—especially racialized folks. For this reason, it's both good science and good in general to consider the ways in which the experiences of disadvantaged groups in a fandom may differ from those of the majority group.

[16] Unfortunately, there were several race categories in which there were only 2-6 participants. As such, quantitative data analysis (as well as potential privacy risks) required that these low-count data be recategorized into a "mixed race/other" category.

[17] This shouldn't be taken to mean that Black and White people in general are equally likely to be bullied. Rather, the data suggest that, at least within this already stigmatized community, Black and White people experience approximately comparable levels of bullying. One possible interpretation is that Black participants already experience a considerable amount of stigma and bullying, and so the additional stigma of being an anime fan may do little to increase what is already a high level of bullying. In contrast, for White people, who typically experience less stigma in general because they exist as part of a privileged group, the stigma of being an anime fan may be felt more impactfully. This is speculation for now, and future research is needed to test this idea.

data that it would be a mistake to treat all anime fans as one and the same and to overlook the importance of who anime fans are beyond their identity as anime fans.

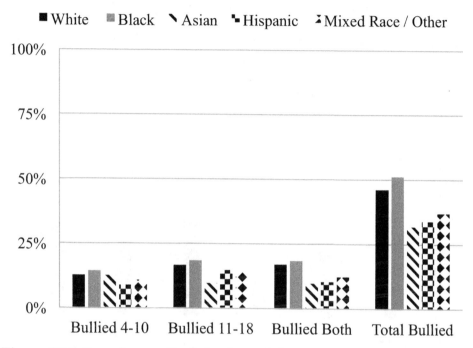

Figure 18.6. Prevalence of bullying by racial category.

Bullying and Specific Fan Behavior

Throughout this book we've repeatedly found differences in the way different anime fans engage with the fandom and we've found a myriad of factors that predict which fans are more likely to engage in which activities. With this in mind, we wondered whether anime fans who engaged in certain fan activities were also more likely to have a history of having been bullied.[18]

---

[18] As a reminder, this is not to suggest that engaging in these activities would *cause* anime fans to be more likely to be bullied, or that being bullied would necessarily *cause* anime fans to engage in these activities. Either direction of causation (or both or neither!) are plausible.

We asked anime fans to rate how frequently they engaged in different anime-related activities in the past year on a scale from 0 = *never* to 7 = *many times each day*. As shown in Figure 18.7, the extent to which anime fans consume anime content (reading manga, watching shows) is largely unrelated to how frequently they're bullied. In contrast, other facets of fandom interaction—which go beyond "mere consumption"—were positively associated—albeit modestly so, with being bullied.

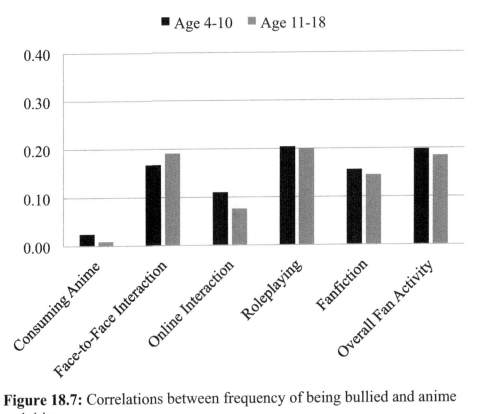

Figure 18.7: Correlations between frequency of being bullied and anime activities.

One possible explanation for this discrepancy has to do with the distinction between simply watching anime—which may or may not make a person a fan—and other, far more "uniquely anime fan" activities. For example, while a person who doesn't consider themselves to be a fan may nevertheless watch a particular anime series, it's unlikely that the non-fan would find themselves going to anime clubs or conventions, roleplaying as anime characters, or writing fanfiction. The very activities that distinguish anime fans from "casual viewers" may be the very activities that identify them as targets for stigma.[19] Speaking to this idea, the activities that are most likely to be done in the privacy of one's home, away from prying eyes, is both consuming anime and online interaction. Face-to-face interaction—at a convention or club—may "out" someone as an anime fan, making it easier for them to be targeted by bullies. In contrast, someone who only consumes anime online at home may be better able to conceal their identity and avoid being identified—and thus targeted—as an anime fan.

As a final note, it's worth pointing out that, for the most part, the magnitude of the correlation between anime consumption and bullying was comparable regardless of age. This could be interpreted as suggesting that the bullying "happened in the past," and largely does not affect one's current levels of fan engagement today. Another possible interpretation is that anime fans get picked on for being anime fans regardless of age (e.g., whether it's a 10-year-old being picked on for watching *Pokémon* or a 17-year-old being picked on for watching *One Piece*).

---

[19] To be clear: This doesn't make the stigmatization or bullying justified in any way—merely that bullies and bigots may latch onto these "distinctly fan" activities as a signal that this is a person for whom stereotypes about anime fans might apply.

Bullying, Well-Being, and Self-Esteem

As we mentioned at the start of this chapter, part of the reason for the steadily-increasing research interest in bullying is a greater appreciation for the myriad of devastating effects that bullying can have on those who experience bullying (e.g., poor psychosocial adjustment: Nansel et al., 2001, 2004; self-esteem: Sharp, 1995).[20]

For this reason, we examined the link between bullying, well-being, and self-esteem in anime fans.[21] Because well-being is such a complex and multi-pronged construct, we used a scale that took into account participants' psychological (e.g., "I feel that I am able to enjoy life"), physical (e.g., "I am satisfied with my physical health"), relationship (e.g., "I am satisfied with my friendships and personal relationships") and overall well-being (Kinderman et al., 2011) on a scale from 1= *strongly disagree* to 7 = *strongly agree*. Overall well-being took into account all of these items. Finally, self-esteem was measured using items from the most popular self-esteem scale used in psychology (Rosenberg, 1965).

The results, shown in Figure 18.8, reveal that, as one might expect, those who were bullied in the past currently experienced reduced well-being as compared to those who were not bullied.[22] No other differences were found among the bullied groups (bullied in childhood, adolescence, both childhood and adolescence). Importantly, the effects were observed regardless of whether one chose to measure well-being in terms of physical health, psychological health, relationship quality, overall well-being, or self-esteem.

---

[20] In fact, poor self-esteem is tied to both being bullied and being a bully (e.g., Guerra et al., 2011).

[21] We ran a series of analyses comparing those who were bullied to bullies themselves. We found relatively few notable differences between them. For simplicity's sake, we're presenting just the results for those who were bullied here.

[22] There did not, however, seem to be a difference between whether fans were bullied in their childhood, adolescence, or both.

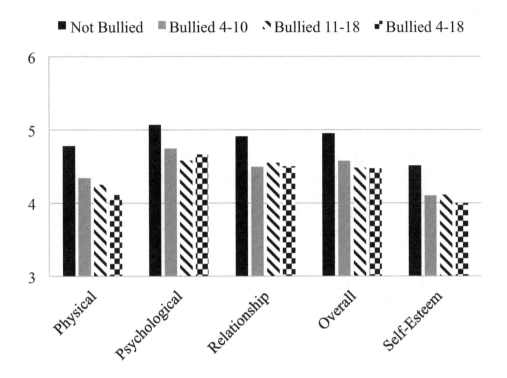

Figure 18.8. Anime fans' well-being scores and prior bullying.

Conclusion

Throughout this chapter, our research consistently found that the average anime fan has a history of experiencing some bullying (e.g., verbal bullying), particularly among convention-going anime fans. Contrary to prior research suggesting that bullying tends to lessen with time (e.g., Smith et al., 1999) or, at very least, remain about the same (Smith & Gross, 2006), bullying seems to get worse for anime fans as they get older. Later analyses revealed the importance of considering other factors when assessing anime fans' experienced stigma and bullying. This can range from seemingly trivial distinctions, like the specific activities that anime fans engage in, to far more salient and central psychological factors, like the stigmatized identities one may simultaneously hold (e.g., their race or gender). As the data make clear, not all anime fans have the same experience when it comes to bullying.

We finished the chapter with an analysis that leads nicely into the final chapter of this book: a look at the relationship between being bullied and well-being. In a finding that likely surprised no one, we found, consistent with past research, that a history of bullying is associated with reduced well-being, regardless of how you measure well-being (e.g., Nansel et al., 2001, 2004; Sharp, 1995; Guerra et al., 2011). This raises an important question: Are anime fans doing okay, or are they as dysfunctional as stereotypes and unflattering media portrayals make them out to be?

Chapter 19
Well-Being Through Fandom

Throughout this book we've focused on the many ways anime fans get involved with the anime fandom and the ties between that fandom involvement and the way fans think, feel, and behave. Some of these connections have been largely positive (e.g., making friends in Chapter 11, or global citizenship in Chapter 12), while others have been far more negative (e.g., bullying in Chapter 18, or elitism in Chapter 13). Despite this seemingly mixed bag of results, we hope that readers have nevertheless picked up on our sincere belief, and our data support, that being an anime fan is, altogether, a net positive for most fans.

With this in mind, we want to end this book on a high note and formally spell out the argument that's been teeming beneath the surface throughout this book, that anime fans benefit from their involvement in their fan interest and in the fandom surrounding it. We'll discuss what we mean by well-being and how fan communities improve the well-being of their members through their connection to both their interests and the fandom as a whole. We'll also discuss research on mental health and stress, as well as how fans, like anyone else, turn to their surrounding community for resilience in times of need.

Defining Well-Being and its Connection to Fandom

If you ask five different people what it means to be "doing well," chances are you'll get five different answers. Some may define "doing well" as being happy and surrounded by friends and family. Others may define it as living a purposeful and productive life. It's even possible to define "doing well" as the mere absence of stress and sickness.

Who's right?

Well, all of those positions have a point. We're not really qualified to be arbiters of great philosophical questions like "what does it mean to live the good life?," since philosophers and other great thinkers far smarter than us have tried—and failed—to reach a consensus on the matter. Similarly, psychologists fail to see eye to eye on the question. Some focus on feelings of health (physiological well-being), others on happiness and satisfaction in life, and still others on the extent to which one's needs (psychological, social, physical) are being met.

Instead of trying to argue which is the most important, we'll instead recognize that well-being—whatever it entails—likely involves some aspect of all of these different facets. In other words, however we decide to judge the well-being of anime fans, it's going to have to be nuanced and multi-pronged, to take this variability of definition into account. Rather than having a single measure of well-being, we'll look at well-being from a number of different angles.

Let's take a step back and ask whether there's any reason to even suspect that fandom is related to well-being in the first place. After all, being a fan of something just means having a hobby, and we often trivialize the things others do in their leisure time. Since during time spent in leisure you're not spending time making a living, fulfilling obligations, or generally trying to make the world a better place, why should we expect it to have any more impact on us than it does on the rest of the world?

Put simply, research on leisure activities more generally, and on fans more specifically, has consistently shown that these activities can provide benefits to a person's well-being and the ability to cope through difficult times.[1] For example, Daniel Wann (2006) proposed a model linking sport team identification (fanship) with psychological well-being. This model posits that being a fan of something increases our likelihood of forming both enduring, long-term, friendships that, in turn, improve various facets of well-being, including trusting others (Wann & Polk, 2007), feeling a sense of group self-esteem (Wann et al., 2008), and feeling less lonely and more positive (Wann, Martin et al., 2008).

In short, the research suggests that having a fan interest and being part of a fan community carries with it some benefits, something that, as we'll see, is just as evident with anime fans as it is with other fans.

Fan Stress and Mental Health

Most of us, fans and non-fans alike, experience stress. In fact, Gen Z, or the cohort following the Millennial generation, may be the most stressed-out generation in recent history, being constantly saturated with news about mass shootings, a global pandemic, and the increasing instability of many essential social systems, all while trying to figure out how to make a living,

---

[1] It's important to note that we're not suggesting that hobbies or fandoms are a replacement for therapy and professional help. However, our fan communities can help to relieve stress and aid in the coping process alongside other coping techniques.

find a place to live, and whether or not they'll be able to afford health care, education, or be able to afford to have children in the most financially bleak future we've seen in decades (APA, 2018).[2] Younger generations—who arguably make up the vast majority of the anime fan community—struggle with mental health issues, with less than half of Gen Z (45%) and barely over half of Millennials (56%) describing their own mental health as excellent or very good.

It's against this background of considerable stress that prior studies have tested whether fan communities are related to psychological well-being (Reysen et al., 2017d). For example, in a relatively recent paper we examined the prevalence of mental illness, including mood disorders,[3] anxiety disorders, attention deficit/hyperactivity disorder (ADHD), and autism spectrum disorder in members of various communities, including anime fans (Reysen, Plante, Chadborn et al., 2018). Given that fans are, as a group, relatively young compared to the general population, and given that younger generations seem to experience greater stress overall, one might expect to find higher rates of mental illness among fans.[4]

As seen in Figure 19.1 however, anime fans report lower mood and anxiety disorders, as well as lower ADHD compared to the U.S. lifetime population.[5] Anime fans were, however, significantly more likely to have been diagnosed on the autism spectrum.[6] Anime fans were, however, about twice as likely to take psychiatric medication (e.g., antidepressants) as the U.S. population average (30% versus 17%), which may be a result of younger Americans being more likely to seek out mental health care.

---

[2] It's no wonder Millennial humor is often characterized as cynical and tinged with more than a hint of existential dread, including one meme that simply reads "Guess I'll die."

[3] Such as Major Depressive Disorder and Bipolar Disorder.

[4] It's worth keeping in mind that nearly half of the U.S. population will have a diagnosable mental illness at some point in their life (Kessler & Wang, 2008).

[5] With the exception of female anime fans who showed no difference from than U.S. population with respect to ADHD diagnosis.

[6] We suspect this may be a feature of fandoms in general, not specifically anime fans, as one of the characteristics of many people on the autism spectrum is engaging in persistent, repetitive behaviors, which could make them especially likely to become a fan of those particular activities.

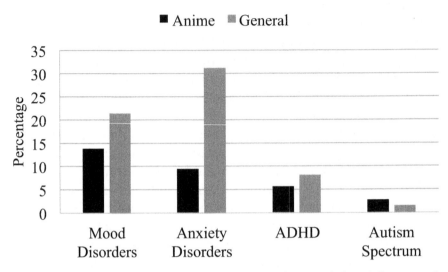

Figure 19.1. Prevalence of diagnoses in anime fans and the U.S. general population (lifetime).

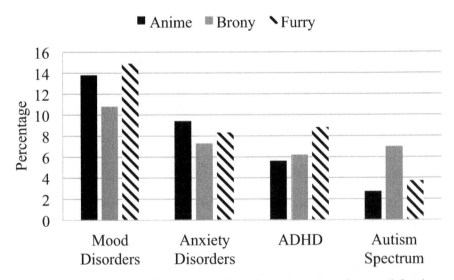

Figure 19.2. Prevalence of diagnoses in anime fans, bronies, and furries.

Findings like these support the idea that anime fans, despite having a non-mainstream interest, are not defined by being any more dysfunctional (at least with respect to mental illness) as the general population. The findings are hardly unique to anime fans either: Figure 19.2 shows comparable levels of diagnoses in members of other fan groups as well.

Sources of Stress

The previous section looked at extreme, diagnosable levels of mental illness, the sorts one might associate with extreme levels of dysfunction and extremely stressful life situations. What about the ability to function with typical, day-to-day forms of stress?

For anime fans, our research indicates that while a minority of fans report some issues with day-to-day coping, the majority of anime fans get through their day just fine. Among those who do show problems with coping, experienced stigma for being an anime fan, immaturity, and wishing to be like their favorite anime character were among the strongest predictors.

Speaking to the first connection, it makes sense that experiencing more stigma would be associated with more stress and greater coping difficulty. These are findings in-line with what we described earlier (Chapters 16, 17, 18) where negative stereotypes about a group contributes to stigma and bullying of group members. This, in turn, may create stress—based on the fear of being victimized or the need to conceal and monitor one's own behavior to avoid being "outed" as a member of a stigmatized group.

Immaturity could be tied to some anime fans' reduced coping for a similar reason. In general, immaturity is not looked upon favorably in most cultures. As such, immature people may feel stigmatized for engaging in activities that others might deem inappropriate for someone of their age (e.g., watching cartoons, cosplay). Not living up to the ideals of others, in turn, may create feelings of disconnect between one's actual and ideal selves, which can lead to feelings of anxiety.[7]

In fact, these same feelings of not living up to a societal standard may well drive the feelings of wishful identification underlying some fans wanting to identify with their favorite anime character. For fans struggling

---

[7] We discussed this idea—which derives from a psychological theory known as self-discrepancy theory—in Chapter 7.

with stress and failing to live up to the expectations of others, they may be especially attracted to characters who would live up to these same demands. Or, alternatively, such characters may provide anime fans with a sense of wish fulfillment and escapism, as a way of temporarily distracting themselves from the stresses they're experiencing.

Moving beyond struggles to cope in day-to-day life, we've also asked anime fans about their overall well-being—a composite of how they're doing physically, psychologically, and in terms of their relationships. In particular, experiencing bullying, basing one's identity extensively on anime, and having the bulk of one's friends be online are all tied to this reduced well-being.

With respect to bullying, Chapter 18 reviewed just some of the research showing the harm that bullying does to people—not just anime fans. After all, bullying not only increases a person's anxiety, but it also undermines their self-esteem, hinders their development of a stable and coherent sense of identity, might lead to physical injury, and can hurt their ability to form social interactions with others due to ostracism.

Beyond bullying, however, we found that having one's anime fan identity be a central facet of one's identity may undermine their well-being. At first glance, this might seem like a bit of a contradiction in a chapter espousing the benefits of fandom. To understand these findings, it's essential to distinguish between fandom and fanship (see Chapter 10). Recall that fandom refers to a sense of felt belongingness and connection to a community of others who, research consistently shows, provide social support, self-esteem, and a myriad of other benefits. In contrast, fanship refers to the extent of one's interest in something, which fails to offer many of the social benefits of fandom while also making a person more likely to use one's fan interest as a means of escapism.

Finally, in a point we will return to near the conclusion of this chapter, while friendships and a sense of community are absolutely essential components for a human's overall well-being, these benefits are largely derived from face-to-face interactions with friends in-person. This isn't to say that there aren't benefits to be had from online friendships—indeed, the literature on the subject is rather contentious. However, there is little doubt that face-to-face friendships confer the strongest benefits, and insofar as higher proportions of online friends means having proportionately fewer face-to-face friends, one would therefore expect people with more online friends to have fewer in-person friends who are there to provide them with tangible, in-person support when coping with life's difficulties.

Fandom and its Association with Well-Being

Up to this point in this chapter we've focused on some of the stressors and predictors of reduced well-being in anime fans. Let's now shift our focus to the positives of being an anime fan, paying particular attention to those anime fans who belong to the broader community of anime fans in particular.

In some of our more recent studies we assessed fan well-being in a multi-faceted way, based on a model proposed Carol Ryff (Ryff & Keyes, 1995). Ryff's six-factor model focuses less on feeling good specifically and more on the extent to which people score high on variables that, themselves, cause them to feel good: self-acceptance, personal growth, purpose in life, environmental mastery, autonomy, and having positive relationships with others. We asked anime fans to complete a measure of these facets—which we combined into a single index of well-being, and tested a number of variables to see which ones are the best at predicting the anime fans who scored lowest and highest on the well-being scale.

Many of the results are in line with findings we've presented earlier in this book. For example, in line with our discussion of stigma in Chapter 17, anime fans who felt more confident in their ability to disclose their anime identity to those around them also scored the highest on Ryff's dimensions of well-being. In contrast, fans who perceived stigma from the world around them and who were less-likely to openly identify as anime fans tended to score lower on measure of overall well-being. This may represent a distinction between "closeted" fans and fans who are "out in the open" about their interests (Chaudoir & Quinn, 2010).[8]

Most presently relevant, however, fandom involvement predicted well-being, especially with respect to social facets of well-being (e.g.,

---

[8] This may also lead to divisions in the fandom about whether it is or is not appropriate for one to openly be a fan. Anecdotally speaking from some of our research on other fan groups, we've noted arguments about how appropriate it is for fans to wear fan-related t-shirts in public or to surround themselves with images and merchandise of their fan interest in the workplace. The line between "fan pride" and "cringe" may be an especially narrow and contentious one for some fans!

maintaining positive relations with others). In fact, many community-related activities are, themselves, positively associated with well-being, including attending fan conventions, where one is likely to encounter other fans.

None of these factors—fandom, having face-to-face friends, being able to freely disclose one's fan interest to others—is unique to the anime fandom. As such, we can ask how anime fans stack up against other fan groups with respect to their well-being?

In short, anime fans are fairly comparable to members of other fan groups, although the evidence suggests that they may score slightly lower in well-being than other fans (see Figure 19.3). For example, both anime fans and furries scored higher than fantasy sport fans on measures of depression and anxiety, which one would expect from non-mainstream fan groups that, by virtue of being seen as atypical fans, are perceived as deviant (see Chapter 16). This, in turn, would explain why anime fans score slightly lower than fantasy sport fans in terms of life satisfaction and self-esteem—though it's notable that they still score above the midpoint on these scales on average. Nevertheless, despite experiencing somewhat less stigma than furries, anime fans do score somewhat lower than furries on life satisfaction and self-esteem measures. For now, we can only speculate on a reason for this: perhaps furries, as a fandom, are simply a closer, more tightly-knit community that provides even greater social support in the face of considerable stigma.

While fandom in general—and its ties to having friends who are anime fans and engaging in anime-themed activities—may be associated with well-being, it's worth noting the cosplay community as a particularly poignant example of the fandom's role in well-being (Reysen et al., 2018d). For one thing, the time, effort, thought that goes into creating a cosplay costume represents considerable devotion to the interest and may solidify one's identity as an anime fan. This, coupled with the fact that cosplayers disclose their fan identity more[9] and feel a stronger sense of connection to the anime fandom (see Chapter 7), illustrates how, beyond the benefits the

---

[9] Think about it. You spend dozens of hours crafting a cosplay costume or spending money on one, at that point it becomes harder and harder to rationalize not embracing your identity.

388

anime fandom provides as a whole, specific subgroups within the anime fandom may especially benefit from it.

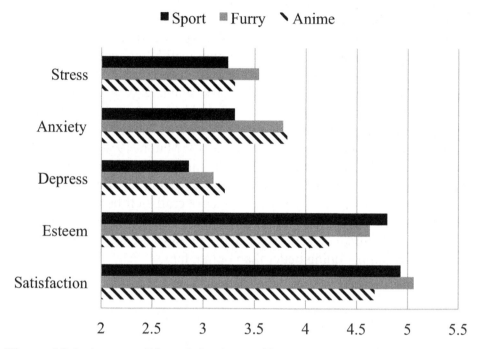

Figure 19.3. Average life satisfaction, self-esteem, and well-being factor comparisons between fantasy sport fans, furries, and anime fans.

The Con High: Well-Being and Con Attendance

Previous research supports the idea that being a part of group activities increases in one's sense of belonging, knowledge, social status, and empathy towards others (Baym, 2006; Kollock, 1999; Wellman & Gulia, 1999). While this has generally been studied with respect to any group interaction, some scholars have distinguished between online group interactions and face-to-face interactions, especially amongst fans (Ray et al., 2018). Emphasizing this point, throughout this book we've repeatedly compared convention-going fans to online fans[10] and routinely find striking differences between them. As we wrap up this book, we can focus on one last comparison between these two groups, comparing them on their well-being, as an illustration of the potential benefits of becoming more involved in-person with the anime fandom.

Looking at research outside of anime fans specifically, sport fans have consistently been shown to experience higher well-being when they engage with other fans face-to-face at a sporting event as opposed to watching the game from home (Wann, Martin et al., 2008; Wann & Weaver, 2009). Other benefits for well-being have been found in groups as disparate as people with multiple sclerosis, people in overeaters anonymous, and people attending religious services (Ivtzan et al., 2013; Maton, 1988).

Across several years of studies on anime fans, we found essentially the same results, a consistent pattern of higher well-being for convention-going fans (see Figure 19.4). Whether we consider overall well-being or look at specific facets of well-being (e.g., psychological, relationship) or at factors related to well-being (e.g., self-esteem), the findings are the same: Con-going fans are simply doing better than online fans.

---

[10] As described previously the comparison between fans in a high salience environment (con) vs. online allows us to examine the effects of salient identity and categorization more readily.

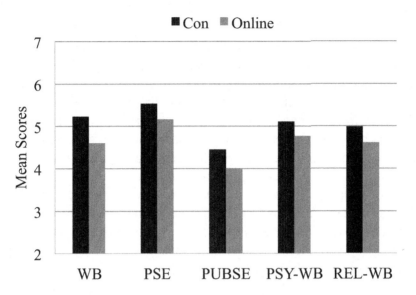

Figure 19.4. Differences in general well-being (WB), private (PSE) and public (PUBSE) collective self-esteem, and psychological (PSY-WB) and relationship (REL-WB) well-being. All differences were significant $p < .05$.

This association between face-to-face fan interaction and well-being may even be responsible—or be a product of—a phenomenon known as the "con high"—a sense of high emotional and physiological excitement tied to being surrounded by so many ingroup members. Of course, the reverse, "post-con depression," has also been noted after fan conventions (Plante et al., 2016). Nevertheless, despite this dip in mood afterward, fans continue to make their way to conventions, often paying hundreds or even thousands of dollars to do so. If we assume that fans aren't in the business of throwing away their money for nothing,[11] we can say that fans themselves recognize these benefits and consider them to be far greater than the temporary slump in mood that follows or the occasional bout of drama that being around so many other people may potentially spark.

---

[11] Although, looking at some of the more… "questionable" fan purchases we've seen over the years, this can't always be taken as a given!

Conclusion

Being part of a fandom offers anime fans numerous benefits. For fans who may be experiencing life stressors, psychological distress, or other personal issues, being part of a larger community offers benefits to their well-being, which may include anything from having a shoulder to cry on to an affirmation of their value and a boost to their self-esteem to tangible, practical resources (e.g., like a couch to crash on for the night). In this chapter we discussed these benefits and the numerous ways they can be measured, doing so within the context of other fan groups and showing that the anime fandom, despite seeming odd and unusual to outsiders, is surprisingly unremarkable among other fandoms. We also revealed that the benefits of fan culture are strongest for those who make the effort to interact in-person with fans. Put simply: Despite the apparent chaos and weirdness of fan conventions, most anime fans can't think of a better way to spend a weekend, and their well-being scores certainly agree!

Conclusion

We've learned a lot about anime[1] and about anime fans in the past seven years, but the project is far from over. As is typical in science, every time you find an answer to one question, you discover two more questions! In other words, you can expect us to be at this for many more years to come!

The International Anime Research Project is about answering questions about anime fans, but also part of a larger goal. We're psychologists, interested in understanding the quirks and characteristics that people share. As such, we study anime fans—just as we study furries, bronies, sport fans, and *Star Wars* fans—to help us answer questions about all fan groups.

We also realize that most of the people reading this book aren't psychologists—they're fans themselves wanting to answer questions about their own fandom. We endeavor to answer those questions too, because we value the symbiotic relationships we have with the fans who help to support our work: They help us answer our boring, lame psychology questions, and we, in turn, help them answer their far-more-interesting questions about waifus and body pillows.

Whenever we conduct a survey and present its results to the anime community, we get ideas from fans themselves for what to study next. For example, after a presentation at AnimeFest, a fan asked about the prevalence of autism in the community. The result was a published article about individuals on the spectrum. At another presentation we mentioned that one of the top reasons why furries leave the furry fandom is fatigue over community drama. A fan asked whether the same was true for anime fans. We realized that the only way to answer that question is with a longitudinal study, and so we just began a longitudinal study to answer this question.[2]

To put it simply, as long as fans continue to ask questions and participate, we'll continue this project. Perhaps in another seven years we'll update this book with many new findings from all manner of new studies, and new and

---

[1] At least one of the authors will attest to the fact that they've discovered several new favorite shows precisely because of this research!

[2] Sorry to that particular fan—it's going to be a few years before you get your answer, but know that we're working on it!

interesting questions to explore. It's in that spirit that we conclude this book, with a look to the future of our research and some of the questions waiting to be explored.

Longitudinal Research

All of the research described in this work is cross-sectional—looking at anime fans here and now, as a snapshot in time. While this methodology has the benefit of being fairly easy to do, it does prevent us from making causal claims about any of our results (see Chapter 2 for more on this!).

One way around this problem is to conduct a longitudinal study, which examines changes in people and in groups over time. We're currently organizing such a project as we write this book. As noted above, the impetus for this study is to answer a question from a fan about why people may leave the anime fandom. However, a good scientist is always resourceful, and we realize that a longitudinal study presents all sorts of opportunities to answer other questions. For example, do fans change genre preferences over time? (e.g., do shonen fans stay shonen fans for life, or do they shift toward slice of life stories as they get older?) When and why do fans leave the fandom? Is there a mass exodus from the anime fandom for those in their mid-to-late 20s, and if they do leave, is it because they're busy with other obligations, or do they simply grow bored and seek out new hobbies? Do fans start as cosplayers and fall into the anime fandom, or do they get into cosplay after joining the anime fandom? These are just a few of the many questions we're kicking around.

We're not alone in being interested in this endeavor! At the end of the survey in 2020 we asked for volunteers to sign up for the longitudinal study. As we write this, we've already got over 400 fans who have completed the first wave of the longitudinal study, which we plan to conduct for at least three years.

Japanese Sample

The majority of participants in the present research are from Western, English-speaking countries.[3] This is due to the survey being administered in English. As mentioned in Chapter 5, otaku in Japan are considered distinct from otaku in the West. However, just how different are Japanese anime

---

[3] This is a common problem in psychology, the oversampling of participants from Western nations, from which psychologists make claims about all of humanity (Henrich et al., 2010).

fans compared to Western fans? After all, in other psychological studies Japanese participants have been found to respond dramatically different from Western participants (e.g., thinking more holistically).

For this reason, a cross-national comparison is desperately needed. We were planning to do exactly that in 2020, however our efforts are currently stalled by the global pandemic. In the future, however, you can expect us to travel to Japan and gather data from the Japanese anime fandom in-person.[4]

Cosplayers

Cosplayers are the most visible aspect of the anime fandom. We've found that cosplayers choose a favorite character that is both similar to them, yet also represents an idealized version of them. A variety of researchers have suggested that cosplayers may learn to act more in line with their ideal self over time (e.g., Lamerichs, 2018). Or as Napier (2007) suggests, cosplayers may change their personality by putting on the costume. Do cosplayers really change over time through their engagement with cosplay? Does a person who cosplays the same character repeatedly begin to take on that character's traits themselves? It's an interesting question that deserves some empirical attention.

Fan Tourism and Culture

Fan tourism is a quickly growing area of the academic literature. For example, Mason (2016) noted that a city experienced a business boom after *Silver Spoon* became popular. Related to this topic is the question of whether the "Cool Japan" campaign has worked: Do non-Japanese fans of anime want to spend money to visit sites where their favorite anime was based? Do fans have a more positive image of the country? After becoming anime fans, do fans take the time to learn more about Japan's history and culture? How does one's attachment with another country impact how they identify with their own country? The continuing growth and popularity of anime/manga exports, coupled with research showing that anime fans desire to visit the country suggest the initiative is working (Agyeiwaah et al., 2019), but it would be interesting to test just how effective the campaign has been through a converted effort to study it.

---

[4] We're also always on the lookout for fans who are fluent in both Japanese and English to translate our surveys and help with recruiting online fans. If anyone is interested in spending lots of time on a research project for no money, contact us!

Genre Preferences

As shown in this book, genre preferences tend to cluster together into about five dimensions. One's genre preferences can tell us all sorts of things about their attitudes and beliefs, from their belief in the paranormal to their sexism and endorsement of traditional gender norms. To date, however, we've only barely tapped the potential for what we can learn about fans from their genre preferences. Do these preferences change, and why? Do attitudes change along with them? Are one's preferred tropes related to their genre preferences? Is there a difference between fans who stick to one or two genres and fans who consume anime from all genres?

Parasocial Relationships

Parasocial relationships are experienced by viewers as real relationships. When a show ends, a character dies, or an actor leaves the show, fans experience relationship dissolution, a "parasocial breakup" (Cohen, 2003). The thought of losing a favorite character can lead to negative emotions, just as the loss of a real world relationship does (Cohen, 2004). Perhaps such negative emotions are lower within the anime fandom, given that most shows only take place across one season with around 12 episodes. However, what about fans of long-running shows (e.g., *One Piece*)? Would they report greater distress after losing a favorite character?

Post-Con Depression

Anime fans show a well-being "high" while attending an anime convention compared to fans who are surveyed at home (Ray et al., 2018). Sport fans report similar boosts to their well-being when surveyed at a game instead of at home (Wann, Martin et al., 2008). Plante and colleagues (2016) surveyed furries at a furry convention and again either 3 days or 7 days after the convention. Regardless of whether the survey was 3 or 7 days after the con, participants tended to show a depressed mood (less happy, more depressed). Participants lamented leaving the con to return to a mundane life (Roberts et al., 2017).

We suspect a similar phenomenon occurs in the anime fandom. However, we hope to build on the existing research by not only measuring well-being at the convention and after it, but also by measuring well-being before the convention and in the months following a convention.

A related phenomenon may be found in post-show depression, where anime fans report feeling worse when a favorite show ends. Further research regarding the emotional investment and toll linked to a show would be interesting. Perhaps one way to mitigate such a phenomenon would be to continue in a fandom related to the show (e.g., the K-On! fandom is still lively), something also known as post-object fandom (Williams, 2015).

Conclusion

As we've seen, there are still plenty of questions to ask and phenomena to observe in the anime fandom. Many of these questions revolve around the ways that anime fans compare to other fans. Many of the same psychological processes appear to be similar regardless of the fandom (e.g., identification with a sport team works the same as identification with anime), but the way those processes manifest often differ in surprising and informative ways.

This book has been a chance for us to stop and take stock of where we've come in the past seven years, as well as assess where we're going in the next seven. We're nowhere close to being done with our research on the anime fandom, and we hope that the future brings with it not only new answers and new puzzles to solve, but also, if any young, budding researchers are reading, new collaborators and colleagues with whom to share this journey.[5]

---

[5] Or, at very least, someone else to help us write the next edition of the book!

References

Abrams, D. (2009). Social identity on a national scale: Optimal distinctiveness and young people's self-expression through musical preference. *Group Processes and Intergroup Relations, 12*(3), 303-317. https://doi.org/10.1177/1368430209102841

Adams, G., Biernat, M., Branscombe, N. R., Crandall, C. S., & Wrightsman, L. S. (2008). Beyond prejudice: Toward a sociocultural psychology of racism and oppression. In G. Adams, M. Biernat, N. R. Branscombe, C. S. Crandall, & L. S. Wrightsman (Eds.), *Commemorating Brown: The social psychology of racism and discrimination* (pp. 215-246). APA Books. https://doi.org/10.1037/11681-012

Agcaoili, M. D. (2011). Hybrid identities: Filipino fansubbers of Japanese media and self-construction. *Asian Studies, 47,* 1-28.

Agyeiwaah, E., Suntikul, W., & Carmen, L. Y. S. (2019). 'Cool Japan': Anime, soft power and Hong Kong generation Y travel to Japan. *Journal of China Tourism Research, 15*(2), 127-148. https://doi.org/10.1080/19388160.2018.1540373

Ahn, J. (2008). *Animated subjects: Globalization, media, and East Asian cultural imaginaries* (Publication No. 3311139) [Doctoral dissertation, University of Southern California]. ProQuest Dissertations and Theses Global.

Aiken, K. D., Bee, C., & Walker, N. (2018). From passion to obsession: Development and validation of a scale to measure compulsive sport consumption. *Journal of Business Research, 87,* 69-79. https://doi.org/10.1016/j.jbusres.2018.02.019

Allen, M. S., & Robson, D. A. (2020). Personality and body dissatisfaction: An updated systematic review with meta-analysis. *Body Image, 33,* 77-89. https://doi.org/10.1016/j.bodyim.2020.02.001

Allen, M. S., & Walter, E. E. (2018). Linking big five personality traits to sexuality and sexual health: A meta-analytic review. *Psychological Bulletin, 144*(10), 1081-1110. https://doi.org/10.1037/bul0000157

American Community Survey. (2017). *Asian alone or in any combination by selected groups. Universe: Total Asian alone or in any combination population (the total groups tallied).* Retrieved July 27, 2020, from

https://archive.vn/20200213004629/https://factfinder.census.gov/bkmk/t
able/1.0/en/ACS/17_1YR/B02018

APA: American Psychological Association. (2018, October). Stress in
America 2018: Stress and Generation Z. *Stress in America Press Room.*
Retrieved October 15, 2020, from
https://www.apa.org/news/press/releases/stress

Anderson, C. A., Shibuya, A., Ihori, N., Swing, E. L., Bushman, B. J.,
Sakamoto, A., Rothstein, H. R., & Saleem, M. (2010). Violent video
game effects on aggression, empathy, and prosocial behavior in Eastern
and Western countries: A meta-analytic review. *Psychological Bulletin,*
136(2), 151-173. https://doi.org/10.1037/a0018251

Andrijiw, A. M., & Hyatt (2009). Using optimal distinctiveness theory to
understand identification with a nonlocal professional hockey team.
Journal of Sport Management, 23(2), 156-181.
https://doi.org/10.1123/jsm.23.2.156

Ang, S., Van Dyne, L., & Koh, C. (2006). Personality correlates of the
four-factor model of cultural intelligence. *Group and Organization*
Management, 31(1), 100-123.
https://doi.org/10.1177/1059601105275267

Anime Expo. (n.d.). In Wikipedia. Retrieved November 12, 2020, from
https://en.wikipedia.org/wiki/Anime_Expo

Anime Trending. (n.d.). Anime Trending. *Facebook.* Retrieved November
12, 2020, from https://www.facebook.com/Anitrendz/

Annett, S. (2011). *Animating transcultural communities: Animation fandom*
in North America and east Asia from 1906-2010 (Publication No.
NR78886) [Doctoral dissertation, University of Manitoba]. ProQuest
Dissertations and Theses Global.

Annett, S. (2014). *Anime fan communities: Transcultural flows and fictions.*
Palgrave Macmillian.

Ashcraft, B., & Plunkett, L. (2014). *Cosplay world.* Prestel.

Ashmore, R. D., Deaux, K., & McLaughlin-Volpe, T. (2004). An
organizing framework for collective identity: Articulation and
significance of multidimensionality. *Psychological Bulletin, 130*(1), 80-
114. https://doi.org/10.1037/0033-2909.130.1.80

Astro Boy. (n.d.). *Wikipedia.* Retrieved October 9, 2020, from
https://en.wikipedia.org/wiki/Astro_Boy

Atkinson, L. (2015). *Down the rabbit hole: An exploration of Japanese lolita fashion* (Publication No. 10005441) [Master's thesis, University of Ottawa]. ProQuest Dissertations and Theses Global.

Azuma, H. (2009). *Otaku: Japan's database animals*. University of Minnesota Press.

Bachen, C. M., Hernández-Ramos, P., Raphael, C., & Waldron, A. (2016). How do presence, flow, and character identification affect players' empathy and interest in learning from a serious computer game? *Computers in Human Behavior, 64,* 77-87. https://doi.org/10.1016/j.chb.2016.06.043

Bainbridge, J., & Norris, C. (2013). Posthuman drag: Understanding cosplay as social networking in a material culture. *Intersections: Gender and Sexuality in Asia and the Pacific, 32,* 1-11. http://ecite.utas.edu.au/85941

Bakker, A. B. (2008). The work-related flow inventory: Construction and initial validation of the WOLF. *Journal of Vocational Behavior, 72*(3), 400-414. https://doi.org/10.1016/j.jvb.2007.11.007

Baldry, A. C., & Winkel, F. W. (2003). Direct and vicarious victimization at school and at home as risk factors for suicidal cognition among Italian adolescents. *Journal of Adolescence, 26*(6), 703-716. https://doi.org/10.1016/j.adolescence.2003.07.002

Ballew, M. T., Pearson, A. R., Goldberg, M. H., Rosenthal, S. A., & Leiserowitz, A. (2020). Does socioeconomic status moderate the political divide on climate change? The roles of education, income, and individualism. *Global Environment Change, 60,* Article 102024. https://doi.org/10.1016/j.gloenvcha.2019.102024

Barajas, A. (2018). *Pros and cons: Anime conventions and cosplayers* (Publication No. 13855850) [Master's thesis, University of Texas at Austin]. ProQuest Dissertations and Theses Global.

Bargh, J. A., Chen, M., & Burrows, L. (1996). Automaticity of social behavior: Direct effects of trait construct and stereotype activation on action. *Journal of Personality and Social Psychology, 71*(2), 230-244. https://doi.org/10.1037/0022 3514.71.2.230

Barefoot, J. C., Beckham, J. C., Haney, T. L., Siegler, I. C., & Lipkus, I. M. (1993). Age differences in hostility among middle-aged and older adults.

Psychology and Aging, 8(1), 3-9. https://doi.org/10.1037/0882-7974.8.1.3

Basil, M. D., & Brown, W. J. (2004). Magic Johnson and Mark McGwire: The power of identification with sports celebrities. In L. R. Kahle & C. Riley (Eds.), *Sports marketing and the psychology of marketing communication* (pp. 159-174). Lawrence Erlbaum Associates.

Baym, N. (2006). Interpersonal life online. In L. A. Lievrouw & S. Livingstone (Ed.), *Handbook of new media: Social shaping and social consequences of ICTs, Updated student edition* (pp. 35- 54). SAGE Publications.

Bender, K. (2014, February 4). 11-year-old boy attempts suicide after being bullied for *My Little Pony* passion. *People.com.* Retrieved January 17, 2021, https://people.com/celebrity/11-year-old-boy-brony-attempts-suicide-after-bullying-over-my-little-pony/

Benino, J. A. R. (2014). *The shifts in the Filipino youth's perceptions of Japan through cosplay* [Unpublished master's thesis]. De La Salle University-Manila.

Berger, K. S. (2007). Update on bullying at school: Science forgotten? *Developmental Review, 27*(1), 90-126. https://doi.org/10.1016/j.dr.2006.08.002

Bessière, K., Seay, A. F., & Kiesler, S. (2007). The ideal elf: Identity exploration in World of Warcraft. *CyberPsychology and Behavior, 10*(4), 530-535. https://doi.org/10.1089/cpb.2007.9994

Biernat, M., & Crandall, C. S. (1999). Racial attitudes. In J. Robinson, P. R. Shaver, & L. S. Wrightsman (Eds.), *Measures of social psychology: Volume 2. Measures of political attitudes* (pp. 297-411). Academic Press.

Billard, T. J. (2019). (No) shame in the game: The influence of pornography viewing on attitudes toward transgender people. *Communication Research Reports, 36*(1), 45-56. https://doi.org/10.1080/08824096.2018.1549539

Bloem, W. (2014). *Japanese fanspeak in the Anglophone manga and anime fan culture* [Master's thesis, Leiden University]. Leiden University. http://hdl.handle.net/1887/29529

Bobowik, M., Basabe, N., Páez, D., Jiménez, A., & Bilbao, M. A. (2011). Personal values and well-being among Europeans, Spanish natives and immigrants to Spain: Does the culture matter? *Journal of Happiness Studies, 12,* 401-419. https://doi.org/10.1007/s10902-010-9202-1

Bogardus, E. (1928). *Immigration and race attitudes.* Heath.

Bogardus, E. S. (1933). A social distance scale. *Sociology and Social Research, 17,* 265-271.

Bornstein, R. F. (1989). Exposure and affect: Overview and meta-analysis of research, 1968-1987. *Psychological Bulletin, 106*(2), 265-289. https://doi.org/10.1037/0033-2909.106.2.265

Branscombe, N. R., & Wann, D. L. (1991). The positive social and self concept consequences of sports team identification. *Journal of Sport and Social Issues, 15*(2), 115-127. https://doi.org/10.1177/019372359101500202

Brenner, R. E. (2007). *Understanding manga and anime.* Libraries Unlimited.

Brewer, M. B. (1991). The social self: On being the same and different at the same time. *Personality and Social Psychology Bulletin, 17*(5), 475-482. https://doi.org/10.1177/0146167291175001

Brown, W. J., & Basil, M. D. (1995). Media celebrities and public health: Responses to "Magic" Johnson's HIV disclosure and its impact on AIDS risk and high-risk behaviors. *Health Communication, 7*(4), 345-370. https://doi.org/10.1207/s15327027hc0704_4

Brown, W. J., & de Matviuk, M. A. C. (2010). Sports celebrities and public health: Diego Maradona's influence on drug use prevention. *Journal of Health Communication, 15*(4), 358-373. https://doi.org/10.1080/10810730903460575

Bueno, A. F. (2016). *Media consume Tokyo: Television and urban place since the bubble* (Publication No. 10632932) [Doctoral dissertation, Harvard University]. ProQuest Dissertations and Theses Global.

Burkett, M. E. (2009). *Pop-diplomacy: Anime and manga as vehicles of cultural context, identity formation, and hybridity* (Publication No. 1484436) [Master's thesis, American University]. ProQuest Dissertations and Theses Global.

Buunk, A. P., Gibbons, F. X., & Visser, A. (2002). The relevance of social comparison processes for prevention and health care. *Patient Education and Counseling, 47*(1), 1-3. https://doi.org/10.1016/S0738-3991(02)00054-X

Cain, S. (2012). *Quiet: The power of introverts in a world that can't stop talking*. Crown Publishers.

Carlson, R. L. (2018). *"More Japanese than Japanese": Subjectivation in the age of brand nationalism and the internet* (Publication No. 10984352) [Doctoral dissertation, University of Pittsburgh]. ProQuest Dissertations and Theses Global.

Carney, J. V. (2000). Bullied to death: Perceptions of peer abuse and suicidal behaviour during adolescence. *School Psychology International, 21*(2), 213-223. https://doi.org/10.1177/0143034300212007

Chadborn, D., Edwards, P., & Reysen, S. (2017). Displaying fan identity to make friends. *Intensities: The Journal of Cult Media, 9,* 87-97.

Chadborn, D., Edwards, P., & Reysen, S. (2018). Reexamining differences between fandom and local sense of community. *Psychology of Popular Media Culture, 7*(3), 241-249. https://doi.org/10.1037/ppm0000125

Chadborn, D. P., Plante, C. N., & Reysen, S. (2016). Perceived stigma, social identity, and group norms as predictors of prosocial giving in a fandom. *International Journal of Interactive Communication Systems and Technologies, 6*(1), 35-49. https://doi.org/10.4018/IJICST.2016010103

Chandra, A., Mosher, W. D., & Copen, C. (2011). Sexual behavior, sexual attraction, and sexual identity in the United States: Data from the 2006-2008 National Survey of Family Growth. *National Health Statistics Reports, 36,* 1-36. Retrieved from http://www.cdc.gov/nchs/data/nhsr/nhsr036.pdf

Chaudoir, S. R., & Quinn, D. M. (2010). Revealing concealable stigmatized identities: The impact of disclosure motivations and positive first-disclosure experiences on fear of disclosure and well-being. *Journal of Social Issues, 66*(3), 570-584. https://doi.org/10.1111/j.1540-4560.2010.01663.x

Chen, J.-S. (2003). The comic/anime fan culture in Taiwan: With a focus on adolescents' experiences. *Journal of Social Theory in Art Education, 23,* 89-103. https://scholarscompass.vcu.edu/jstae/vol23/iss1/8/

Chen, J.-S. (2007). A study of fan culture: Adolescent experiences with anime/manga doujinshi and cosplay in Taiwan. *Visual Arts Research, 33*(1), 14-24. https://www.jstor.org/stable/20715430

Chowning, K., & Cambpell, N. J. (2009). Development and validation of a measure of academic entitlement: Individual differences in students' externalized responsibility and entitled expectations. *Journal of Educational Psychology, 101*(4), 982-997. https://doi.org/10.1037/a0016351

Christensen, P. N., Rothgerber, H., Wood, W., & Matz, D. C. (2004). Social norms and identity relevance: A motivational approach to normative behavior. *Personality and Social Psychology Bulletin, 30*(10), 1295-1309. https://doi.org/10.1177/0146167204264480

Cialdini, R. B., Borden, R. J., Thorne, A., Walker, M. R., Freeman, S., & Sloan, L. R. (1976). Basking in reflected glory: Three (football) field studies. *Journal of Personality and Social Psychology, 34*(3), 366-375. https://doi.org/10.1037/0022-3514.34.3.366

Cialdini, R. B., Reno, R. R., & Kallgren, C. A. (1990). A focus theory of normative conduct: recycling the concept of norms to reduce littering in public places. *Journal of Personality and Social Psychology, 58*(6), 1015-1026. https://doi.org/10.1037/0022-3514.58.6.1015

Cialdini, R. B., & Trost, M. R. (1998). *Social influence: Social norms, conformity and compliance.* In D. T. Gilbert, S. T. Fiske, & G. Lindzey (Eds.), *The handbook of social psychology* (pp. 151-192). McGraw-Hill.

CIRCLE: Center for Information & Research on Civic Learning and Engagement. (2018, October 24). *Young people's ambivalent relationship with political parties.* Retrieved from https://circle.tufts.edu/latest-research/young-peoples-ambivalent-relationship-political-parties

Clements, J. (2018). *Anime: A history.* Bloomsbury.

Clements, J., & McCarthy, H. (2015). *The anime encyclopedia: A century of Japanese animation* (3rd ed.). Stone Bridge Press.

Coats, S., Smith, E. R., Claypool, H. M., & Banner, M. J. (2000). Overlapping mental representations of self and in-group: Reaction time evidence and its relationship with explicit measures of group identification. *Journal of Experimental Social Psychology, 36*(3), 304-315. https://doi.org/10.1006/jesp.1999.1416

Cohen, A. (2009). A value based perspective on commitment in the workplace: An examination of Schwartz's basic human values theory among bank employees in Israel. *International Journal of Intercultural Relations, 33*(4), 332-345. https://doi.org/10.1016/j.ijintrel.2009.04.001

Cohen, J. (2003). Parasocial breakups: Measuring individual differences in responses to the dissolution of parasocial relationships. *Mass Communication and Society, 6*(2), 191-202. https://doi.org/10.1207/S15327825MCS0602_5

Cohen, J. (2004). Parasocial break-up from favorite television characters: The role of attachment styles and relationship intensity. *Journal of Social and Personal Relationships, 21*(2), 187-202. https://doi.org/10.1177/0265407504041374

Cohn, D., Passel, J., Wang, W., & Livingston, G. (2011). Barely half of U.S. adults are married—A record low. *Pew Research Center*. Retrieved July 28, 2020, from https://www.pewsocialtrends.org/2011/12/14/barely-half-of-u-s-adults-are-married-a-record-low/

Condry, I. (2013). *The soul of anime: collaborative creativity and Japan's media success story*. Duke University Press.

Connor-Smith, J. K., & Flachsbart, C. (2007). Relations between personality and coping: A meta-analysis. *Journal of Personality and Social Psychology, 93*(6), 1080-1107. https://doi.org/10.1037/0022-3514.93.6.1080

Cook, C. R., Williams, K. R., Guerra, N. G., Kim, T. E., & Sadek, S. (2010). Predictors of bullying and victimization in childhood and adolescence: A meta-analytic investigation. *School Psychology Quarterly, 25*(2), 65-83. https://doi.org/10.1037/a0020149

Cooper, B., Cox, D., Lienesch, R., & Jones, R. P. (2016, September 22). Exodus: Why Americans are leaving religion—and why they're unlikely to come back. *Public Religion Research Institution*. Retrieved from https://www.prri.org/research/prri-rns-poll-nones-atheist-leaving-religion/

Copen, C. E., Chandra, A., & Febo-Vazquez, I. (2016). Sexual behavior, sexual attraction, and sexual orientation among adults aged 18-44 in the United States: Data from the 2011-2013 National Survey of Family Growth. *National Health Statistics Reports, 88,* 1-14. https://pubmed.ncbi.nlm.nih.gov/26766410/

Crosby, F. (1984). The denial of personal discrimination. *American Behavioral Scientist, 27*(3), 371-386. https://doi.org/10.1177/000276484027003008

Csíkeszentmihályi, M. (1975). *Beyond boredom and anxiety.* Jossey-Bass.

Csíkeszentmihályi, M. (1990). *Flow: The psychology of optimal experience.* Harpers Perennial.

Cuddy, A. J. C., Fiske, S. T., & Glick, P. (2007). The BIAS Map: Behaviors from intergroup affect and stereotypes. *Journal of Personality and Social Psychology, 92*(4), 631-648. https://doi.org/10.1037/0022-3514.92.4.631

Cuddy, A. J. C., Fiske, S. T., & Glick, P. (2008). Warmth and competence as universal dimensions of social perception: The stereotype content model and the BIAS Map. *Advances in Experimental Social Psychology, 40*, 61-149. https://doi.org/10.1016/S0065-2601(07)00002-0

Daspe, M. È., Vaillancourt-Morel, M. P., Lussier, Y., Sabourin, S., & Ferron, A. (2018). When pornography use feels out of control: The moderation effect of relationship and sexual satisfaction. *Journal of Sex and Marital Therapy, 44*(4), 343-353. https://doi.org/10.1080/0092623X.2017.1405301

Davis, C. R. (2017). *The formation of temporary communities in anime fandom: A story of bottom-up globalization* (Publication No. 10604452) [Master's thesis, California State University, Fullerton]. ProQuest Dissertations and Theses Global.

Davis, J. C. (2008). *Japanese animation in America and its fans* [Master's thesis, Oregon State University]. Oregon State University. https://ir.library.oregonstate.edu/concern/graduate_thesis_or_dissertations/4t64gr636

Davis, N. (2016). *Manga and anime go to Hollywood.* Bloomsbury.

Deci, E. L., & Ryan, R. M. (2000). The "what" and "why" of goal pursuits: Human needs and the self-determination of behavior. *Psychological Inquiry, 11*(4), 227-268. https://doi.org/10.1207/S15327965PLI1104_01

De Cremer, D., & Leonardelli, G. J. (2003). Cooperation in social dilemmas and the need to belong: The moderating effect of group size. *Group Dynamics: Theory, Research, and Practice, 7*(2), 168-174. https://doi.org/10.1037/1089-2699.7.2.168

DeDominicis, K. (2015). *Imagining virtual community: Online media fandom and the construction of virtual collectivity* [Unpublished doctoral dissertation]. University of Edinburgh.

Devos, T., & Banaji, M. R. (2005). American = white? *Journal of Personality and Social Psychology, 88*(3), 447-466. https://doi.org/10.1037/0022-3514.88.3.447

Devos, T., & Mohamed, H. (2014). Shades of American identity: Implicit relations between ethnic and national identities. *Social and Personality Psychology Compass, 8*(12), 739-754. https://doi.org/10.1111/spc3.12149

Dinnie, T. (2012, December 5). Anime club addresses stereotypes. *The Big Red*. Retrieved from http://bigredhawks.com/?p=5548

Dion, K. L., & Kawakami, K. (1996). Ethnicity and perceived discrimination in Toronto: Another look at the personal/group discrimination discrepancy. *Canadian Journal of Behavioural Science, 28*(3), 203-213. https://doi.org/10.1037/0008-400X.28.3.203

Donovan, C. (2014, October 4). Get to know a manga artist: The unstoppable Hiromu Arakawa. *The Mary Sue*. https://www.themarysue.com/hiromu-arakawa-part-1/

Dowler, K. (2002). Media influence on attitudes toward guns and gun control. *American Journal of Criminal Justice, 26*(2), 235-247. https://doi.org/10.1007/BF02887829

Drazen, P. (2014). *Anime explosion!: The what? why? and wow! of Japanese animation*. Stone Bridge Press.

Dunbar, C. (2011, November 30). *The obligatory stereotyping discussion* [Web log post]. Retrieved from http://www.studyofanime.com/2011/11/obligatory-stereotypingdiscussion.html

Dunlap, K., & Wolf, C. (2010). Fans behaving badly: Anime metafandom, brutal criticism, and the intellectual fan. *Mechademia, 5*, 267-283. https://www.muse.jhu.edu/article/400561

Dziesinski, M. J., II (2014). *Cool vocations in Japan's global pop culture industries: From young fans to skilled animators and manga artists* (Publication No. 3648529) [Doctoral dissertation, University of Hawaii at Manoa]. ProQuest Dissertations and Theses Global.

Edwards, P., Chadborn, D. P., Plante, C., Reysen, S., & Redden, M. H. (2019). *Meet the bronies: The psychology of adult* My Little Pony *fandom.* McFarland & Company.

Eidelman, S., & Biernat, M. (2002). Derogating black sheep: Individual or group protection. *Journal of Experimental Social Psychology, 39*(6), 602-609. https://doi.org/10.1016/S0022-1031(03)00042-8

Emma's Pen. (2013, October). *Fan entitlement and celebrity culture* [Web log post]. Retrieved from https://emmaspen.wordpress.com/2013/10/05/fan-entitlement-and-celebrity-culture/

End, C. M., Kretschmar, J., Campbell, J., Mueller, D. G., & Dietz-Uhler, B. (2003). Sport fans' attitudes toward war analogies as descriptors for sport. *Journal of Sport Behavior, 26*(4), 356-367.

Eng, L. (2006). *Otaku engagements: Subcultural appropriation of science and technology* (Publication No. 3232607) [Doctoral dissertation, Rensselaer Polytechnic Institute]. ProQuest Dissertations and Theses Global.

Eng, L. (2012). Strategies of engagement: Discovering, defining, and describing otaku culture in the United States. In M. Ito, D. Okabe, & I. Tsuji (Eds.), *Fandom unbound: Otaku culture in a connected world* (pp. 85-104). Yale University Press.

Erdem, C., & Uzun, A. M. (2020). Smartphone addiction among undergraduates: Roles of personality traits and demographic factors. *Technology, Knowledge and Learning.* Advance online publication. https://doi.org/10.1007/s10758-020-09467-1

Ettinger, B. (2015, September 25). Akado Suzunosuke. *Anipages.* http://www.pelleas.net/aniTOP/index.php/akado-suzunosuke

Facebook. (n.d.). Facebook. Retrieved November 12, 2020, from https://www.facebook.com/search/groups/?q=anime

Feiler, D. C., & Kleinbaum, A. M. (2015). Popularity, similarity, and the network extraversion bias. *Psychological Science, 26*(5), 593-603. https://doi.org/10.1177/0956797615569580

Fennell, D., Liberato, A. S., Hayden, B., & Fujino, Y. (2013). Consuming anime. *Television and New Media, 14*(5), 440-456. https://doi.org/10.1177/1527476412436986

Festinger, L., Schacter, S., & Back, K. (1963). *Social pressure in informal groups: A study of human factors in housing.* Sanford University Press.

Finneran, C. M., & Zhang, P. (2005). Flow in computer-mediated environments: Promises and challenges. *Communications of the Association for Information Systems, 15,* 82-101. https://doi.org/10.17705/1CAIS.01504

Fisher, P. (2020). Generational cycles in American Politics, 1952-2016. *Society, 57,* 22-29. https://doi.org/10.1007/s12115-019-00437-7

Fiske, S. T., Cuddy, A. J. C., Glick, P., Xu, J. (2002). A model of (often mixed) stereotype content: Competence and warmth respectively follow from perceived status and competition. *Journal of Personality and Social Psychology, 82*(2), 878-902. https://doi.org/10.1037/0022-3514.82.6.878

Flatt, S. (2015). *Cosplay in the USA* [Honor's thesis, Middle Tennessee State University]. Middle Tennessee State University.

Flores, A. R., Herman, J. L., Gates, G. J., & Brown, T. N. T. (2016). How many adults identify as transgender in the United States? *The Williams Institute.* Retrieved July 27, 2020, from https://williamsinstitute.law.ucla.edu/wp-content/uploads/Trans-Adults-US-Aug-2016.pdf

Fry, R. (2016, May 24). For the first time in modern era, living with parents edges out other living arrangements for 18-to-34-year-olds: Share living with spouse or partner continues to fall. *Pew Research Center: Social & Demographic Trends.* Retrieved from http://www.pewsocialtrends.org/2016/05/24/for-the-first-time-in-modern-era-living-with-parents-edges-out-other-living-arrangements-for-18-to-34-year-olds/

Fryar, C. D., Carroll, M. D., & Ogden, C. L. (2018). Prevalence of overweight, obesity, and severe obesity among adults aged 20 and over: United States, 1960-1962 through 2015-2016. *Report from the National Center for Health Statistics, Division of Health Interview Statistics.* Retrieved July 29, 2020, from https://www.cdc.gov/nchs/data/hestat/obesity_adult_13_14/obesity_adult_13_14.pdf

Fu, J. (2013). For love and money: Professionalism and community in anime and manga artists' alleys. *The Phoenix Papers, 1*(2), 155-192.

Fukukawa, K., Shafer, W. E., & Lee, G. M. (2007). Values and attitudes toward social and environmental accountability: A study of MBA students. *Journal of Business Ethics, 71,* 381-394. https://doi.org/10.1007/s10551-005-3893-y

Funder, D. C., & Fast, L. A. (2010). Personality in social psychology. In S. T. Fiske, D. T. Gilbert, & G. Lindzey (Eds.), *Handbook of social psychology* (5th ed., pp. 668-697). John Wiley & Sons.

Furnham, A., Richards, S. C., Paulhus, D. L. (2013). The dark triad of personality: A 10 year review. *Social and Personality Psychology Compass, 7*(3), 199-216. https://doi.org/10.1111/spc3.12018

FurryLife Online. (2020, August 29). *Hello all! Venthas here again. The staff have decided that we will not, now or ever, condone or accept zoophilia or zoophiles. We do have a couple of questions regarding NSFW feral content. Please take a moment to respond* [Tweet]. Twitter. https://twitter.com/FurrylifeOnline/status/1299857201205518337

FurScience. (2017). *Anthrocon 2017 Summary.* FurScience. Retrieved July 30, 2020, from https://furscience.com/research-findings/appendix-1-previous-research/anthrocon-2017-summary/

Fyock, J., & Stangor, C. (1994). The role of memory biases in stereotype maintenance. *British Journal of Social Psychology, 33*(3), 331-343. https://doi.org/10.1111/j.2044-8309.1994.tb01029.x

Galbraith, P. W. (2009). *The otaku encyclopedia: An insider's guide to the subculture of cool Japan.* Kodansha USA.

Galbraith, P. W. (2014). *The moé manifesto: An insider's look at the worlds of manga, anime, and gaming.* Tuttle.

Galbraith, P. W. (2019). *Otaku and the struggle for imagination in Japan.* Duke University Press.

Gates, G. J. (2017, January 11). In U.S., more adults identifying as LGBT. *Gallup Social & Policy Issues.* Retrieved from https://news.gallup.com/poll/201731/lgbt-identification-rises.aspx

Gerbasi, K. C., Roberts, S. E., Reysen, S., Plante, C. N., & McHugh, R. (2020). The lion, the wolf and the ~~wardrobe~~ fursuit: Do furries attending a furry convention have animal/fursona, furry, and convention themed dreams? In T. Howl (Ed.), *Furries among us 3: Essays by furries about furries* (pp. 62-84). Thurston Howl Publications.

Giluk, T. L. (2009). Mindfulness, big five personality, and affect: A meta-analysis. *Personality and Individual Differences, 47*(8), 805-811. https://doi.org/10.1016/j.paid.2009.06.026

Gini, G. (2006). Bullying as a social process: The role of group membership in students' perception of inter-group aggression at school. *Journal of School Psychology, 44*(1), 51-65. https://doi.org/10.1016/j.jsp.2005.12.002

Glick, P., & Fiske, S. T. (1996). The ambivalent sexism inventory: Differentiating hostile and benevolent sexism. *Journal of Personality and Social Psychology, 70*(3), 491-512. https://doi.org/10.1037/0022-3514.70.3.491

Gn, J. (2011). Queer simulation: The practice, performance and pleasure of cosplay. *Continuum: Journal of Media and Cultural Studies, 25*(4), 583-593. https://doi.org/10.1080/10304312.2011.582937

Goffman, E. (1963). *Stigma: On the management of spoiled identity.* Prentice-Hall.

Goldberg, L. R. (1990). An alternative "description of personality": The big-five factor structure. *Journal of Personality and Social Psychology, 59*(6), 1216-1229. https://doi.org/10.1037/0022-3514.59.6.1216

Gordon, B. S., Yoshida, M., Nakazawa, M., & Bass, J. (2019). The role of pride feelings in the team and fan community identification process: An empirical examination in professional sport. *Corporate Reputation Review.* Advance online publication. https://doi.org/10.1057/s41299-019-00092-y

Gosling, S. D., Rentfrow, P. J., & Swann, W. B., Jr. (2003). A very brief measure of the big-five personality domains. *Journal of Research in Personality, 37*(6), 504-528. https://doi.org/10.1016/S0092-6566(03)00046-1

Grassmuck, V. (1990, December). *"I'm alone, but not lonely": Japanese otaku-kids colonize the realm of information and media: A tale of sex and crime from a faraway place.* Retrieved from https://www.cjas.org/%7Eleng/otaku-e.htm

Green, M. C., & Brock, T. C. (2000). The role of transportation in the persuasiveness of public narrative. *Journal of Personality and Social Psychology, 79*(5), 701-721. https://doi.org/10.1037/0022-3514.79.5.701

412

Grieve, R., Indian, M., Witteveen, K., Tolan, G. A., & Marrington, J. (2013). Face-to-face or Facebook: Can social connectedness be derived online? *Computers in Human Behavior, 29*(3), 604-609. https://doi.org/10.1016/j.chb.2012.11.017

Grigoryev, D., Fiske, S. T., & Batkhina, A. (2019). Mapping ethnic stereotypes and their antecedents in Russia: The stereotype content model. *Frontiers in Psychology, 10,* Article 1643. https://doi.org/10.3389/fpsyg.2019.01643

Guerra, N. G., Williams, K. R., & Sadek, S. (2011). Understanding bullying and victimization during childhood and adolescence: A mixed methods study. *Child Development, 82*(1), 295-310. https://doi.org/10.1111/j.1467-8624.2010.01556.x

Gunderson, E. A., Ramirez, G., Levine, S. C., & Beilock, S. L. (2012). The role of parents and teachers in the development of gender-related math attitudes. *Sex Roles, 66,* 153-166. https://doi.org/10.1007/s11199-011-9996-2

Gwinner, K., & Swanson, S. R. (2003). A model of fan identification: Antecedents and sponsorship outcomes. *Journal of Services Marketing, 17*(3), 275-294. https://doi.org/10.1108/08876040310474828

Hack, B. (2016). Subculture as social knowledge: A hopeful reading of otaku culture. *Contemporary Japan, 28*(1), 33-57. https://doi.org/10.1515/cj-2016-0003

Hackenbracht, J., & Gasper, K. (2013). I'm all ears: The need to belong motivates listening to emotional disclosure. *Journal of Experimental Social Psychology, 49*(5), 915-921. https://doi.org/10.1016/j.jesp.2013.03.014

Hald, G. M., Malamuth, N. M., & Yuen, C. (2010). Pornography and attitudes supporting violence against women: Revisiting the relationship in nonexperimental studies. *Aggressive Behavior, 36*(1), 14-20. https://doi.org/10.1002/ab.20328

Hamburger, M. E., Basile, K. C., & Vivolo, A. M. (2011). Measuring bullying victimization, perpetration, and bystander experiences; a compendium of assessment tools. *Centers for Disease Control and Prevention.* http://www.cdc.gov/violenceprevention/pdf/bullyCompendiumbk-a.pdf

Han, Y. (2020). *Yaya Han's world of cosplay: A guide to fandom costume culture.* Sterling Publishing Co.

Hedlund, D. P. (2014). Creating value through membership and participation in sport fan consumption communities. *European Sport Management Quarterly, 14*(1), 50-71. https://doi.org/10.1080/16184742.2013.865775

Hellekson, K. (2010). History, the trace, and fandom wank. In H. Urbanski (Ed.), *Writing and the digital generation: Essays on new media rhetoric* (pp. 58-69). McFarland & Company.

Heere, B., & James, J. D. (2007). Stepping outside the lines: Developing a multi-dimensional team identity scale based on social identity theory. *Sport Management Review, 10*(1), 65-91. https://doi.org/10.1016/S1441-3523(07)70004-9

Hegarty, P., & Bruckmüller, S. (2013). Asymmetric explanations of group differences: Experimental evidence of Foucault's disciplinary power. *Social and Personality Psychology Compass, 7*(3), 176-186. https://doi.org/10.1111/spc3.12017

Hegarty, P., Stewart, A. L., Blockmans, I. G., & Horvath, M. A. (2018). The influence of magazines on men: Normalizing and challenging young men's prejudice with "lads' mags". *Psychology of Men and Masculinity, 19*(1), 131-144. https://doi.org/10.1037/men0000075

Henrich, J., Heine, S. J., & Norenzayan, A. (2010). The weirdest people in the world? *Behavioral and Brain Sciences, 33*(2-3), 61-135. https://doi.org/10.1017/S0140525X0999152X

Hertz, M. F., Donato, I., & Wright, J. (2013). Bullying and suicide: a public health approach. *Journal of Adolescent Health, 53*(1), S1-S3. https://doi.org/10.1016/j.jadohealth.2013.05.002

Hess, G., Schredl, M., & Goritz, A. S. (2017). Lucid dreaming frequency and the big five personality factors. *Imagination, Cognition and Personality, 36*(3), 240-253. https://doi.org/10.1177/0276236616648653

Hesse, C., & Floyd, K. (2019). Affection substitution: The effect of pornography consumption on close relationships. *Journal of Social and Personal Relationships, 36*(11-12), 3887-3907. https://doi.org/10.1177/0265407519841719

414

Higgins, E. T. (1987). Self-discrepancy: A theory relating self and affect. *Psychological Review, 94*(3), 319-340. https://doi.org/10.1037/0033-295X.94.3.319

Higgins, E. T., Bond, R. N., Klein, R., & Strauman, T. (1986). Self-discrepancies and emotional vulnerability: How magnitude, accessibility, and type of discrepancy influence affect. *Journal of Personality and Social Psychology, 51*(1), 5-15. https://doi.org/10.1037/0022-3514.51.1.5

Hill, N. L. (2017). *Embodying cosplay: Fandom communities in the USA* [Master's thesis, Georgia State University]. Georgia State University. https://scholarworks.gsu.edu/anthro_theses/119

Hills, M. (2014). Returning to 'becoming-a-fan'stories: theorising transformational objects and the emergence/extension of fandom. In L. Duits, K. Zwaan, & S. Reijnders (Eds.), *The Ashgate research companion to fan cultures* (pp. 9-22). Ashgate. https://doi.org/10.4324/9781315612959-2

Hilton, J. L., & Von Hippel, W. (1996). Stereotypes. *Annual Review of Psychology, 47*(1), 237-271. https://doi.org/10.1146/annurev.psych.47.1.237

Hinduja, S., & Patchin, J. W. (2010). Bullying, cyberbullying, and suicide. *Archives of Suicide Research, 14*(3), 206-221. https://doi.org/10.1080/13811118.2010.494133

Hinkle, S., Taylor, L. A., Fox-Cardamone, L., & Crook, K. F. (1989). Intragroup identification and intergroup differentiation: A multicomponent approach. *British Journal of Social Psychology, 28*(4), 305-317. https://doi.org/10.1111/j.2044-8309.1989.tb00874.x

Hinton, P. R. (2014). The cultural context and the interpretation of Japanese 'lolita complex' style anime. *Intercultural Communication Studies, 23*(2), 54-68.

Hirt, E. R., Zillmann, D., Erickson, G. A., & Kennedy, C. (1992). Costs and benefits of allegiance: Changes in fans' self-ascribed competencies after team victory versus defeat. *Journal of Personality and Social Psychology, 63*(5), 724-738. https://doi.org/10.1037/0022-3514.63.5.724

Ho, M. H. S. (2018). *An ethnography of crossdressing: Gender politics and Queer belongings in contemporary Japan* (Publication No. 10822930)

[Doctoral dissertation, State University of New York at Stony Brook]. ProQuest Dissertations and Theses Global.

Hoff, E. W. (2012). Cosplay as subculture: In Japan and beyond. *Bulletin of Tokai Gakuen University: Studies in Humanities, 17,* 149-167.

Hogg, M. A., Hardie, E. A., & Reynolds, K. J. (1995). Prototypical similarity, self-categorization, and depersonalized attraction: A perspective on group cohesiveness. *European Journal of Social Psychology, 25*(2), 159-177. https://doi.org/10.1002/ejsp.2420250204

Hogg, M. A., & Reid, S. A. (2006). Social identity, self-categorization, and the communication of group norms. *Communication Theory, 16*(1), 7-30. https://doi.org/10.1111/j.1468-2885.2006.00003.x

Hogg, M. A., & Williams, K. D. (2000). From I to we: Social identity and the collective self. *Group Dynamics: Theory, Research, and Practice, 4*(1), 81-97. https://doi.org/10.1037/1089-2699.4.1.81

Hokusai. (1814). *Tako to Ama* [Woodblock print]. In *Kinoe no Komatsu* Vol 3.

Horbinski, A. (2019). What you watch is what you are? Early anime and manga fandom in the United States. *Mechademia, 12*(1), 11-30.

Hornsey, M. J. (2008). Social identity theory and self-categorization theory: A historical review. *Social and Personality Psychology Compass, 2*(1), 204-222. https://doi.org/10.1111/j.1751-9004.2007.00066.x

Hu, T.-Y. G. (2010). *Frames of anime culture and image-building.* Hong Kong University Press.

Igarashi, R. (2002, August). *Ru's 6th annual rec.arts.anime "what are we like?" fan survey.* Ru's Annual Anime Fan Questionnaire. https://web.archive.org/web/20070326035612/http://members.shaw.ca/ru.igarashi/Surveys/fans/fan0208/results.html

Igarashi, R. (2007, September). *Ru's 10th annual anime fan survey.* Ru's Annual Anime Fan Questionnaire. https://web.archive.org/web/20071023201004/http://members.shaw.ca/ru.igarashi/Surveys/fans/fan0709/results.html

Ito, K., & Crutcher, P. A. (2014). Popular mass entertainment in Japan: Manga, pachinko, and cosplay. *Society, 51,* 44-48. https://doi.org/10.1007/s12115-013-9737-y

Ivtzan, I., Chan, C. P. L., Gardner, H. E., & Prashar, K. (2013). Linking religion and spirituality with psychological wellbeing: Examining self-actualization, meaning in life, and personal growth initiative. *Journal of Religion and Health, 52*(3), 915-929. https://doi.org/10.1007/s10943-011-9540-2

Jackson, S. A., & Marsh, H. W. (1996). Development and validation of a scale to measure optimal experience: The flow state scale. *Journal of Sport and Exercise Psychology, 18*(1), 17-35. https://doi.org/10.1123/jsep.18.1.17

Jacobs, K. (2013). Impersonating and performing queer sexuality in the cosplay zone. *Participations: Journal of Audience and Reception Studies, 10*(2), 22-45.

Jenkins, H. (1992). *Textual poachers: Television fans and participatory culture*. Routledge.

Jenkins, H. (2007). Afterward: The future of fandom. In C. Harrington, J. Gray, & C. Sandvoss (Eds.), *Fandom: Identities and communities in a mediated world* (pp. 357-364). NYU Press.

Jenkins, S. T., Reysen, S., & Katzarska-Miller, I. (2012). Ingroup identification and personality. *Journal of Interpersonal Relations, Intergroup Relations and Identity, 5,* 9-16.

Jetten, J., Spears, R., & Manstead, A. (1996). Intergroup norms and intergroup discrimination: Distinctive self-categorization and social identity effects". *Journal of Personality and Social Psychology, 71*(6), 1222-1233. https://doi.org/10.1037/0022-3514.71.6.1222

Jindra, M. (1994). *Star Trek* fandom as a religious phenomenon. *Sociology of Religion, 55*(1), 27-51. https://doi.org/10.2307/3712174

John, O. P. (1990). The "big five" factor taxonomy: Dimensions of personality in the natural language and in questionnaires. In L. A. Pervin (Ed.), *Handbook of personality: Theory and research* (pp. 66-100). Guilford Press.

Jonason, P. K., & Webster, G. D. (2010). The dirty dozen: A concise measure of the dark triad. *Psychological Assessment, 22*(2), 420-432. https://doi.org/10.1037/a0019265

Jones, J. (2020, March 29). *10 Largest anime conventions in the United States.* https://largest.org/entertainment/anime-conventions-usa/

Jordan, P. J., Ramsay, S., & Westerlaken, K. M. (2017). A review of entitlement: Implications for workplace research. *Organizational*

Psychology Review, 7(2), 122-142.
https://doi.org/10.1177/2041386616647121

Josephy-Hernández, D. E. (2017). Fansubbing hentai anime: Users, distribution, censorship and ethics. In D. Orrego-Carmona & Y. Lee (Eds.), *Non-professional subtitling* (pp. 171-197). Cambridge Scholars Publishing.

Judge, T. A., & Ilies, R. (2002). Relationship of personality to performance motivation: A meta-analytic review. *Journal of Applied Psychology, 87*(4), 797-807. https://doi.org/10.1037/0021-9010.87.4.797

Jussim, L. (2012). *Social perception and social reality: Why accuracy dominates bias and self-fulfilling prophecy.* Oxford University Press.

Jussim, L., Eccles, J., & Madon, S. (1996). Social perception, social stereotypes, and teacher expectations: Accuracy and the quest for the powerful self-fulfilling prophecy. In M. P. Zanna (Ed.), *Advances in experimental social psychology* (Vol. 28, pp. 281-388). Academic Press. https://doi.org/10.1016/S0065-2601(08)60240-3

Kaichiro, M., & Washburn, D. (2013). おたく Otaku/Geek. *Review of Japanese Culture and Society, 25,* 56-66. https://doi.org/10.1353/roj.2013.0002

Kam, T. H. (2013). The common sense that makes the 'otaku': Rules for consuming popular culture in contemporary Japan. *Japan Forum, 25*(2), 151-173. https://doi.org/10.1080/09555803.2012.743481

Kane, L. (2017). *Why cosplay? Motivations behind participation and use of social media among cosplayers who maintain Facebook artist pages* [Doctoral dissertation, Oregon State University]. Oregon State University.
https://ir.library.oregonstate.edu/concern/graduate_thesis_or_dissertatio
ns/j098zd59k

Karasawa, M. (1991). Toward an assessment of social identity: The structure of group identification and its effects on in-group evaluations. *British Journal of Social Psychology, 30*(4), 293-307. https://doi.org/10.1111/j.2044-8309.1991.tb00947.x

Katz, E., Blumler, J. G., & Gurevitch, M. (1974). Uses and gratifications research. *The Public Opinion Quarterly, 37*(4), 509-523. https://doi.org/10.2307/2747854

Kelly, S. U., Sung, C., & Farnham, S. (2002). Designing for improved social responsibility, user participation and content in on-line communities. *Proceedings of the SIGCHI Conference on Human Factors in Computing Systems,* 391-398. https://doi.org/10.1145/503376.503446

Kelts, R. (2006). *Japanamerica: How Japanese pop culture has invaded the U.S.* Palgrave Macmillan.

Kessler, R. C., & Wang, P. S. (2008). The descriptive epidemiology of commonly occurring mental disorders in the United States. *Annual Review of Public Health, 29,* 115-129. https://doi.org/10.1146/annurev.publhealth.29.020907.090847

Kim, Y., Kim, S., & Kim, Y.-M. (2017). Big-five personality and motivations associated with sport team social networking site usage: A cluster analysis approach. *Journal of Global Sport Management, 2*(4), 250-274. https://doi.org/10.1080/24704067.2017.1389249

Kim, Y. S., & Leventhal, B. (2008). Bullying and suicide. A review. *International Journal of Adolescent Medicine and Health, 20*(2), 133-154. https://doi.org/10.1515/IJAMH.2008.20.2.133

Kinderman, P., Schwannauer, M., Pontin, E., & Tai, S. (2011). The development and validation of a general measure of well-being: The BBC well-being scale. *Quality of Life Research, 20,* 1035-1042. https://doi.org/10.1007/s11136-010-9841-z

Kinsella, S. (1998). Japanese subculture in the 1990s: Otaku and the amateur manga movement. *Journal of Japanese Studies, 24*(2), 289-316. http://www.jstor.org/stable/133236

Klimmt, C., Hefner, D., Vorderer, P., Roth, C., Blake, C. (2010). Identification with video game characters as automatic shifts of self-perceptions. *Media Psychology, 13*(4), 323-338. https://doi.org/10.1080/15213269.2010.524911

Kohnen, M. (2014). 'The power of geek': fandom as gendered commodity at Comic-Con. *Creative Industries Journal, 7*(1), 75-78. https://doi.org/10.1080/17510694.2014.892295

Kohut, T., Baer, J. L., & Watts, B. (2016). Is pornography really about "making hate to women"? Pornography users hold more gender egalitarian attitudes than nonusers in a representative American sample.

The Journal of Sex Research, 53(1), 1-11.
https://doi.org/10.1080/00224499.2015.1023427

Kollock, P. (1999). The economies of online cooperation: Gifts and public goods in cyberspace. In M. A. Smith & P. Kollock (Eds.), *Communities in cyberspace* (pp. 220-239). Routledge.
http://hdl.handle.net/10535/3824

Koufaris, M. (2002). Applying the technology acceptance model and flow theory to online consumer behavior. *Information Systems Research, 13*(2), 205-223. https://doi.org/10.1287/isre.13.2.205.83

Kwon, H. H., Trail, G., & James, J. D. (2007). The mediating role of perceived value: Team identification and purchase intention of team-licensed apparel. *Journal of Sport Management, 21*(4), 540-554.
https://doi.org/10.1123/jsm.21.4.540

Lai, K., Xiong, X., Jiang, X., Sun, M., & He, L. (2020). Who falls for rumor? Influence of personality traits on false rumor belief. *Personality and Individual Differences, 152,* Article 109520.
https://doi.org/10.1016/j.paid.2019.109520

Lamarre, T. (2006). Otaku movement. In T. Yoda & H. Harootunian (Eds.), *Japan after Japan: Social and cultural life from the recessionary 1990s to the present* (pp. 358-394). Duke University Press.

Lamarre, T. (2009). *The anime machine: A media theory of animation.* University of Minnesota Press.

Lamarre, T. (2013). Cool, creepy, moé: Otaku fictions, discourses, and policies. *Diversité Urbaine, 13*(1), 131-152.
https://doi.org/10.7202/1024714ar

Lamerichs, N. (2013). The cultural dynamic of doujinshi and cosplay: Local anime fandom in Japan, USA and Europe. *Participations: Journal of Audience and Reception Studies, 10*(1), 154-176.

Lamerichs, N. (2016). Otaku: Representations of fandom in Japanese popular culture. In L. Bennett & P. Booth (Eds.), *Seeing fans: Representations of fandom in media and popular culture* (pp. 251-261). Bloomsbury.

Lamerichs, N. (2018). *Productive fandom: Intermediality and affective reception in fan cultures.* Amsterdam University Press.

Langsford, C. (2014). *Cosplay in Australia: (Re)creation and creativity: Assemblage and negotiation in a material and performative practice*

[Doctoral dissertation, University of Adelaide]. University of Adelaide. http://hdl.handle.net/2440/94401

Larsen, M. R. (2018). Fandom and otaku. In P. Booth (Ed.), *A companion to media fandom and fan studies* (pp. 277-288). Wiley Blackwell.

Lawn, R. B., Slemp, G. R., & Vella-Brodrick, D. A. (2019). Quiet flourishing: The authenticity and well-being of trait introverts living in the west depends on extraversion-deficit beliefs. *Journal of Happiness Studies, 20,* 2055-2075. https://doi.org/10.1007/s10902-018-0037-5

Leary, M. R., Twenge, J. M., & Quinlivan, E. (2006). Interpersonal rejection as a determinant of anger and aggression. *Personality and Social Psychology Review, 10*(2), 111-132. https://doi.org/10.1207/s15327957pspr1002_2

Leavitt, J. D., & Christenfeld, N. J. S. (2011). Story spoilers don't spoil stories. *Psychological Science, 22*(9), 1152-1154. https://doi.org/10.1177/0956797611417007

Lee, P. S. N., Leung, L., Lo, V., Xiong, C., Wu, T. (2011). Internet communication versus face-to-face interaction in quality of life. *Social Indicators Research, 100,* 375-389. https://doi.org/10.1007/s11205-010-9618-3

Leonardelli, G. J., Pickett, C. L., & Brewer, M. B. (2010). Optimal distinctiveness theory: A framework for social identity, social cognition, and intergroup relations. *Advances in Experimental Social Psychology, 43,* 63-113. https://doi.org/10.1016/S0065-2601(10)43002-6

Leshner, C., Reysen, S., Plante, C. N., Chadborn, D., Roberts, S. E., & Gerbasi, K. C. (2018). "My group is discriminated against but I'm not": Denial of personal discrimination in furry, brony, anime, and general interest fan groups. *The Phoenix Papers, 4*(1), 130-142. https://doi.org/10.17605/OSF.IO/27PZG

Levenson, A. R. (2010). Millennials and the world of work: An economist's perspective. *Journal of Business and Psychology, 25,* 257-264. https://doi.org/10.1007/s10869-010-9170-9

Li, J. (2012). *Global geekdom: The rise of anime and otaku in the information age* (Publication No. 3546450) [Doctoral dissertation, New York University]. ProQuest Dissertations and Theses Global.

Lockwood, P., & Kunda, Z. (1997). Superstars and me: Predicting the impact of role models on the self. *Journal of Personality and Social Psychology, 73*(1), 91-103. https://doi.org/10.1037/0022-3514.73.1.91

Lotecki, A. (2012) Cosplay culture: The development of interactive and living art through play [Doctoral dissertation, Ryerson University]. Ryerson University.

Lounsbury, J. W., Loveland, J. M., & Gibson, L. W. (2003). An investigation of psychological sense of community in relation to big five personality traits. *Journal of Community Psychology, 31*(5), 531-541. https://doi.org/10.1002/jcop.10065

Lynn, S. J. & Rhue, J. W. (1988). Fantasy proneness: Hypnosis, developmental antecedents, and psychopathology. *American Psychologist, 43*(1), 35-44. https://doi.org/10.1037/0003-066X.43.1.35

Major, B., & Eccleston, C. P. (2004). Stigma and social exclusion. In D. Abrams, M. A. Hogg, & J. M. Marques (Eds.), *The social psychology of inclusion and exclusion* (pp. 63-87). Psychology Press.

Major, B., & O'Brien, L. T. (2005). The social psychology of stigma. *Annual Review of Psychology, 56,* 393-421. https://doi.org/10.1146/annurev.psych.56.091103.070137

Maltby, J., Day, L., McCutcheon, L. E., Gillett, R., Houran, J., & Ashe, D. D. (2004). Personality and coping: A context for examining celebrity worship and mental health. *British Journal of Psychology, 95*(4), 411-428. https://doi.org/10.1348/0007126042369794

Manion, A. (2005). *Discovering Japan: Anime and learning Japanese culture* (Publication No. 1430397) [Doctoral dissertation, University of Southern California]. ProQuest Dissertations and Theses Global.

Maraboli, S. (2013). *Unapologetically You: Reflections on Life and the Human Experience.* Better Today Publishing.

Martinsen, Ø. L. (2011). The creative personality: A synthesis and development of the creative person profile. *Creativity Research Journal, 23*(3), 185-202. https://doi.org/10.1080/10400419.2011.595656

Maslej, M. M., Oatley, K., & Mar, R. A. (2017). Creating fictional characters: The role of experience, personality, and social processes. *Psychology of Aesthetics, Creativity, and the Arts, 11*(4), 487-499. https://doi.org/10.1037/aca0000094

Mason, M. M. (2016). Dishing out *Silver Spoon*: Agricultural tourism in the Tokachi-Obihiro area of Hokkaido. *International Journal of Contents Tourism, 1*(2), 31-43. http://hdl.handle.net/2115/62624

Maton, K. I. (1988). Social support, organizational characteristics, psychological well-being, and group appraisal in three self-help group populations. *American Journal of Community Psychology, 16*(1), 53-77. https://doi.org/10.1007/BF00906072

Matthias, P. (2018, May 16). Meet Emma the Tiger: A showcase of fandom love from BLFC 2018. *Dogpatch Press*. Retrieved August 31, 2020, from https://dogpatch.press/tag/emma.

Mazar, R. (2006). Slash fiction/fanfiction. In J. Weiss, J. Nolan, J. Hunsinger, & P. Trifonas (Eds.), *The international handbook of virtual learning environments* (pp. 1141-1150). Springer. https://doi.org/10.1007/978-1-4020-3803-7_45

McCain, J., Gentile, B., & Campbell, W. K. (2015). A psychological exploration of engagement in geek culture. *PloS ONE, 10*(11), Article e0142200. https://doi.org/10.1371/journal.pone.0142200

McCarthy, H., & Ashmore, D.-J. (Eds.) (2021). *Leiji Matsumoto: Essays on the manga and anime legend*. McFarland.

McKee, A. (2007). The positive and negative effects of pornography as attributed by consumers. *Australian Journal of Communication, 34*(1), 87-104.

McLelland, M. (2005, July). *A short history of 'hentai'*. Paper presented at Sexualities, Genders and Rights in Asia: 1st International Conference of Asian Queer Studies. Bangkok, Thailand: AsiaPacifiQueer Network, Mahidol University; Australian National University. http://hdl.handle.net/1885/8673

Mendelson, S. (2013, September 5). 'Batfleck', 'Fifty Shades of Grey' and fan entitlement syndrome. *Forbes*. Retrieved from http://www.forbes.com/sites/scottmendelson/2013/09/05/batfleck-fifty-shades-of-grey-and-fan-entitlement-syndrome/

Meyer, I. H. (2003). Prejudice, social stress, and mental health in lesbian, gay, and bisexual populations: Conceptual issues and research evidence. *Psychological Bulletin, 129*(5), 674-697. https://doi.org/10.1037/0033-2909.129.5.674

Miller, D. J., Kidd, G., Raggatt, P. T., McBain, K. A., & Li, W. (2020). Pornography use and sexism among heterosexual men. *Communication Research Reports, 37*(3), 110-121. https://doi.org/10.1080/08824096.2020.1777396

Mills, C., Guerin, S., Lynch, F., Daly, I., & Fitzpatrick, C. (2004). The relationship between bullying, depression and suicidal thoughts/behaviour in Irish adolescents. *Irish Journal of Psychological Medicine, 21*(4), 112-116. https://doi.org/10.1017/S0790966700008521

Miyamoto, Y., Nisbett, R. E., & Masuda, T. (2006). Culture and the physical environment: Holistic versus analytic perceptual affordances. *Psychological Science, 17*(2), 113-119. https://doi.org/10.1111/j.1467-9280.2006.01673.x

Mock, S. E., Plante, C. N., Reysen, S., & Gerbasi, K. C. (2013). Deeper leisure involvement as a coping resource in a stigmatized leisure context. *Leisure/Loisir, 37*(2), 111-126. https://doi.org/10.1080/14927713.2013.801152

Moore, D. W. (2005, June 16). Three in four Americans believe in paranormal. *Gallup.* Retrieved from http://www.gallup.com/poll/16915/three-four-americans-believeparanormal.aspx

Moors, A. C., Selterman, D. F., & Conley, T. D. (2017). Personality correlates of desire to engage in consensual non-monogamy among lesbian, gay, and bisexual individuals. *Journal of Bisexuality, 17*(4), 418-434. https://doi.org/10.1080/15299716.2017.1367982

Morrison, K. R., & Ybarra, O. (2009). Symbolic threat and social dominance among liberals and conservatives: SDO reflects conformity to political values. *European Journal of Social Psychology, 39*(6), 1039-1052. https://doi.org/10.1002/ejsp.606

Mycella. (2012, November 21). Psychology behind anime and stereotypes towards anime fans [Web log post]. Retrieved from http://mycellary.blogspot.com/2012/11/psychology-behind-anime-andstereotypes.html

Nakamori, A. (1983). A study of otaku. *Manga Burikko, 2*(7), 200-201.

Nansel, T. R., Craig, W., Overpeck, M. D., Saluja, G., & Ruan, W. J. (2004). Cross-national consistency in the relationship between bullying behaviors and psychosocial adjustment. *Archives of Pediatric and*

Adolescent Medicine, 158(8), 730-736.
https://doi.org/10.1001/archpedi.158.8.730

Nansel, T. R., Overpeck, M., Pilla, R. S., Ruan, W. J., Simons-Morton, B., & Scheidt, P. (2001). Bullying behaviors among US youth: Prevalence and association with psychosocial adjustment. *Journal of the American Medical Association, 285*(16), 2094-2100.
https://doi.org/10.1001/jama.285.16.2094

Napier, S. J. (2001). Peek-a-boo Pikachu: Exporting an Asian subculture. *Harvard Asia Pacific Review, 5,* 13-17.

Napier, S. J. (2005). *Anime: From* Akira *to* Howl's Moving Castle. Palgrave MacMillian.

Napier, S. J. (2006). The world of anime fandom in American. *Mechademia, 1,* 47-63. https://doi.org/10.1353/mec.0.0072

Napier, S. J. (2007). *From impressionism to anime: Japan as fantasy and fan cult in the mind of the West.* Palgrave Macmillan.

National Film Archive of Japan (n.d.). *Seitaro Kitayama.* Retrieved November 4, 2020, from
https://animation.filmarchives.jp/en/writer06.html

Nettle, D. (2006). Psychological profiles of professional actors. *Personality and Individual Differences, 40*(2), 375-383.
https://doi.org/10.1016/j.paid.2005.07.008

Newitz, N. (1994, April). Anime otaku: Japanese animation fans outside Japan. *Bad Subjects,* 13. Retrieved July 29, 2020, from
https://pdfs.semanticscholar.org/e557/9a190a07ddfa3c96e29619a299ee441c9803.pdf

Nichols, A. L., & Webster, G. D. (2013). The single-item need to belong scale. *Personality and Individual Differences, 55*(2), 189-192.
https://doi.org/10.1016/j.paid.2013.02.018

Noftle, E. E., & Robins, R. W. (2007). Personality predictors of academic outcomes: Big five correlates of GPA and SAT scores. *Journal of Personality and Social Psychology, 93*(1), 116-130.
https://doi.org/10.1037/0022-3514.93.1.116

Norris, A. L. & Orchowski, L. M. (2020). Peer victimization of sexual minority and transgender youth: A cross-sectional study of high school students. *Psychology of Violence, 10*(2), 201-211.
https://doi.org/10.1037/vio0000260

Norris, P. (2000). Global governance and cosmopolitan citizens. In J. S. Nye Jr. & J. D. Donahue (Eds.), *Governance in a globalizing world* (pp. 155-177). Brookings Institution Press.

Nozawa, S. (2009). Ensoulment and effacement in Japanese voice acting. In P. W. Galbraith & J. G. Karlin (Eds.), *Media convergence in Japan* (pp. 169-199). Kinema Club.

Odell, C., & Le Blanc, M. (2013). *Anime*. Kamera Books.

Ojala, K., & Nesdale, D. (2004). Bullying and social identity: The effects of group norms and distinctiveness threat on attitudes toward bullying. *British Journal of Developmental Psychology, 22*(1), 19-35. https://doi.org/10.1348/026151004772901096

Okabe, D. (2012). Cosplay, learning, and cultural practice. In M. Ito, D. Okabe, & I. Tsuji (Eds.), *Fandom unbound: Otaku culture in a connected world* (pp. 225-248). Yale University Press.

O'Luanaigh, C. (2010, July 21). Osamu Tezuka: Father of manga and scourge of the medical establishment. *The Guardian*. https://www.theguardian.com/science/blog/2010/jul/21/medical-manga-osamu-tezuka

Oshio, A., Taku, K., Hirano, M., Saeed, G. (2018). Resilience and big five personality traits: A meta-analysis. *Personality and Individual Differences, 127,* 54-60. https://doi.org/10.1016/j.paid.2018.01.048

Ozer, D. J., & Benet-Martínez, V. (2006). Personality and the prediction of consequential outcomes. *Annual Review of Psychology, 57,* 401-421. https://doi.org/10.1146/annurev.psych.57.102904.190127

Pachankis, J. E. (2007). The psychological implications of concealing a stigma: A cognitive-affective-behavioral model. *Psychological Bulletin, 133*(2), 328-345. https://doi.org/10.1037/0033-2909.133.2.328

Paré, J. (2004). *Beyond boredom: The importance of the dull in information overload* (Publication No. MQ94617) [Master's thesis, Concordia University]. ProQuest Dissertations and Theses Global.

Parry, K. D., Jones, I., & Wann, D. L. (2014). An examination of sport fandom in the United Kingdom: A comparative analysis of fan behaviors, socialization processes, and team identification. *Journal of Sport Behavior, 37*(3), 251-267.

Paulhus, D. L., & Williams, K. M. (2002). The dark triad of personality: Narcissism, Machiavellianism, and psychopathy. *Journal of Research in Personality, 36*(6), 556-563. https://doi.org/10.1016/S0092-6566(02)00505-6

Pavalache-Ilie, M., & Cazan, A.-M. (2018). Personality correlates of pro-environmental attitudes. *International Journal of Environmental Health Research, 28*(1), 71-78. https://doi.org/10.1080/09603123.2018.1429576

Peirone, A., & Maticka-Tyndale, E. (2017). "I bought my degree, now I want my job!": Is academic entitlement related to prospective workplace entitlement? *Innovative Higher Education, 42,* 3-18. https://doi.org/10.1007/s10755-016-9365-8

Peirson-Smith, A. (2013). Fashioning the fantastical self: An examination of the cosplay dress-up phenomenon in Southeast Asia. *Fashion Theory, 17*(1), 77-111. https://doi.org/10.2752/175174113X13502904240776

Peplau, L. A., & Perlman, D. (1982). *Loneliness: A sourcebook of current theory, research and therapy.* Wiley.

Perry, S. L., & Whitehead, A. L. (2020). Do people in conservative states really watch more porn? A hierarchical analysis. *Socius, 6.* https://doi.org/10.1177/2378023120908472

Peterson, J. C., Smith, K. B., & Hibbing, J. R. (2020). Do people really become more conservative as they age? *The Journal of Politics, 82*(2), 600-611. https://doi.org/10.1086/706889

Pimentel, R. W., & Reynolds, K. E. (2004). A model for consumer devotion: Affective-commitment with proactive sustaining behaviors. *Academy of Marketing Science Review, 5,* 1-45.

Pinquart, M. & Sörensen, S. (2000). Influences of socioeconomic status, social network, and competence on subjective well-being later in life: A meta-analysis. *Psychology and Aging, 15*(2), 187-224. https://doi.org/10.1037/0882-7974.15.2.187

Plante, C., Anderson, C. A., Allen, J. J., Groves, C., & Gentile, D. A. (2019). *Game on! Sensible answers about video games and media violence.* ZenGen LLC.

Plante, C. N., Chadborn, D., Groves, C., & Reysen, S. (2018). Letters from Equestria: Prosocial media, helping, and empathy in fans of My Little Pony. *Communication and Culture Online, 9*(1), 206-220. https://doi.org/10.18485/kkonline.2018.9.9.11

Plante, C. Chadborn, D., & Reysen, S. (2018). When entertaining isn't enough: Fan motivation and word of mouth spreading of fan interests. *Journal of Digital and Social Media Marketing, 6*(2), 168-180.

Plante, C. N., Reysen, S., Chadborn, D., Roberts, S. E., & Gerbasi, K. C. (2020). 'Get out of my fandom newbie': A cross-fandom study of elitism and gatekeeping in fans. *Journal of Fandom Studies, 8*(2), 123-146. https://doi.org/10.1386/jfs_00013_1

Plante, C. N., Reysen, S., Groves, C. L., Roberts, S. E., & Gerbasi, K. (2017). The fantasy engagement scale: A flexible measure of positive and negative fantasy engagement. *Basic and Applied Social Psychology, 39*(3), 127-152. https://doi.org/10.1080/01973533.2017.1293538

Plante, C. N., Reysen, S., Roberts, S. E., & Gerbasi, K. C. (2016). *FurScience! A summary of five years of research from the International Anthropomorphic Research Project*. FurScience.

Plante, C. N., Roberts, S. E., Reysen, S., & Gerbasi, K. C. (2012). *International Anthropomorphic Research Project: Anthrocon 2012 and 2-Year Summary*. Retrieved from https://sites.google.com/site/anthropomoprhicresearch/past-results/anthrocon-2012-iarp-2-year-summary

Plante, C. N., Roberts, S., Reysen, S., & Gerbasi, K. C. (2014). "One of us": Engagement with fandoms and global citizenship identification. *Psychology of Popular Media Culture, 3*(1), 49-64. https://doi.org/10.1037/ppm0000008

Plante, C. N., Roberts, S., Reysen, S., & Gerbasi, K. (2015). "By the numbers": Comparing furries and related fandoms. In J. W. Thurston (Ed.), *Furries among us: Essays on furries by the most prominent members of the fandom*. Thurston Howl Publications.

Plante, C. N., Roberts, S. E., Reysen, S., & Gerbasi, K. C. (2020). "Here comes the drama llama": Drama within the furry fandom. In T. Howl (Ed.), *Furries among us 3: Essays by furries about furries* (pp. 50-61). Thurston Howl Publications.

Plaschke, B. (2005, December 14). It's a case of addition by subtraction. *Los Angeles Times*. Retrieved from http://articles.latimes.com/2005/dec/14/sports/sp-plaschke14/2

Poitras, G. (2001). *Anime essentials: Every thing a fan needs to know*. Stone Bridge Press.

Ponzo, M. (2013). Does bullying reduce educational achievement? An evaluation using matching estimators. *Journal of Policy Modeling, 35*(6), 1057-1078. https://doi.org/10.1016/j.jpolmod.2013.06.002

Potter, W. J. (2011). Conceptualizing mass media effect. *Journal of Communication, 61*(5), 896-915. https://doi.org/10.1111/j.1460-2466.2011.01586.x

Prentice, D. A., & Miller, D. T. (1993). Pluralistic ignorance and alcohol use on campus: Some consequences of misperceiving the social norm. *Journal of Personality and Social Psychology, 64*(2), 243-256. https://doi.org/10.1037/0022-3514.64.2.243

Putnam, R. D. (2000). *Bowling alone: The collapse and revival of American community.* Simon & Schuster.

Quinn, D. M., & Chaudoir, S. R. (2009). Living with a concealable stigmatized identity: The impact of anticipated stigma, centrality, salience, and cultural stigma on psychological distress and health. *Journal of Personality and Social Psychology, 97*(4), 634-651. https://doi.org/10.1037/a0015815

Quinn, D. M., & Earnshaw, V. A. (2013). Concealable stigmatized identities and psychological well-being. *Social and Personality Psychology Compass, 7*(1), 40-51. https://doi.org/10.1111/spc3.12005

Rahman, O., Wing-Sun, L., & Cheung, B. H.-M. (2012). "Cosplay": Imaginative self and performing identity. *Fashion Theory, 16*(3), 317-341. https://doi.org/10.2752/175174112X13340749707204

Rain, M., Cilento, E., MacDonald, G., & Mar, R. A. (2017). Adult attachment and transportation into narrative worlds. *Personal Relationships, 24*(1), 49-74. https://doi.org/10.1111/pere.12167

Ramirez, M. (2017). *From the panels to the margins: Identity, marginalization, and subversion in cosplay* (Publication No. 10260027) [Master's thesis, University of South Florida]. ProQuest Dissertations and Theses Global.

Ray, A., Plante, C. N., Reysen, S., Roberts, S. E., & Gerbasi, K. C. (2018). "You had to be there": Convention attendance and well-being in anime fans. *The Phoenix Papers, 3*(2), 20-30.

Rentfrow, P. J., & Gosling, S. D. (2003). The do re mi's of everyday life: The structure and personality correlates of music preferences. *Journal*

of Personality and Social Psychology, 84(6), 1236-1256.
https://doi.org/10.1037/0022-3514.84.6.1236

Reyes, M. E. S., Davis, R. D., Panlilio, S. L. D., Hidalgo, P. R. A. S.,
Ocampo, M. C. D., Opulencia, M. R. D., & Que, J. R. P. (2017).
Filipino cosplayers: Exploring the personality traits linked with fantasy
proneness and dissociative experiences. *North American Journal of
Psychology, 19*(3), 525-540.

Reynolds, K. J., Bizumic, B., Subasic, E., Turner, J. C., Branscombe, N.,
Mavor, K. I., & Batalha, L. (2012). Social identity and personality
processes: Non-Aboriginal Australian identity and neuroticism.
European Journal of Social Psychology, 42(2), 252-262.
https://doi.org/10.1002/ejsp.1841

Reysen, S., & Branscombe, N. R. (2010). Fanship and fandom:
Comparisons between sport fans and non-sport fans. *Journal of Sport
Behavior, 33*(2), 176-193.

Reysen, S., & Katzarska-Miller, I. (2013). A model of global citizenship:
Antecedents and outcomes. *International Journal of Psychology, 48*(5),
858-870. https://doi.org/10.1080/00207594.2012.701749

Reysen, S., & Katzarska-Miller, I. (2018). *The psychology of global
citizenship: A review of theory and research.* Lexington Books.

Reysen, S., Katzarska-Miller, I., Nesbit, S. M., & Pierce, L. (2013). Further
validation of a single-item measure of social identification. *European
Journal of Social Psychology, 43*(6), 463-470.
https://doi.org/10.1002/ejsp.1973

Reysen, S., Katzarska-Miller, I., Plante, C. N., Roberts, S. E., & Gerbasi, K.
C. (2017). Examination of anime content and associations between
anime consumption, genre preferences, and ambivalent sexism. *The
Phoenix Papers, 3*(1), 285-303.

Reysen, S., Katzarska-Miller, I., Plante, C. N., Roberts, S. E., Gerbasi, K.
C., Brooks, T. R., & Tague, A. (2020). Anime and global citizenship
identification. *The Phoenix Papers, 4*(2), 48-61.
https://doi.org/10.17605/OSF.IO/JXPTQ

Reysen, S., Larey, L. W., & Katzarska-Miller, I. (2012). College course
curriculum and global citizenship. *International Journal of
Development Education and Global Learning, 4*(3), 27-39.
https://doi.org/10.18546/IJDEGL.04.3.03

Reysen, S., & Plante, C. N. (2017). Fans, perceived maturity, and willingness to form a romantic relationship: Application of a short maturity measure. *Communication and Culture Online, 8*(1), 154-173. https://doi.org/10.18485/kkonline.2017.8.8.8

Reysen, S., Plante, C., & Chadborn, D. (2017). Better together: Social connections mediate the relationship between fandom and well-being. *AASCIT Journal of Health, 4*(6), 68-73.

Reysen, S. Plante, C. N., Chadborn, D., Roberts, S. E., Gerbasi, K. C., Miller, J., Gamboa, A., & Ray, A. (2018). A brief report on the prevalence of self-reported mood disorders, anxiety disorders, attention-deficit/hyperactivity disorder, and autism spectrum disorder in anime, brony, and furry fandoms. *The Phoenix Papers, 3*(2), 64-75.

Reysen, S., Plante, C. N., Roberts, S. E., & Gerbasi, K. C. (2015a). A social identity perspective of personality differences between fan and non-fan identities. *World Journal of Social Science Research, 2*(1), 91-103.

Reysen, S., Plante, C. N., Roberts, S. E., & Gerbasi, K. C. (2016). Optimal distinctiveness and identification with the furry fandom. *Current Psychology, 35*(4), 638-642. https://doi.org/10.1007/s12144-015-9331-0

Reysen, S., Plante, C. N., Roberts, S. E., & Gerbasi, K. C. (2017a). Anime genre preferences and paranormal beliefs. *The Phoenix Papers, 3*(1), 327-343.

Reysen, S., Plante, C. N., Roberts, S. E., & Gerbasi, K. C. (2017b). Optimal distinctiveness needs as predictors of identification in the anime fandom. *The Phoenix Papers, 3*(1), 25-32.

Reysen, S., Plante, C. N., Roberts, S. E., & Gerbasi, K. C. (2017c). Accuracy of perceived prejudice toward one's fan group. *The Phoenix Papers, 3*(1), 122-129.

Reysen, S., Plante, C. N., Roberts, S. E., & Gerbasi, K. C. (2017d). Anime fans to the rescue: Evidence of Daniel Wann's team identification-social psychological health model. *The Phoenix Papers, 3*(1), 237-247.

Reysen, S., Plante, C. N., Roberts, S. E., & Gerbasi, K. C. (2018a). Motivations of cosplayers to participate in the anime fandom. *The Phoenix Papers, 4*(1), 29-40. https://doi.org/10.17605/OSF.IO/UT4FB

Reysen, S., Plante, C. N., Roberts, S. E., & Gerbasi, K. C. (2018b). "Who I want to be": Self-perception and cosplayers' identification with their favorite characters. *The Phoenix Papers, 3*(2), 1-7.

Reysen, S., Plante, C. N., Roberts, S. E., & Gerbasi, K. C. (2018c). A brief report on differences in big five personality dimensions between anime cosplayers and non-cosplayers. *The Phoenix Papers, 3*(2), 46-53.

Reysen, S., Plante, C. N., Roberts, S. E., & Gerbasi, K. C. (2018d). "Coming out" as an anime fan: Cosplayers in the anime fandom, fan disclosure, and well-being. *The Phoenix Papers, 4*(1), 1-9. https://doi.org/10.17605/OSF.IO/HUJGS

Reysen, S., Plante, C. N., Roberts, S. E., & Gerbasi, K. C. (2020). Psychology and fursonas in the furry fandom. In T. Howl (Ed.), *Furries among us 3: Essays by furries about furries* (pp. 86-104). Thurston Howl Publications.

Reysen, S., Plante, C. N., Roberts, S. E., Gerbasi, K. C., Mohebpour, I., & Gamboa, A. (2016). Pale and geeky: Prevailing stereotypes of anime fans. *The Phoenix Papers, 2*(1), 78-103.

Reysen, S., Plante, C. N., Roberts, S. E., Gerbasi, K. C., Schroy, C., Gamboa, A., Gamboa, J., & McCarter, T. (2017). Routes to fandom discovery and expression of fan identity in furry, anime, and fantasy sport fans. *The Phoenix Papers, 3*(1), 373-384.

Reysen, S., Plante, C. N., Roberts, S. E., Gerbasi, K. C., & Shaw, J. (2016). An examination of anime fan stereotypes. *The Phoenix Papers, 2*(2), 90-117.

Reysen, R., Reysen, M., & Reysen, S. (2021). Academic entitlement predicts smartphone usage during class. *College Teaching, 69*(1), 52-57. https://doi.org/10.1080/87567555.2020.1803192

Reysen, S., & Shaw, J. (2016). Sport fan as the default fan: Why non-sport fans are stigmatized. *The Phoenix Papers, 2*(2), 234-252.

Reysen, S., Shaw, J., & Brooks, T. R. (2015). Heterosexual missionary as the sexual default and stigmatization of perceived infrequent sexual activities. *Advances in Social Sciences Research Journal, 2*(5), 93-104. https://doi.org/10.14738/assrj.25.1181

Rhodes, R. E., & Smith, N. E. I. (2006). Personality correlates of physical activity: A review and meta-analysis. *British Journal of Sports Medicine, 40*(12), 958-965. https://dx.doi.org/10.1136/bjsm.2006.028860

Richler, J. (2013, March 21). Scientific explanations for why spoilers are so horrible. *The Atlantic.* Retrieved from https://www.theatlantic.com/entertainment/archive/2013/03/scientific-explanations-for-why-spoilers-are-so-horrible/274227/

Richman, L. S., & Learly, M. R. (2009). Reactions to discrimination, stigmatization, ostracism, and other forms of interpersonal rejection: A multimotive model. *Psychological Review, 116*(2), 365-383. https://doi.org/10.1037/a0015250

Roberts, S. E., Chong, M.-M., Shea, S., Doyle, K., Plante, C. N., Reysen, S., & Gerbasi, K. C. (2017). The highs, the lows, and post-con depression: A qualitative examination of furries' return home following an anthropomorphic convention. In T. Howl (Ed.), *Furries among us 2: More essays on furries by furries* (pp. 129-141). Thurston Howl Publications.

Roccas, S., Sagiv, L., Schwartz, S. H., & Knafo, A. (2002). The big five personality factors and personal values. *Personality and Social Psychology Bulletin, 28*(6), 789-801. https://doi.org/10.1177/0146167202289008

Rosen, L. D., Whaling, K., Carrier, L. M., Cheever, N. A., & Rokkum, J. (2013). The media and technology usage and attitudes scale: An empirical investigation. *Computers in Human Behavior, 29*(6), 2501-2511. https://doi.org/10.1016/j.chb.2013.06.006

Rosenberg, M. (1965). *Society and the adolescent self-image.* Princeton University Press.

Rosenberg, R. S., & Letamendi, A. M. (2013). Expressions of fandom: Findings from a psychological survey of cosplay and costume wear. *Intensities: The Journal of Cult Media, 5,* 9-18.

Rubin, A. M., & Rubin, R. B. (1985). Interface of personal and mediated communication: A research agenda. *Critical Studies in Mass Communication, 2*(1), 36-53. https://doi.org/10.1080/15295038509360060

Rushton, J. P., Fulker, D. W., Neale, M. C., Nias, D. K., & Eysenck, H. J. (1986). Altruism and aggression: the heritability of individual differences. *Journal of Personality and Social Psychology, 50*(6), 1192-1198. https://doi.org/10.1037/0022-3514.50.6.1192

Ryan, C. (2002). Stereotype accuracy. *European Review of Social Psychology, 13*(1), 75-109. https://doi.org/10.1080/10463280240000037

Ryff, C. D., & Keyes, C. L. M. (1995). The structure of psychological well-being revisited. *Journal of Personality and Social Psychology, 69*(4), 719-727. https://doi.org/10.1037/0022-3514.69.4.719

Saito, H. (2004). Hentai - H. In I. Shōichi & K. S. Kenkyūkai (Eds.), *Sei no yōgoshū* (pp. 45-58). Kōdansha.

Saroglou, V. (2002). Religion and the five factors of personality: A meta-analytic review. *Personality and Individual Differences, 32*(1), 15-25. https://doi.org/10.1016/S0191-8869(00)00233-6

Sayehmiri, K., Kareem, K. I., Abdi, K., Dalvand, S., & Gheshlagh, R. G. (2020). The relationship between personality traits and marital satisfaction: A systematic review and meta-analysis. *BMC Psychology, 8,* Article 15. https://doi.org/10.1186/s40359-020-0383-z

Schäfer, M., Korn, S., Smith, P. K., Hunter, S. C., Mora-Merchán, J. A., Singer, M. M., & Van der Meulen, K. (2004). Lonely in the crowd: Recollections of bullying. *British Journal of Developmental Psychology, 22*(3), 379-394. https://doi.org/10.1348/0261510041552756

Schiappa, E., Gregg, P. B., & Hewes, D. E. (2004). Can a television series change attitudes about death? A study of college students and *Six Feet Under*. *Death Studies, 28*(5), 459-474. https://doi.org/10.1080/07481180490437581

Schimmel, K. S., Harrington, C. L., & Bielby, D. D. (2007). Keep your fans to yourself: The disjuncture between sport studies' and pop culture studies' perspectives on fandom. *Sport in Society, 10*(4), 580-600. https://doi.org/10.1080/17430430701388764

Schmitt, M. T., Branscombe, N. R., Postmes, T., & Garcia, A. (2014). The consequences of perceived discrimination for psychological well-being: A meta-analytic review. *Psychological Bulletin, 140*(4), 921-948. https://doi.org/10.1037/a0035754

Schneider, D. J. (2005). *The psychology of stereotyping*. Guilford Press.

Schodt, F. L. (2007). *The Astro Boy essays: Osamu Tezuka, Mighty Atom, manga/anime revolution*. Stone Bridge Press.

Schroy, C., Plante, C. N., Reysen, S., Roberts, S. E., & Gerbasi, K. C. (2016). Different motivations as predictors of psychological connection to fan interest and fan groups in anime, furry, and fantasy sport fandoms. *The Phoenix Papers, 2*(2), 148-167.

Schuster, G. P. (2010). *Unmasking mecha identities: Visual media perspectives on posthumanism in Japanese popular culture* [Undergraduate honors thesis, University of Redlands]. Retrieved from https://inspire.redlands.edu/cas_honors/61

Schwartz, S. H. (1992). Universals in the content and structure of values: Theoretical advances and empirical tests in 20 countries. *Advances in Experimental Social Psychology, 25,* 1-65. https://doi.org/10.1016/S0065-2601(08)60281-6

Schwartz, S. H., & Sortheix, F. M. (2018). Values and subjective well-being. In E. Diener, S. Oishi, & L. Tay (Eds.), *Handbook of well-being* (pp. 1-25). DEF Publishers.

Scott, S. (2019). *Fake geek girls: Fandom, gender, and the convergence culture industry.* New York University Press.

Sharp, S. (1995). How much does bullying hurt? The effects of bullying on the personal wellbeing and educational progress of secondary aged students. *Educational and Child Psychology, 12*(2), 81-88.

Shaw, J., Plante, C. N., Reysen, S., Roberts, S. E., & Gerbasi, K. C. (2016). Predictors of fan entitlement in three fandoms. *The Phoenix Papers, 2*(2), 203-219.

Shen, C., & Williams, D. (2011). Unpacking time online: Connecting internet and massively multiplayer online game use with psychological well-being. *Communication Research, 38*(1), 123-149. https://doi.org/10.1177/0093650210377196

Shen, L. F. (2007). *The pleasure and politics of viewing Japanese anime* (Publication No. 3286809) [Doctoral dissertation, Ohio State University]. ProQuest Dissertations and Theses Global.

Shirky, C. (2003, July 1). A group is its own worst enemy. Clay Shirky's Writings about the Internet. Retrieved May 31, 2019, from http://www.shirky.com/writings/group_enemy.html

Shweder, R. A. (1990). Cultural psychology—what is it? In J. Stigler, R. Shweder, & G. Herdt (Eds.), *Cultural psychology: Essays on comparative human development* (pp. 1-46). Cambridge University Press.

Sibley, C. G. (2010). The dark duo of post-colonial ideology: A model of symbolic exclusion and historical negation. *International Journal of Conflict and Violence, 4*(1), 106-123. https://doi.org/10.4119/ijcv-2818

Smahel, D., Brown, B. B., & Blinka, L. (2012). Associations between online friendship and internet addiction among adolescents and emerging adults. *Developmental Psychology, 48*(2), 381-388. https://doi.org/10.1037/a0027025

Smith, A. (2020). *What do manga depict? Understanding contemporary Japanese comics and the culture of Japan* (Publication No. 27834637) [Doctoral dissertation, Indiana University of Pennsylvania]. ProQuest Dissertations and Theses Global.

Smith, E. R., & Henry, S. (1996). An in-group becomes part of the self: Response time evidence. *Personality and Social Psychology Bulletin, 22*(6), 635-642. https://doi.org/10.1177/0146167296226008

Smith, G. J., Patterson, B., Williams, T., & Hogg, J. (1981). A profile of the deeply committed male sports fan. *Arena Review, 5*(2), 26-44.

Smith, R. (2014, October 24). Does a rising sense of fan entitlement devalue football loyalties? [Web log post]. Retrieved from http://www.espnfc.com/blog/espn-fc-unuted-blog/68/post/2107266/rising-sense-of-fan-entitlement-devalues-football-loyalties

Smith, R. G., & Gross, A. M. (2006). Bullying: Prevalence and the effect of age and gender. *Child & Family Behavior Therapy, 28*(4), 13-37.

Smith, P. K., Madsen, K. C., & Moody, J. C. (1999). What causes the age decline in reports of being bullied at school? Towards a developmental analysis of risks of being bullied. *Educational Research, 41*(3), 267-285. https://doi.org/10.1080/0013188990410303

Snyder, C. R., Lassegard, M., & Ford, C. E. (1986). Distancing after group success and failure: Basking in reflected glory and cutting off reflected failure. *Journal of Personality and Social Psychology, 51*(2), 382-388. https://doi.org/10.1037/0022-3514.51.2.382

Sohr-Preston, S., & Boswell, S. S. (2015). Predicting academic entitlement in undergraduates. *International Journal of Teaching and Learning in Higher Education, 27*(2), 183-193.

Soutter, A. R. B., & Hitchens, M. (2016). The relationship between character identification and flow state within video games. *Computers in Human Behavior, 55,* 1030-1038. https://doi.org/10.1016/j.chb.2015.11.012

436

Spindler, W. J. (2010). *Anime and manga, Japanese foreign language students, and the assumption popular culture has a place in the classroom* (Publication No. 1481212) [Master's thesis, University of California, Davis]. ProQuest Dissertations and Theses Global.

Spitzberg, B. H., & Cupach, W. R. (2008). Fanning the flames of fandom: Celebrity worship, parasocial interaction, and stalking. In J. R. Meloy, L. Sheridan, & J. Hoffman (Eds.), *Stalking, threatening, and attacking public figures: A psychological and behavioral analysis* (pp. 287-319). Oxford University Press.

Spriggs, A. L., Iannotti, R. J., Nansel, T. R., & Haynie, D. L. (2007). Adolescent bullying involvement and perceived family, peer and school relations: Commonalities and differences across race/ethnicity. *Journal of Adolescent Health, 41*(3), 283-293. https://doi.org/10.1016/j.jadohealth.2007.04.009

Stangor, C. (2010). *Introduction to psychology.* FlatWorld.

Star Blazers. (n.d.). *Wikipedia.* Retrieved November 13, 2020, from https://en.wikipedia.org/wiki/Star_Blazers

Statistics Canada. (2017, November 29). Does education pay? A comparison of earnings by level of education in Canada and its providences and territories. Retrieved July 28, 2020, from https://www12.statcan.gc.ca/census-recensement/2016/as-sa/98-200-x/2016024/98-200-x2016024-eng.cfm

Steele, C. M., & Aronson, J. (1995). Stereotype threat and the intellectual test performance of African Americans. *Journal of Personality and Social Psychology, 69*(5), 797-811. https://doi.org/10.1037/0022-3514.69.5.797

Sterling, J. [Jim Sterling] (2019). A difficult subject (The Jimquisition). Retrieved May 31, 2019, from https://www.youtube.com/watch?v=nIWivb-8C1w

Stever, G. S. (2009). Parasocial and social interaction with celebrities: Classification of media fans. *Journal of Media Psychology, 14*(3), 1-39.

Stever, G. S. & Lawson, K. (2013). Twitter as a way for celebrities to communicate with fans: Implications for the study of parasocial interaction. *North American Journal of Psychology, 15*(2), 339-354.

Stewart, J. (1964). 378 U.S. at 197 (Stewart, J., concurring).

Stone, J., Lynch, C. I., Sjomeling, M., & Darley, J. M. (1999). Stereotype threat effects on Black and White athletic performance. *Journal of Personality and Social Psychology, 77*(6), 1213-1227. https://doi.org/10.1037/0022-3514.77.6.1213

Stone, J., Perry, W., & Darley, J. M. (1997). "White men can't jump": Evidence for the perceptual confirmation of racial stereotypes following a basketball game. *Basic and Applied Social Psychology, 19*(3), 291-306. https://doi.org/10.1207/s15324834basp1903_2

Stoner, J. A. F. (1968). Risky and cautious shifts in group decisions: The influence of widely held values. *Journal of Experimental Social Psychology, 4,* 442-459.

Stony Brook University. (n.d.). *1940s and Princess Iron Fan. The effects of politics and society on Chinese animation.* Retrieved November 5, 2020, from https://you.stonybrook.edu/teamred/1940s-and-princess-iron-fan/

Storrs, C. (2016, January 6). Bisexuality on the rise, says new U.S. survey. *CNN Health.* Retrieved from https://www.cnn.com/2016/01/07/health/bisexuality-on-the-rise/index.html

Stricker, J., Buecker, S., Schneider, M., & Preckel, F. (2019). Multidimensional perfectionism and the big five personality traits: A meta-analysis. *European Journal of Personality, 33*(2), 176-196. https://doi.org/10.1002/per.2186

Sullivan, J. (2005). *Anime: The cultural signification of the otaku* [Master's thesis, McMaster University]. McMaster University. http://hdl.handle.net/11375/8450

Sun, T. (2010). Antecedents and consequences of parasocial interaction with sport athletes and identification with sport teams. *Journal of Sport Behavior, 33*(2), 194-217.

Swift, J. (n.d.). Mudken incident. *Britannica.* Retrieved November 13, 2020, from https://www.britannica.com/event/Mukden-Incident

Tabacchi, M. E., Caci, B., Cardaci, M., & Perticone, V. (2017). Early usage of Pokémon Go and its personality correlates. *Computers in Human Behavior, 72,* 163-169. https://doi.org/10.1016/j.chb.2017.02.047

Tajfel, H., & Turner, J. C. (1979). An integrative theory of intergroup conflict. In W. Austin & S. Worchel (Eds.), *The social psychology of intergroup relations* (pp. 33-47). Monterey, CA: Brooks/Cole.

Takatalo, J., Häkkinen, J., Kaistinen, J., & Nyman, G. (2010). Presence, involvement, and flow in digital games. In R. Bernhaupt (Ed.), *Evaluating user experience in games: Concepts and methods* (pp. 23-46). Springer.

Taylor, J. R. (2009). *Convention cosplay: Subversive potential in anime fandom* [Master's thesis, University of British Columbia]. University of British Columbia. http://hdl.handle.net/2429/7116

Tezuka Osamu Official. (n.d.). *Astro Boy*. Retrieved October 9, 2020, from https://tezukaosamu.net/en/anime/30.html

Thorson, K., & Wells, C. (2015). How gatekeeping still matters: Understanding media effects in an era of curated flows. In T. Vos & F. Heinderyckx (Eds.), *Gatekeeping in transition* (pp. 25-44). Routledge.

Tobacyk, J. J. (2004). A revised paranormal belief scale. *The International Journal of Transpersonal Studies, 23,* 94-98.

Trail, G. T., Robinson, M. J., Dick, R. J., Gillentine, A. J. (2003). Motives and points of attachment: Fans versus spectators in intercollegiate athletics. *Sport Marketing Quarterly, 12*(4), 217-227.

Turner, J. C., Hogg, M. A., Oakes, P. J., Reicher, S. D., & Wetherell, M. (1987). *Rediscovering the social group: A self-categorization theory.* Blackwell.

Twenge, J. M. (2006). *Generation me: Why today's young Americans are more confident, assertive, entitled—and more miserable than ever before.* Free Press.

Twenge, J. M., & Campbell, W. K. (2009). *Living in the age of entitlement: The narcissism epidemic.* Free Press.

Twenge, J. M., Spitzberg, B. H., & Campbell, W. K. (2019). Less in-person social interaction with peers among U.S. adolescents in the 21st century and links to loneliness. *Journal of Social and Personal Relationships, 36*(6), 1892-1913. https://doi.org/10.1177/0265407519836170

u/Impressive-Pin [Reddit screen name]. (2019, December 18). *It's unsettling how many famine fans will defend lolicon* [Online forum post]. Retrieved September 1, 2020, from https://www.reddit.com/r/GamerGhazi/comments/ecf970/its_unsettling_how_many_anime_fans_will_defend/

Ullén, F., de Manzano, Ö., Almeida, R., Magnusson, P. K. E., Pedersen, N. L., Nakamura, J., Csíkeszentmihályi, M., & Madison, G. (2012).

Proneness for psychological flow in everyday life: Associations with personality and intelligence. *Personality and Individual Differences, 52*(2), 167-172. https://doi.org/10.1016/j.paid.2011.10.003

University of Montreal. (2009, December 1). Are the effects of pornography negligible? *ScienceDaily.* Retrieved September 19, 2020, from www.sciencedaily.com/releases/2009/12/091201111202.htm

van Driel, I. I., Gantz, W., & Lewis, N. (2019). Unpacking what it means to be—or not be—a fan. *Communication and Sport, 7*(5), 611-629. https://doi.org/10.1177/2167479518800659

Vignoles, V. L., Regalia, C., Manzi, C., Golledge, J., & Scabini, E. (2006). Beyond self-esteem: Influence of multiple motives on identity construction. *Journal of Personality and Social Psychology, 90*(2), 308-333. https://doi.org/10.1037/0022-3514.90.2.308

von Feigenblatt, O. F. (2010). A socio-cultural analysis of romantic love in Japanese harem animation: A Buddhist monk, a Japanese knight, and a samurai. *Journal of Asia Pacific Studies, 1*(3), 636-646. https://ssrn.com/abstract=1760643

Wang, P.-T. (2010). *Affective otaku labor: The circulation and modulation of affect in the anime industry* (Publication No. 3426892) [Doctoral dissertation, City University of New York]. ProQuest Dissertations and Theses Global.

Wang, Q., Fink, E. L., & Cai, D. A. (2008). Loneliness, gender, and parasocial interaction: A uses and gratifications approach. *Communication Quarterly, 56*(1), 87-109. https://doi.org/10.1080/01463370701839057

Wann, D. L. (1995). Preliminary validation of the sport fan motivation scale. *Journal of Sport and Social Issues, 19*(4), 377-396. https://doi.org/10.1177/019372395019004004

Wann, D. L. (2006). Understanding the positive social psychological benefits of sport team identification: The team identification-social psychological health model. *Group Dynamics: Theory, Research, and Practice, 10*(4), 272-296. https://doi.org/10.1037/1089-2699.10.4.272

Wann, D. L., Allen, B., & Rochelle, A. R. (2004). Using sport fandom as an escape: Searching for relief from under-stimulation and over-stimulation. *International Sports Journal, 8*(1), 104-113.

Wann, D. L., & Branscombe, N. R. (1990). Die-hard and fair-weather fans: Effects of identification on BIRGing and CORFing tendencies. *Journal of Sport and Social Issues, 14*(2), 103-117. https://doi.org/10.1177/019372359001400203

Wann, D. L., & Branscombe, N. R. (1993). Sports fans: Measuring degree of identification with their team. *International Journal of Sport Psychology, 24*(1), 1-17.

Wann, D. L., Grieve, F. G., Zapalac, R. K., & Pease, D. G. (2008). Motivational profiles of sport fans of different sports. *Sport Marketing Quarterly, 17*(1), 6-19.

Wann, D. L., Hunter, J. L., Ryan, J. A., & Wright, L. A. (2001). The relationship between team identification and willingness of sport fans to consider illegally assisting their team. *Social Behavior and Personality, 29*(6), 531-536. https://doi.org/10.2224/sbp.2001.29.6.531

Wann, D. L., Martin, J., Grieve, F. G., & Gardner, L. (2008). Social connections at sporting events: Attendance and its positive relationship with state social psychological well-being. *North American Journal of Psychology, 10*(2), 229-238.

Wann, D. L., Melnick, M. J., Russell, G. W., & Pease, D. G. (2001). *Sport fans: The psychology and social impact of spectators.* Routledge.

Wann, D. L., Metcalf, L. A., Adcock, M. L., Choi, C.-C., Dallas, M. B., & Slaton, E. (1997). Language of sport fans: Sportugese revisited. *Perceptual and Motor Skills, 85*(3), 1107-1110. https://doi.org/10.2466/pms.1997.85.3.1107

Wann, D. L., Peterson, R. R., Cothran, C., & Dykes, M. (1999). Sport fan aggression and anonymity: The importance of team identification. *Social Behavior and Personality, 27*(6), 597-602. https://doi.org/10.2224/sbp.1999.27.6.597

Wann, D. L., & Polk, J. (2007). The positive relationship between sport team identification and belief in the trustworthiness of others. *North American Journal of Psychology, 9*(2), 251-256.

Wann, D. L., Royalty, J., & Roberts, A. (2000). The self-presentation of sport fans: Investigating the importance of team identification and self-esteem. *Journal of Sport Behavior, 23*(2), 198-206.

Wann, D. L., Schrader, M. P., & Wilson, A. M. (1999). Sport fan motivation: Questionnaire validation, comparisons by sport, and relationship to athletic motivation. *Journal of Sport Behavior, 22*(1), 114-139.

Wann, D. L., & Weaver, S. (2009). Understanding the relationship between sport team identification and dimensions of social well-being. *North American Journal of Psychology, 11*(2), 219-230.

Wellman, B., & Gulia, M. (1999). Virtual communities as communities: Net surfers don't ride alone. In M. A. Smith & P. Kollock (Eds.), *Communities in cyberspace* (pp. 167-194). Routledge.

Wenzel, M. (2001). A social categorization approach to distributive justice: Social identity as the link between relevance of inputs and need for justice. *British Journal of Social Psychology, 40*(3), 315-335. https://doi.org/10.1348/014466601164858

Williams, K. L. (2006). *The impact of popular culture fandom on perceptions of Japanese language and culture learning: The case of student anime fans* (Publication No. 3245796) [Doctoral dissertation, University of Texas at Austin]. ProQuest Dissertations and Theses Global.

Williams, R. (2015). *Post-object fandom: Television, identity and self-narrative*. Bloomsbury.

Wilson, S. C., & Barber, T. X. (1983). The fantasy-prone personality: Implications for understanding imagery, hypnosis, and parapsychological phenomena. In A. A. Sheikh (Ed.), *Imagery: Current theory, research and application* (pp. 340-390). Wiley.

Wilson, T. D., & Gilbert, D. T. (2005). Affective forecasting: Knowing what to want. *Current Directions in Psychological Science, 14*(3), 131-134. https://doi.org/10.1111/j.0963-7214.2005.00355.x

Winge, T. (2006). Costuming the imagination: Origins of anime and manga cosplay. *Mechademia, 1,* 65-76. https://doi.org/10.1353/mec.0.0084

World Cosplay Summit. (n.d.). World Cosplay Summit. *Facebook.* Retrieved November 12, 2020, from https://www.facebook.com/WorldCosplaySummit/

World Cosplay Summit. (n.d.). In Wikipedia. Retrieved November 12, 2020, from https://en.wikipedia.org/wiki/World_Cosplay_Summit#:~:text=This%20year%20the%20WCS%20gained,more%20attended%20the%20Cosplay%20Parade

Wright, P. J., & Bae, S. (2013). Pornography consumption and attitudes toward homosexuality: A national longitudinal study. *Human Communication Research, 39*(4), 492-513. https://doi.org/10.1111/hcre.12009

Wu, K., Chen, C., & Greenberger, E. (2019). Nice guys and gals can finish first: Personality and speed-dating success among Asian Americans. *Journal of Social and Personal Relationships, 36*(8), 2507-2527. https://doi.org/10.1177/0265407518790103

Wynne, J. (2017). How casual gamers are indirectly and objectively ruining gaming for gamers. *Common Sense Gaming, 25*. Retrieved May 31, 2019, from https://csgmagazine.com/2017/10/25/how-casual-gamers-are-indirectly-and-objectively-ruining-gaming-for-gamers/

Xu, S. (2016). *A platform for otakus to gradually learn to adapt to social conventions* (Publication No. 10181157) [Master's thesis, Purdue University]. ProQuest Dissertations and Theses Global.

Yamato, E. (2013). The otaku identification in Malaysia. In R. Machart, C. B. Lim, S. N. Lim, & E. Yamato (Eds.), *Intersecting identities and interculturality: Discourse and practice* (pp. 130-147). Cambridge Scholars.

Yamato, E. (2016). 'Growing as a person': experiences at anime, comics, and games fan events in Malaysia. *Journal of Youth Studies, 19*(6), 743-759. https://doi.org/10.1080/13676261.2015.1098769

Yasuo, Y. (2013, December 20). The evolution of the Japanese anime industry. *Nippon*. https://www.nippon.com/en/features/h00043/

Yergin, M. A. (2017). *Shared enthusiasm: Social cohesion with in the anime fandom* (Publication No. 10639235) [Master's thesis, Northern Illinois University]. ProQuest Dissertations and Theses Global.

Yoshida, M., Gordon, B., Heere, B., & James, J. D. (2015). Fan community identification: An empirical examination of its outcomes in Japanese professional sport. *Sport Marketing Quarterly, 24*(2), 105-119.

Yoshida, M., Heere, B., & Gordon, B. (2015). Predicting behavioral loyalty through community: Why other fans are more important than own intentions, our satisfaction, and the team itself. *Journal of Sport Management, 29*(3), 318-333. https://doi.org/10.1123/jsm.2013-0306

Zeng, C. (2018). Living in a virtual reality: Anime and manga fandom. In C. L. Wang (Ed.), *Exploring the rise of fandom in contemporary consumer culture* (pp. 244-253). IGI Global.

Zielinski, T. M.-M. (2014). *Of broken wings and otaku empathy: repairing fractured relationships using anime to reconnect disenfranchised youth with the gospel* (Publication No. 3664420) [Doctoral dissertation, United Theological Seminary]. ProQuest Dissertations and Theses Global.

Zubernis, L., & Larsen, K. (2012). *Fandom at the crossroads: Celebration, shame, and fan/producer relationships.* Cambridge Scholars Publishing.

Index